Imagining Zion

Imagining Zion

Dreams, Designs, and Realities in a Century of Jewish Settlement

S. Ilan Troen

Yale University Press   New Haven & London

Set in Swift and Syntax types by Achorn Graphic Services.
Printed in the United States of America

Library of Congress Cataloging-in-Publication Data

Troen, S. Ilan (Selwyn Ilan), 1940–
    Imagining Zion : dreams, designs, and realities in a century of Jewish settlement / S. Ilan Troen.
        p.   cm.
Includes index.
    ISBN 978-0-300-17853-1

    1. Zionism—Palestine—History. 2. Jews—Colonization—Palestine—History.
3. Agricultural colonies—Palestine—History. 4. Jews—Palestine—Economic conditions—19th century. 5. Jews—Israel—Economic conditions—20th century. 6. Moshavim—History. 7. Kibbutzim—History. 8. Urbanization—Israel—History.   I. Title.
    DS149.5.I75 T76 2003
    956.9405—dc21

                                                                                    2002151900

A catalogue record for this book is available from the British Library.

For Carol

זכרתי לך חסד נעוריך
אהבת כלולותיך
לכתך אחרי במדבר
בארץ לא זרועה

I remember the devotion of your youth,
your love as a bride,
how you followed me in the wilderness,
to a land not sown.
   —*Jeremiah* 2:2

Contents

Acknowledgments   ix

Introduction   xiii

PART I: **The Zionist Village**

CHAPTER 1. *Covenantal Communities*   3

CHAPTER 2. *Trial and Error in the Village Economy*   15

CHAPTER 3. *The Economic Basis for Arab/Jewish Accommodation*   42

CHAPTER 4. *The Village as Military Outpost*   62

PART II: **Urban Zion**

CHAPTER 5. *Tel Aviv: Vienna on the Mediterranean*   85

CHAPTER 6. *Urban Alternatives: Modern Metropolis, Company Town, and Garden City*   112

CHAPTER 7. *"Imagined Communities": The Zionist Variation*   141

PART III: **Post-Independence Opportunities and Necessities**

CHAPTER 8. *The Science and Politics of National Development*   163

CHAPTER 9. *From New Towns to Development Towns*   184

CHAPTER 10. *Israeli Villages: Transforming the Countryside*   208

CHAPTER 11. *Establishing a Capital: Jerusalem, 1948–1967*   233

CHAPTER 12. *Contested Metropolis: Jerusalem After the 1967 War*   259

Epilogue: Israel into the Twenty-First Century   281

Notes   293

Index   325

Acknowledgments

Long before I immigrated to Israel, interest in the establishment of a Jewish state was embedded in the discourse and collective imagination of my parents, Rose and Aleck Troen, and of my family and community, and was a subject of formal and informal study. Israel did not become the focus of my professional research until the mid-1980s when I joined the Ben-Gurion Research Center in Sede Boker. Prior to this, I had concentrated on American and European social and urban history. This research on frontier settlement, immigration, cities, and planning informed the way in which I came to think about the Zionist settlement experience.

My first explorations in this area brought me to topics that had been relatively untreated by Israeli colleagues and that appeared to me to reflect local variations of phenomena familiar to students of the modern history of the west. I remain fascinated by issues of normality and uniqueness and by how social ideas that are transported across space and cultures are preserved, adapted, or discarded. After pursuing this kind of inquiry, I began to weave my studies into a coherent story that was necessarily cast within the context of the Jewish/Arab and Israeli/Palestinian conflict. To create such an account required learning from individuals whose fields were outside Israeli history, others who were deeply involved with it, and the few who were engaged in integrating the two domains.

Early in this course, I came to rediscover what I had learned about social history and the transfer of ideas across cultures while a student at the University of Chicago with two master scholars: Daniel Boorstin and Richard Wade. I doubt either could have imagined, any more than I could have, that my training with them in American history would have laid the foundation for a study of Zionist settlement, although I believe their imprint is here. Inspired teaching and scholarship often lead to unforeseen consequences. From the beginning of this project, I benefited from the insight, criticism, and friendship of the late Gordon Cherry, who enhanced my interest in and knowledge of planning history, a topic that runs throughout this book. Another dear friend, the late Daniel Elazar, shared his encyclopedic knowledge and interest in frontiers, cities, and planning in both America and Israel. His insightful criticism of an earlier draft saved me from premature publication of this study. Yehoshua Ben-Arieh, the dean of Israeli historical geographers, offered criticism and advice during the early stages, and his own work and that of his students have had a deep impact on my reconstruction of Jewish colonization. Yosef Gorny's research in Jewish settlement as well as his studies on the labor movement have been valuable, as has his personal interest in this undertaking. Walter Ackerman, whose cable "start packing" signaled that a position was available at Ben-Gurion University, followed and encouraged this project from its inception. I am very grateful to Sam Aroni, Arnold Band, and Howard Morley Sachar, whose thoughtful reading and valuable criticism of a complete manuscript greatly improved the final result.

In carrying out this research, I was also fortunate to be able to meet with and learn from experts who participated in the events described in this book. The most significant were Ra'anan Weitz, who headed the Rural Settlement Department of the Jewish Agency, Jean Gottmann, the geographer probably best known for his work on megalopolis but who had a long professional connection and personal commitment to Zionist settlement, and Robert Nathan, a New Deal economist who came to study the future state at a crucial period and remained its devoted friend for the rest of his long life.

Most sections of this book benefited from repeated visits to the Kressel Collection and the library at the Oxford Centre for Hebrew and Jewish Studies, where I enjoyed the generosity and friendship of David Patterson and collaboration with Noah Lucas. I am also grateful to Alan Crown, Kenneth Jackson, Jack Lassner, Roger Owen, David Ruderman, and David Thelen, who provided venues for presenting and refining different parts of this work.

The most important locale for research and writing has been the Ben-Gurion Research Center at Sede Boker. I have benefited from interaction with colleagues, particularly Allon Gal, Zvi Shilony, and Nahum Karlinsky, and the opportunity to share ideas with the Center's scholars. The ongoing seminars have been a source of continuing education with multidisciplinary and divergent political perspectives. I am particularly grateful to Tuvia Friling, who as a young scholar in charge of the Ben-Gurion Archives and later my successor as Director of the Center, pointed me toward appropriate documentation. So, too, I am happy to acknowledge the assistance of Hanna Pinshow and Leana Feldman of the Ben-Gurion Archives and Lili Adar of the center's library, who unfailingly provided indispensable materials. Other libraries and archives were, of course, essential. Most important were the Central Zionist Archives and Israel State Archives in Jerusalem and the Lavon Archives in Tel Aviv. Foreign archives contained much pertinent material, especially the Scottish National Library in Edinburgh, the Public Record Office and the British Library in London, the National Archives in Washington, and Harvard University's superb resources on Israel.

Through much of the research I was ably and creatively assisted in the collection of materials and in their evaluation by Natan Aridan and Ran Or-Ner, students who have become friends and colleagues.

I am grateful to Pieter Louppen of the cartography unit of Ben-Gurion University's Department of Geography and Environmental Development and to Patrice Kaminski of the archaeological technical services unit of the Department of Bible and Ancient Near East Studies, who prepared the maps and numerous illustrations. I very much appreciate permission to publish other illustrations and the assistance of the staffs of the photo archives of the National Press Office, the Jewish National Fund, and Yad Yitzhak Ben-Zvi in Jerusalem and of Nadav Mann of "Bitmunah" in Kibbutz Merhavia. Ellen Blair, the daughter of Sam and Anna Lopin who established the chair I hold at Ben-Gurion University, provided needed funding and encouragement at a critical time. I am also grateful to various university funds that supported the assembling and preparation of illustrations and maps. Special thanks are due Robert Flynn and Erin Carter of Yale University Press, who received the book proposal and guided it through to publication with professional expertise and personal courtesy. So, too, am I grateful to Lauren Shapiro and Nancy Moore Brochin, whose close professional attention contributed to an improved final product.

The greatest debt is to my wife, Carol Rosenberg Troen. Even beyond moral support during the long course of producing this book, she has been a collaborator in reflecting on the research and in refining and transforming the findings into a worthy text. This book is a product of an intellectual undertaking in which she has been a genuine partner. It would not have been accomplished without her. The verse on the dedication page only partially expresses my thanks for her role in this shared journey and adventure. Finally, I would like to express my appreciation to our children, Lisa, Aron, Joshua, Deborah, Judah, and Abraham, who endured their father's many absences, even when physically at home, and accepted with understanding their mother's involvement with my work. They, too, encouraged and discussed the project and read portions of the manuscript. I hope they will find this interpretation of the past useful as they assume responsibility for Israel's future.

Introduction

The return of Jews to their homeland is a central event in contemporary history and a continually vexing issue in world affairs. While there has been a small but constant Jewish presence in Palestine, the center of Jewish life, culture, and learning moved for nearly two millennia from one Diaspora community to another. In 1900, less than one-half of 1 percent of world Jewry, or only approximately 50,000, lived in the *Yishuv* (the Jewish community in Palestine). In the course of the twentieth century, the Yishuv increased a hundredfold, to nearly 5 million. By the end of the first decade of the twenty-first century, Israel is likely to contain the largest Jewish community in the world. Not since the Romans destroyed Jerusalem in 70 c.e. and the subsequent eclipse of Jewish sovereignty have Jews been such a significant majority in the country. (Israel's population in 2000 numbered 6.3 million, of whom 4.9 million were Jews and 1.1 million were Arabs.) This "ingathering of the exiles," whether one believes it is the fulfillment of a Divine promise or a necessary pragmatic response of Jews to persecution in the lands where they sojourned, has signified an unprecedented opportunity and challenge. An ancient people—long dispersed, linguistically and culturally diverse, usually marginalized and restricted in occupation and residence—Jews set out toward the end of the nineteenth century to reconstitute themselves as a modern and sovereign nation living in their own land.

Between 1880 and the end of the twentieth century, the Zionist movement established nearly 700 villages, towns, and cities. About 250 were built prior to independence in 1948 and more than 450 during the first fifty years of statehood. This was not a haphazard development fueled by private capital and carried out by individuals acting primarily for personal gain. Nor was it the product of a directed and well-financed policy of an imperial power. Rather, during the crucial stage prior to statehood, the Jewish settlement of Palestine was conceived by a corps of professional planners, architects, and officials recruited by organizations bent on achieving national purposes. Most were immigrant Jews from Europe, but there were also a few Americans, gentiles as well as Jews. Many were professionals employed by bureaucracies, but there were also visionaries, architects, social scientists, military officers, and politicians. Some are familiar figures in Israeli history, while others are known primarily to those in the field. Bringing with them the best of contemporary planning and design ideas primarily from Europe, these experts aspired to implement their plans in Zion even as they were challenged to adapt their concepts to the realities and requirements of the country's physical and political environment.

Imagining Zion is a history of the ideas of these colonizers and how they attempted to implement them. I have placed their story within Jewish and Zionist history and the history of the Arab/Israeli conflict. And I have set it within another historiography as well: the expansion of European societies into non-European worlds that began about 500 years ago. Understood in this way, *Imagining Zion* is both a particularistic history of *Eretz Israel* (the Land of Israel), the ancient term for Palestine, and a chapter in the history of a larger phenomenon. Indeed, Zionists may have been the last Europeans to colonize distant lands. Nevertheless, their experience was unique, for there was no "mother country" in the conventional sense. For this reason and for others, as I shall argue, their history is a deviation from the familiar categories of imperialism and colonialism found in other instances of European emigration. It is a unique story of a people rediscovering their past and returning to an ancient homeland. They did so with an increasing awareness that the other people in the country, Palestine's Arabs, opposed them. Their program therefore attempted to placate and accommodate opposition and to confront it when it became violent. The phases in this process are also necessarily part of this history.

Like other European settlers, Zionists transplanted European ideas in a process of experimentation and adaptation. Initially, they planned agricultural colonies, but they soon added towns and cities to the inventory of their colonization program. The first model for agricultural settlement was the *moshava*, a colony of independent property owners. This was superseded by the *moshav*, a cooperative farming village, and the *kvutza* and *kibbutz*, or collective settlements. More recently, planners have set nonagricultural colonies in the countryside. On Zion's urban frontiers they designed metropolises, regional cities, new towns, company towns, garden suburbs, and discrete housing estates. The balance between urban and rural colonization changed, as did the preferred models within these categories.

The continuous revisions and adjustments in settlement planning were a response to the interplay of three distinct factors that determined which design concept was given priority. These factors are social and political ideologies, the need for productivity and economic independence, and the problem of ensuring security in a hostile environment. Ideological, economic, and security objectives competed with one another for primacy and affected the plans of colonizers in different ways at different periods. By examining the dynamic relationship among these three variables, this study creates a unique prism through which to view Israel's history.

Imagining Zion tells this large story in an efficient compass. It begins in the 1880s with the establishment of a loose network of small farming villages. Zionist planning at that time reflected a popular attempt to escape the abnormalities of exile and to enable a "return to history" by embracing the romantic ideal of transforming Jews into peasants. By the 1930s, security and strategic concerns had emerged as paramount in the thinking of planners, and had come to dominate the design of Zionist Palestine. Only at the start of the twentieth-first century, more than a half-century later, with negotiations for peace and normalization of relations with Arabs within and beyond Israel's borders, is there a possibility that Zionist planning may finally become relatively unexceptional. Our story ends fifty years after the establishment of the State of Israel with discussion over a new Master Plan for the year 2020 as the independent Jewish state continues to seek "normality." This plan reflects what many Israelis believe an advanced industrial state should look like in the future.

Whether Israel can emulate the course of development conceived for other modern nations will depend on the significance of the third variable, security, in Israeli society. If Palestinian Arabs do not become reconciled to a Jewish state, strategic concerns will continue to shape and even distort Israel's development, and the beginning of the second century may be a chronological marker and nothing more. However, if amicable relations and secure borders can be achieved, Israeli planning may come to approximate that of other modern states. The end of the first century would be a watershed in Israel's history and a new departure in imagining Zion.

Imagining Zion

Part I
The Zionist Village

CHAPTER 1

Covenantal Communities

The stream of modern life draws the countryman to the town. To exchange the town for the country is to swim against the stream. For a people which was uprooted from its land two thousand years ago and which has become attached with every fibre of its being to town-life, for such a people to return to the soil is to swim against the current of double strength. An effort of quite unusual intensity is required to overcome the obstacles.
—YITZHAK ELAZARI-VOLCANI, 1927

F ROM the 1880s, Jews who swam against the stream and returned to Palestine came with increasingly precise and practical conceptions of how the country could be settled. The first generation of pioneers and planners imagined a land filled with villages in imitation of the Europe they had known before emigration. They assumed that the European experience could be applied directly to changing European Jewry into a Middle Eastern peasantry. Jewish agricultural colonization did transform Palestine from a poorly developed and backward country into a land that supports hundreds of villages and boasts one of the most modern and efficient agricultural systems in the world. But this result was not achieved merely by transplanting European models. Nearly fifty years of systematic experimentation and adaptation were necessary to produce the methods by which a modern nation based on villages might be established. In the course of a process of trial and error, the economy and agricultural technology of the Zionist village were necessarily transformed. By the 1930s Zionist colonizers had begun to redesign these pastoral villages as paramilitary outposts necessary for penetrating and holding territory in a hostile countryside.

From the 1880s until Israel was granted statehood in 1948, about 250 villages of various types were established. With recruits drawn from the massive post-Independence immigration of the 1950s and the enlarged territory and financial resources generated with statehood, 400 more settlements were founded until the Six-Day War in 1967, when agricultural colonization largely ended. Thus, in less than a century, from 1882 to 1967, Zionist colonizers established more than 650 villages.[1]

During the initial stage of this process, from the 1880s until the First World War, Jewish settlement was concentrated almost exclusively in the *moshava*, a traditional kind of colony whose members farmed their land independently. The early *moshavoth* (plural of moshava) failed to achieve economic independence and did not develop quickly enough to enable large-scale colonization within a reasonable time. Attempts at reform and experimentation led to the design of the *kibbutz*, or *kvutza* (collective settlements), and the *moshav* (cooperative farming village) just before the outbreak of the First World War.

There were prior movements to resettle Jews in Palestine. Disciples of the Gaon of Vilna (1720–1797), a spiritual and rabbinic authority among Eastern European Jewry, constituted one of the first and certainly largest early organized migrations of European Jews. Believing that omens indicated the imminent arrival of the Messiah, they thought they could hasten Redemption if they settled in Eretz Israel, and several thousand immigrated between 1807 and 1847. In an effort to attract more Jews, they even dispatched a messenger to Yemen to encourage the ingathering of that remote community. Their preferred locations for settlement were Jerusalem and Safed, where they established institutions for study and worship, most notably the Hurva synagogue in the Old City of Jerusalem. They looked forward to the year 1840 (5600 in the traditional Jewish reckoning), when it was widely predicted that the Messiah would come. His failure to appear at the appointed time caused great frustration and led them to abandon the belief that by taking action "from below," Jews could ensure and even hasten Redemption. The disappointed disciples of the Gaon retreated into the ideology of "If God does not build the house, its builders labor in vain."

Other Jews took personal responsibility for "rebuilding ruins" and called for an "awakening from below," including the establishment of productive farming colonies.[2] Perhaps the best known was Moses Montefiore, the English philanthropist, who in 1855 contributed funds for moving Jews out of Jerusalem to become farmers. In 1870, the French-Jewish philanthropic organization, the Alliance Israélite Universelle, established Mikve Israel outside of Jaffa as a training farm for Jews whom they hoped would work the land. In 1878, a group of largely Jerusalem-based Hungarian Jews established a colony on the coastal plain that soon disbanded. Not until 1882 did a sustained movement of rural Jewish settlement begin. In that year recent arrivals founded Petach Tikva, Rishon le-Zion, and Zichron Ya'acov along the coast and Rosh Pina at the base of the Upper Galilee. A year later, settlers established Ness Ziona in the coastal plain and Y'sod Hama'ala in the north, followed in 1884 by Gedera in the south. By the outbreak of the First World War, approximately 12,000 Jews were living in some 30 moshavoth. They understood themselves as engaged in a new departure that would change the character of Jewish society in Eretz Israel from an object of charity to a thriving, independent community and thereby begin a new page in Jewish history. They viewed themselves as pioneers of a new Jewish society rooted in the ancient homeland.[3]

Yet for all their differences, colonists who undertook to cultivate a barren land shared significant similarities with settlers who established themselves in "holy cities" to await the Messiah. Neither disciples nor pioneers saw themselves as individual pioneers on a frontier. Both sought to live within a communal framework. Most founders of moshavoth were traditional Jews, although they did not choose to live under an uncompromising regime supervised by religious authorities. Moreover, although pioneers who settled in moshavoth, unlike their religious counterparts in the cities, sought and anticipated ultimate economic independence, they also assumed that they would require significant temporary financial support from sponsors abroad. Thus, Zionist villages were conceived as communities, rooted in a common religious tradition and dependent on external support.

Covenantal Traditions

The founding and the travails of the moshavoth have been documented often and well. The salient issue in the present discussion is the intention of the founders to create communities or, to borrow a relevant phrase from the Puritan experience in the seventeenth and eighteenth centuries, "miniature commonwealths."[4] The source of this communitarianism has usually been traced to various streams of European cooperative, socialist, or communist ideologies. However, upon closer examination, the covenants of the moshavoth suggest that Zionist communal thought was rooted in the religious experience, imaginations, and predilections of early planners and pioneers, and that their colonies recreated traditional patterns of bonding along national and/or religious lines. By the First World War, the collective imperative was secularized, and it transcended regnant ideologies from socialism on the left to free-enterprise capitalism. Still, it is noteworthy that Zionist colonizers from all ideological perspectives built villages rather than latifundia, plantations, ranches, or homesteads.[5]

The communitarian and religious roots of this phenomenon prefigure the moshava. At the beginning of the nineteenth century there were about 3 million Jews in the world, and only 5,000, most of whom were Sephardim, or Oriental Jews, lived in Palestine. Thereafter, Ashkenazim, or European Jews, began to arrive in steady if small numbers, contributing significantly to the growth of Jewish communities in the "holy cities" of Safed, Tiberias, Hebron, and, above all, Jerusalem. By 1880, the Jewish population had increased about fivefold to perhaps 24,000 as a result of emigration from Eastern Europe.[6] But these new arrivals did not cultivate the land. Many neighborhoods and housing estates were established as the city expanded westward from the ancient core. Individual homes were rare. Nearly 90 percent of all building was constructed by or for Jews who organized themselves according to a communal contract with specific regulations and rules. They joined or created *kollelim,* religious communities devoted to the study of Torah and committed to a rigorous adherence to religious law and custom. Coreligionists abroad supported them and their institutions through an extensive charity network. These early neighborhoods provided considerable local experience in community-building. Some of the founders of the first moshavoth were themselves involved in the organization of Jerusalem's new housing estates and were members of them. The Jerusalem experience followed a pattern common to Jewish community-building across the centuries and throughout the Diaspora. They easily and naturally transplanted deeply rooted practices to nineteenth-century Palestine.[7]

The moshava's founding covenants (*brithoth,* or *brith* in the singular) and regulations (*takanoth*) provide a clear statement of the intentions of both planners and pioneers. The ubiquity of these documents testifies to their significance. One major collection of covenants and regulations is contained in seven substantial volumes.[8] Together and individually they reflect the aspirations and intentions of Jews from the small towns and cities of Eastern and Western Europe as well as those who emigrated from them to America and Palestine.

The fundamental purposes put forward in these documents and the plans for their realization are remarkably similar. It is as if a recognized and agreed archetype for community design had emerged without the deliberations and formal adoption of an international association. There was no single planner, group of planners, or planning authority in this initial stage of Zionist colonization. Not until 1897, when Theodor Herzl organized the first Zionist Congress and established the World Zionist Organization, did an international Zionist authority undertake to coordinate and implement a coherent policy of colonization. There were attempts that anticipate the work of the WZO including regional conferences of the Hovevei Zion (Lovers of Zion) and the efforts of individuals, notably Baron Edmund de Rothschild of France. But in the first generation, Zion was planned according to a common blueprint that reflected the aspirations of a multitude of Jews.

Covenantal Societies: Social Ideals

Individuals became members of a community in Palestine by entering into contracts replete with largely standardized bylaws, or takanoth. These documents affirmed social and religious bonds among the members. Social ties were paramount, while economic distinctions were blurred, so that bylaws typically made no distinctions between poor and rich. The crucial marker was the differentiation of Jews on the basis of country of origin or religious practice. There were, for example, separate neighborhoods of Jews from Bukhara in Asia and from Hungary in Europe. Community members adhered to the teachings of a particular rabbi or religious movement such as a Hasidic sect. The takanoth ensured that neighborhoods and housing would be societies of like-minded people dedicated to the same purposes. Like the miniature commonwealths of New England—which were also framed by covenants—the early settlements in Palestine were exclusive societies with democratic elements only for those permitted to join.

Like the Puritans, who understood themselves as latter-day Israelites, the Zionists, too, framed their compacts, covenants, and founding documents with Biblical precedents as they returned to their Promised Land. The takanoth resonate with biblical imagery, often echoing the experience of the Patriarchs. Many explicitly use the word "brith" (covenant), a term that appears frequently in the documents of colonizing societies in Eastern and Central Europe during the last two decades of the nineteenth century. Whether in the masthead, the opening statement, or a specific article identifying the purpose of the proposed society, covenants usually employ quotations from the Bible foretelling the time when Jews will take their destiny in their own hands and reclaim the land from which they have been exiled.

When Me'a She'arim was constructed beyond the walls of the Old City of Jerusalem (1874), the takanoth quoted Isaiah to address problems of urban overcrowding: "Enlarge the site of thy tents, and let them stretch forth the curtains of thy dwellings; spare not, lengthen thy cords, and strengthen thy stakes" (Isaiah 54:2). Pioneers who ventured beyond the city walls to work the land and those who supported them found inspiration in other verses. The society organized to establish Ness Ziona invoked Ezekiel (36:8, 24): "But ye, O Mountains of Israel, ye shall shoot forth your branches, and yield your fruit to My people Israel, for they are at hand to come."[9] Redeeming the land through the toil of the pioneers is the dominant motif of the bylaws of the rural moshava.

The Bible also provided founders of the moshavoth with a call for collective action. The organizers of Rehovoth (1890) begin their founding document, *The Book of the Covenant of Menuchah ve-Nachalah* (Rest and inheritance), with a quotation from Isaiah (65:21–22):

> And they shall build houses, and inhabit them;
> And they shall plant vineyards, and eat the fruit of them.
> They shall not build, and another inhabit,
> They shall not plant, and another eat;
> For as the days of a tree shall be the days of My people.[10]

The society of Hovevei Zion in Warsaw, in September 1883, rallies its members with a call for self-help, also from Isaiah (63:5):

> In the name of G-D who dwells in Zion!
> And I looked and there was none to help,
> And I beheld in astonishment, and there was none to uphold;
> Therefore, Mine own arm brought salvation unto Me.[11]

This Warsaw constitution, framed in the aftermath of an outbreak of particularly violent pogroms, demands a solution to imminent national calamity. The Jews must save themselves by joining forces in rebuilding their national homeland as workers of the land in Zion. Their urgent call to action, too, is cast in the language of ancient prophecy: "Living in the city of Warsaw we have seen the signs of the present time, the burning sword of hatred, that is turning over today in human society. We have observed the plight of our people and its ruin. We are totally frustrated with the position of the nation . . . and we shall listen to the voice of God from the voices of the torches that are so powerfully calling the children of the scattered and separated people saying: 'gather together children of Jacob, understand the matter and understand what you see!' "[12]

The recourse to Biblical motifs is consistent with the traditional religious orientation of the early colonists and their supporters. Bylaws made provisions for the employment of a rabbi and a teacher for religious instruction as well as literacy training; a ritual slaughterer who would be able to provide the colonists with kosher meat; the construction of a communal ritual bath, a synagogue, and a house of study.

Many covenants correctly refer to the intended colony as a "kehillah kedoshah," or a "holy community." Adherents of traditional religious culture could not otherwise imagine life in the Holy Land, or perhaps anywhere. In Judaism, there are commandments that can only be fulfilled and even prayers that may only be uttered within communities. By tradition and religious law, group worship offers greater possibilities than does individual prayer. Moreover, most institutions essential to the conduct of Jewish life require communities. It was therefore natural to envision themselves and their coreligionists in Palestine as members of communities rather than individuals venturing forth in pursuit of personal objectives.

When secular pioneers, infused with secular socialist ideologies, came during the Second Aliyah ("aliyah" meaning "immigration," literally "going up" to the Land) (1904–1913) and the Third Aliyah (1919–1923), they also set out as members of groups. They, too, went to great lengths to work out and write down the arrangements of the communities they intended to create. Although the pioneers of the First Aliyah (1882–1904) anchored their beliefs and actions in religious tradition, their successors based their communities on socialist conceptions of brotherhood and on a commitment to national solidarity. Traditional settlers of the First Aliyah and their secular, socialist successors shared a commitment to collective ambitions. What is striking, then, is that all Zionist villagers in this formative period of agricultural colonization framed their communities in terms of national purposes and couched their preferences in terms of which model served those purposes best. Entirely absent were alternative models where individuals would settle rural areas primarily for personal benefit.

During the First Aliyah, religious law also figured in the regulations governing agriculture. Returning to the land meant Jews could fulfill *mitzvoth,* or religious commandments, that could not be performed in the Diaspora or even when resident in a city in the Holy Land. The laws most frequently mentioned in the covenants concern the observance of the sabbatical year (*sh'mitah*) and of the fiftieth or jubilee year (*yovel*) when Biblical injunctions prohibit cultivation. Occasionally there are regulations about leaving a portion of the harvest for the poor, as indicated by Biblical law and reflected in the Book of Ruth. There are also references to tithing. In sum, European supporters and early colonists intended to shape their agricultural economy in accordance with ancient legislation that had been studied continuously in the abstract during centuries of exile.

Traditional law also influenced the design of Jerusalem's communal neighborhoods. The *Shulkhan Aruch* (the code of Jewish law), for example, specifies that windows may not look out on neighbors. So in Jerusalem's new neighborhoods, windows opened onto the alleys in back of the houses. Also, as stipulated in the *Shulkhan Aruch,* synagogues were placed at the center of the housing estate. It is revealing that even laws regarding sanitation are anchored in *Halakha* (Jewish law based on Biblical injunctions) rather than drawing on the contemporary sanitary and urban planning movements in Europe. Any correspondence between communal design and purpose and contemporary secular conceptions was unintentional.

This commitment to community animated even avowedly secular pioneers. Perhaps the most famous group in the mythology of early Zionist pioneering is the *Bilu'im,* who took their name from the acrostic: B-I-L-U, or *Beit Ya'acov Lechu V'nelcha* (Isaiah 2:5: "O House of Jacob, Come ye and let us go"). With a strong sense of the first-person plural—"let US go"—they constituted themselves into a community. Lacking financial resources and practical skills, this group of largely secular and socialistically inclined young people suffered great privation in an unsuccessful effort to achieve a shared objective. Many left Palestine, and only a handful actually became farmers.

Far more numerous and successful were the founders of Hadera (1890), a moshava organized by four different subgroups who joined forces to establish their colony. One of these groups originated in Vilna, where they invited a broad spectrum of Jewish youth to join in a shared enterprise. These included "suitable" men and women, followers of Hasidism or traditional orthodoxy, and even secularists "that go with the spirit of the day." Although they did not define themselves as a disciplined religious society, their objectives are stated within a traditional framework that could embrace many potential members. Exiles are called to return to the land after being dispersed for nearly two thousand years: "The purpose of the association Ohavey Zion is to spread knowledge of Eretz-Israel with the objective of exiles returning to work the land, to plant it with all their hearts, to support the immigrants to the land of Israel in cultivating the land and in working its mountains and valleys, and to support them with a generous hand; and also to translate step by step the settlement of Eretz Israel from the idea to the deed and from the potential to the reality."[13]

The founders of Rehovoth (1890) were perhaps the least explicitly religious of the pioneers of the First Aliyah moshavoth. Yet, even their takanoth draw extensively on Jewish traditions. Organized by largely middle-class pioneers who sought to further their wealth within a communal framework, their regulations contain no mention of a rabbi, ritual bath, synagogue, and other religious functionary or institutions. Nevertheless, such offices and officials were instituted in the new colony. In the spectrum of societies that the first generation of Zionists created, a recognizable similarity developed. The inherent and even intended congruence of these societies is anticipated in the takanoth of one of the first moshavoth, Rishon le-Zion. Its purpose as defined by the founders was "to improve the material and moral condition of the congregation, and to be a sign for our brothers the Children of Israel who are coming to take hold in the Holy Land, to stir the hearts of our people in settling Eretz Israel and in upbuilding the national ruins, and to assist with all their might the founders of other moshavoth with counsel and action."[14]

The covenants of these colonies, then, reflected a common culture rooted in tradition. Thus, the Vilna colonization society that supported the establishment of Hadera ordains in their takanoth that "The Association will celebrate annually (in Vilna) its establishment on the Sabbath of Nachamu." That is, they plan to assemble in late summer to chant Isaiah 40 and subsequent chapters that foretell the return to Zion after a national catastrophe. The takanoth go on to provide: "On this day, three active members shall come to the main synagogue to pray and one of them shall recite the prophetic portion, *kaddish* [memorial prayer] shall be recited for the members who have died and a candle shall be lit for them." Moreover, they determine that on one of the days of Hannukah they will assemble for a review of accounts and for a cultural program, including reading portions of the Bible relevant to pioneering and chapters from the Book of *Hasmoneans* (Maccabees). Several members were to discuss settlement in Eretz Israel after which the takanoth carefully stipulate that "they then dine at their own expense."[15] Often, arrangements for public convocations that were originally conceived by covenant-makers in Europe were transferred and incorporated in the life of the moshavoth.[16]

Covenantal Communities: Self-Government

Jewish settlers in Palestine, whether rural or urban and religious or secular, viewed themselves as separate from the surrounding society. In part, this might have been a consequence of how the Ottomans related to foreigners and members of non-Muslim religions. Jews were a separate community, as were Christians and others. As in most cases where separation is enforced, it is rarely accompanied by equality.[17] The British, who supplanted the Ottomans as Palestine's rulers after World War I, also viewed Jews and Arabs as members of separate communities. Typically, the British assembled statistics and published their census with people divided by religion: Moslems, Christians, and Jews.[18] However, these distinctions were not strange or remarkable to Jewish immigrants, particularly those from Eastern Europe. Jews who came from Russia, Poland, Romania, and the lands of the Austro-Hungarian empire were accustomed to viewing themselves and others as members of distinct communities who enjoyed or endured differential status defined by law. They brought with them well-developed traditions and patterns of self-government within the parameters established by local rulers and readily translated these into covenants.[19]

Thus, although there was no supervising authority that imposed a standard format, the moshavoth developed common provisions for self-government. As was customary in the small towns where Jews lived in Europe, the rabbi was not only a learned authority on religious matters but also the judicial authority in the event of disputes between settlers. All colonies established community courts of from three to five members, depending on their size. This practice became so firmly incorporated that after the First World War a court of appeals emerged to adjudicate disputes between moshavoth on matters where local courts failed to satisfy the litigants. Jews stayed away from Ottoman justice whenever possible. Independent courts were part of a larger mechanism envisaged in the earliest covenants. Depending on size, each moshava had a council of up to seven elected members, one of whom was elected as its head.[20] Nearly all elections were conducted by the membership of the General Assembly, which was open to all men and women who had been resident in the colony for at least a year and who paid taxes to the moshava. Candidates for office had to be resident longer, from two or three years, and had to be older, at least twenty-five in most settlements.

A major function of the council was to serve as an intermediary between the moshava and the Ottoman government on such issues as taxation and military service. As in Europe, local committees were responsible for communal services including education, health, security, and the library. Elected council members supervised and paid employees such as the doctor, pharmacist, midwife, and teachers. In addition, special needs were met by voluntary groups that organized to grant small loans and assist the poor and visit the sick.

With their own institutions for handling social, health, and education needs, the moshavoth became miniature commonwealths. Given the inherent similarities between these miniature societies, the shared general purposes, and the common origins of the settlers, it was natural that there should be attempts to establish cooperative frameworks among them. In the decade before the First World War, common security problems led to cooperation in self-defense through the organization of ha-Shomer (The Watchman). Shared economic problems led to cooperative organizations such as in 1905 both Pardes, the association of citrus-growers, and Agudat ha-Kormim, the association of vine-growers, for marketing wines and producing almonds, and even associations for digging wells and irrigating fields and orchards. Cooperation also led to the establishment of common political institutions and communal frameworks. At the end of two generations, on the eve of the First World War, the moshavoth were connected to one another in a loose federation.

For all their success in forging communal institutions and building societies on shared values, the moshavoth were beset by forces that pushed toward disintegration and failure. The primary challenge to maintaining these village communities through the First World War was economic. The moshavoth had to achieve economic independence or they could not survive. It is to the impact of economic imperatives on the Zionist village that we now turn.

CHAPTER 2

Trial and Error in the Village Economy

INIATURE commonwealths—*moshava, kibbutz,* or *moshav*—could
not survive without a solid economic basis. Achieving this was
far more difficult than the first generation of sponsors and
settlers imagined. Crucial debates began in earnest in the 1920s over
which economic system was best suited for Zionist villages. During that
decade, both the moshav and the kibbutz models were refined, and assumed their now recognizable form of social and economic organization. By the early 1930s, there were attempts to combine the advantages
of the kibbutz and the moshav in the *moshav shitufi* (smallholder's settlement). In subsequent decades, further modifications took place, although no new labels were applied to established forms. Throughout
this second stage, planners within the international network created
by the World Zionist Organization (WZO), including leading American
experts, challenged European-born professionals in Palestine in an effort to find the most economically viable model for the Zionist village.

Indeed, settlements were rarely profitable in the short term. Their
establishment and viability depended on substantial and continuing
external support and a willingness to forgo short-term gains for long-
term goals.[1] In order to understand how settlements achieved economic

solvency after extended dependencies on philanthropic or public bodies, it is necessary to examine the work of the professional planners employed by Zionist colonization authorities. It was they who controlled the design of settlements and influenced the distribution of funds on which further colonization depended.[2]

The Changing Economy of the Zionist Village

As the preferences of planners changed from the moshava to the kibbutz, moshav, and moshav shitufi, settlers debated vigorously their distinctions and relative merits. For the purposes of this analysis, I will not dwell on the ideological debates of the settlers themselves. They have been amply documented, and their story has been told.[3] Rather, I will focus here on the interests and objectives of settlement experts. In this perspective, the differences between the various types of village are less consequential than their similarities. Common to the plans for all these various colonies is a formula for planting Jews on the land in relatively small communities. Indeed, a kind of "magic" number emerged of how large a farming colony ought to be.

This settlement formula evolved in response to a chronic lack of adequate land and, at the same time, the imperative that the villages become economically independent as soon as possible. An apparent exception is the *kvutza,* a greatly expanded kibbutz composed of thousands of members. However the kvutza, postulated in the 1920s, is only an ostensible deviation from the common design, the "exception" that proves the rule. Like the kibbutz and moshav, the kvutza enshrined agriculture as the highest value even though many members actually worked outside the community in nonagricultural activities and projects because not enough land was available for cultivation. What is remarkable about Zionist rural colonization schemes from the beginnings through the present is the relative stability of the ideal: a Middle Eastern countryside dotted with modest communities of pioneers engaged in agriculture.

The uniqueness of the Zionist approach to settlement becomes apparent when it is viewed within the larger context of European colonization. At the same time that European Jews were imagining villages spreading throughout Palestine, American colonizers were acting on the Jeffersonian ideal of individualism codified in the Homestead Act of 1862. Much of the vast territory of the United States beyond the Appalachians was dotted with individual homesteads separately and neatly placed in the continental geometric grid. The English in Australia, the Boers in South Africa, the French in North Africa, and colonists in Argentina established private and often large estates or plantations. In contrast to most of these transplanted Europeans, Zionists consciously chose perhaps the most traditional form of European settlement. They clustered in villages of modest population where farmers cultivated relatively small plots of adjacent land, and explicitly rejected the individualistic pattern of settlement of large family farms dispersed across the countryside.

Calling on Jews to abandon urban areas for rural life, early Zionist planners resisted fundamental trends characteristic of western societies and their colonial offshoots. Determined to reverse the flight of peasants from the countryside, they rejected the modern pattern of ever fewer farmers producing more through the advantages of mechanization, economies of scale, scientific innovations, and improved storage methods. They held to the archaic ideal of a traditional rural economy based on communities of peasants and stubbornly maintained the farming village as central to the organization of agriculture and society as a whole. Elsewhere, small towns or villages became service centers catering to agriculturalists in outlying areas. In Zionist Palestine, farmers continued to live proximate to their fields even when there was no longer a technological or economic justification for doing so.[4] These colonies were taken as evidence that Jews could overcome their historic condition, and were seen as an achievement by Jews who settled in Palestine's cities as well as by sympathizers in the Diaspora. The arcadian and obsolescent character of this aspiration is captured in the iconography of the Zionist movement. It typically featured a brawny farmer standing in the midst of vineyards and orchards against a barren biblical landscape. Urban representations occupied a decidedly secondary place in the rhetoric of Zionist propaganda. The heroic rebirth of the Jews as a modern people in their own land was widely represented in agrarian terms.[5]

The comparative perspective of the present study usefully underscores the audacity of this revolutionary ambition. Back-to-the-land movements emerged elsewhere in the modern, industrializing world but typically did not succeed. The chance of success was particularly daunting for European Jews. Few had experience as farmers. Most were urban and becoming increasingly so. Even those who lived in small towns were artisans or engaged in commerce, not agriculture. Indeed,

Jews were probably the most urbanized part of the population in all the lands in which they lived. This was true even in the relatively under-developed Russia of 1900, where 90 percent of the non-Jewish popula-tion were peasants and only 10 percent were urbanized. Among Russian Jews, the reverse was true: only 10 percent were farmers in an over-whelmingly traditional, agrarian society. Of the large number of Jews who were emigrating to the advanced and industrialized Western Euro-pean states, almost all relocated in the largest cities. Indeed, in nearly all the countries of the Diaspora, Jews are still overwhelmingly concen-trated in capital cities or major metropolises. In these respects, the Zion-ist village was an antihistorical and romantic ideal. To impose such an impractical model challenged the skills and commitment of the settlers and the financial and organizational resources of their supporters.

From the founding of the first moshavoth in the 1880s, European-based colonization societies provided the initial grants for acquiring the land, obtaining equipment, and assisting settlers in establishing themselves. Colonization of Palestine was supported through the lar-gesse of Diaspora Jewry, from philanthropists such as the Baron Ed-mund de Rothschild to the contributions of small donors who put away zlotys, centimes, pfennigs, pence, and pennies in little blue collection boxes—the "*pushkes*" of the Jewish National Fund. Capital from these sources was vital, because the first moshavoth were unable to sustain themselves. Within the first decade it became apparent that the individ-ual Hovevei Zion societies of Eastern Europe could not provide adequate support. Hence the role of particularly wealthy European philanthro-pists such as Baron Rothschild became crucial from nearly the begin-ning of the settlement process. Although some private companies as well as Hovevei Zion groups tried to maintain resource-poor pioneers, only the Baron was able or willing to sustain a network of moshavoth for extended periods.[6] By 1900 he decided to diminish his direct involve-ment and transferred responsibility to the Palestine Jewish Coloniza-tion Association. By the first decade of the twentieth century, the most important patrons were the "national institutions" of the WZO, espe-cially the Keren Kayemeth (Jewish National Fund, 1901), the Palestine Office of the WZO (1908) and its successors, and the Keren Hayesod (Pal-estine Foundation Fund, 1920).[7] One can appreciate the crucial, continu-ing significance of outside support by noting that, even after Israel's establishment, settlement agencies within the Israeli government and the WZO expected that a period of ten to twenty years might be required to nurture new villages to economic independence. Although chronic insolvency generated impatience with settlers in the early years of Zionist colonization, experience lead to greater understanding and tolerance.

The prolonged economic dependence of the moshava presaged what would repeatedly occur in establishing all other forms of villages. Settlers lacked sufficient funds not only for equipping and developing their colonies but even for personal maintenance. Benefactors soon concluded that financial assistance alone was not a solution. Pioneers were largely ignorant of what ought to be grown and the techniques necessary for cultivating the desired crops in the unfamiliar and relatively arid conditions of Palestine. Indeed, lack of farming skills and knowledge of the country were a far greater threat to colonization than was inadequate funding. This perception led to the establishment of numerous training institutions for future pioneers in Europe (*hachsharoth*) and throughout the Yishuv.

Ignorance of farming among European Jews was addressed as early as 1870, when French philanthropists founded Mikve Israel outside Jaffa. Before the first moshava was established, they created this agricultural training school for Jewish youth and a rudimentary agricultural research center. When Rothschild became involved in supporting colonization he, too, created schools for educating the settlers in agriculture. He also went a step further, stipulating control over the training of farmers and the right to determine what crops they would grow as a requirement for financial support. Together with generous infusions of money, the Baron imposed a bureaucracy of administrators, educators, and other experts who shaped overall agricultural policy and intervened in the management of the colonists' affairs. He recruited experts from the Mikve Agricultural School and later imported others from Algeria and France and placed them under the authority of a managing director. These experts included engineers, hydraulic mechanics, botanists, and agronomists. From this early period, the outside planner, the expert, and the administrator became permanent fixtures of Zionist colonization.

Like other enlightened philanthropists in Western European liberal societies who favored the worthy over the unworthy poor, Rothschild distinguished between charity and assistance to those in temporary need. He was convinced that the moshavoth could be made viable if the colonists could be equipped not only with idealism and diligence but also with the knowledge of what and how to cultivate. Otherwise, giving funds to the moshavoth would become merely another form of *haluka,* the charitable dole that had maintained pious Jews in the Holy Land over the generations. Rothschild had no intention of assuming permanent responsibility for the financial problems of the colonists. His aim was to nurture the colonists to self-sufficiency. This approach became the paradigm for every succeeding private society and public agency of the WZO and of the State of Israel.[8]

The outright paternalism of this approach appears arrogant and alien today. Consider the following affidavit concerning the engagement of a settler at the moshava of Ekron: "[I promise] to submit myself totally to the orders which the administration shall think necessary in the name of M. le Baron in anything concerning the cultivation of the land and its service and if any action should be taken against me I have no right to oppose it."[9] But the Baron's experts and administrators considered such utter control necessary and natural given the inexperience and ignorance of the settlers. Without signing this or similar documents, the residents could get no help and could be removed.

The settlers may have lacked knowledge and skills, but the experts lacked important information. European-trained, and with experience in European colonization in other parts of the world, they imported varieties of "plantation" economies to Palestine. They envisioned extensive fields with vines, almond and olive trees, mulberry plants for silk, plants and flowers for a perfume industry, and finally, citrus orchards. They proposed food-processing plants and invested substantial sums in the wineries of Rishon le-Zion and Zichron Ya'acov. The Baron and his experts clearly imagined Jewish agriculture as serving an export market and foreign consumers. Like other European colonies, Palestine would become a classic exporter of foodstuffs and agricultural products.

This conception of Palestine dominated the thinking and informed the allocation of resources of most Zionist organizations until well into the British Mandate. The accepted perspective was that Palestine lacked natural resources except for land, and much of that was arid or swampridden. Few saw a basis for nonagricultural industry. A noted exception was Theodor Herzl, the founding leader of the WZO. Herzl wrote extensively in his influential utopian novel, *Altneuland* (Old-New Land) (1902), of a modern urban and industrial New Society in Palestine, but his was a minor voice until the 1920s. Until then, Zionist planners concentrated their efforts on developing a multitude of small villages engaged in plantation-like agriculture for external markets. A succession of scenarios that featured different crops failed until after the First World War when the "Jaffa orange" succeeded and became Palestine's major export.[10]

There is a caveat to the linearity of this evolution. After the First World War, when Palestine's cities began to grow at a rapid rate, Zionist planners tried to adapt village agriculture with a view to serving and profiting from a new domestic urban market. They recognized that diversification could be a practical solution to Zionist agriculture. This is an important topic that will occupy us later in this chapter. Here, it is enough to observe that two developments—citrus groves and truck farming, or the "mixed" farm—transformed the Jewish sector of Palestinian agriculture by moving it away from the initial emphasis on field or plantation crops.

An early failure that illustrates the gap between plans conceived in Europe and the realities in the Yishuv (the Jewish community in Palestine) is the attempt to introduce silk-growing. Europeans had long imagined that silk production was appropriate to temperate areas outside their continent. This notion may also be related to conceptions of the Orient, a vague geographic designation that sometimes included Palestine. By investing in silk, European philanthropists expected to earn profits while alleviating poverty. Rothschild, who visited Safed in 1887, had been appalled at the poverty and squalor among the city's Jews. Uncleanliness was rampant, mendicancy was ubiquitous, and few were gainfully employed. In contrast, but a short distance away, small groups of colonists were struggling in the new moshavoth of Rosh Pina and Y'sod Hama'alah. In an attempt to help these worthy colonists, in 1890–91 the Baron had his experts supervise the planting of approximately 10,000 dunams (a dunam is 1/4 acre) with French mulberry trees at Y'sod Hama'alah. In addition, he dispatched a French educator, Lazar Lévy, to establish a school for girls and another for boys. These were to be based on the model institutions adjoining textile factories like those established by Robert Owen at the model workers' town of New Lanark, Scotland, early in the nineteenth century. In this model, children worked in the factory and were provided with free education in company-controlled schools. Although the trees fared well, the transplanted model did not take root in Palestine. Jewish parents resisted having their children forgo study of traditional, sacred texts for demeaning manual labor and an education they considered irreligious and potentially pernicious. Consequently, although there was an abundance of silkworms feasting on the Baron's mulberry leaves, there were no little hands to weave the silk. Without local labor the industry atrophied and died. As in the case of English Quaker philanthropists, who imagined a thriving silk industry in colonial Georgia, the Baron's initiative was a disaster.[11]

Other attempts to produce varieties of grapes and fruits for wines and preserves and plants for a perfume industry were stymied by problems with disease, plant adaptation, or marketing. Palestine's fledgling wine industry was stunted by overproduction of French wines and a preferential policy toward Algerian growers. In addition, the vines suffered from an attack of phylloxera.[12] The Baron continued to pour in money. He invested both in agriculture and in people. He dug wells, had fields plowed, experimented with varieties of seeds, plants, and livestock. He also built schools, hospitals, and homes. The colonies did not fail for lack of capital. In Zichron Ya'acov alone, the Baron spent 11 million francs in the first sixteen years.[13] But despite the efforts of the colonists and the enlightened and expensive schemes of their supporters, the colonies did not achieve self-sufficiency.

The Search for New Models

The failure of the moshava to achieve economic independence prompted a search for alternatives. After inspecting the moshavoth during a tour of Palestine in 1898 and noting the unsatisfactory state of colonization, Theodor Herzl envisaged a more radical and substantial approach.[14] He postulated in *Altneuland* that in the Palestine of 1923 the country would be organized into a commonwealth called the New Society. He coined the term "mutualism" to describe this utopia "where the individual is neither ground between the millstones of capitalism, nor decapitated by socialistic leveling."[15] Deeply influenced by the English Rochdale cooperative movement of the latter half of the nineteenth century, Herzl conceived of the New Society as a giant cooperative that owned capital, machinery, and land. This grand organization was to be democratically run through a congress composed of delegates from the smaller cooperatives in which members lived and worked. Included in these building blocks were rural cooperatives of which the archetype was the model village of Neudorf (new village).[16] Herzl described this village as a cooperative "commonwealth" with about 100 members. Beyond that, "new settlements are founded on its outskirts." Interestingly, Herzl's plan was in keeping with the communitarian or covenantal ideas of other European utopians and planners, and conceived at the same time Ebenezer Howard proposed limiting the size of garden cities that he sited in clusters. Controlling expansion and consciously locating defined societies across the landscape had become a widely held idea. Observing the results of the first efforts at creating a Jewish society of small villages, Herzl imagined reforming and improving the individual villages and their relationships to one another. The ideal, then, was Jewish farmers living in miniature commonwealths. What was needed to realize this goal was to make them economically viable.[17]

Herzl's conception was based on ideas available to European intellectuals. In *Altneuland,* he singled out Etienne Cabet, who imagined Icaria; Charles Fourier, who invented the phalansteries; Edward Bellamy, who outlined "a noble communistic society" in *Looking Backward;* Theodor Hertzka, who created Freiland; the English cooperative experiment at Rochdale; and Franz Oppenheimer, a professor of sociology and economic theory who wrote extensively on cooperative agricultural settlement. Herzl was so impressed with Oppenheimer (1864–1943) that he invited him to speak before the 1903 Zionist Congress in Basle on the application of cooperative ideas to Zionist colonization. Oppenheimer had a profound effect and is credited with being the spiritual father of the first moshav, Merchavia (1911), and its influential successor Nahalal (1921).[18]

The historical literature of Zionist colonization is particularly rich on cooperative settlements as they began to take shape just before the First World War. Among the most illuminating documents on settlement history are the writings of Yitzhak Elazari-Volcani (Yitzhak Wilkansky: 1880–1955). Volcani, a leading Zionist planner, was one of the foremost agricultural colonization experts. The analyses of this participant-observer are singularly important for understanding the transformation and spread of the Zionist village, because he was actively engaged in planning from the period of experimentation with the moshav and kibbutz during the Second Aliyah (1904–1913) through the massive settlement program in post-Independence Israel. Born in Lithuania and trained as an agronomist in Germany, he arrived in Palestine in 1908. Within a year he was appointed by Arthur Ruppin, the head of the WZO office in Palestine, to a number of key administrative and advisory posts. Volcani first directed the training farms at Ben-Shemen and Hulda. In 1921, he helped found and then directed the WZO agricultural research station in Tel Aviv that was later moved to

Rehovoth. He held this central position until 1951, when the research institute—which now bears his name—was taken over by the Israeli Ministry of Agriculture. He also became the founding director and first professor of agricultural economics when the Hebrew University established a faculty of agriculture in Rehovoth.

In 1927, when the WZO was undertaking an official review of the relative merits of three models—the "individualistic" moshava versus the cooperative moshav and collective kibbutz—Volcani set the discussion in historical perspective. According to Volcani's analysis, the first stage of Zionist colonization began in 1870 with the establishment of the Mikve Israel training school, which he termed the "new Yavneh." The original Yavneh had been a settlement of scholars on the coastal plain that survived the Roman suppression of the Jewish rebellion in 70 c.e. when Jerusalem was destroyed and Jews began nearly two millennia of exile. Yavneh symbolized the power of a small, elite community to sustain and rejuvenate Jewish culture in the face of surrounding catastrophe. During the first stage of colonization, Volcani noted, only 8,000 settlers had been placed on 350,000 dunams. From the point of view of a settlement planner, the crucial test of the value and importance of any model—moshava, moshav, or kibbutz—was how well it contributed to an expansive colonization policy. In this respect, the moshava had been a failure.[19]

The second stage, according to Volcani, began in 1908 with Ruppin's decision to support the farm at Degania, near the Sea of Galilee, with WZO funds. Financial sponsors and experts like himself had considered Degania a pilot project, designed to test community structures as well as agricultural methods.[20] Initially, the project employed only seven workers hired on the basis of strict equality in work and wages. Their numbers soon increased to thirty permanent laborers, and they worked for subsistence wages of 50 francs each per month. They also shared in half the net profit after deductions were made for expenses like seed, food for cattle, security, and medical care. The Degania experiment was a marriage of convenience between idealistic socialists anxious to work the land and middle-class settlement officials and wealthy philanthropists similarly concerned about furthering colonization. They were all bound together in a shared commitment to a national objective.[21]

During the first years the farm grew winter cereals, largely barley and wheat. Diversification came later through experiments to identify more profitable crops. Dairy production was introduced in 1920, and it soon surpassed cereals as a major source of income. Vegetables were successfully introduced in 1922. These new departures were undertaken when planners determined that the farm had reached its maximum potential in cereal production. With these changes came a fundamental shift in the village's agricultural system, from nearly complete concentration on field crops to truck farming. In Volcani's formulation, the colonies had to shift emphasis toward *meshek me'ourav* ("diversified" farming). This change was carefully calibrated for, as Volcani observed, "only after the success of one branch is assured can another be added."[22] In contrast to the Baron's experts who imposed foreign concepts on the moshava, the new generation of WZO planners undertook a careful and programmatic search for appropriate crops. Yet, the dependency of the pioneers on their WZO patrons gave Zionist planners as much leverage as it did the Baron in implementing ideas throughout the new settlements.

Because the amount of land available for cultivation was limited, WZO experts sought ways of augmenting productivity and profitability without increasing the number of dunams allotted each village. At a time when some moshavoth were evolving into towns and even cities, planners insisted that the moshav and kibbutz adhere to the communitarian village ideal. With the exception of those who supported the expanded kibbutz, or kvutza, most settlers supported the objective of retaining the modest size of the village, in terms of population and territory, for ideological reasons.

Three illustrations indicate the distinctive communal characteristics of these types of settlements. In the moshava Rehovoth (Figure 2.1), private fields of varying size are located largely outside the village core. This relatively successful community, founded in 1890, is characterized by well-built and often ample private homes and communal institutions and by substantial orchards in the surrounding area. The sketch of the model moshav (Figure 2.2) is also intended as a village, but, with its homes and facilities closer to one another, its village core is more compact than that of the moshava. At least in the initial phase, land is farmed by families in sections that are fairly equal. The model kibbutz (Figure 2.3), too, has all agricultural lands outside a relatively small residential nucleus. There are no private plots. All land, agricultural and residential, is controlled by the entire commune.

By the 1920s, with forty years of experience establishing and maintaining villages, planners had arrived at workable formulas for Zionist

2.1. A moshava: Rehovoth, 1918. Courtesy of Dr. Dov Gavish, Aerial Photography Archives, Department of Geography, Hebrew University of Jerusalem.

colonization. They would continue to build small villages whose size they could now define in precise, scientific terms. By calculating the amount of land needed to sustain a family unit, they intended to contain the size of the village, and at the same time to ensure that the community would become self-sufficient on its limited allotment after an initial period of support. Behind their plans lurked the specter of the moshava's failure as an instrument of an expansive settlement policy. The WZO had limited funds and was under intense pressure from Jewish youth anxious to immigrate to Palestine from an increasingly hostile Europe. Planners responded to this urgent need by constantly experimenting with ways to support increasing numbers of people on smaller tracts of land.

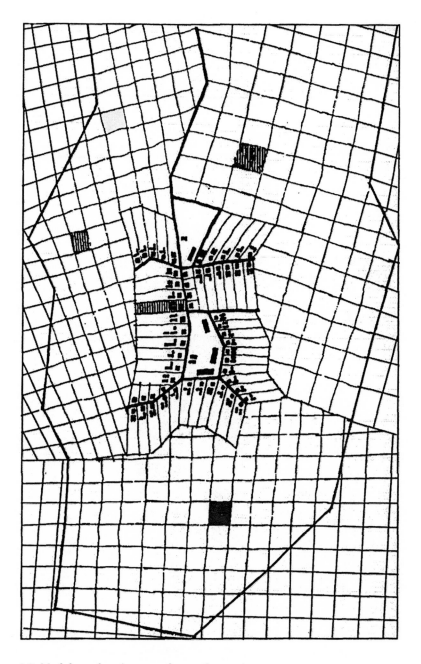

2.2. Model moshav (cooperative settlement).

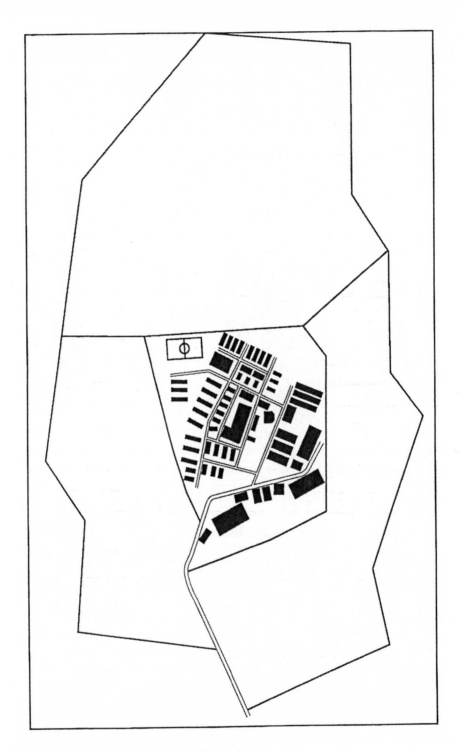

2.3. Model kibbutz (collective settlement).

Competing Models: Modern America versus Medieval Europe

Economics became a central factor in the calculation of WZO experts. Because the formula adopted by Volcani and his colleagues had fixed the number of residents in a village as well as the amount of land the settlers could cultivate, the crucial variables to be negotiated were what would be grown and how the community would be organized. A profound debate emerged over these issues. Volcani represented a school that explicitly celebrated the agrarian culture of medieval Europe, while others advocated emulating modern America.

When the WZO emerged as the primary patron of colonization in the decade before the First World War, the source of expertise shifted. The Baron, with his extensive agricultural holdings in France, had naturally drawn on the French agricultural and colonial experience. The WZO, in the twenty years between its founding and the Balfour Declaration (1917), looked to the German colonization experience. This is hardly surprising. Most of the leaders of the Zionist movement were German or had studied in German universities. Otto Warburg, the president of the WZO from 1911 to 1920, had even worked as a botanist in the German imperial service. Arthur Ruppin, an accomplished social scientist and the chief administrator in charge of settlement from 1908 as founding director of the WZO's Palestine Office until his death in 1943, was trained in Germany. Volcani, too, though born in Lithuania, was one of a number of German-trained specialists recruited to further the settlement program.[23] With the defeat of Germany, the Balfour Declaration in 1917, and the initiation of the British Mandate in 1922, the British capital replaced Berlin as the headquarters of the Zionist movement, and the center of organization shifted once again, this time to London.

In large measure, this shift of locale reflects a far larger phenomenon. The center of power and influence among Diaspora Jewry was moving gradually but insistently across Europe. When, after the First World War, it crossed the Atlantic, the American experience for the first time suggested alternative conceptions for the design of Zionist society. Although planning became a transnational endeavor, based on a fund of social and scientific ideas that were common to western culture, important distinctions emerged among the different national cultures.[24] Despite commonalities, the social and scientific ideas of French, German, and American experts bore the imprints of distinctive national experiences. Thus, even though it had no "mother country" in the conventional sense, Zionist colonization bears the imprint of various national historical experiences of western states at different periods.

The United States was an excellent source of expertise, particularly in areas related to agriculture in arid or semi-arid zones. Conditions in Palestine were similar to those in many parts of the American West, Australia, and elsewhere. American agricultural experts and engineers who had experience with irrigation and building water projects had developed new technologies to make America's deserts bloom. A corps of experts had transformed large sections of the West, particularly Southern California, into fabulously successful oases and had gone on to reclaim deserts from China to the Middle East. With this in mind, Louis Brandeis, the leader of American Zionists, urged Chaim Weizmann, President of the WZO, to invite American experts to Palestine.

In February 1920, Brandeis wrote to Weizmann, suggesting that H. T. Cory, a recognized expert in irrigation and water power, be sent to Palestine. Brandeis emphasized that Cory was "one of the most eminent civil and hydraulic engineers in the United States; and his present work in Egypt will place him among the foremost of his profession in the world." In addition to working in the Aswan region along the Nile, he had worked on controlling the Colorado River and in bringing irrigation to the Imperial Valley in Southern California.

Cory was more than willing to go. Like other gentiles well-disposed to the Zionist effort, he was eager to participate in what he and other experts of that generation perceived as one of the great, historic planning missions of their time, and he employed friends to present him to prominent Zionist leaders. Recognizing that in addition to good technical advice there were public relations benefits to inviting non-Jewish experts like Cory, a Zionist advocate predicted that "upon his return to the United States you will find him [Cory] ready to cooperate with you in arousing and extending the interest in the Zionist movement—speaking not as a Jew, but as a great engineer who has studied the problems of Palestine in precisely the same spirit that he is now studying the problems of the Nile. Might he not be very influential in augmenting popular interest and support for the cause which strongly appeals alike to his mind and his heart?"[25]

Cory's invitation, then, was one of many extended to American experts, Jews and non-Jews, who carried out research and wrote reports on Palestine during the Mandate. Among the more widely circulated studies were those produced by two gentiles, Elwood Mead, an agricultural specialist, and Walter Clay Lowdermilk, an irrigation expert. Both provided estimates of the number of people who could be supported by the land, suggestions as to the kinds of technologies that ought to be employed, and proposals for the form of social and political organization best suited to implementing these technologies. Mead argued for the transfer of the American model of homesteading. Lowdermilk pressed for a Jordan Valley Authority (JVA), which he proposed as a Palestinian equivalent of the New Deal's Tennessee Valley Authority (TVA). Such studies are interesting not only for what they indicate about Palestine's problems and prospects but also for what they reflect about their authors' experiences and about American society. American experts were exporting not socially neutral technologies but the social and economic values underlying America's development of its own frontiers. The most far-ranging American model, the report of Elwood Mead and his associates, was put forward as an alternative to the cooperative Labor Zionist conceptions of colonization championed by Volcani and his colleagues.

An American Model for Agricultural Colonization: The Road Not Taken

The Report of the Experts (1928) was officially a joint British and American effort initiated by Chaim Weizmann, President of the World Zionist Organization, and Mark Schwartz, Director of the Palestine Department of the Zionist Organization of America. They proposed the creation of a joint Anglo-American commission of professionals, most of whom were American, to study the changes in agricultural colonization since 1923. Proponents of the study wanted to stem pressure from settler groups to adopt the kibbutz as the preferred model for Zionist settlement.[26] The commission's chairman and perhaps leading figure was Elwood Mead, a former professor at the University of California and then Commissioner of Reclamation of the Department of the Interior in Washington, D.C., who conducted research on Palestine in 1923 at the behest of the WZO. His findings on the potential of the Yishuv were acclaimed, and Mead was touted before American audiences by Arthur Ruppin as "the best living authority on agricultural colonization." It was a reputation that extended even to Australia, where Mead was a leading consultant proposing much the same kind of program he was to bring to Palestine.[27]

Most of the 1928 report is appropriately technical. It identifies good soils, assesses water resources, evaluates suitable crops, and suggests the kinds of modern technologies required to make farming not only possible but profitable. The report also touches on Arab-Jewish tensions. The authors address the economic implications of a situation where many landholders are Arabs and opposed to Jewish settlement. They observe that there are numerous difficulties in acquiring land and that, even when available, its price is exaggerated relative to productive value. Writing prior to the violent Arab protests of 1929 and the consequent *White Papers* that restricted Jewish immigration and land purchases, the authors are hopeful for relations sufficiently amicable to permit Jewish agriculture to expand.

The remainder of the report is concerned with the cultural, political, and economic problems of transforming European Jews into farmers. In a brief review of assistance programs from Germany to Australia, the experts evaluate strategies throughout the world that were designed to enable individuals to settle and remain on their own land. Their evaluation is based on a belief in private ownership. This is what had occurred in the United States. American agriculture was based on the ideal of independent homesteaders who had title to their own farms. The American experts contended that this model could and should be replicated by Jews in Palestine.

The commission's proposals for Palestine derive from their analysis of what afflicted American agriculture. From the Greenbackers of the 1870s through the Populists and to the agricultural crisis of the 1920s, American farmers had sought technical, political, and economic assistance to enable them to remain on the land. It had been a losing struggle. The 1920 census officially announced that the United States was an urban nation and confirmed the diminishing proportions of Americans engaged in farming. The deteriorating situation in America gave urgency to the conviction that Palestine could and must be different.

Mead and his commission understood that it was a daunting challenge to achieve in Palestine what was difficult to achieve in the United States. In America, which began and expanded as an agricultural nation, the primary problem was holding people to the land. In Palestine, Jews had yet to become farmers. They urged that instruction prior to and subsequent to immigration as well as continuing education could compensate for technical ignorance. However, in their assessments, the most serious impediment to the success of the Zionist colonization effort was cultural and ideological: "Another intangible, but serious difficulty, in the creation of a solvent Jewish agriculture, is the appeal this [agricultural settlement] movement makes to emotional people—poets, reformers, labor and social leaders, men with keen minds and lively imaginations, but lacking the rural traditions, practical experience and balanced judgment so necessary to success in farming. The tendency of people so equipped is to try experiments."[28]

Indeed, it was the tendency of "poetic" Zionist farmers to engage in ideologically motivated social experimentation that the American observers viewed as the most serious obstacle to widespread, private ownership and successful colonization. Thus, beyond the technical aspects of the report, the most important item on the agenda is rebutting the socialist alternatives to capitalist agriculture. Drawing on the American experience, Mead and his associates advocate homesteading as the key to establishing an agricultural society in Palestine.

It is in this sense that the report may be read as a brief against the growing commitment of Zionist settlement authorities to the kibbutz. Despite the Baron's unsuccessful efforts to foster a village community of independent farmers more than a generation earlier, this report argued for continuing the method but without the communitarian framework. Mead sought to save the system by training the farmers and improving their technologies. His report called for the transfer of agricultural expertise, and maintained the basic free-enterprise ethos that had motivated earlier colonization schemes.

The American experts, who saw socialist colonization as both impractical and incompatible with American values, buttressed their report by citing alternative forms of colonization that had proved successful in Palestine. The prosperity of the Templers, German religious societies that had settled in Palestine in the latter half of the nineteenth century, was persuasive evidence in support of private ownership of land: "These (Templer settlements) are not merely self-sustaining, they are decidedly prosperous. The neat two-story stone houses, their large barns usually of stone and their plantations, livestock and equipment make a pleasing rural picture which is enhanced by closer examination. . . . In one of their colonies not a single farmer is in debt . . . they are educating their children and living in better homes than the average farmer in Europe or America. This shows that farming in Palestine carried on by Europeans who are both good workers and good managers can be made profitable."[29]

The other useful model was the Palestine Jewish Colonization Association (PICA) colonies founded by the Rothschilds, where Jews were pragmatic enough to put irrelevant ideological considerations aside: "Those in charge of PICA colonies realize that enduring agricultural success in Palestine calls for industry, thrift and good management, as in other countries. They pay no attention to social theories, or to claims that the Jew has a peculiar temperament that places him outside the influence of economic and business facts which prevail elsewhere. They have had a trying experience in substituting business for philanthropy. . . . What is important, is that they have made progress in the direction that Zionist colonization must travel. . . . There is a complete absence of the peculiar social experiments so conspicuous in the Zionist colonies."[30]

The homestead model was also viable, the commission argued, as demonstrated by the personal experience of a Mr. Broza, who came to Palestine around 1890 and pioneered in the hill country outside Jerusalem. The fact that "a Jewish farmer can, without outside help, overcome all local obstacles, acquire a farm and prosper in its cultivation in direct competition with Arabs, is shown by the case of Mr. Broza. . . . Mr. Broza has prospered because he exercises all the faculties with which his race is so richly endowed. He is a worker, an organizer and a business man."[31]

Broza's experience could be replicated if only Zionists remained faithful to what had motivated colonizers in other places in the world: "As a rule, the governing motive in colonization is to build up a permanent and prosperous rural life with broad opportunities for qualified people of small means to become home owners." Instead of adopting such a well-tried approach, the commission lamented, Zionist authorities were subordinating success in colonization "to the creation of a new economic and social order, with a strong antagonism to Capital." The villain was the *Histadrut* (Jewish Federation of Labor): "It is the view of the Commission that . . . the influence of the Jewish Federation of Labor is giving these colonies a character not in harmony with the ideals and aspirations of the Jewish race." The report musters scientific arguments to support the vision of a Jewish homeland with independent farms owned by inherently bourgeois Jews, and free of the taint of socialism.[32]

Transplanting Medieval Europe to Palestine

The American-initiated report in favor of the private farm failed to change the direction of Jewish settlement. Labor Zionism succeeded in rallying support for cooperative and collective models during the 1920s, in part, because middle-class Jews were not coming to Palestine in sufficiently large numbers and most of those who came did not invest in the countryside. This was abundantly clear to the European bourgeois lay leadership of the WZO and to experts in Palestine. Experience and necessity required adjusting preconceptions and preferences to realities. On this basis, they made a shift to noncapitalist agriculture in the 1920s. In the view of a growing lobby within the Zionist movement, particularly among colonists already in Palestine, primarily the moshav and secondarily the kibbutz offered the best hope for ensuring large-scale settlement of the country.[33]

Rejecting the model derived from the American frontier, Volcani and local WZO experts worked from an interpretation of the European experience. Volcani was familiar with American farming. He had visited the United States and Canada in 1921 as part of a WZO program to send experts resident in Palestine to study agriculture in a variety of countries in America, Europe, and North Africa.[34] Although he found much to appreciate in American agricultural technology, he rejected the American rural settlement model. He argued Zionist colonization had more to learn from European agricultural society in the Middle Ages than from the United States in the modern period.

Volcani's somewhat curious historical perspective was related to the dangers of mechanization.[35] In his view, modern, mechanized agriculture led to a fundamentally undesirable and perhaps dangerous social and economic order. The use of machines generally required and fostered big farms that Volcani viewed as vestiges of a feudal system dominated by large landowners. Moreover, the introduction of machines resulted in the displacement of rural populations, and this was precisely contrary to what Zionist colonizers were trying to achieve. In effect, farmers were impoverished so that large landowners could prosper. Volcani observed that "machines such as reapers, binders, threshing machines and elevators do not create, do not increase production; they simply help to economise in taking the place of manual labour, or in certain cases to make the labour itself easier and more agreeable."[36] The result, while maintaining production and increasing profits of the landholders, was to push agricultural laborers to the cities.

Mechanization had been crucial in the development of American agriculture, because there was not enough labor to work the virgin lands of the West. Palestine was different. Zionist planners had to place people on the land and keep them there. The most effective course was to train farmers in scientific techniques and provide them with light and handy implements to increase productivity. If this were done, Volcani maintained, Zionist planners could combine in Palestine the relatively dense countryside of a labor-intensive, medieval agriculture with the productivity of modern farming. "From the point of view of the national economy," Volcani argued, "a large farm, however well run and managed, is never to be recommended, as it would always bring in more [income] if it were divided into small farms. . . . From the point of view of the national economy, national assets are wasted through large farms."[37] As noted above, Volcani saw this approach, so strangely anachronistic to a modern reader, as a pragmatic response to urgent problems. The Jewish claim to Palestine would be difficult if not impossible to maintain if Palestine's countryside were not populated with Jews. Planners required a model that could justify and accommodate a mass immigration of Jewish settlers and ensure that they would spread across the land. It was in this context that the moshava based on individualistic agriculture was rejected.

The delicate and complicated dilemma for colonizers was how to fulfill national goals and at the same time satisfy the needs and ambitions of individuals. This problem was manifest in a number of related areas. For example, many moshavoth used less expensive Arab labor rather than employ immigrant Jews. Undoubtedly, this was an economically rational decision for capitalist farmers. But from the perspective of Zionist planners, the use of Arab labor contained the seeds of a national disaster. It was an issue on which both planners and landless socialist pioneers who came on the Second Aliyah and after could readily agree.[38] Volcani chides those who ignore the danger of individual Jewish farmers building up their holdings by employing Arabs to work the land, reminding them that "we aim at increasing our numbers in order to secure and fortify our position, and we are in fact creating a new Galuth [exile]. Every owner collects round him a number of non-Jewish working families. Settlement of this kind will not open a path to an extensive immigration, the dense population we are looking for will not be formed, and no original culture will be developed."[39]

Without large numbers of Jews working the land themselves, Zionists would have a fragile hold on the country and might be unable to build a stable society in it. Pointing out that "ownership even if it is fully secured by law" would be insufficient to ensure the permanent transfer of land to Jewish control, Volcani concludes that Jewish labor "is therefore for us not a dictate of the higher morality but of stern necessity."[40] From this same national perspective, "socialistic" settlements were superior. They were more stable and therefore the investment of scarce resources in such communities was less risky. For example, in the event of personal or natural disasters, the individual might lose title to his land. This would also entail damage to national interests. Because communal enterprises such as the moshav or kibbutz were better able to sustain temporary losses, they were a more reliable method of national settlement and investment.

Much of Volcani's analysis hinges on the fact that the success of Zionist agriculture depended on poor but idealistic immigrants. It had become clear that the expectation of early colonization societies that future pioneers would have their own resources or contribute their share of settlement costs on the installment plan was not going to be realized in the dimensions required by an ambitious national project. Those middle-class immigrants who decided to try farming settled in the coastal regions. They did not readily venture forth and expand the Yishuv's frontiers.[41] It became apparent that in order to extend frontiers to new regions that were difficult to cultivate, initial models of settlement would have to be altered. In large measure, Herzl's *Altneuland,* for all its utopianism, accurately captured the class structure of the Zionist reality. Herzl envisioned a first wave of poor pioneers who would have to be supported. The middle and the upper classes would follow later. This progression remained a widely held expectation. After more than forty years of experience, pioneers and pioneering as the initial step in colonization still had to be supported.

Size of the Zionist Village

By the 1920s, a half-century after founding the Mikve Israel school, Zionist colonizers had successfully trained several generations of Jews to farm even inhospitable and arid lands. The moshava was no longer the preferred model, and the moshav and the kibbutz had come to replace it. Of the two, the moshav was the planners' village of choice until the mid-1930s when the kibbutz—for reasons we shall explore in a later chapter—superseded it. Aside from the question of community form, the size of the community was the most important feature remaining to be determined. This was not a mere technical or ideological question. It went to the core of the economic problems that had beset Jewish villages from the start. In Volcani's terms, establishing "farms of the right size" entailed determining what was to be produced on a minimum amount of land while still avoiding mechanization.[42] How to sustain and satisfy pioneers on the smallest possible plot was the paramount challenge for Volcani's agricultural experimental station from its founding in 1921 and for similar institutions through well after Independence.

During the first half of the 1920s, experts introduced a variety of new branches of agriculture such as bees, poultry, and cows to the villages under WZO sponsorship. The dairy industry received perhaps the greatest attention because it appeared to be a natural and familiar way for the small farmer to diversify. This assessment appears justified in light of the results: while dairy farmers had produced only 60,000 liters of milk before the First World War, output reached more than 3 million by 1930.[43] Dairy farming was attractive because it required little mechanization. The fact that the basic unit of production was the family made it economical as well. Volcani reasoned: "The price of milk does not depend on the two extra minutes that the farmer's wife spends on milking the cow."[44] Relatively small farms could count on the labor of women and would not require hired labor. They could be sustained by the working capacity of a single family. This was crucial in Volcani's formulation, which stipulated that "the size of the holding must not exceed the area which can be properly cultivated by the settler and his family. The type of cultivation must be such as to provide occupation for all members of the family during all seasons of the year."[45]

Another important advantage of family farming was that it required a smaller initial investment. As calculated by the WZO, the cost of settling a family in a moshav or kibbutz, exclusive of the price of land and of preliminary reclamation works and of building roads, was about 500 pounds. This was only half the amount spent by other colonizing agencies in assisting immigrants in traditional villages. Part of the WZO savings stemmed from the introduction of the *meshek ezer*, a small piece of land attached to the house where the settler could raise vegetables and keep a cow, fowl, and fodder. Such attachments were intended not only for farmers in distant settlements, but also for workers living in housing estates in the suburbs of Tel Aviv, Haifa, and Jerusalem.[46]

Indeed, the land allotment could sometimes be as little as 20 dunams (about 5 acres) per family for agricultural workers or other laborers who derived additional employment in nearby towns and cities. This minimum was justified in a study prepared for the Zionist leadership in 1929 by Volcani and Levi Eshkol (Shkolnik) (1895–1969), who held a variety of key positions in the administration of Zionist settlement before becoming Prime Minister (1963–1969). Their report, entitled "Key for the Settlement of Various Zones in Palestine," was initially designed for the Nakhalat Yehuda housing estate near Rehovoth. It sets forth the three issues that had to be weighed in matters of size: that there was not enough land to settle all the immigrants who wished to become farmers; too small an allotment would impoverish the settler; and too large a grant would necessarily diminish the chances of others who wanted to become farmers.

The magic formula arrived at for this workers' suburb near Rehovoth was only 20 dunams. Nakhalat Yehuda was to be divided into 8 dunams for citrus (primarily oranges), 5 for fodder (for dairy cows), 2 for vegetables, and 5 for other purposes. The remaining income would come from wages settlers earned as laborers in nearby towns or farms. Volcani and Eshkol's "key" for colonies that were proximate to urban areas also applied to distant rural areas where Zionist organizations owned large tracts of land, as in the Valley of Jezreel and the Galilee. However, in these remote regions, where supplemental income was unavailable, family farms were allowed 100 dunams each.[47]

Allotments of 100 dunams appear as a regular feature of settlement plans from the early 1920s, although occasionally this figure is mentioned as much as 40 years earlier by the Baron's experts. There is one interesting exception, a plan by members of ha-Shomer (The Watchman) for communities of families on only 40 dunams, but this never materialized. By and large, the planners of the first generation of colonies including the Baron's experts had calculated that as much as 400 dunams were required per family. In effect, an inexorable downward push reduced the allotments to 100 dunams by the 1920s. By then WZO experts were confident that by settling families on 100 dunams they could achieve their goal of a numerous, densely settled, independent, and self-sufficient Jewish peasantry.[48]

Mead's 1928 *Report of the Experts* was one of the last assessments that still called for larger figures. Mead was convinced that 100 dunams were inadequate for assuring the all-important goal of settler self-sufficiency, yet he fully recognized the Zionist predicament of insufficient land to settle potential farmer/pioneers. His succinct formulation could not have been better articulated by official Zionist planners: "There were weighty social and political reasons for reducing the farm unit in Palestine to the lowest economic area. The smaller the farms the larger the number of settlers who can be cared for in a given colony."[49]

Though Mead appreciated the pressures and principles that influenced the actions of Zionist settlement officials, he criticized them for settling more colonists on land "than can reasonably be maintained thereon." He predicted that their policy would result in impoverishment. Families would be forced to work for wages or to rent additional land outside the village. On the other hand, if they remained tied solely to cultivating their allotments, he believed, they could never become economically self-sufficient. Both outside work and renting additional land, he feared, would compromise the integrity of the farming community and settlement officials would have only themselves to blame for the failure of the colonization program.[50]

Yet, even the 100-dunam framework was hard to maintain, and there were constant pressures on Zionist planners to lower that figure. Between 1927 and 1931, for example, 6,300 new pioneers, primarily Polish Jews, joined those already dependent on the WZO. These immigrants were distributed among new moshavim, kibbutzim, teaching farms, and experimental stations because there were insufficient resources to set up new colonies for them. At the same time, planners sketched out schemes for settling 55,000 additional families they hoped would be able to leave an increasingly ominous political situation in Europe. They also hoped that there would be land and funds to accommodate them. In the sketches that they made for this potential influx, planners took into account an allotment of no more than 100 dunams per family and resisted pressures to consider smaller allocations. In effect, they had found what they believed was a workable formula and expected to remain faithful to it.

One last observation should be made here concerning the optimal size of the Zionist village. Although some independent colonization societies continued to organize moshavoth when settlement resumed after the disruptions of the First World War, the WZO focused on the moshav and the kibbutz. Both could conform to the formula of 100 dunams per family. Volcani, like most Zionist planners, preferred the moshav. As we have noted, Herzl himself had envisioned Neudorf as the ideal settlement, incorporating many English cooperative principles associated with the Rochdale plan. Convinced that some form of ownership is part of human nature and both a useful inducement as well as a goal in colonization, Volcani expected that kibbutz members would first acquire farming skills and then join a moshav. In his appraisal, "The worker of today is the owner of tomorrow." He pointed to the example of California's schemes for assisting white small landowners lest their lands go over to "coloured" workers, admitting that, in Palestine, too, "our national aspirations cannot be realised without a dash of socialism." It was perhaps this "dash" that he applauded in Ruppin's support for the establishment of the first kibbutz at Degania before the First World War. World Zionist Organization planners would support any model that settled Jews on the land, even the socialist kibbutz, especially because it was expected to be only a transient phenomenon.[51]

Volcani and his colleagues confidently gave priority to the moshav. They did not suspect the kibbutz would emerge in the 1930s as the WZO's preferred means of settlement in frontier regions and that it would maintain this role until the early 1950s when it would again be superseded by the moshav. However, after the 1930s, political and strategic concerns rather than economic or ideological preferences motivated a change in favor of the kibbutz. It was political issues raised by the growing success of the Zionist village that increasingly focused attention on the problem of defense.

CHAPTER 3

The Economic Basis for Arab/Jewish Accommodation

No one will deny that, whether based upon a specific document or not, the well-being of *all* the inhabitants of Palestine is a prime consideration. . . . Official bodies have consistently found that the development of the [Jewish] National Home has fostered rather than hindered the well-being of the whole population. The [Mandatory] Government in its recent Memorandum is forced to make the same admission.
—*The Jewish Plan for Palestine; Memoranda and Statements*, 1947

The Jews come to Palestine to execute not a colonial, but a colonization policy.
—ABRAHAM GRANOVSKY, 1931

ZIONISM achieved international recognition and legitimacy on the eve of Britain's conquest of Palestine. The Balfour Declaration proclaimed in November 1917 that "His Majesty's Government views with favour the establishment in Palestine of a National Home for the Jewish people." The way appeared clear for the expansion and development of the Yishuv (the Jewish community in Palestine). However, the Balfour Declaration also maintained that "nothing shall be done which may prejudice the civil and religious rights of existing non-Jewish communities in Palestine." The Covenant of the League of Nations reiterated the Balfour Declaration's commitment that a Jewish "national home" would be built, while at the same time it stipulated the obligation to safeguard "the civil and religious rights of all the inhabitants of Palestine, irrespective of race and religion."[1] Thus, Jewish rights and prospects were tied to those of Palestine's Arab communities. Simple logic would suggest that as more Jews settled in Palestine and purchased more land, less land and opportunity would be available for Arabs. Zionist experts were challenged to prove that large-scale Jewish settlement could be accomplished without jeopardizing the rights of the Arab population.

Zionists assumed that confrontation with the Arabs could be avoided. Based on the experience of the Zionist village, experts calculated the land could become so productive that it would provide a good standard of living to both peoples. If the benefits of Zionist technology were made available to everyone in Palestine, causes of conflict rooted in competition could be eliminated. The common assumption of the early settlers was that Palestine could support both Arabs and Jews, and it appears that they were correct. The population of Palestine has grown by nearly tenfold in the course of the twentieth century, and the standard of living has continually risen. Nevertheless, by the 1920s it was becoming apparent that whatever theories Zionists might hold and whatever economic incentives they might offer, Palestine's large Arab majority viewed their presence as a threat, and the very success of Jewish settlements was a source of anxiety.

The campaign to vindicate Jewish colonization proceeded on many fronts. Zionists laid claim to Eretz Israel by appealing to history and invoking the collective memory of Judeo-Christian civilization. At a time when the right of national self-determination had been consecrated into a paramount international principle, Jews, a people whose very existence was threatened, could demand the chance to resettle the land promised to the Children of Israel. Zionists also claimed Palestine as part of their reward for their role in the First World War and promised further support for the victorious side. They also invoked the ideal of the pioneer engaged through the "conquest of labor" in "redeeming the land" and "making the desert bloom." Their rhetoric depicted them as virtuous settlers engaged in a heroic and moral enterprise. These arguments and others became part of the international discourse the Zionist movement engaged in through the establishment of the state. They are evident in wonderfully succinct and expressive form in the first part of Israel's Declaration of Independence.

None of the above, however, dealt with the issue raised by the Balfour Declaration or the terms of the Mandate under the League of Nations. Was there room in Palestine for two peoples? Was there any way to ensure that the development of the Yishuv would not impinge on the opportunities of Arabs for a good life? It must be pointed out that these international declarations neither mentioned nor recognized Palestinians as a distinct people with their own national rights. They were treated as "natives," residents in the land but people whose political identity derived from membership in the larger Arab nation that had only recently been granted numerous states with the dissolution of the Ottoman Empire. From both the international and the Zionist perspective, then, justice to Arabs meant ensuring civil, religious, and economic rights within a non-Arab-dominated Palestine. It fell to Zionism's large corps of planning experts to propose a persuasive formula to address the economic issue.

The question was defined in terms of the "economic absorptive capacity" of Palestine. Agricultural experts and planners had to prove that Palestine could be sufficiently productive to support immigrant farmers without compromising Arabs already settled on the land. Their challenge was not only to provide a technical solution. They also had to present their case in moral terms that could satisfy the scrutiny of the world community and even the doubtful among the Zionists. The "economic absorptive capacity" also figures in the effort to remodel Palestine into a modern, urban-industrial society capable of absorbing millions of Jewish immigrants in the generation following the Second World War. At that time, experts from a variety of fields including archaeology and history, geography, economics, and other social sciences were enlisted to prove a large number of refugees could be successfully absorbed. This topic is discussed in Chapter 8. Here, the emphasis is on how agricultural planners tried to establish a basis for accommodation with the Arabs by assuring mutual benefit. Indeed, the search for an economic or any other realistic framework for cooperation among Jews and Arabs continues through the present.

International Context

Zionist agricultural planners did not initially identify Palestine's Arab population as an item of concern. From the 1880s through the establishment of Israel, their prime objective was to create vibrant and successful agrarian communities rooted in the land. The widespread appeal of this imperative among Jews was based on their collective historical memory, a calendar of festivals, and everyday rituals intimately bound up with the land and the desire to return to Zion. Colonization was the realization of this desire, an internal affair to be debated within the world Jewish community.[2]

During the beginning stages of settlement, experts of the First Aliyah worked for a private individual such as the Baron and a loose international network of local Hovevei Zion societies. After the convening of the World Zionist Organization in 1897, their work was sponsored and controlled by an increasingly efficient international organization whose membership, though primarily European and led largely by German Jews, stretched across the Atlantic and the Mediterranean to include Jews and Jewish organizations in many countries. For most of this period, references to advantages for non-Jews from the Return to Zion were couched in Biblical or historical language largely anchored in the universalistic visions of the Hebrew prophets. No one thought to discuss with Palestine's Arabs the problems and prospects of Zionist ambitions. When problems arose, Zionist leaders turned to officials of the Ottoman Empire, who were often located outside Palestine.

In the decade prior to the First World War, the needs and problems of Jewish colonization began to earn recognition and legitimacy beyond the world Jewish community. From its founding by Theodor Herzl, the WZO persistently sought and ultimately succeeded in obtaining international support and recognition without which re-creating a large, let alone independent, Jewish community in Palestine would have been impossible. Early achievements before the First World War were due to interventions negotiated through Germany, on which Zionist leadership had influence and which, in turn, had considerable influence with the Ottomans. The Balfour Declaration, issued by Britain toward the conclusion of the war, was the next and essential step in this process.[3] Moreover, other countries including the United States, Italy, and France endorsed the declaration. The League of Nations, through the Mandate granted Britain in 1922, capped this development by establishing a specific framework that sanctioned the status of Zionist planners and set the terms for their mission of settling Jews in Palestine. Thus, by the 1920s, Zionist experts worked under the auspices, stipulations, and inspection of international authorities.

The frame of reference for their work was clearly defined by international agreements. The Mandate anticipated that Palestine would remain a country divided into Jewish and Arab communities living and working in separate villages. The country was clearly not intended to become one of ranches, plantations, or even large farms as in other lands colonized by Europeans. Article 11 of the League of Nations' Covenant enjoins the Mandatory government to "introduce a land system appropriate to the needs of the country, having regard, among other things, to the desirability of promoting *the close settlement and intensive cultivation of the land.*"[4] A landscape of dense agricultural populations was envisaged for both Arabs and Jews.

The Covenant regarded the country as underdeveloped but assumed that Jews would be able to undertake a far larger share of their own development than the Arab population, who required extensive assistance. In language infected with claims to Western superiority, Article 22 enjoined the Mandatory government to nurture the independence of those "peoples not yet able to stand by themselves under the strenuous conditions of the modern world." This was defined as "a sacred trust of civilisation." It went on to assert that the "best method of giving practical effect to this principle is that the tutelage of such peoples should be entrusted to advanced nations who by reason of their resources, their experience or their geographical position, can best undertake this responsibility, and who are willing to accept it, and that this tutelage should be exercised by them as Mandatories on behalf of the League." In practice this meant that the Mandatory government in Palestine worked through the local arm of the World Zionist Organization, which was charged with considerable responsibility. Article 4 viewed the WZO as the "public body for the purpose of advising and cooperating with the Administration of Palestine in such economic, social and other matters as may affect the establishment of the Jewish national home and the interests of the Jewish population in Palestine, and, subject always to the control of the administration, to assist and take part in the development of the country." In 1929, this local body became the Jewish Agency for Palestine.

The Jewish Agency was the institutional forerunner of the State of Israel, with its officials assuming parallel positions after independence. For example, its Chairman, David Ben-Gurion, became Prime Minister. Similar continuities took place in law and security matters. Jewish Agency professionals in settlement work or economic planning continued in comparable official capacities after the state was created. Yitzhak Elazari-Volcani, for example, began his career as a planner and expert prior to the First World War in the employ of the Palestine Office of the private and voluntary World Zionist Organization, a body without recognition in the Ottoman Empire. With the Mandate, he became an official in a recognized quasi-governmental body. At the end of his career, he worked for the independent and sovereign Jewish State of Israel.

It should be emphasized that colonization through rural settlement was but one function of the Jewish Agency. It was also charged with contributing to economic development in general. Article 11 enjoined the WZO to undertake "public works, services and utilities, and to develop any of the natural resources of the country, in so far as these matters are not directly undertaken by the Administration." The Jewish Agency was also to engage in the provision of social services, including education, health, and welfare services to the Yishuv. In time, it would engage in defense activities that led to the formation of the Israel Defense Forces. Constant negotiations with the Mandatory and other international bodies required the development of officials with diplomatic skills and an international bureaucracy. In sum, the colonization activities of the Jewish Agency, in its manifold aspects and as sanctioned by international agencies and agreements, became the basis for the establishment of an independent Jewish state. Zionism directed its attention toward the outside world, primarily Britain and the Jewish Diaspora. The Arabs of Palestine existed in parallel and increasingly in competition with Jewish settlement. Contact occurred when there was friction between the two national groups.

Socioeconomic Division

In Zionist thought and policy, the Jewish state was envisioned as containing an Arab population. During the deliberations over partition by the Peel Commission, the British suggested transfer of Arabs from sectors designated for Jews and this possibility was explored by Zionist authorities. Then and subsequently, such scenarios occasionally appear. Nonetheless, Zionist planners worked on the assumption that a Jewish state would necessarily include an Arab population. When Zionist authorities accepted the United Nations plan for partition of Palestine, they accepted de facto that Arabs would constitute about 40 percent of the Jewish state, although it was expected that a sovereign Jewish state would open its borders to extensive Jewish immigration and thereby achieve a very substantial majority.[5] Suggestions that Zionists secretly or privately sought the "transfer" of the Arab population out of Palestine are erroneous.[6] Extended, active, and public discussion of how

Arabs could share in the development of the country belie such charges. During these years of the Mandate, Zionist experts developed arguments on how Arabs could improve their agriculture, their chief occupation, by emulating the Zionist example.

As we have seen, the 100-dunam allotment grew out of competing claims for land in what has become an extended Arab/Jewish conflict. Despite the growth of Arab and Jewish Palestine under the Mandate, the country remained underdeveloped and underpopulated with large unsettled and uncultivated areas. The British promise of support for a Jewish national homeland as expressed in the Balfour Declaration and in the terms of the Mandate did not include land grants. Jews continued to acquire land under the British as they had under the Ottomans, through purchase from wealthy and often absentee Arab landowners. As much as 90 percent of Jewish-owned land was acquired in this fashion. As Jewish pioneers moved into lands that were under cultivation, they necessarily uprooted Arab tenant farmers. Wherever this occurred it posed a moral dilemma as well as a political obstacle to Zionist colonization.

The prime proposition offered by Zionist experts was that much land was being poorly cultivated or not cultivated at all. Consequently, the country could support new Jewish villages without displacing Arabs. They reasoned that if Arabs improved their farming methods, they could limit a family's holding to 100 dunams, even as Jews did, and still raise their standard of living. In this fashion, Palestine would have enough fertile land to support a far larger population of both Arabs and Jews. They argued that in the long term, Jewish agricultural development was advantageous to Arabs as well. Traditional techniques, including the use of the primitive plow, were already being superseded, and many Arab farmers had already adopted more modern methods of farming. Modern fertilizers, seeds, and irrigation systems could cross communal and sectarian boundaries. The citrus industry, whose best-known product was the Jaffa orange, was a prime example. Initially cultivated by Arabs, the industry had been enormously stimulated and developed by Jewish experts to the benefit of both Jewish and Arab growers.[7]

Statements about the superiority of Zionist farming predate the First World War, but they become more frequent during the Mandate in official suggestions that, with modern methods, both Jews and Arabs could cultivate lands in Transjordan and in other unsettled areas of Palestine.

These claims became urgent in response to a series of *White Papers*. Beginning with the Hope Simpson Report of 1930, which heralded a retrenchment of the British commitment to Zionism, Britain moved to bar Jews fleeing Europe from entering Palestine and suspended the legal right of Jews to buy land. These official reports were in effect a reversal of the promise given Jews of a chance to build a national homeland. They justified limiting Jewish immigration and land purchases because they were said to be damaging to Arab interests. The British position raised a formidable challenge, and Volcani and his colleagues set out to undermine and disprove the evidence on which the *White Papers* were based.

The success of the Zionist village whose economy had been revolutionized provided an abundance of data to support Zionist claims. The Jewish cooperative marketing organization for dairy products and juices, Tnuvah, the Biblical term for produce, reported that between 1931 and 1938 milk production and citrus exports increased by 600 percent and eggs by 1,000 percent. Growth continued at substantial rates following the outbreak of the Second World War when transportation difficulties between Britain and the eastern Mediterranean led the British to use Palestine as their main supplier of many items, including foodstuffs. Zionist agriculture had by then come of age and was able to provide for a surging local population as well as the needs of a large military establishment. This burgeoning Jewish rural economy sustained steadily increasing numbers of settlements and settlers. By 1939, there were 140 settlements with a population of 32,000, or an average of 280 individuals each. During the next decade, or by Independence, about 100 more villages would be established.[8]

The settlements were maintained and stimulated by a host of institutions that built the physical infrastructure and provided financial and marketing support as well as agricultural research and training. These included water and electricity companies, banks and credit institutions, purchasing and marketing agencies, and research stations and schools. For example, in addition to Tnuvah, there were sixty-four rural credit societies and sixty-one cooperative local water societies. There were also national companies and associations that served a large number of individual settlements. Many directed their services to discrete and often competing segments of the Yishuv. Nevertheless, all operated under the comprehensive umbrella of political institutions created by the Jewish Agency that provided official representation before the Mandate authorities.[9]

A distinctive industrial sector complemented the achievements of rural colonization. The two largest nonpetroleum-related industrial firms in the Middle East—the Palestine Electric Corporation and the Palestine Potash Company, both established during the Mandate—developed so rapidly that they employed approximately 1,500 workers each by the end of the 1930s.[10] The management of these companies were Jews and identified with Zionist purposes. Yet, unlike the rural settlements that were ideologically committed to exclusive use of Jewish labor, they had mixed Arab and Jewish labor forces, though these were typically separated by crafts organized along religious and national lines. A similar phenomenon took place in the large industries of Haifa, where apparent shared proletarian interests could not supersede national ones. As one student of the boundaries between Jewish and Arab workers concluded: "Class interests could not and did not transcend national interests."[11]

Smaller Jewish enterprises were also springing up in a multitude of areas that were new to Palestine: foods, textiles, clothing, metal goods, pharmaceuticals, optics, machinery, timber products, leather goods, printing and paper products, stone and cement, and electrical machinery. However, these smaller enterprises tended to be based on exclusively Jewish labor as found in the agricultural colonies. Arab firms did not compete in these areas but were concentrated in commodities that had been established before the Mandate—such as soap, cigarettes, shoes, and some articles of apparel—and they employed exclusively Arab labor. Virtually no competition or duplication existed between Jewish and Arab manufactures. Indeed, Arabs consumed only 10 percent of Jewish industrial production, most of it electricity.[12]

Whether in agriculture, industry, or commerce, then, Palestine's Arabs and Jews continued to occupy different niches. In the vivid expression coined by Moshe Lissak, a leading Israeli sociologist, nearly the entire organized Yishuv lived in a "Jewish bubble"—a discrete society that functioned in parallel to Arab society. In addition to working in separate economies, they lived in segregated urban neighborhoods and rural communities, participated in particularistic political institutions and ideological movements, and enjoyed the educational and health services they provided. Palestine, at least in socioeconomic terms, was already a partitioned country.[13] The Jewish side of the divide was extraordinarily dynamic, far outstripping the Arab side in assets and prosperity. The magnitude of the challenge facing the experts was considerable.

Socioeconomic Inequalities

The succession of studies undertaken during the Mandate's quarter century reported the steady and, in fact, spectacular development of the Yishuv.[14] Its numbers were initially small, but the potential for rapid and significant growth was recognized. Indeed, it was the very success of the Yishuv that increasingly threatened the country's Arab population. Jews represented one-tenth of Palestine's population on the eve of the First World War, and one-third at the outbreak of the Second World War. Particularly during the years immediately preceding the Arab uprising of 1936–39, Jewish immigration numbers were very large. In 1929 Jews were but 17 percent of the population. After Hitler rose to power, the numbers swelled, especially from Central Europe. Sixty-one thousand entered legally in 1935 alone, and others entered without legal documents. By 1936, Jews constituted 31 percent of the population. At this rate, it appeared that in the foreseeable future Jews would become a majority in Palestine and would attempt to realize the *Judenstaat* Herzl had envisioned. This, in fact, was anticipated by world leaders including Lloyd George, Winston Churchill, Woodrow Wilson, and individual members of the League of Nations. The more concrete the achievements of Jewish colonization, the greater the expectation that a Jewish state or "commonwealth" would be established.[15]

The gap between Jews and Arabs was evidenced in many indicators including geographic distribution and residence, levels of literacy and education, occupational structure, and income. For example:

- Rural communities were completely segregated. Although Arab and Jewish settlements might be quite close to each other, none had a mixed Arab-Jewish population.
- More than 50 percent of all Arab town dwellers lived in "all-Arab towns." The remainder lived in "mixed" towns: Jerusalem, Jaffa, Haifa, Tiberias, and Safed. But even there, Jews and Arabs lived in separate neighborhoods. Tel Aviv, Palestine's largest city by the end of the 1930s, as well as other rapidly growing towns were entirely Jewish.
- The Arab community remained primarily rural. In 1880, 79 percent of Palestine's Arabs were rural. This proportion declined to 64 percent in 1946. At the same time, less than 1 percent of the Jewish population was rural in 1880, rising to 26 percent by 1931 and declining thereafter. In sum, despite the enormous effort in rural colonization, Jews came to the country as an urban people and so largely remained.

- 99.5 percent of all Jews worked in Jewish enterprises, were employed in Jewish institutions, or were self-employed. Less than one-half of 1 percent worked for Arabs or provided professional services only to Arabs. In contrast, large numbers of Arabs were employed in Jewish agriculture, commerce, and industry.

Thus, Palestine had become a divided country with a "dualistic" economy even prior to the Peel Commission's recommendation in 1937 for partition. A network of relationships emerged that reflected this fact. Among its features was an intercommunal trade characterized by an Arab sector that provided unskilled labor, services, agricultural produce, and raw building materials as well as land to Jews, while Jews purchased land and provided manufactured goods, professional services, and wages to Arabs.[16] This imbalance was expressed in the considerably greater per capita wealth among Jews than among Arabs. As early as 1931 the far smaller Yishuv had an income 15 percent higher than that of the Arab sector. By 1944, after the First World War had brought considerable prosperity to the country, the gap widened to 25 percent.

These figures must be placed against the background of a rapidly developing country during the interwar period. The Arab economy grew quickly, but the Jewish economy grew twice as fast: 13.2 percent annually as opposed to 6.5 percent.[17] Indeed, the relative growth of Jewish Palestine ranks sixth in the world in a representative sampling of thirty-nine economies during the 1920s and 1930s. Only oil-producing Venezuela, France, Czechoslovakia, Finland, and Austria outperformed the Yishuv. As economic historian Jacob Metzer has concluded: "Mandatory Palestine was by far the most vibrant Middle Eastern economy in the first half of the twentieth century."[18]

The same disparities were reflected in social services. In 1921, of the physicians in Palestine, 44 percent were Jews; the figure had risen to 90 percent by the end of the decade. Indeed, Jews enjoyed a higher proportion of physicians per capita than any country in the world. The same sharp differentiation was found in education. Immigrant Jews re-created the educational system they had experienced in Europe. Around 75 percent of Jewish youth between ages 5 and 19 were enrolled in schools during the 1930s and 1940s. Among Arabs, the figures rose from 19 percent to about 25 percent in the same period. Moreover, Jewish institutions, from elementary schools to universities and research institutes, were funded by Jews in the Yishuv or by external Jewish sources. The Mandatory government or foreign ecclesiastical and charitable institutions provided for Arab schools. Arab Palestine had serious if declining rates of illiteracy, comparable to those in such then underdeveloped countries as India and Egypt, whereas Jewish schooling was at the high end of the European norm.

Potential Contribution to the Arab Population

It was precisely these disparities that challenged Zionist planners and politicians to bring economic advantages to the country's Arab population. A wide spectrum of observers were certain this would happen. T. E. Lawrence (Lawrence of Arabia) predicted that "The success of their [the Zionists] scheme will involve inevitably the raising of the present Arab population to their own material level, only a little after themselves in point of time, and the consequence might be of the highest importance for the future of the Arab world."[19] Official British evaluations as well as many surveys and reports confirmed that this was taking place. Among items often cited were:

- Importation of significant capital for the country's development from which all benefited.
- Extraordinary expansion of the Arab citriculture industry that followed from advances in technology, financing, and marketing introduced by Jews.
- Increased employment in urban areas and improved health standards and medical care throughout the country, including for Arabs.
- Greater revenues to the Mandatory government, of which a higher share was raised from the Jewish sector and redistributed to the Arab sector including greater investment in Arab education and, as a result, reduced illiteracy among Arab men and women.
- A very significant increase in the standard of living. Thus, even as the Yishuv came to enjoy the highest standard of living in the region, Palestine's Arabs became better off than Arabs in neighboring countries.[20]

Data of this kind, supporting the assertion that Jewish settlement benefited the region, have been advanced from the first Zionist Congress in 1897 through the present. Herzl, in the utopian plan detailed in his book *Altneuland*, typically imagined that Jewish science, experience, and enterprise would transform Palestine and the Middle East. Thus, toward the conclusion of the novel he locates his heroes in the "Peace Palace" situated in a modern, prosperous, and westernized Jerusalem: "Wherever in the world a catastrophe occurs—earthquake, flood, famine, drought, epidemic—the stricken country wires to this centre for help."[21]

This theme was treated over the next generation by a host of writers including Ahad Ha-Am, Menachem Ussishkin, Leo Motzkin, Max Nordau, and Ber Borochov. It was discussed among intellectuals of the right and the left, religious and secular. Throughout is an explicit assumption that much of the country's fertile soils were already under cultivation. Yitzhak Epstein, perhaps the first Zionist theoretician who, in 1907, wrote about the need for accommodation with Arabs, called for institutionalized cooperation wherein Jews would open to Arabs their hospitals, schools, research facilities, and all the other components of a modern society. Arabs would appreciate that their improved standard of living was due to the Zionist colonists, and this would lead to acceptance of an active Jewish presence in the country. Epstein was convinced that "this [Arab] nation occupies such a broad swath of territory that it can allow us, an ancient people so close to it in blood, language, and many spiritual traits, to occupy that part of the land of our fathers that it does not yet occupy. And it not only can, but also must for its own good, let the Jews into their country, because it is powerless to lift itself up alone and to end its poverty and ignorance, but with us alone it can overcome its deficiencies."[22]

Abraham Granovsky (Granot) and his generation of experts on this argument were to demonstrate that the amount of land available was far greater than originally believed and that it could be far more productively cultivated by Jews and certainly Arabs. By the 1930s, Zionist experts were propagating this more expansive view of Palestine's potential wealth and prosperity. Also, the advantages of Zionist colonization to Palestine's Arabs were quantified and no longer relied on declarations of good intentions.[23]

At century's end, Shimon Peres, a former Prime Minister and Foreign Minister, echoed these claims in his book *The New Middle East* (1993), which appeared at the time of the Oslo Accords between the Palestine Liberation Organization and the State of Israel. The book, a best-seller translated into more than thirty languages, heralds an era of peace and shared prosperity in which Zionist science, business acumen, and initiative will play the central role. While Granovsky and his generation offered a vastly expanded view of prosperity brought to an essentially agricultural Palestine, Peres evokes the picture of an advanced industrial society where wealth is no longer primarily set in fixed and limited resources such as land. Peres promises that Israel will share its human, intellectual, and financial resources with neighboring peoples in creating an unlimited modern economy of continual growth. This activity will bring prosperity to all. Peace and harmony will thereby be a possible consequence.

The refrain Peres employed is repeated throughout the twentieth century: Zionism is not a threat to Arabs in Palestine or to the Middle East. On the contrary, the Yishuv should be viewed as a common resource that can improve the condition of all peoples. Moreover, a higher standard of living would encourage social and political change that would solidify a shared commitment to peace and accommodation. Peres advised that the proper view of the Oslo Accords is "as a historic commitment with an economic lining." Under conditions of peace, the successfully established Jewish National Home would realize the promise of the Balfour Declaration and the Mandate to all of Palestine's peoples.[24]

In retrospect, the difficulty with these expectations is that until the Oslo Agreements of 1993, Zionism did not treat Palestine's Arabs as a people with aspirations for political independence in their own, exclusive homeland. This attitude was widely shared. As late as 1947, in the formal report of the United Nations that studied the problems of Palestine and again recommended partition, a discrete Palestinian national identity was treated as a recent development. The report claimed that a distinctive Palestinian consciousness did not appear until after the Balfour Declaration and the establishment of the Mandate, or only after Zionism emerged and gained recognition for its claims and programs. Paragraph 166 of the UNSCOP (United Nations Special Committee on Palestine) report provided a succinct summary of this view, arguing that the "desire of the Arab people of Palestine to safeguard their national existence is a very natural desire. However, Palestinian nationalism, as distinct from Arab nationalism, is itself a relatively new phenomenon which appeared only after the division of the 'Arab rectangle' by settlement of the First World War. The National Home policy and the vigorous policy of immigration pursued by the Jewish leadership has sharpened the Arab fear of danger from the intruding Jewish population."[25]

Recent academic scholarship pushes the awakening of a discrete Palestinian identity perhaps to the decade before the First World War and locates the evidence for this in newspaper editorials and interpretation of the sometimes violent protests of Arab peasants on land Jews had begun to work. Other scholars find a distinctive Palestinian identity even earlier.[26] Still, as these peasants lacked differentiated political institutions based on an explicitly identifiable Palestinian polity, it is not surprising that both Zionists and the agencies of the international community viewed Palestine's Arabs as integral parts of the larger Arab nation. Indeed, there is ample testimony that that is how they viewed themselves. The gamut of institutions and activities—raising taxes, maintaining democratically elected political institutions that performed many of the services of a modern national government, creating a discrete and manifest national culture with distinctive, visible symbols—had no parallel among Palestine's Arabs. The development of such manifest and visible expressions of national identity came in large measure after the establishment of the State of Israel, and, some have suggested, in response to it. Palestinian Arabs have only relatively recently gained recognition in official Israeli consciousness as a separate nationality with political rights. Such recognition came slowly, over the course of a generation, spanning the activities of the Palestine Liberation Organization—who published a comprehensive and explicit Charter in 1968—through the *intifada* at the end of the 1980s.[27]

Sharing such widespread perceptions of Arabs in Palestine before the creation of Israel, Zionist advocates during the Mandate concentrated on providing evidence for the actual and potential advantages from Jewish colonization without reference to the impact of Zionist settlements on a Palestinian polity.

100 Dunams for Arab Farmers

A particularly precise statement of the advantages of Zionist settlement was articulated by Granovsky—like Volcani, an agricultural expert and economist. Using statistics to support his social and political analysis, Granovsky responded to the Hope Simpson Report of 1930 with the argument that Palestine had much room for development beyond the relatively concentrated settled areas in the hill country to the north and south of Jerusalem.[28] He calculated that, west of the Jordan River, there was a potential for 156,012 agricultural families. In 1931, there were 55,429 Arab households and 7,325 Jewish ones, for a total of 62,754. Employing the 100-dunam-per-family formula, Granovsky concluded that 93,258 more families could be settled. Assuming each farming family included about six members, Palestine's total agricultural population could be increased by approximately 600,000.[29] In Granovsky's words: "Palestine still has much land which is awaiting settlement, and offers many opportunities for a substantial enlargement of its absorptive capacity. And, on the other hand, Jews and Jewish capital are waiting only for the call in order to transform the waste places of the land into fertile and closely settled areas."[30]

Granovsky refuted Hope Simpson's assessment that Arabs needed more land. He claimed that the problems and the poverty of the *fellahin* (peasants) were a consequence of deficient methods rather than lack of land. For example, whereas Arab farmers had yields of only 105 pounds of wheat from a dunam, Jewish farmers achieved 158 pounds. The figures were similarly dramatic with other crops: 138 pounds per dunam for barley on Arab farms as opposed to 244 on Jewish farms; 97 pounds of Durra wheat as opposed to 141, and so on.[31] Clearly, it was in the self-interest of Jews that Arabs would learn from and emulate Jewish agriculture by adopting the methods Jewish agronomists and other experts proposed. If this were done, they predicted, there would ultimately be an equalization of income and standard of living between Jews and Arabs. Thus, if, as Volcani and others argued, Jews could achieve a European standard of living on 100 dunams, so could the Arab population.

The Zionist intention to share their settlement experience had an explicit political element. According to Granovsky: "A distinction should be drawn between colonial policy and colonization policy. Colonial policy is aimed primarily at exploiting the natural resources of a country, and is little concerned with its settlement. It has prejudicial results in various respects: the enrichment of a small group of European immigrants who establish enterprises in which natives do all the work; exploitation of the aborigines and creation of deep-lying differences between the two classes of the population. In the end, all this tends to check the development of a country, especially if it is thinly populated. Colonization policy, on the contrary, is bound up with settlement on a large scale: room must be found for the largest possible number of immigrants who will take a personal share in every field of activity."[32]

Granovsky and his generation explicitly described themselves as engaged in colonization (establishing settlements), not colonialism (dominating another people): "The Jews come to Palestine to execute not a colonial, but a colonization policy." This distinction was crucial in the political debates of that era, even as it is now in the controversies among pro-Zionist, anti-Zionist, and post-Zionist scholars. Zionism was a moral movement that could bring prosperity to everyone. Moreover, it could accomplish this without exploiting the native population.[33]

As Granovsky's statement and others like it demonstrate, Jewish settlement authorities were sensitive to the charge of usurpation and exploitation. Perhaps paradoxically, this led them to justify deepening
the social and economic divide between Jews and Arabs. In this context,
the ideological decision not to employ Arab labor at low wages was both
a practical step to ensure there would be work for Jewish immigrants
and an ideological position that valued labor and rejected exploitation.
As Volcani insisted, Jews would do the hard work themselves. Jewish
youth would engage in the most difficult and dangerous physical labor,
from clearing land and drying swamps to cultivating fields and tending
animals. Jewish labor was to "conquer" and, in an expression that reso-
nates with Biblical promise, "redeem" the land.

The moshava, where bourgeois Jewish farmers had sometimes exploited cheap Arab labor rather than hire Jewish immigrants, was dero-
gated. Not only was this form of settlement compromised by its failure to expand, it was morally tainted. The moshav and the kibbutz, in
contrast, were designed to settle the maximum number of pioneering
youth on a limited amount of land, at once transforming European
Jewry into an honest peasantry and rooting Jews in the land as no mere
legal document or political pronouncement could.

Zionists celebrated the fact that they neither made Arabs into tenant
farmers nor exploited them as laborers. Unlike in other lands to which
the Europeans came, in Palestine "natives" were not pushed off the land
by force nor were they reduced to modern bondage by employment on
colonial plantations.[34] Abraham Granovsky claimed: "In no event is it
possible to say that the economic position of Palestine has become
worse because of the Jewish immigration. The Jewish immigrants have
not crowded the Arabs out from any occupation. Not one enterprise can
be pointed out where Arabs were employed before the Jewish colonization was begun, and were later displaced by Jews."[35]

It was on this basis that the WZO mobilized political and financial
support from Jews throughout the world. This capital was not raised
and expended for the profit of investors. Rather, it was used to enable
Jews to return to the land and revive its ancient beauty and fertility.
The end result of this process was to be not only a modern "Jewish
national homeland" but an example, "a light unto the nations." This
message is reiterated throughout Zionist thought. Herzl's *Altneuland* begins with a solution to the problems of a particular national group but
concludes with a vision of Jewish/Arab harmony and cooperation that
would radiate throughout the world. Paradoxically, the exclusive "Jew-

ish bubble" was designed to be economically productive, to advance Zionist interests, and, at the same time, to serve universal ends. Zionism held then, as now, that Jewish self-interest and the self-interest of its neighbors were compatible.

Limits and Necessity of Economic Analysis

This vision now appears at once naive and imperfect. Had Arab villages and early Zionist settlements been microcosms of late-twentieth-century individualistic, civil societies in which individuals are independent and equal, without reference to community of origin, tensions between Jews and Arabs might have been attenuated and a costly and painful human conflict might have been avoided. Having injected itself into a social and cultural landscape dominated by Arabs, Zionism incurs blame for setting political priorities on a sectarian basis. However, such a critique errs in two fundamental ways. It anachronistically privileges the rights of the individual over the needs of community and nation. It also delegitimates the desire for collective rejuvenation through village life with a distinctive communal culture, which was so fundamental to Zionist pioneering. Even the sharpest critics within the Zionist camp, such as philosopher Martin Buber and his colleagues in B'rith Shalom (Covenant of Peace, an association of largely Central European immigrant intellectuals) accepted the legitimacy of Jewish settlement. Buber praised the development of the exclusive "Hebrew village," in particular the kibbutz, and proclaimed it the best example of a utopian community in the modern world.[36]

The moshav and the kibbutz, the two creations of Zionist planners that took shape during the postwar period, were homogeneous societies for cultural reasons. They were designed as communities in which an authentic, modern Jewish society would be regenerated. There were many versions of what this might mean. The history of settlement, and particularly of the kibbutz, is rife with ideological conflict and communal fragmentation. Nevertheless, the common bond was a commitment to re-creating modern Jewish culture, necessarily expressed in Hebrew and, to greater or lesser degrees, secularized and socialistic depending on the particular branch of the settlement movement. Zionist villages were intended as cradles and laboratories where modern Jewish culture might be nurtured and tested. In this sense, they remained covenantal societies even without the religious commitments of the first pioneers.

Zionism saw itself readily and naturally aligned to universal values and rights while at the same time holding to the validity of national identity.[37] Many of Israel's founders had grown up in Europe having witnessed how socialism had everywhere blended a commitment to universal class interests with the interests of nation states. Certainly no alternative, nonparticularistic model suggested itself in the Middle East, where Moslem societies gave primacy to religion and nationality.[38] Mixed villages would have been as inconceivable to Arabs as they were to Jews. Partition of Palestine's countryside by religion and nationality was but one instance of a wider phenomenon that afflicted Cyprus, India, much of Africa, and Europe itself. To try to resolve the Arab/Jewish conflict by dividing the country made perfect sense to the British, who initiated the process. By 1937, when the Peel Commission first proposed partition, the British, experienced with sectarian conflicts throughout the world, concluded that Palestine, too, would have to be partitioned. A decade later, the United Nations resolved that an Arab and a Jewish state should be established in Palestine. Today, more than a half-century later, Israelis and Palestinians are engaged in trying to negotiate terms for the same result. Domination by one of the parties over the other has proven impossible. Creating an admixture within the same national framework appears to be an elusive fantasy shared only by a limited group of largely Jewish intellectuals who would ask both communities to submerge national/religious identities and interests for the sake of an abstraction beyond the experience or desires of both peoples and, indeed, most peoples everywhere.

In the Middle East of the late nineteenth and early twentieth century, the model of the homogeneous Zionist village, employing only Jewish labor and operating within a "Jewish bubble," was a normal and perhaps the only viable way of imagining settlement. In retrospect, Zionist planners were naive in expecting that if they limited land to 100-dunam allotments for Arabs and Jews and if they shared agricultural expertise they could persuade Arabs there was nothing to fear from the spread of Jewish settlements. However, the arguments of Zionist experts did have demonstrable impact on world opinion and on the international bodies that determined Palestine's future, persuading them that Jewish colonization did not necessarily prejudice the economic well-being of Palestine's Arabs. Ironically, seventy years after Granovsky's writings and during the current controversy between Israeli and Palestinian negotiators over the "Right of Return" of Arabs to their former homes inside Israel, some Palestinian Arabs have adopted a minimalist view of how much land is necessary for the maintenance of a family. It is they who now argue that there is ample room for Jews and Arabs on the same land.[39]

Despite the success of their technical work and its moral and political value, Zionist agricultural planners came to recognize that the promise of shared economic productivity was not enough to ensure the survival of their villages. Armed attacks during the Arab uprisings of 1936–1939 demonstrated they could not persuade Arabs there was nothing to fear. However successful their arguments and convincing their data in the world arena, they could not mollify opposition in Palestine. To secure the fate of the Yishuv, Zionist planners began to redesign their villages as military outposts whose structure and locations were determined in strategic terms.

CHAPTER 4

The Village as Military Outpost

Song of the Valley
Rest comes to the weary
And refreshment to the toiler
A pale night spreads
On the fields of the Valley of Jezreel.
Dew below and the moon above,
From Beit Alpha to Nahalal

Mist envelops Mount Gilboa
A horse gallops from shadow to shadow.
A shout rises upwards
From the fields of the Valley of Jezreel.
Who shot and who fell
Between Beit Alpha and Nahalal

Refrain:
Oh, oh, from night to night
Silence in Jezreel
Sleep, O valley, splendid land
We stand guard over you.
—NATAN ALTERMAN

ALTHOUGH earlier designs of Jewish villages did not seriously or effectively take self-defense into account, this concern became paramount in the 1930s. Responding to the increasing outbreaks of conflict and growing competition with the country's Arabs, planners gave unanticipated preference to the kibbutz as the instrument for expanding settlement. For approximately twenty years, from the mid-1930s through the early 1950s, the kibbutz was the spearhead of Zionist settlement policy. After the establishment of the state when an army was available to defend borders, the moshav displaced the kibbutz, again becoming the preferred model. Thus, the colony of 100 families was shaped not only by religion, ideology, and economics but, eventually, also by compelling strategic and political considerations that evolved from the growing conflict with Palestine's Arab population.

First the *Haganah* (Defense—the leading pre-state military organization), prior to Independence, and then the Israeli army, at its highest command level, have engaged actively in planning villages. From the 1880s to 1948, the process of planning that began with the imaginations of visionaries proceeded to the drawing boards of professional experts and planners and finally to the map rooms of military strategists. The involvement of the military continues to be a peculiar feature of Israeli national planning at the beginning of the twenty-first century. It is especially strategic considerations that contributed to making Israel exceptional in modern village development. Israel is the only noncommunist country that adopted collective farming as the preferred form for organizing agriculture. Zionist planners recognized that such communities, particularly the kibbutz, were well-suited to perform police and security functions, and the design of these Zionist villages was then further altered to root their population in a hostile countryside and to enable pioneers to hold their gains in a protracted and increasingly violent contest.[1]

As noted earlier, the process of establishing Jews in villages was not straightforward. Preconceived ideas had to be reexamined, modified, and abandoned even as innovative strategies were invented and implemented. The early planners of the moshava, moshav, and kibbutz did not anticipate the transformation of villages into military outposts. Defense requirements and strategic advantages were not even discussed until about half a century into the process of planting Zionist villages across the landscape of Eretz Israel. The crucial period for considerations of defense was the twenty years from the 1930s into the first decade of the state. Prior to this time, means to reduce the vulnerability of Jewish settlements were not evident in their design. Beginning with the outbreak of sustained Arab attacks in 1936, a new type of settlement emerged with the appearance and purpose of a military outpost. After the first decade of Independence the military function of these settlements was greatly diminished, because the new state now maintained an army to defend borders. Moreover, the successful Sinai Campaign of 1956 reduced the threat from the regular armies of neighboring Arab states and from irregular infiltrators (*fedayeen*), so there was less need for settlements, particularly along the Egyptian border. Israel's successes in the 1967 Six-Day War reduced the strategic role of border kibbutzim even further.

The emergence of the kibbutz as the preferred mode of colonization for particularly strategic purposes is readily apparent in comparative data. Between 1927 and 1935, 31 moshavim, 22 moshavoth, and 8 middle-class agricultural settlements were established—but only 20 kibbutzim.[2] During 1936–1939, 80 settlements were laid out in the Sharon coastal plain between Tel Aviv and Haifa and in the Judean Mountains leading to Jerusalem. It is during this period that the kibbutz emerges as the preferred village model. From 1943 to 1948, another 80 settlements were established—56 kibbutzim and 24 moshavim. In the five years after Independence 213 settlements, of which 79 were kibbutzim, were founded and most of these were planted along Israel's armistice lines. The strategic function of kibbutzim was crucial. The War of Independence did not yield internationally recognized borders with neighboring states. It resulted in armistice lines that were often tense with the threat of armed violence by intruders if not actual invasion of a regular enemy army. The kibbutz was the village designated to define and maintain borders in the face of this continuing danger.[3]

The evolution of the defensive character of the Zionist village is reflected in the innovations in the design of the moshav and kibbutz. Prior to the First World War, most settlements had no walls and were open to the surrounding countryside. Village streets and paths led into the fields or joined with the few roads that crossed the countryside. There were virtually no walls or other structural means for self-defense. Planting small groups of pioneers in distant and isolated locales became increasingly risky by the 1920s. In response to the changing circumstances, Richard Kauffmann, one of the leading planners for the WZO to emerge during this decade, planned in 1921 the moshav Nahalal with a clearly defensive design. The circular form offered security advantages even as it limited the size of the village. Figure 4.1, a photograph taken in 1997, indicates how resistant to change was the initial design.

By the mid-1930s, the kibbutz superseded the moshav as the preferred settlement, and a crucial reason for the change is reflected in its design. With the increasing incidence of violence against Jewish rural settlements, walls were erected. The result was the "stockade and tower" design that characterized the kibbutzim built over the next decade or until Independence. Figure 4.2, a photograph of Ein Gev under

4.1. Nahalal, 1997. Courtesy of the National Photo Collection, Government Press Office. Photo by Moshe Milner.

construction in 1937, not only illustrates the fundamental design features but the popular place that the kibbutz captured in the public imagination. Volunteers from settlements and even distant cities came to this remote site on the shores of the Sea of Galilee at a prearranged time and in the course of a night and a day erected the tower and walls with prefabricated parts they had carried with them.

This growing attention to security led to the formulation of the "Security Principles in the Planning of Agricultural Settlements and Workers' Villages," drafted during the War of Independence by the Settlement Department of the Operations Branch of the General Staff.[4] This document defined where settlements were to be located, and how they should be organized and constructed. The rationale grew out of the cumulative experience in planting frontier colonies during the pre-state period. As we shall see when we consider "Israeli Villages" in Chapter 10, these principles were refined further in post-Independence Israel through the design of the unique "rurban" villages established in Judea and Samaria, or the West Bank, after the Six-Day War of June 1967.

4.2. Volunteers erecting the stockade and tower at kibbutz Ein Gev, 1937. Courtesy of the National Photo Collection, Government Press Office. Photo by Zoltan Kluger.

Nahalal, planted in the eastern end of the Jezreel Valley, offers a preview of how the need to defend an outlying settlement affected design. The inner ring housed the village center and the educational, social, and technical services the settlers required as well as homes for resident artisans. In the outer ring were the farmhouses attached to medium-sized plots. Along the spokes of the wheel Kauffmann designated sections for irrigation and farmyards. Dry farming took place on larger plots farther away from the houses. Together with the social and economic benefits of this layout, there are carefully planned defensive advantages. Buildings, principally the cowsheds that were shared by two neighbors, are erected parallel to the ring road and serve as a protective barrier. Moreover, bunkers are located but a few paces from the cowsheds. In effect these form an outer wall. The community is thus concentrated together at the hub in a manifestly defensive position, with the fields radiating out from the protected core. Only in 1952, when there was no longer a security threat, did planners recommend breaking through the ring and relocating the buildings according to strictly agricultural requirements.[5] Kauffmann's plan was "closed." The design explicitly limited the opportunities for expansion, in keeping with the thinking of contemporary European planners, particularly proponents of Ebenezer Howard's garden city concept. Additional population would have to be accommodated in other controlled communities.[6]

The circular form was not unique to Jewish Palestine. American pioneers typically set up circular wagon camps to protect themselves when they crossed the West against hostile flat-trajectory, light weapon fire from Native Americans. In the Middle Ages, Germans had located their Rundling villages in frontier regions. The circle of settler homes and structures for work and livestock was a logical choice for isolated villages in frontier regions.

Experience indicated that the ring pattern had limitations. The space between the houses on the outer ring was larger than between those in the inner ring. When an attacker penetrated the outer ring, defenders could find it difficult to discriminate between hostile forces and friendly ones. The army investigated this issue and then instructed planners to site homes in frontier moshavim at no more than 30 or 40 meters from each other. Another solution was organizing settlements according to a star-shaped or finger-shaped plan (Figure 4.3). In this pattern, it was possible to develop flanking fire in the areas between the axes. It was also possible to withdraw from the end axes to the more secure core. Using the image of a ship built with watertight compart-

4.3. Star-shaped settlements in the Jezreel Valley, 1950s.

ments, it was expected that "even if some compartments are damaged the ship remains afloat." Defense strategy also figured in plans for settlements in the Ta'anakh region in another portion of the Jezreel Valley, designed in the 1950s, which provided for "the possibility of opening flanking fire from two of the units to protect the third and enable a retreat to the common center."[7]

The idea of a compact community in a defensive mode—whether in a ring, a square, or any other shape—was explicit in the design of the kibbutz in the mid-1930s. Indeed, one of the reasons the kibbutz became the preferred means of settlement on the frontier was its organizational structure. Unlike the family-based moshav, the kibbutz encouraged the concentration of living quarters with the children housed together and dining and recreational facilities organized in common. This meant that kibbutz members were concentrated in discrete structures rather than dispersed among the separate farming plots of cooperative or individualistic villages. When the moshav replaced the kibbutz in the 1950s as the predominant form of settlement, planners reduced the space between houses in border settlements in order to impede infiltration by fedayeen. Where such spaces did exist, they were assumed to be temporary in the expectation that children of moshav pioneers would eventually establish homes near their parents.

Planning the Kibbutz: Strategic Imperatives

The kibbutz came to the fore in Zionist settlement policy as a consequence of the "disturbances" that began in 1936 and lasted until the outbreak of the Second World War. In 1936, Tel Amal, the first of the "stockade and tower" settlements, was established where the Beit She'an Valley connects with the eastern end of the Jezreel Valley. An initial attempt to settle at this location failed when violence erupted in early 1936. The settlers retreated to a relatively nearby kibbutz, Beit Alpha in the Jezreel Valley, and returned to Beit She'an in the fall of 1936 to reestablish the settlement. They employed a method called *homa 'umigdal* (stockade and tower), which has since become enshrined in heroic versions of the struggle to build the state.[8]

The establishment of this kibbutz became an act of popular resistance and cooperation. With volunteers assisting the small band of actual settlers, in one day they erected a prefabricated settlement that featured a tower with a searchlight and a protective wall around a modest compound. Additional construction was undertaken within the protective shield of the walls and the tower's searchlight. Homa 'umigdal was then replicated in other frontier regions.[9] This initiative was a response both to new dangers and obstacles to settlement in the Palestinian countryside in a period of anti-Jewish violence and to political decisions made in London. In January 1937, the Peel Commission, appointed to cope with the apparently irreconcilable inter-communal conflict in Palestine, proposed dividing Palestine between Jews and Arabs. With the prospect of partition, Zionist planners devised a settlement policy to obtain the most generous borders possible. This entailed the extensive use of settlements as instruments for staking out frontiers. As Moshe Shertok (Sharett), one of the preeminent leaders of the Yishuv, noted, "From the political point of view, I know of no more pressing tasks, no more effective weapon, than founding settlements in [border] areas, and thereby creating facts."[10]

The creation of such "facts" had long been part of settlement policy, but until 1936 ideological conceptions and economic issues had been paramount. Since Arthur Ruppin became director of the WZO office in Palestine in 1908, planners had attempted to create clusters of Jewish villages to enhance the security of each. Yet, nothing as strategically comprehensive as the post-1936 settlement policy had ever been undertaken.

"Creating facts" led to an immediate increase in settlement activity. In the five years between 1932 and 1936, on average one settlement was created per month, for a total of sixty-six. During the disturbances and until the outbreak of the Second World War, fifty-three settlements, or nearly two per month, were established under more difficult financial and security conditions. This enormous effort was widely supported by the public at large and by the leadership of the Yishuv, as well as by Zionist leaders abroad.

The results of this policy can be readily seen in maps 4.1 and 4.2. The clustering of settlements in a discernible pattern is a characteristic of Zionist colonization. By and large, since the First Aliyah, Jews had settled in the plains of Eretz Israel: the coastal plain, the Jezreel Valley, the Beit She'an Valley below the Sea of Galilee, and up into the finger of the Upper Galilee. This created the base for the "N" of settlement. With the Arab population located largely in the hills and mountains of Palestine, land could be purchased and settled more readily in the valleys where absentee landlords were willing to sell to Jews. Moreover, Jews often settled in undesirable land such as arid areas or in the swamps of the coast and Lower Galilee. Nevertheless, the pace of acquisition increased during the 1930s despite growing opposition from Arabs and legal restrictions imposed by the British Mandatory government.[11] While small numbers of colonists attempted to move into the mountains including the Golan Heights and areas around Jerusalem, the bulk of settlement activity since the first moshavot was in the lower areas— on the plains and in the valleys. The violence inaugurated in 1936 gave urgency to filling vacant areas within these regions and extending out the boundaries from the already existing "N" of settlement.

- First: Ten kibbutzim were established in the Beit She'an Valley and five in the area on the western and southern shore of the Sea of Galilee. In effect, these clusters, added to existing settlements, represent a drive to break beyond the boundaries designated by the Peel Commission. A Jewish presence along the Jordan could also perform several strategic functions: protect Palestine's most important electric power plant, which had been built by Zionist entrepreneur and engineer Pinhas Ruttenberg on the Jordan south of the Sea of Galilee; ensure access to scarce water resources; and create a Jewish presence

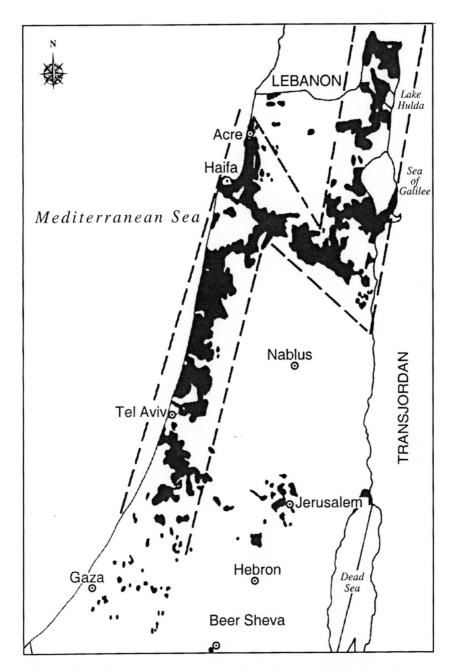

Map 4.1. The "N" of Jewish settlement. The shaded areas within the "N" represent land purchased or settled by Jews prior to Independence. The map also indicates selected purchases and settlements outside this region: near Jerusalem, north of the Dead Sea, the northern Negev and the Western Galilee near the Lebanese border. Zionist planners consciously invested their resources and energies outside the West Bank until after the 1967 war.

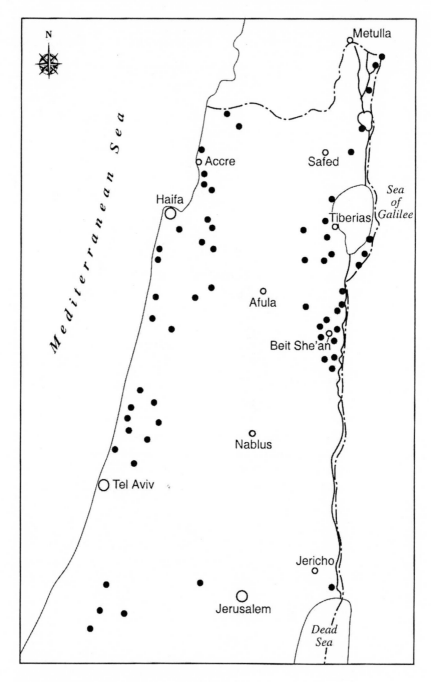

Map 4.2. Sixty new settlements, 1936–1939.

on the route from the Mediterranean through the Jezreel Valley eastward across to the rich Mosul oilfields in Iraq.

- Second: A cluster of four kibbutzim was established in the area of
the Huleh swamp in the Upper Galilee proximate to the Jordan north
of the Sea of Galilee. These kibbutzim reinforced a Jewish presence
at Lake Huleh, which Jews had a concession from the British to drain.
Here, too, there was concern for placing Jewish settlements adjacent
to the most important source of water in the region.
- Third: Twelve kibbutzim were established in the region of Haifa extending back to the east and around Haifa Bay to the north, thereby
forging links between the city and established Jewish settlements.
As we shall see in subsequent discussions, Haifa was a burgeoning
urban center perceived by the British and Zionists as potentially the
most important commercial and industrial center in the eastern
Mediterranean. It was crucial to ensure a strong Jewish presence in
this area, and kibbutzim were an important element in this plan.
- Fourth: Zionist colonizers also pushed into the Negev, which the Peel
Commission had excluded from a possible Jewish state. Settlement
names such as Sha'ar Ha-Negev (gateway to the Negev) and Negba (to
the Negev) give expression to their intended function. In one night in
1946, eleven additional kibbutzim were set up to penetrate the region and establish a Jewish presence. This action enabled the incorporation of the Negev into Israel, which both the Peel Commission
and later the United Nations had intended to exclude from the territory of a Jewish state.
- Fifth: Regions sparsely populated with Jews but designated by the
Peel Commission as potential parts of a Jewish entity became targets
of colonization. Thus three kibbutzim were established near the
Mediterranean around the solitary moshav of Naharia just below
what was to become the border with Lebanon and Israel. Indeed,
Hanita (spear), the northernmost kibbutz of the cluster, marked the
western border with Lebanon, even as kibbutzim in the Upper Galilee were placed along the eastern border. Similarly, seventeen settlements were established in other important areas in order to achieve
an even greater Jewish presence in various sections of the country.
For example, two kibbutzim were placed near Kiryat Anavim and
Motza, two relatively isolated settlements on the road from the
coastal plain to Jerusalem.

The overriding principle was that legal ownership of land alone did
not ensure control over territory or a moral right to it. Only actual settlements and the physical presence of Jews who were themselves engaged in productive labor could provide the necessary moral and political weight in the growing controversy over the fate of the country and

the practical means for realizing and defending political objectives.[12] The kibbutz became the prime instrument in a well-planned campaign to circumvent unfavorable political decisions regarding the future state and to force developments in the desired direction.

It is clear that planners and the public appreciated this. Indeed, the popular reputation and the myth of the kibbutz as the essential avant-garde of colonization probably originated at this time. It was not until the "disturbances" of 1936–1939, when the highly disciplined and motivated graduates of youth movements undertook to expand and defend the frontiers, that the kibbutz became elevated in fact as well as in myth. Idealistic youth answered the call and placed themselves in the service of settling the land, accepting *din ha-tenu'ah* (the decree of the movement) in the arduous and dangerous tasks of pioneering for national purposes. This change in status of the kibbutz and of pioneering reflected a new ethos succinctly expressed by a historian of the kibbutz movement: "A young pioneer who left the kibbutz in 1934 was betraying his friends and his movement. In 1937–9, he would feel that he was also betraying his country."[13]

Anticipating conflict with the local Arab population as well as regular armies from neighboring Arab states, Yishuv authorities exploited the strategic value of kibbutzim and invested in them accordingly. Among the most dramatic applications of the stockade and tower principle occurred during the night of October 5/6, 1946, at the conclusion of Yom Kippur (the Day of Atonement), when eleven groups of settlers built new kibbutzim at selected points in the northern Negev. Most points of embarkation were themselves settlements established between 1937 (Negba and Kfar Warburg) and 1944 (Ruhama). Three had been established as recently as 1943 with the kind of strategic logic that had come to dominate the thinking of planners. In one coordinated campaign, the national authorities set up Gvulot, to the west of Beer-Sheva, Beit Eshel to the east of the city, and Revivim to the south. It is perhaps surprising, then, that by 1947 the kibbutz population reached its zenith, making up about 7 percent of the country's total Jewish population.

Josef Weitz (1890–1976), for many years the chief planner of the Jewish National Fund, proposed this imaginative program for settling the Negev. In 1943, he presented a memorandum to the Yishuv leadership explaining his overall strategy. Although only the three *mitzpim* (observation points) that became the kibbutzim mentioned above—Gvulot, Beit Eshel, and Revivim—were actually established, his plan called for

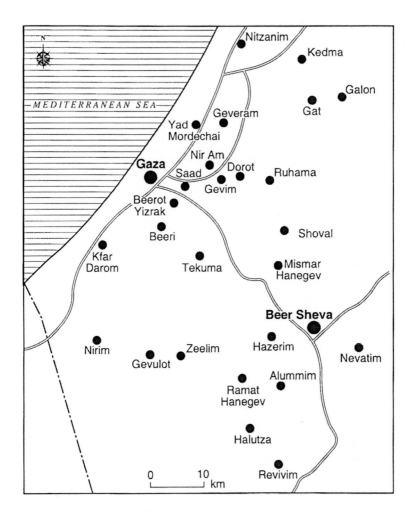

Map 4.3. Settlements established in the Negev desert, 1941–1947.

settling ten mitzpim. He suggested a deviation from the usual stockade and tower design, given the isolated locations, actual numbers of settlers, and other particular needs. Weitz called for fortified enclosures that would have a minimum of buildings, one of which would be at least two stories to provide an overview of the surrounding area. These relatively small structures would include largely public space including a dining room and kitchen, and a room for weapons and ammunition. He also planned for minimally protected structures for animals and farm implements.[14]

The primary purpose of mitzpim was to support the planning of additional Jewish settlements. Settlers would be responsible for surveying the land, identifying owners of desirable tracts and negotiating their purchase, planting test crops, and drilling for water. In addition, they would protect themselves. Initially such a community would have only ten or twelve members. They were not expected to be self-sustaining, but rather were to be paid wages by the settlement authorities. An additional five persons might be added if the Mandatory government would give them permission to serve in an official policing capacity. Weitz expected it would take two or three years for the settlers to gain enough information on lands suitable for purchase and on what they might profitably grow. He then anticipated the mitzpim would become permanent kibbutzim. This is, in fact, what happened.[15]

Weitz's strategy coincided with the plans of the leaders of the Yishuv, especially Ben-Gurion, for incorporating the Negev within a Jewish state. The area was not included in the Peel Commission partition plan of 1937 and the United Nations partition plan of 1947. In the War of Independence, Ben-Gurion determined to wrest control of the Negev in accordance with a conception he had held at least since the 1930s. His plan succeeded in large measure because of the presence and infrastructure provided by the mitzpim and kibbutzim.

Indeed, kibbutzim that were established in the western Negev after 1943, such as Kfar Darom, Yad Mordechai, and Negba, played a crucial role in slowing down and ultimately blocking the advance of the Egyptian army headed for Tel Aviv. In addition, the experience of kibbutzim in the Negev was replicated along the borders with Lebanon, Syria, and Jordan, giving rise to the reputation of the kibbutz as the heroic spearhead of Jewish settlement in the struggle to establish the state.[16]

The role of the kibbutz as the key instrument both in defining the borders of Jewish settlement and in defending them was widely and publicly appreciated. To aid in the acquisition and development of land, the Jewish National Fund distributed collection boxes, called "blue boxes," to tens of thousands of homes worldwide. The box shown in Figure 4.4 was sent to thousands of homes in Great Britain during the early 1940s. Significantly, the map on the front accurately displays the extent of Jewish purchases from Arab landowners at that time.

At the same time, it was clear that the same lands were vulnerable. Figure 4.5 depicts youthful pioneers as "the shield of the homeland." This election poster, drawn by kibbutz artist Shraga Weill for a 1949 campaign to the first Knesseth of Mapam, a party strongly identified

4.4. Jewish National Fund collection box, Britain, early 1940s. Courtesy of the Photo Archive–Jewish National Fund–K.K.L.

with the kibbutz movement, also provides the settlement map that became the basis of the State of Israel. In the background are dots representing the villages that, the poster proclaims, are "strongholds on the country's borders." There was nothing secret or mysterious about the purpose of the kibbutz. Its role in creating the outline of a Jewish state was understood and widely supported.

4.5. Mapam election poster by Shraga Weill, 1949. Courtesy of the Ben-Gurion Research Center, Sede Boker.

The Army and the Planners

Aside from such instances as the wall built around the moshava Kfar Tabor, there was little relation between physical design of villages and defense until after the First World War. Settlers depended upon themselves and, in the early stages, also hired guards, generally Bedouins, to protect their produce, property, and families. When this proved inadequate, immigrant Jews who had been active in self-defense organizations in Europe set up counterpart organizations in Palestine: Bar-Giora (named for a Jewish leader who fought the Romans in 70 c.e.) in 1907 and ha-Shomer (The Watchman) in 1909. During and after the First World War, Jews who had served in European armies and Zionist political leaders conceived a permanent, professional force. This departure enjoyed support by Zionist thinkers who urged Jews to take their destiny into their own hands, including self-defense, rather than wait for Divine intervention.

With the transfer of Palestine from Ottoman to British control, the first steps in establishing what would become the Haganah were taken. Yochanan (Eugen) Ratner, a leading figure among Zionist architects in the Yishuv as well as a high-ranking officer, participated in developing the Haganah from its earliest stages and helped transform it into a modern army after Independence.[17] Ratner had acquired military experience in the Russian army and served as an officer before immigrating to Palestine. After immigration, he became a successful practicing and academic architect. The founding dean of the School of Architecture at the Technion in Haifa as well as a senior officer in the Haganah and the Israeli army, he held important posts in the pre-state period. The career of this architect-soldier is a case study for how military concerns interacted with Zionist planning. He served as advisor for security matters in the Settlement Department of the Jewish Agency through various staff and command positions including Head of the Planning Department in the Haganah and in the Israeli Defense Forces during the War of Independence. After the inauguration of statehood, he was not only a professor of architecture but held senior positions on the General Staff, achieving the rank of 'Aluf (major general).

Ratner's professional involvement with settlement planning began in the aftermath of the 1929 riots when he was invited by Col. Frederick Kisch, Chairman of the Zionist Executive, to tour settlements in order to advise on means for protecting them and to allay the fears of settlers. Like Ratner, Kisch had military experience and relevant professional skills. Born in India, he had served as a commander of engineers in a British army camp in northern Africa. In Palestine, neither Kisch nor Ratner could solve the problems they observed. Indeed, in an amusing and revealing anecdote, Ratner recounts the exchange with settlers over the level of defensive planning at the time of the 1929 Arab riots:

> After the initial words of welcome, the representative of the kibbutz, moshav or moshava—it was the same in all of these, the settlers would begin with the following: "Although we are not professional soldiers and do not understand strategy and tactics but . . ." and Kisch would always butt in at precisely this moment and ask: "And do you have a dog?" In this manner Kisch brought things down to earth by getting the discussion directed to priorities and practicalities. . . . The issue of a dog was raised to begin a discussion on a warning system, then moved to water and only later to talk about arms. . . . Incidentally, there were no dogs. So Kisch had to patiently overcome the traditional Jewish hostility to dogs by explaining that for a watchman or guard patrolling at night without an animal was like taking a step towards suicide. . . . The settlers generally paid little attention and believed this was but a way to distract them from their request for arms and a water tower.[18]

After such meetings, Kisch and Ratner would tour the settlement. Often they discovered that an unguarded orchard bordered the homes of the settlers or that a wadi was so nearby that an infiltrator could enter the community unobserved. Wherever they went they encouraged settlers to take steps to protect themselves, especially by constructing fences and changing the location of buildings. When settlers turned the conversation back to armaments, searchlights, and better buildings, Kisch reluctantly informed them that there was not enough money. He could offer only canines, not cannons.

By 1936, funds had become available. In addition, Ratner and his colleagues had begun to develop technologies and concepts that led to the stockade and tower design and subsequent refinements. Ratner moved up the ladder of the relatively limited professional corps of officers who shaped the Israeli army and its operational doctrines. In the early 1950s, he was a leading advocate of a strategy for fortifying small outposts, including kibbutzim, that could secure internal lines and serve as staging areas for defense or assault by small, flexible, and mobile forces. This strategy built on the role that villages played in expanding and defending designated territories. These ideas were shared by many Palmach (Pelugot Mahatz, or "shock troops"—the striking arm of the Haganah) and Haganah officers who participated in the kibbutz experience.[19]

From the late nineteenth century through the establishment of the state, the Zionist village underwent a continual and insistent process of evolution and adaptation. Initial colonization was by communities of religious or traditional Jews in moshavoth. In the twentieth century, planners struggled to maintain the most efficient number of settlers in small communal villages, the moshav and kibbutz. Sidestepping the modern age of individualism and mechanization, they drew on insights gleaned from feudal Europe. When strategic needs became paramount, particularly the kibbutz was transformed into an efficient instrument in the political and military struggle that extended into statehood. As villages of one type were supplanted by another to meet new challenges, successive generations of planners and pioneers gradually populated, cultivated, and transformed the landscape of Eretz Israel with hundreds of productive and defensible colonies. Abjuring patterns of agricultural settlement found elsewhere in the modern world, Zionist colonizers maintained their commitment to villages of modest size as they designed communities that would reinforce shared national aspirations.

Part II
Urban Zion

CHAPTER 5

Tel Aviv

Vienna on the Mediterranean

For the workers they build apartment houses in the Bauhaus style, like the ones built by the Werksbund in the Weissenhofsiedlung in Stuttgart (they remind me so poignantly of working-class neighborhoods at home that I am surprised when I draw closer and hear a babble of foreign tongues—Yiddish, Russian Polish, and Hebrew—instead of German).
—NATHAN SHAHAM, 1987

The most important cultural enterprise in the country is the recently established symphony orchestra. One of the reasons for this is the universal language that it speaks (an irony which the Zionist culture lover prefers to ignore). . . . The orchestra was founded with the express purpose on the part of its founder, the Polish violinist Bronislaw Huberman, of "strengthening the ties between Eretz Israel and Europe," so that we wouldn't be doomed to live here in a "cultural exile." So he said, and he knew what he was talking about.
—NATHAN SHAHAM, 1987

THE discussion of urban Zionism properly begins with Theodor Herzl's *Altneuland (Old-New Land)* (1902), a suggestive blueprint for Zionist colonization thought. Written between 1898 and 1902, *Altneuland* is a political tract in the form of a utopian novel, and immediately recognizable as a contemporary, political/literary genre. The primary purpose of the book was to suggest possible solutions to the practical problems that had stymied colonization efforts in Palestine over the past twenty years. The novel's pervasive optimism regarding colonization is articulated in a phrase that has since echoed through Zionist discourse: "If you will it, it is no legend" (Wenn Ihr wollt, ist es kein Märchen).[1]

"It" is a utopian vision of what Palestine could become as a consequence of Zionism. As is common with books of this genre, the reader is led to examine two societies. The first, which exists in the present with its problems and deficiencies, is contrasted with a vision of what that society could become. In the case of *Altneuland,* revolutionary change takes place in only twenty years while the traveling observer is on a voyage to the distant Pacific. At the opening of the novel the reader is exposed to Palestine as encountered by the European traveler at the time of the book's publication. The reader is then invited to revisit the Palestine transformed by Zionism in 1923.

As is customary in such novels, the reader accompanies a guide who undergoes a process of enlightenment and personal transformation. *Altneuland*'s traveling hero is Dr. Friedrich Loewenberg, a spiritually fatigued Viennese intellectual of Jewish origins who may be identified partially with Herzl himself. With the exception of Mr. Kingscourt, an Anglicized Prussian gentlemen, all the other Europeans are readily identifiable as members of Herzl's circle of Central European Jews. As one critic has commented, *Altneuland* "resembles a contemporary Viennese melodrama," and the novel's atmosphere is suffused with the dreams of Hugo von Hofmannsthal's poetry and the mood of Gustav Mahler's music. The setting is the salons of Europe and Palestine as well as Palestine's rural landscape. The conversation is permeated with the social and political ideas that informed the planning of the new society. Drawn from a large fund of reform thought, these ideas were no doubt familiar and congenial to educated, urban, Jewish bourgeois readers. Indeed, Herzl's utopia was intended to be inhabited by settlers drawn precisely from this group.[2]

Like other Zionists of the period, Herzl did not see the middle classes as predominant in the first wave of pioneers. He assumed the poor would leave Europe first and that the middle classes would follow. In the first stage, Jewish philanthropists would send the poor to Palestine to relieve their communities of dependents as well as to provide for the establishment of a working class on which Palestine's development could be based.[3] The second wave of immigrants would be composed of educated and upwardly mobile young people, including engineers, administrators, architects, city planners, and jurists, whose training was necessary to develop the country:

The trained men graduated from universities, technical, agricultural and commercial colleges had brought with them every type of skill required for building up the country. The penniless young intelligentsia, for whom there were no opportunities in the anti-Semitic countries and who there sank to the level of a hopeless, revolutionary-minded proletariat, these desperate, educated young men had become a great blessing for Palestine, for they had brought the latest methods of applied science into the country.

Emigration would solve two problems. It would provide employment for "educated young men who in the anti-Semitic times had no sphere for the exercise of their skill" as well as provide a cadre of workers for upbuilding the country.[4]

The Jewish settlers who streamed into the *Altneuland* "brought with them the experience of the whole civilized world," in order to create an extension of western civilization in the Middle East. Indeed, one of Herzl's protagonists explains that "everything you see here already existed in Europe and America a quarter of a century ago." In effect, the successful colonization of Palestine involved transplanting western science and technology as well as western social and political ideas.[5]

Science was necessary for developing the economy of a backward country. In the tradition of the period's utopian novels, Herzl projects daring and innovative applications of modern technology to create wealth. Among his futuristic proposals is transforming the Dead Sea into a base for an international chemical industry. *Altneuland*'s engineers were also to establish hydroelectric plants and a national electricity network to power trains and industries and illuminate cities. The net result of these "science fiction" speculations was the creation of the technologically driven cornucopia common to the period's utopian literature.

While *Altneuland*'s prosperity is created by modern science, its society is shaped by attention to social justice and regulated by cooperative principles that had precedents in the English Rochdale system and Oppenheimer's cooperative socialism. However, it is primarily a society based on the middle-class belief in the ethical and economic value of individualism, a belief shared by Herzl's circle of friends in Vienna: "The Jews had, as a matter of fact, long been among the most ingenious entrepreneurs . . . we could be no less enterprising in Palestine than elsewhere."[6] Zionist Palestine is an improved version of the European world known to Herzl and his generation of Central and Western European Zionists. Implicitly, at least, this meant an urban society. Herzl fully

5.1. Port of Jaffa, 1909. Courtesy of the Photo Archive—Jewish National Fund—K.K.L.

expected the country to have an extensive artistic culture including even an opera house, and he clearly imagined a transplanted German-speaking society, one that would prove attractive and congenial to a Viennese intellectual.

A sense for the magnitude of the change he imagined can be gleaned by comparison with what Herzl observed when he arrived in the Holy Land in 1898. He arrived via Jaffa, the main port of entry to pilgrims coming to the Holy Land. By European standards, it was hardly even a port. Ships had to moor some distance from the shore and both passengers and cargo had to be ferried by lighters in order to avoid the rocks that made the approach to shore hazardous. The lack of modern facilities reflected the relatively primitive nature and needs of the country's economy (Figure 5.1).

There was also no real transportation system once one reached land. Only a single, narrow-gauge railway went the fifty miles from Jaffa to Jerusalem. There were no connecting roads to Haifa to the north or to El-Arish and the Sinai to the south. At that time Palestine had 4,000 Jews living in 16 agricultural colonies. Nearly all were administered by Rothschild's overseers and dependent on his largesse. For Jaffa's population of 32,000, only a tenth of whom were Jews, there were no large-scale industries, only primitive manufacturing carried on in small workshops. Urban life was limited and unimpressive. There were no distinguished civic art or public buildings, and there was no opera house. In sum, Herzl had to invent a great deal in order to fill his utopian vision with people, cities, and productive occupations and public culture to engage them.

Herzl's futuristic Zion stimulated other Zionists to imagine life in Palestine. Like other European colonizers since the time of Columbus who imagined their extra-European land could be made to conform to the images and ideas of the lands of their birth, they set out to impose the familiar on the new.

The Bourgeois Metropolis

As with other cities founded in the modern period, Tel Aviv did not just happen to appear. It was imagined and realized through conscious decisions and actions undertaken with specific purposes. In this sense, Tel Aviv is an example of the classic nineteenth-century entrepreneurial, commercial-industrial city. Such cities were established on the frontiers of North America, Australia, and elsewhere to establish control over an area; to serve as capitals or scientific or educational centers; or to promote specialized economic purposes from textile manufacturing to entertainment. By and large such cities were created to further commerce, industry, and profit. These were places that attracted expectant capitalists.

The founders of Tel Aviv expected the first, modern, all-Jewish city in two millennia to become an entrepôt of Middle Eastern commerce and industry. Their model was clearly European and the experience in building the city has parallels on other frontiers settled by Europeans. Indeed, Tel Aviv was settled and developed by "boosters," the American term for entrepreneurs who knew the value of advertising their plans. Of course there were differences between American and Zionist boosters, perhaps the most significant of which was the commitment among Zionists to a national ideology and a shared rather than individualistic meaning and purpose. Tel Aviv was not established for satisfying personal ambitions alone.[7]

The above interpretation was consistently and continually stressed by Mayor Meir Dizengoff and other early chroniclers of Tel Aviv. According to their account, Tel Aviv was conceived in 1906 when sixty merchants and professionals organized a private building society dedicated to realizing a shared dream of creating a "Jewish suburb." In contradistinction to Jaffa, they wanted "something clean, beautiful and healthy." It seemed wrong—"anti-Zionist"—to exchange the conditions of a European ghetto for a Middle Eastern one. In Jaffa dwellings lacked sufficient air, streets were dirty, the water was unclean. There was little greenery and inadequate space for children to play. Jewish women, when they strolled through the town, suffered the insulting inspection of onlookers who expected women to wear the veil. Insofar as they had a text, it was Ebenezer Howard's *Tomorrow: A Peaceful Path to Reform*, the garden city treatise that was being implemented at Letchworth and elsewhere in England at about the same time.[8]

Dizengoff's view was affirmed by a well-known British planner who spent considerable time in Palestine between the world wars. Clifford Holliday, in a 1933 review on "Town and Country Planning in Palestine," found that Zionism's preference for garden cities even predated Howard, and that the basis for welcoming his ideas was inherent in Zionist colonization. Holliday notes that already at the beginning of the First Aliyah in the 1880s, Jews attempted to change the form of rural settlement by rejecting the Arab villages they found. In effect, according to Holliday, "pioneer settlements were the genesis of ordered planning in Palestine." They were organized in the form of a grid—that is, a rectangle with broad, straight streets crossing at right angles. Houses were placed on individual plots with large gardens attached. These colonies generally had a small town square surrounded by a green agricultural belt. "In contrast," Holliday observes, "the typical Arab village was gardenless, overcrowded and unsanitary, made up of masses of closely packed, ill-ventilated houses and a maze of dirty narrow alleys. Its one asset being the picturesque appearance when seen from a distance."[9]

Zionist planners filled a vacuum. Local Arabs were traditional and uninterested in innovative community design, while the "Turks hardly touched the towns of Palestine and did nothing for the villages." Indeed, prior to British control there was virtually no government involvement in regulating land use, little health and sanitary control, and no controls on the building of private dwellings or public structures. There were few significant public works projects except in transportation, especially the development of a rail line and a few roads that were considered useful for asserting imperial control. The country suffered from an absence of government responsibility as well as local initiative, Holliday concludes, because "Both central and local administration was corrupt and the population was indolent."[10] To European eyes, Turkish Palestine was an empty landscape, one that invited Herzl and other Europeans to fill it. In the absence of regulatory agencies that could have contributed to community design, and with local models perceived as squalid and unaesthetic, new settlers had a wide-open field for imagining Palestine in alternative terms. As Holliday observes, with the minor exception of German Templar farming communities, it was Zionism that introduced modern, European planning to Palestine. Under the umbrella of the British Mandate, Zionist planning came to full flower in the urban landscape.

Tel Aviv's founders, most of whom had lived in or were familiar with the moshavoth that had been established during the twenty-five years prior to building of their city, were practiced in drawing up plans for new communities. They, too, signed a covenant and articles regulating their community. Beyond the written articles, they imagined Tel Aviv not as a farming village but as a city that emulated a variety of European models with which they were familiar. For some it was to be a Palestinian Odessa. For others it was to be Vienna on the Mediterranean. All envisioned a European city rising out of the desolate sand dunes on the shores of the Mediterranean.[11] The Europeanness of the property owners is reflected in their dress as they gather on the dunes to the north of Jaffa on 11 April 1909 to cast lots for the selection of plots on the site of their future city (Figure 5.2).

Yosef Klausner, a historian and Zionist leader who was part of a circle of Zionist intellectuals residing in Odessa, described the newly founded city on a visit in 1912: "Tel Aviv is surrounded by sand, in front and in back of the city. And when one considers that but three years earlier sand covered the site on which this charming community stands, you begin to become proud of the movement for national revival. . . . Come see the place in the world where Jews are 'carriers of culture.' . . . in place of Jaffa's sand dunes they created the community of 'Tel-Aviv' with its wide and beautiful streets, with sidewalks of marble, with beautiful boulevards, with villas that contain all that one could find in urban dwellings in the largest European city. Is this not the most authentic culture that is worthy of its name—which the children of Israel are bringing from Europe to Asia?"[12]

These yearnings became articulated in a plan to develop "a European city" that would spread out along the seashore and back into the dunes with wide boulevards, a generous water supply of its own, gardens, public places, and schools. With considerable pride, Tel Aviv's boosters ex-

5.2. Choosing lots in Tel Aviv, 1909. Courtesy of the National Photo Collection, Government Press Office.

plained that the city's citizens relied on their own resources, and aside from a loan from the Jewish National Fund, which was repaid, they "did not turn for help to any institution or private individual." With satisfaction it was told and retold how when Baron Rothschild offered to make a charitable contribution as the city tried to recover from the neglect and expulsions incurred at the hands of the Ottomans during the First World War, the city fathers refused the philanthropist's largesse and remained true to their commitment to self-sufficiency. Tel Aviv was lauded as a triumph of private enterprise. Given the Mandatory government's benign neglect and the national Zionist institutions' preferential support for agricultural colonization, it could not have been otherwise.[13]

An aerial view of Jaffa and Tel Aviv in 1917, just prior to their capture by the British, reflects the size and character of the site (Figure 5.3). At bottom center is the German colony, with its church and spire on a site initially settled in the 1860s by a group of American millenarians. To the lower right is the spreading city of Tel Aviv, which in the first years after its founding had a suburban appearance that belied the me-

5.3. Aerial view of Jaffa and Tel Aviv in 1917. Courtesy of Yad Ben-Zvi.

tropolis it was to become. In the corner is a modest railroad station on the line that leads to Jerusalem. During the following two decades Tel Aviv rapidly spread along the shore and inland to surpass Jaffa and become the leading city on Palestine's Mediterranean shore.

Booster accounts of Tel Aviv's development were generally accompanied by statistics demonstrating the vitality of individual initiative. The extraordinary boom in population was endowed with particular significance. Despite the expulsion of most of the city's Jews by the Turks during the First World War, Tel Aviv had virtually been reestablished, reaching 50,000 by the end of the 1920s and then tripling to 150,000 by the outbreak of the Second World War. In the course of this interwar expansion, Tel Aviv came to constitute about a third of the Yishuv. Dizengoff predicted, in the tradition of "boosters" on other urban frontiers, that there would be 500,000 residents by the city's Jubilee, an accurate estimate if one includes the metropolitan region. Moreover, there were very impressive statistics on the value of thousands of newly constructed buildings, calculations of the wealth of commercial and industrial enterprises, and figures on the city's territorial expansion as a result of the incessant acquisition of adjacent land.

No less worthy in the hierarchy of achievements was the development of Tel Aviv into Zion's cultural capital. By 1930 there were more than 13,000 Hebrew-speaking children in municipal schools. This remarkable figure supported the Zionist claim that an ancient people could be revitalized in its historic land even as its ancient language, once limited to prayer or unspoken scholarly prose, could once again resound in the living chatter of children. Further visual testimony to this achievement was found in Tel Aviv's street signs, which bore in Hebrew script the names of ancient and modern heroes. Moreover, the city could boast the establishment of a host of major cultural institutions such as Hebrew-language theaters, a symphony orchestra, an opera company, and a museum. Perhaps the statistic that best indicates the level of cultural achievement is that by 1930, Tel Aviv had already published 2,500 titles and was producing new books at the rate of 600 per year and was touted as "the second Leipzig," a Hebrew publishing center in Europe. Tel Aviv, not Jerusalem, had emerged as the Zionist cultural capital and home of most of the country's poets, novelists, painters, sculptors, and political writers.[14]

Another indicator of the kind of culture Tel Aviv's founders managed to create was the existence of at least as many cafés and restaurants per person as in European cities. The appreciation for this civic amenity is captured in discussions in the City Council over the appropriate way to represent Tel Aviv to the world. The city elders waxed proud over their "Casino," situated on the boardwalk along the Mediterranean. This was not a locale for gambling but the greatest café of them all—a picturesque, pink structure that featured widely in the city's promotional material. Indeed, as a symbol the Casino vied with the lighthouse that was set on the official city seal indicating Tel Aviv was, for Jews, a beacon, the gateway to Palestine.[15]

This view constitutes a conservative alternative to the radical, Labor Zionist version of the purposes of agrarian Zionist colonization. In *Altneuland,* Herzl depicted Zionists as transplanted middle-class Europeans. The Zionist settlement he described was not merely an agricultural society of dreamy poets and young radicals committed to beginning anew, unconnected with or denying the urban Diaspora. It derived in large measure from middle-class Vienna, and it was the center of a Jewish universe sharing many of the values and virtues of the Jewish bourgeoisie and the Ringstrasse (the elegant civic core within the road encircling Vienna's center). This was the kind of city Tel Aviv's leaders imagined. Their decision to establish an opera, symphony orchestra, theater, and museum for what was still a frontier city is consistent with a stream of thought at the vital center of the Zionist movement.[16] Tel Aviv's significance as the epicenter for a new Jewish culture was celebrated by two of its most famous residents, the national poets Chaim Nachman Bialik (1861–1934) and Shaul Tschernichowsky (1875–1943). Bialik, for example, wrote eloquently in 1933 of Tel Aviv as the mother *shtetl* (town) of Jews the world over. By this he meant that Tel Aviv had achieved a significance far beyond the Yishuv. It was the inheritor of Jewish culture through the ages as well as its new center, and the entire Jewish world was its hinterland. He regarded Tel Aviv as a successful and authentic expression of Zionist aspirations.[17]

Support for this urban Zion was grounded in an alternative view of the practical priorities of Zionist colonization. Taking issue with the agrarian model of the social and economic restructuring of Jewish society, the mainspring of Labor Zionist ideology and action, the city's founders voiced concern that the entire Zionist enterprise was vulnerable; celebration of the achievement of building Tel Aviv was accompanied by warnings of possible disaster to Zionist settlement as a whole. While appreciating the commitment to distribute population on the land in small settlements, they contended that building Tel Aviv was equally crucial to the interests of Zionist colonization. This analysis was based on a fundamental objection to the method of colonization adopted by the national institutions. They were supporting costly agrarian communes that could absorb only a limited number of pioneers. Cities and not farms had the capacity to attract and absorb a large-scale Jewish immigration, without which, Dizengoff warned, "others" would settle the land.[18]

These apprehensions and sense of foreboding were voiced in response to the Balfour Declaration, which promised that the reestablishment of a Jewish national home in Palestine was at hand. The declaration, Dizengoff believed, had placed the Yishuv in a dangerous and possibly untenable position: between unrealistic expectations of rapidly developing the country and the growing hostility of a restive Arab population opposed to an expanding Jewish presence. He urged channeling resources to building the economic infrastructure of Jewish society as quickly as possible so the Yishuv could absorb a large number of immigrants and provide them with a satisfactory standard of living. This meant diverting energy and resources to developing a modern and efficient urban-industrial society as exemplified in the projections for Tel Aviv. To do anything less would threaten the Zionist enterprise.[19]

According to Dizengoff's analysis, agrarian communes did not absorb and retain large numbers of pioneers. They were costly to maintain and did not address the fundamental goal of the Yishuv, which was to create wealth that would generate work. He argued that a system for financing individual mortgages could solve the problem of those who had and would come. At the same time, a construction boom would create jobs even as the establishment of banks of commerce and industry would fuel needed economic expansion. Only in this manner could large-scale immigration be encouraged and sustained. In this calculation, offering the possibility of private ownership of homes and property was a way to attract large numbers of entrepreneurs and skilled workers.

Dizengoff contended that the skills of Jewish entrepreneurs were at least as important as the labor of the young, idealistic, Polish-Jewish pioneers who were streaming into the country. He argued that the textile manufacturers of Lodz should be courted and induced to immigrate and invest in Tel Aviv. Entrepreneurs would create jobs, without which the highly motivated cadres of Zionist youth movements would be unemployed. Dizengoff frequently cited the example of neighboring Egypt, where local entrepreneurs established a flourishing tobacco industry although their country lacked forests for the production of paper as well as extensive tobacco plantations. In a similar vein, Vladimir Jabotinsky, leader of the anti-socialist movement within Zionism, claimed that "Whether we like it or not, its [Palestine's] future is also that of a trading country." Jabotinsky invoked Manchester's cotton mills, which prospered despite a lack of locally grown raw materials, and Italy's "first-rate machinery despite the absence of coal." He claimed that the key to development was in "the energy and the resourcefulness" of people. It was the "human factor" that made the difference in the development of a region and in the creation of wealth.[20]

Using such illustrations, Dizengoff urged that Tel Aviv become a major industrial and commercial center capable of supporting a large population through the enterprise of its citizens. Placing this perception in the context of internal Zionist politics, he called on government and Zionist institutions to encourage an environment in which liberal, middle-class values could flourish. He opposed plans for financing housing estates for workers, arguing the scheme was similar to the nonproductive, corrupting philanthropy that had weakened the Yishuv prior to the Zionist movement. Scarce resources would be better employed to create credit for large and small entrepreneurs.[21]

In promoting this vision of a city of comfortable burghers, Dizengoff led a middle-class movement that incessantly pressed the national institutions to establish banks and a chamber of commerce. Although the national capital was relatively limited before the Second World War, it was nevertheless important. As the largest single supply of money available for settlement, it could be directed to achieve significant and large-scale objectives. This naturally made control of the national capital an area of bitter contention by all sectors of the Zionist movement. In 1923 when national institutions were not sufficiently forthcoming, Dizengoff took the unorthodox approach of journeying to Wall Street to organize the first sale of municipal bonds. Proclaiming the message that the Yishuv, particularly Tel Aviv, was not a charity but an investment, he sought capital for mortgages and industrial development. Combining in his rhetoric the enthusiasm of an urban "booster" with the passion of a prophet preaching the end of exile, he promised both profits and national redemption. This appeal had great resonance particularly among other European Jews who had chosen to settle in America but who understood and sympathized with the dream of building a modern Jewish city in Zion.[22]

Between 1927 and 1929, the only period when socialist parties controlled the municipal government until well after Independence, Dizengoff assumed the directorship of the World Zionist Organization's newly created Department for Urban and Commercial Development. He lobbied to establish the department so there would be an organizational mechanism for institutionalizing his approach. Conflict over budget and an assessment that there was no real support for this department within the WZO resulted in his resignation and return as mayor of Tel Aviv.[23] In the 1929 campaign to recapture city hall, Dizengoff's coalition charged that continued socialist control would prolong a serious depression, whose cause was acrimoniously disputed by left and center. The election literature colorfully reflects the basic liberal position Dizengoff represented throughout these formative years: "Who would want a municipality organized according to the principle of Marx? Who would want the first of May as a city holiday, a main street named for Lenin, the red flag flying from all municipal buildings and taxes paid only by the property owners? ... The left is seeking control over everything, the Executive of the WZO, other public institutions and now the municipality. ...

5.4. Jewish workers load gravel on camels on the Tel Aviv shore, 1936. Tel Aviv was built largely by manual labor, with local methods applied to constructing a city to European tastes. Courtesy of the National Photo Collection, Government Press Office. Photo by Zoltan Kluger.

5.5. Women constructing a boulevard, King George Street, 1931. Pride in building the first Jewish city in nearly two millennia was widespread and crossed class and gender lines. Courtesy of the National Photo Collection, Government Press Office.

5.6. Convoy of camels passing Tel Aviv's power station, 1946. Electric power did not come to Palestine until the 1920s and reached Tel Aviv in 1925. Despite modernization, camels were still used extensively twenty years later. Courtesy of the Photo Archive—Jewish National Fund—K.K.L. Photo by Zoltan Kluger.

5.7. Promenade on Dizengoff Circle, 1938. The landscaping, the fountain, and the importation of contemporary European fashion in dress, architecture, and design demonstrate that Tel Aviv had become the city founders intended. Courtesy of the National Photo Collection, Government Press Office. Photographer unknown.

We need not Marx or Lenin. We need a centrist position. . . . [Our slogan is] 'Bourgeoisie in Democracy.' "[24] This vision of a capitalistic Zionism was supported by most of Tel Aviv's voters, who reelected Dizengoff to head Ha-Ezrach (The Citizen), the leading force in a coalition of non-labor, middle-class parties until well after Dizengoff's death in 1937.[25]

The planned, physical shape of Dizengoff's Tel Aviv fit this position. The middle class appreciated the plan, formulated by the famous British planner Patrick Geddes, for subdividing the city into lots suitable for middle-class housing, whether substantial, private dwellings or apartment houses for four to six families. Tel Aviv was eminently well-designed for a city of industrious and prosperous burghers and artisans. Private contractors and individuals had sufficient ground on which to erect their preferred structures. The middle-class founders of Tel Aviv succeeded in shaping a city that reflected their social and political aspirations (Figures 5.4–5.7).[26]

Working-Class Metropolis

Yet alongside the bourgeois Tel Aviv of boulevards and cafés was a proletarian ideal of what the city could look like, and it, too, imitated European models. Like the competing models of the moshava, the moshav,
and kibbutz, the pluralism of urban design reflects different priorities
in colonization. In 1909, for example, at the same time that a private
association of Jewish residents in Jaffa began constructing a suburb, the
World Zionist Organization, through its various agencies, purchased
land and equipment and provided the expertise and the subsidies for
establishing Degania on the southern shores of the Sea of Galilee. The
suburb became Tel Aviv, the Yishuv's first modern Jewish city, while
Degania became the prototype kibbutz and the forerunner of communitarian agrarian development. Both settlements were the product of separate initiatives and reflect differing priorities in colonization. Such pluralism characterized not only the country as a whole but also Tel Aviv
itself, as different groups attempted to shape the city in markedly different ways. Even as Tel Aviv became, for some, a bourgeois metropolis,
for others it was the locale for proletarian utopian experimentation.

Pluralism was made possible, in part, by the way Zionist settlement
was financed. Until the Second World War, funds were divided into
private and public, or, to employ the terminology of Zionist colonization, private capital and national capital. The mainstay of Zionist settlement in the period up to the Second World War was private capital.
From 1881, when the first wave of European pioneers arrived, until 1921
when the League of Nations confirmed the British Mandate, £19.4 million was imported into Palestine. National Zionist institutions such as
the World Zionist Organization and its agencies like the Jewish National
Fund brought in only 14 percent of this total. Until the outbreak of the
Second World War, between 1921 and 1939, the capital brought into
Palestine increased very substantially, reaching £80 million. But not
more than 16 percent—or about the same proportion as before the Mandate—was brought in by national Zionist sources.[27]

The largest single area of investment in the interwar period was Tel
Aviv. The funds expended on its construction constituted about half the
total Jewish investment in Palestine, and nearly all was imported by
private individuals. In 1925, at the height of the immigration of Polish
Jews, a peak of 80 percent of all imported Jewish capital was invested
in building the city. One consequence was that, as Dizengoff predicted,
the population of Tel Aviv increased fiftyfold, from approximately 3,000

in 1920 to about 150,000 in 1940, or about one-third of the Jewish population of Palestine. The investment of private capital also meant that Zionism's largest settlement was effectively outside the range of control of national institutions. This helps explain how a liberal, capitalistic program was so influential in Tel Aviv's development. It also helps account for the fact that socialist Zionists, who were almost entirely dependent on national capital earmarked for settling Palestine's countryside, were handicapped in implementing their programs for the city.[28]

While private funds built Tel Aviv and other urban centers, national capital went almost exclusively into developing the rural sector. The Zionist allocation policy favored the planting of collective, agrarian settlements to the near exclusion of any urban project. Thus, a bifurcation of effort developed during the interwar years. Using the contributions of tens of thousands of Jews throughout the world, the Jewish National Fund purchased land that became the focus of official Zionist colonization. Usually through the agency of the Keren Hayesod [Palestine Foundation Fund], the Zionist Organization reclaimed barren land, established agricultural colonies, planted forests, paved roads, built a local fertilizer industry, and established an electric power network. These efforts made possible the settlement of 35,500 pioneers in 119 agricultural colonies by the outbreak of the Second World War.[29]

This allocation policy reflects priorities that were already in place in the decade before the First World War and were later shared by the leadership of the Histadrut, which adopted similar preferential policies after its founding in the early 1920s. The Histadrut was so committed to labor Zionist ideology and to the proposition that control over the country would not be possible unless Jews actually cultivated the land that it relegated the immediate interests of most of its members to secondary importance. Consequently, an atypical labor organization developed. Although approximately 65 percent of the membership in the interwar period were urban workers, most of whom lived in Tel Aviv and Haifa, the Histadrut gave priority to the interests of its agricultural members, who were considered the elite of the Labor movement for undertaking a crucial national assignment. As such, they benefited from the sacrifices of the movement as a whole on their behalf. Not only did the development budget favor the agricultural sector but so did cultural and health funds. Both major Histadrut hospitals, for example, were located close to the farmworkers in rural Afulah and Petach Tikvah. The Histadrut's failure to provide housing for Tel Aviv's burgeoning population of young, immigrant artisans and laborers was an indication of this agrarian bias.[30]

The rapid growth of the Jewish and Arab populations in Palestine's cities had created a housing problem already in the latter part of the nineteenth century. Tel Aviv itself had been built in response to congested conditions in Jaffa. The sudden influx of thousands of young pioneers in the years following the First World War seriously aggravated existing crowding. A constant stream of studies sponsored by the Histadrut and by the municipality graphically described the condition of these young immigrants in a comparative framework that comprehended data on urban populations in Europe and the United States. These analyses demonstrated that Tel Aviv's workers were suffering far more than workers in the world centers with which they were familiar. For example, during the crucial period of the mid-1920s, inflation averaged 20–30 percent annually while housing costs rose by 100 percent. This situation was an outcome of the extraordinary rise in the cost of land, which in some parts of Tel Aviv doubled or tripled each year. The proportion of income that went to housing was enormous. According to the municipality's calculations, Tel Aviv's workers spent 42.5 percent of their earnings on housing, or between two to three times the amount spent in most European countries. In Vienna, for example, the figure was only 5 percent. The result, as all studies repeatedly pointed out, was that the level of congestion was among the worst in the western world. In 1925, Tel Aviv had about 2.2 individuals per room, while in England the figure was only 1 per room, although Birmingham and Edinburgh reached 1.4.[31]

Such overcrowding was exacerbated by high rents that forced many of Tel Aviv's laborers to become boarders. It was common for clerical workers or artisans to sublet a room to one or several laborers in order to pay rents. Moreover, there was a significant class of property owners who benefited from the congestion. While profit from urban rental properties in Europe was typically between 8 percent and 10 percent per annum, in Tel Aviv 30 percent was not uncommon. The anticipation of high profits and continuing demand for limited space kept rentals at an inordinately high level. This cycle helps explain why Tel Aviv's workers spent so much of their income on such inferior housing. With the influx of new population putting increasing pressure on an inadequate housing supply, Tel Aviv spilled over into a tent and barrack city on the dunes along the Mediterranean.[32]

In coping with the housing problem, the workers of Tel Aviv had to rely on their own resources. The British were unwilling to intervene in the internal affairs of the Jewish community. Zionist institutions were investing their limited resources in agricultural colonization. Depending on the municipality to deal with the problem was impractical because, under the Mandate, Tel Aviv lacked the legal instruments to raise funds for expropriating privately held land or initiating building programs. The workers, realizing that the solution would have to come from within Zionist institutions, turned to the Histadrut for leadership. Beginning in 1923, following a sudden and severe economic depression, union members organized conferences, mass meetings, and publications calling for action to alleviate their plight. The practical steps taken to provide for workers' housing were inadequate in relation to the magnitude of the problem. The effort, however, produced a rich yield of ideas for constructing an environment appropriate to pioneers on Zionism's urban frontier.[33]

Responding to the demand to provide better housing and a just society, Labor leaders drew on a world of thought that was deeply infused with the moral vision and technical concepts associated with European planning, especially the garden city movement and municipal socialism. "Red Vienna" in the years prior to the rise of Hitler was adopted as an inspiring and explicit model for action and design.[34]

For proponents of working-class housing, the garden city movement was attractive because of ideas that appeared to be consistent with their own democratic, socialistic, and anti-industrial predilections.[35] The commitment to collective ownership of land was fundamental. Howard's garden city was based on the idea that the people were primarily responsible for the increase in the value of land. This notion of land belonging to the people as a whole was also expressed in numerous Zionist writings and supported by resolutions of the international congresses of the World Zionist Organization. The widespread diffusion of a Hebrew translation of Henry George's *Progress and Poverty* suggests the keen interest in such progressive ideas. In practice, an international fund for the purpose of purchasing land in Palestine was organized by the WZO in 1907 and supported by the modest donations of tens of thousands of individual Jews. The commitment to national ownership of land was so pervasive that there were instances of hard-pressed workers purchasing land and then turning it over to the Jewish National Fund. Drawing on these ideas, housing reformers all at the same time agitated against speculation in property, which pushed the price of building lots out of the reach of urban workers, and demanded that national capital be used to purchase land and to erect suitable housing on their behalf.

5.8. Workers housing estate in Kiryat Avoda, 1938. Courtesy of the National Photo Collection, Government Press Office.

Another garden city idea adopted by advocates of workers' housing was spatially controlled societies. Palestine was still predominantly rural and its industries were operated on a small scale by individual craftsman or small groups of artisans working together. Nevertheless, immigrant socialists carried with them from Europe the specter of the ever-expansive, modern industrial city composed of masses of individuals alienated from one another. Unalterably opposed to the prospect of re-creating such a society, labor leaders embraced the notion of modest-sized societies as optimal for establishing vital and genuine community life in the city as well as in the countryside. In practice, this meant inner-city housing estates were constructed on a modest scale with their backs to the city and with a focus on green interior courtyards shared by the dwelling units. It also led to building workers' housing estates, as in Kiryat Avoda (City of Work) on the southern outskirts of Jaffa (Figure 5.8). This estate, and others like it, came to compose the well-named section called Holon (from *hol,* or "sand"). It contained modest homes with plots attached, in keeping with the garden city ideal and as a means of supplementing the income of residents whose primary employment was in Tel Aviv's offices and factories. Visionaries imagined these communities surrounded by yet-to-be-planted greenbelts in a land still characterized by large regions of desert.

Reformers further viewed the garden city idea, which brought urban and rural occupations and aesthetics into an organic whole, as a useful guide for providing a balanced mix between industry and agriculture. In addition to the naturally beautiful prophylactic of the greenbelt, they sought to endow all communities with a maximum area for planting visually pleasing and economically productive greenery. When possible, as in suburban housing estates, they envisaged that some householders would derive their primary income from agriculture, by supplying urban residents with vegetable, poultry, and dairy products. Most would supplement their income as laborers, clerks, or artisans with the produce of modest gardens. In no case were the suburban estates to be mere dormitory communities. It was evident that even those who earned their livelihood from industrial or commercial occupations would benefit by living in a community that had the economic and aesthetic characteristics of a traditional village.

Finally, Labor Zionist reformers interpreted the garden city movement as fundamentally anti-capitalist, from its principles of land ownership to the expressed preference for agricultural occupations. Their plans provided for communities of like-minded individuals who would share the same socialist ideals. This involved establishing patterns of democratic governance and creating a network of social organizations and educational institutions designed to propagate and perpetuate socialist values. These were meant to be controlled, limited-access socialist communities. Their ideal Tel Aviv was a garden city ringed with modest pastoral neighborhoods whose population would be close to nature even if some were engaged largely in industry and commerce.

While the garden city idea was popular in Palestine even before the First World War, the interest in municipal socialism developed during the 1920s coterminously with the growth of an urban proletariat in Tel Aviv. The Vienna model of the *Wohnhöfe*, a scheme for urban workers' housing that captured the imagination and idealism of the Labor Zionist movement, was viewed as a natural extension and complement of the garden city idea. Here, too, there was a perceived fit between physical design and the shaping of social and political systems.[36]

Viennese courtyards, or *Höfe*, were built in a tradition of the sanitary reform movement that had influenced urban design since the midnineteenth century. It was postulated that the creation of open space for dwellings of urban workers would satisfy both the sanitary need for light and air and aesthetic concerns. These courtyards also served to turn the attention of the residents to the inside of the housing estate and away from the potentially corrupting, capitalistic city outside. In this they reflected the strong impulse to create distinctive communities that were socially and politically segregated.

A feature of the Vienna model was proletarian architecture. The large and imposing buildings were designed as monuments to impress the power of the people on those who passed them. Indeed, they were called *Volkswohnungspaläste* (people's housing palaces) and were explicitly designed to contrast with other urban, aristocratic monuments such as royal palaces and museums. This often meant construction of very large apartment houses that contained many family units. This bias was in keeping with a tradition that began a century earlier with Robert Owen and Charles Fourier, who rejected single-family dwellings as reflecting the petite bourgeoisie and conservative, small peasants. In common with socialist housing schemes, Viennese planners emphasized the group or the collective. Architecturally, the solidarity of the group was expressed in a single structure in contrast to the capitalist ethic, which demonstrated ostentation and individuality through private homes.

These design ideas were debated and transformed in Tel Aviv. The Bauhaus-trained architect Arieh Sharon, for example, persuaded future residents of an early workers' housing estate to scale down the proportions of their dwellings to blend with Tel Aviv's still low-profile and relatively modest skyline. The result was individual buildings that were considerably smaller than their Viennese counterparts. Some of the effect of the *Volkswohnungspaläste* idea was maintained by constructing four three-story rectangles in the shape of a larger rectangle enclosing a courtyard.

Perhaps the most important effect of the Vienna model was on Tel Aviv's inner-city housing estates (*me'onot ovdim*). As in the *Wohnhöfe*, community space was provided for not only in the courtyard, but also in libraries, kindergartens and schools, health centers, meeting halls, recreation spaces, and the like. Even without the useful isolation of greenbelt workers' suburbs, great care was taken to encourage a sense of community that would foster working-class solidarity and nurture the kind of individuals who would grow into and participate in proletarian societies. In Vienna, this was articulated by the socialist philosophy of *Der Neuer Mensch,* or the New Man. In Tel Aviv, Labor Zionism produced an innovative educational system around *Beit HaChinuch* (the House of Education), which was similarly designed to nurture new personalities. In addition to schools embodying the spirit of progressive educational ideals, these communities organized choirs, youth groups, working-class theaters, and political party cells that serviced the residents of the housing estates and were often located in them or at least nearby. In addition, most inhabitants worked within the network of companies and institutions established by the Histadrut. In other words, there was an attempt to create sub-universes of workers committed to the same culture and totally occupied within it. A prime purpose of this arrangement was to infuse this world with the *ha-vay ha'histadruti* (the "Histadrut experience"). This was the Labor Zionist equivalent of an idea widely disseminated in Central Europe by socialists and Bauhaus architects who advocated the design of a new *Gesamtkultur* or *Wohnkultur*. The aim was to provide a total environment, a "cocoon" and a "hothouse," that would create and sustain collective values. It would have the added benefit of contributing to the political unity of the working class.[37]

Many of these features were incorporated into Shchunat Borochov, the first working-class, suburban housing estate. Inaugurated in 1922 outside Tel Aviv by Histadrut-associated companies on land acquired from the Jewish National Fund, it became a model for all subsequent suburban estates, although its social and political principles influenced the inner-city housing estates as well. Intended as a means for withdrawing workers from the city, Shchunat Borochov was based on a mix of garden or truck farming and employment in the city. Every resident was given from 2 to 3 dunams, or one-half to three-quarters of an acre, which was considered suitable for a small house and a productive garden. In 1930, after a process of constant experimentation and revision, Shchunat Borochov adopted a "universal" charter that served as a model for suburban housing estates as well as in-town ones.

A number of features distinguished Shchunat Borochov. The land on which the estate was built belonged to the Jewish National Fund, and householders were required to be members of Achdut Ha'Avodah (The Unity of Labor), a political party dedicated to Labor Zionism. Education was to be free and compulsory beginning with the kindergarten. The pedagogic principles were "progressive" in the western European and American sense, and it was expected that humane, socialist, and nationalistically Jewish personalities would be nurtured. The principle of progressive taxation was adopted as an appropriately equitable and socialist measure that furthered the principle of mutual assistance. In addition, the charter provided that there were to be no independent merchants profiteering from residents. Instead, all residents were required to support consumer cooperatives based on the Rochdale plan, which originated in mid-nineteenth-century England to become a staple of reform programs throughout Europe.

In a further attempt to prevent exploitation of workers and to preclude householders from engaging in the moral and economic crime of speculation, the charter stipulated that there were to be no boarders. Property, in the form of ownership of the house and rights to the land, could be bequeathed to family members or others, but the inheritors had to accept the principles on which the community was based in order to acquire the property.[38]

As explained by the model *takanoth* (regulations), the object was "To establish a complete and comfortable workers' community, in accordance with the laws of sanitation and the cultural needs of the urban worker in the form of a garden city, on the land provided by the Jewish National Fund, on the principle of an absence of speculation." Like Tel Aviv, which was founded a few miles toward the west, this community was intended as a suburban response to overcrowded Jaffa but along explicitly socialist lines. Similar constitutions adopting the relevant principles were drawn up for the inner-city housing estates. The intention was to solve Tel Aviv's housing problem by establishing satellite workers' suburbs and inner-city workers' communities. Whatever the scale of the community, they aimed at creating discrete socialist universes in terms of their architectural, social, economic, and political characteristics. Covenantal societies were located in the urban as well as rural landscape.

By the mid-1920s, the movement for working-class suburbs had spread from the Tel Aviv area to Haifa, Jerusalem, Petach Tikvah, Tiberias, and Hadera. In Palestinian terms of the period, it was a mass movement envisaging the spread of replicas of Shchunat Borochov in a ring around Tel Aviv and throughout the country. In 1925, in Tel Aviv alone, 1,000 workers registered and committed themselves with a down payment for establishing communities modeled after Shchunat Borochov. Yet by 1940, Shchunat Borochov housed only 600 families. In 1940, suburban and inner-city estates together provided accommodations for but 13,000 families, most of them in Tel Aviv and Haifa, with much smaller numbers in Jerusalem and other urban settlements. Given the paucity of resources, it is perhaps remarkable that so much was achieved.

But with the total Jewish population reaching approximately 450,000 throughout Palestine and 150,000 in Tel Aviv, this was far from adequate. The great majority of workers still struggled to find housing in the private marketplace. Congestion and privation remained common.[39]

Despite the pressing need for workers' housing and the interest in implementing planning models intended to create utopian urban communities, Labor Zionism devoted most of its efforts to staking out the

5.9. Tel Aviv in 1997. Modern Tel Aviv still follows the plan for the garden city laid out by Patrick Geddes in 1925. Instead of modest homes on city lots there are now modern hotels, business complexes, and apartment buildings, many of them pushing upward. Dizengoff Circle is still visible below the middle and center. In the upper right is a far larger modern circle. In between is the former Kings of Israel Square, set off by the large city hall, renamed Yitzhak Rabin Square following the assassination of the prime minister on this site in 1995. Courtesy of Yad Ben-Zvi.

Jewish claim to Palestine by building utopian agrarian communities. Its success in creating a similarly influential presence in Palestine's rapidly growing cities was circumscribed. The Histadrut inner-city housing estates and satellite suburbs were overtaken and enveloped by an expansive, bourgeois, urban environment. Ironically, proponents of this alternative model of urban development contended with equal passion that their activities would realize the national purpose.

The kibbutz, enjoying the buffer of space, total control over community governance, strict selection of membership, and the moral and financial support of powerful institutions, was better able to maintain itself and its special "experience." Urban equivalents were fragile and vulnerable creations. While the traces of inner city and of suburban workers' estates are still visible, it is apparent that they have been engulfed in the dominant and manifestly bourgeois culture of Tel Aviv (Figure 5.9).[40]

CHAPTER 6

Urban Alternatives

Modern Metropolis, Company Town, and Garden City

I N the romance of Zionist colonization, European Jews transformed themselves into peasants. Their avowed enthusiasm for life on the land and Zionism's investment of ideological energies and material resources in rural settlement masks the fact that most Jews went to cities.[1] Some were attracted by cultural and economic opportunities, and others could not find a place in the small and limited farming colonies. However romantic, life on the land generally entailed considerable privation and demanded dedication and personal sacrifice. Zionism had to offer more than the moshava, the moshav, and the kibbutz to attract the numbers that could transform Palestine into the Jewish National Homeland.

For those headed to Palestine's cities there were alternatives, as there were for those who preferred the countryside. They could choose established centers such as the traditional "holy" cities of Jerusalem, Hebron, Safed, and Tiberias or they could settle in ancient Jaffa on the Mediterranean coast. They could become pioneers in the establishment of the new totally Jewish centers of Tel Aviv or Afula, or the moshavoth that were being transformed from farming villages to towns, suburbs, and cities, or they could settle in Haifa, a dynamic city on the country's northern coast. Some newcomers were involved in an effort to create a metropolis in the Jezreel Valley that never materialized. And a few even participated in building a successful and attractive company town in Palestine's most remote frontier on the shores of the Dead Sea. The country offered opportunities for many different kinds of urban pioneering.

Urban Zionism also embodied revolutionary elements. Settlers on urban frontiers claimed to be engaged in the reform of society and of themselves just as were their agrarian counterparts. While farmers developed an agricultural economy even as they built ideal communities, urban pioneers created the industry and commerce to sustain cities that conformed to their social and political visions. The founders of Tel Aviv derived the name of the largest and first Zionist city from Theodor Herzl's utopian tract, *Altneuland*. Nachum Sokolow, a Zionist leader and the book's translator into Hebrew, rendered the German "*alt*" into the Hebrew "*tel*," which represents the mound of an ancient city, and translated "*neu*" as "*aviv*," which means "spring" and represents the new. In choosing this name the founders of Tel Aviv expressed their hope that it would become an ideal, modern city in the ancient homeland. Planners dreamed of transforming Haifa, a sleepy coastal town across the ancient and moribund harbor of Acre, into an international port city and industrial center. Their moral, aesthetic, and political ideas were expressed in the innovative physical design with which they attempted to shape that city.

Radical in both social organization and physical design, utopias in the form of workers' housing estates and satellite suburbs were built in and around Tel Aviv and Haifa and, to a lesser extent, Jerusalem. They competed for space and for resources with innovative plans for a modern, bourgeois Zionist city. Afula, in the middle of the Jezreel Valley, was designed to be an ideal garden city and a complement to the agrarian communes that were taking form nearby. Communities of industrial workers were planned for below Jericho on the northern shore of the Dead Sea and near Sodom at the southern end. The extent and range of Zionist urban utopianism is impressive.

The history of the urban and industrial aspirations of Zionist planners and the cities they produced is relatively terra incognita. Utopian, agrarian settlements have enjoyed a far larger scholarship and a more prominent place in popular literature. In Zionist historiography there is no direct correlation between the number of people who settled in a place and the literature historians and chroniclers have generated about it. Indeed, some of the kibbutzim, particularly the older ones, and the movements that sponsored them have a far larger historical literature than do Tel Aviv and Haifa. However, as we have noted, at the turn of the twentieth century Jews were among the most urbanized of all European peoples. At the beginning of the nineteenth century most lived in towns set in the countryside, and by century's end an increasingly large proportion were concentrated in capitals or in other major urban centers. In Palestine, too, they continued to prefer life in cities.

Planners intended Haifa to become a modern European metropolis on the Mediterranean coast, Palestine's most important city and its industrial center. Although it never surpassed Tel Aviv in population, Haifa did become a leading industrial and commercial center and the country's busiest port. As with Tel Aviv, there were distinctive bourgeois and working-class models of settlement. When Haifa became independent of British rule, Labor Zionism won political control of the city, and the characterization "Red Haifa" highlights the distinction from bourgeois Tel Aviv, which was governed largely by successors to the liberal Meir Dizengoff. It was Labor Zionists, along the shore to the north of the city, who constructed the Yishuv's largest concentration of satellite, working-class housing estates.

Attempts by Zionists of any persuasion to control and direct the development and design of the city were limited during the British Mandate. Unlike in Tel Aviv, which was a totally Jewish city, Jews were in a minority in Haifa until the end of the Second World War. Whereas in Tel Aviv Jews were more or less free to develop the city on their own, in Haifa they both benefited and suffered from imperial rule and initiative. Tel Aviv's boosters lacked the resources that a powerful empire might bring, but they were largely free from outside interference. Dreams for a Zionist Haifa could be realized only with the permission and cooperation of others.

Haifa: A Capitalist Metropolis

Haifa had never been an important city in the ancient world, and for long periods over the centuries the site was not even settled. Continuous settlement began as recently as 1761 when a Bedouin sheikh, Dahr-el-'Amar, ordered the construction of a fortified, walled city that strad-

6.1. Druze at the foot of Mount Carmel, 1870s. Photo by Adrien Bonfils. Courtesy of Nadav Mann of Merhavia and of Yad Ben-Zvi.

dled the main route from Acre to Jaffa. He needed to find an alternative to Acre, whose harbor was damaged through conflict, and he appreciated that Mount Carmel protected the new site from winds. Haifa grew slowly. Toward the end of the nineteenth century travelers' accounts depict it as a small, somnolent town across the bay from a dormant Acre.[2]

The same bucolic scene is captured in early photographs. Adrien Bonfils, a photographer from Beirut who made a successful career producing postcards and photographs in the Levant for a largely European market, provided a visual record of the site that would become Haifa (Figure 6.1). In this photograph he focused on a Druze on his donkey in what is today the lower city near the railway station, where the downtown and port of Haifa would develop a half-century later. In the upper left at the edge of Mount Carmel, one can barely discern the monastery Stella Maris. Aside from this structure, Mount Carmel is largely devoid of development. The Mediterranean is in the horizon beyond the Druze and to the right. Aside from the residents in Stella Maris and a small German colony of farmers on the other side of the mountain, the Druze were the most prominent of the site's inhabitants, living in scattered villages on and near Mount Carmel. Haifa was a site waiting to be developed and integrated into the modern world.

Between 1870 and the First World War the town grew fivefold, from about 4,000 to more than 20,000. This was the largest rate of growth of any city in Palestine at that time. Sephardi and Ashkenazi Jews who anticipated commercial development were among the new arrivals. Haifa's fortunes dramatically improved when the Turks decided to link the town with the Hedjaz railway, a project completed in 1905. Herzl sensed the city's possibilities during his visit and, in *Altneuland*, described Haifa as the major metropolis in a prosperous and technologically advanced Palestine. In 1908, the decision of the Hilfsverein der deutschen Juden, a leading German-Jewish philanthropic organization concerned with education, to locate a technical school (first called the Technikum, later Technion) in Haifa gave practical expression to the growing confidence in the city's future. The choice of Haifa rather than Jerusalem was motivated by the perception that universities should be established in advance of colonization or as part of the process of settlement. In fact, when the Technion opened in 1924 there were only 6,000 Jews in the city.

Projections of the city's growth supported the recommendations placed before the Hilfsverein when it deliberated on the site of the Technion. First, it was claimed that Haifa was destined to become the region's great port and Palestine's center for shipping and industry. In addition to geographical advantages, the railway link between the Mediterranean and routes leading to and throughout the Middle East would make the city the regional nexus of land transportation. It was argued that Haifa would therefore require skilled, technical personnel whose training was the prime objective of the proposed institution. It was also understood that the establishment of the Technion would itself stimulate the growth of the Jewish community and thereby contribute to Jewish influence in shaping the future metropolis. The Hilfsverein's vote of confidence was meant to advance German imperial interests related to Ottoman development and thereby bring prosperity to the local Jewish community. On this basis the Hilfsverein voted money, and the Jewish National Fund, the land-purchasing arm of the World Zionist Organization, acquired land for the proposed educational institution.[3]

Given the backward and generally stagnant character of Palestine at the beginning of the twentieth century, even the modest growth experienced by Haifa could readily encourage ambitious dreams. Construction of the first homes in Tel Aviv was still a year away when the decision to invest in Haifa's future was made, and Jaffa was a backward port with limited possibilities of expansion. Zionists appreciated that Palestine would require a port if it were to develop its commerce and industry. Haifa appeared to be the best available site. Nevertheless, it is entirely likely that without British influence, Haifa would have resembled Jaffa, with an undistinguished aggregation of buildings, a population engaged in commerce, and scattered suburbs populated by those with the means and taste for a different form of life.

Prior to British control, Haifa was a small, compact city. The most distinguished buildings had been built by Christian religious institutions, but there were also stone structures that were a blend of European and Arab architecture as found throughout the Levant. The most important planned site was that colonized by German Templers (Figure 6.2). Their community had been designed by a professional architect and was based on the kind of village found in Württemburg, from which many settlers had come. It consisted of a central boulevard set in a grid that featured ample lots with detached homes. Many residences were built of local stone but in a style reminiscent of that in Germany. When viewed from above, the very regularity of the design sets it off from the haphazard way Haifa was developing and suggests a foreign transplant in the local landscape. Beginning in the 1920s, this pastoral definition of the village was lost as factories and offices as well as the port overwhelmed the settlement.[4]

The earliest attempt by Jews to introduce distinctive concepts was in connection with the Technion. On land purchased by the Jewish National Fund near the site of the future institution, they planned a community of twelve houses laid out on a regular grid that was called Herzlia. Like the parallel movement that lead to the founding of Tel Aviv, they wished to create an alternative to the crowded and often squalid conditions in Haifa's quarters, a community with the kinds of amenities available in Europe and even in the nearby Templar commu-

6.2. German colony, Haifa, 1934. Courtesy of the National Photo Collection, Government Press Office. Photo by Zoltan Kluger.

nity. But aside from these German and Jewish initiatives, prior to the First World War Haifa was an undistinguished town located in a very picturesque and increasingly strategically important landscape.[5]

By the time the British wrested Haifa from the Turks in September 1918, the town had grown to nearly 20,000, with a mixed population of Muslims, Christians, Jews, and various Europeans. After 400 years of Ottoman rule, the small, bustling city had only recently surpassed Acre, which nevertheless remained the seat of local government. It was also far smaller than Jaffa, the leading city on the Palestinian coast. Thus it required a real leap of imagination to believe that Haifa was on the verge of a boom and about to become a metropolis of considerable regional importance.[6]

When the Mandate was inaugurated in 1922 Haifa had a population of 24,640, of whom 6,230, or a quarter, were Jews spread over a variety of neighborhoods. According to the 1944 census the population had grown fivefold to 128,800, with Jews making up just over half the total. By then, Haifa's 66,000 Jews had begun to concentrate in new neighborhoods, primarily the Hadar area on Mount Carmel overlooking the harbor, with smaller concentrations on Mount Carmel at Ahuza and on the shore south of the city. By 1948, only 3 percent of Haifa's Jews remained in the old downtown or in the established German colony. Moreover, a considerable Jewish population was now located in new, satellite workers' housing estates, the *krayoth,* along the shore of the bay between Acre and Haifa. Numbering only 50 in 1931, the area's Jewish population swelled to nearly 20,000 by the outbreak of the War of Independence in 1948.[7] Thus, a Jewish majority largely concentrated in distinct, ethnic districts was established in the Haifa region in the quarter century of the British Mandate.

The growth and shape of Jewish settlement in Haifa were explicitly directed and nurtured by Zionist institutions. Even as Zionist authorities planned the development of the moshavoth, the kibbutz, and the moshav in the countryside, they planned for a large Jewish presence in the area the British were going to transform into a major metropolis of international significance.

Imperial Context of Zionist Planning

The British invested in Haifa because of imperial interests. In January 1919, Gen. Edmund Allenby, the commander of the British forces that defeated the Ottomans, wrote to his Secretary of War observing that if the British army were to remain in Palestine it would require a suitable port "from the point of view of military needs."[8] Allenby's communication was the consequence of a "Confidential Memorandum" prepared for him by the newly appointed military governor of Haifa in December 1918, or shortly after Allenby entered Jerusalem. This report suggested that a port at Haifa would provide necessary anchorage for British ships patroling the eastern Mediterranean to ensure a secure channel for provisioning the army. It predicted that Haifa could become the Mediterranean terminus of oil emanating from Iraq as well as a commercial center. In order to accomplish these ends, the report recommended, further professional studies were needed, although it already assumed that the German Templer colony, near the future port, would need to be commandeered for railway yards and other facilities. Mount Carmel, which rose behind the proposed port area, could then become "the future residential European town." The report concluded with the observation that British intervention could result in "making Haifa one of the most flourishing cities and ports in the Mediterranean." All these elements would be found with varying degrees of emphasis in subsequent reports and studies concerning Haifa's development. The British appreciated the potential inherent in Haifa's geographic location and encouraged transforming the site into a modern city.[9]

The idea of a military base as part of a port was obvious and aroused no controversy among the British military and the Foreign Office. The idea of an oil terminus was more complex and became intertwined with very large questions of British imperial strategy and economic interests. The Iraqi oil fields, which were then being developed largely by the British, had to remain accessible in the event of local conflicts or a general war. This required establishing an alternative to the Suez Canal for oil entirely through British-held territory. The British reasoned that in the event of war there could be legal complications if British warships wished to take on oil or use a port such as Tripoli in Lebanon that was within French jurisdiction. Although crossing French-controlled Syria and Lebanon to Tripoli was shorter and more economical, the British wished to avoid having their oil under French protection. The final decision was made in 1927 for an oil pipeline from the Mosul fields through British-controlled Iraq, Transjordan and Palestine to Haifa. A secret memorandum from the acting High Commissioner for Iraq, B. H. Bourdillon, to the Foreign Office indicates British considerations. Arguing that Tripoli or an even more northern route would bring the line into

less secure and more volatile territory, he concluded: "The more south-
erly route . . . is obviously far better from the point of view of security
in war, in time of disorder, and in peace. The section between the Tigris
and the Euphrates is short and little inhabited. . . . The route is quite
remote from Turkish interests and first and foremost traverses throughout territory under British mandate which, over and above war and
disorder risks, forms a very strong insurance to the Company even in
peace time."[10] Considerations of the interpower rivalries for penetration
into the Middle East led British military and political strategists to prefer Haifa.

Once the pipeline's course was determined, other decisions fell into
place, including the integration of Haifa into a proposed regional railway and road network. Here, too, it was imperative that the line from
Baghdad should safely lead to Haifa and on to Europe. Such a line
"would place Iraq in direct contact with the West and enormously increase her potential prosperity by conferring on her the advantages of a
Mediterranean country."[11] Benefits would also accrue to Palestine from
trade with Syria, Transjordan, and Egypt. It was anticipated this would
make Haifa a center of regional commerce and stimulate local industry
because, in colonial fashion, the city would receive raw agricultural
products, especially grains, provide commercial services, and export
manufactured goods. Finally, it was hoped that the railroad linkage
would make Haifa into a tourist center: "The railway would provide
easier access to Moslem holy places for pilgrims. It would substitute a
temperate for a tropical port of access for an appreciable proportion of
the traffic of Iraq and Western Persia and would avoid Suez Canal
dues."[12] The geopolitics of the British Empire elevated Haifa as Palestine's future transportation center to a position of great strategic significance. British historian and Zionist critic Arnold Toynbee observed
in 1934 that "Palestine held a key position in the twentieth century
world, which was not incomparable to the position of Great Britain as
the entrepôt between Europe and the Americas."[13] His view echoed what
Zionists had been propagating. Harry Sacher, an entrepreneur and a
leading British Zionist, claimed in 1928: "Palestine will be an industrial
and commercial country. If you look at the map, you will find Palestine
interestingly situated. Its coastline opens out on two continents. The
Red Sea offers a passageway from Asia to Europe. In the old days, part
of the commerce of Asia came through the Mediterranean. . . . Within
a few years Haifa will be the outlet for the greater part of this vast
hinterland. It will also be the outlet and port for the Iraq oil fields in

Mesopotamia, at present the richest oil fields in the world. . . . Haifa and Palestine will be the connecting commercial link between Europe and Asia."[14]

Zionist Plans for Haifa

We noted above how Central European Jews familiar with German interests in the Middle East, including Herzl and the Hilfsverein, appreciated the significance for the Zionist enterprise of the Turkish decision to connect Haifa to a railroad. A similar phenomenon occurred during the British Mandate among wealthy and influential English Jews with substantial holdings in rails, oil, and chemicals. Bankers Albert and Frederick Stern invested heavily in Middle Eastern railroads, including the line to Baghdad; Waley Cohen of Shell Oil became involved in developing the Haifa terminus for Mosul oil; Alfred Mond (later Lord Melchett) of Imperial Chemical Industries was active in petrochemicals and interested in the extraction of potash and other chemicals from the Dead Sea. While not themselves active leaders in the Zionist movement, they were familiar with leading Zionists, especially Chaim Weizmann, President of the Zionist Organization, who resided in England. They assumed harmony between their investments and the interests of the British Empire and of the Zionist movement. Sacher observed, again in connection with the role of Haifa, that Jews are "peculiarly fitted" for vitalizing imperial connections and cited Jews from Baghdad who sent out trading emissaries to India, Shanghai, Singapore, and Europe.[15]

Other publicly identified Zionists came to appreciate Haifa's prospects under the British Mandate. The Palestine Economic Corporation, for example, counted among its leadership important and wealthy American Jews including Louis Brandeis, Herbert Lehman, Louis Marshall, Felix Warburg, and Robert Szold. In addition to investing in the development of the citrus industry, this group sought out large-scale industrial projects. All ventures were rooted in a rejection of the exclusively philanthropic approach that had characterized the pre-Zionist relationship of Diaspora Jewry with the Yishuv. These American Zionist sympathizers thought that for moral and practical reasons building the country should bring profits to investors. On this basis, they encouraged privately supported, capitalistic enterprises that would strengthen Palestine's economy. Haifa was a favored venue for their activities.[16]

Haifa's population began to burgeon with the building of the city's infrastructure and industrialization. The construction of the British-sponsored petroleum tank area at the end of the Mosul field pipeline was the most significant new venture. The related refineries created the base for a petrochemical industry. On a smaller scale but still important was the establishment of Jewish-owned industries including the Nesher Cement Factory and the Shemen plant, which manufactured edible oils as well as soap, cosmetics, and paint. During the 1930s, particularly after the beginning of the Fifth Aliyah, in 1933, which brought Jews from Germany with capital and industrial experience, about sixty-five large and medium-size factories were erected. These included the Vulcan Foundries (initially Kremener Ltd.), Palmyra Glass, the Mosaica factory, Frutarom Essences, Electric Cable and Wire Works, and Hillel Pharmaceutical Works. The Histadrut also established a variety of industries. At the same time, Pinchas Ruttenberg, a Zionist leader and entrepreneur, spearheaded the development of the Palestine Electric Company, which made industrialization possible in a country without local sources of energy. In a fairly rapid process, industries attracted one another around the developing port, which was protected by the British navy.

One indication of the magnitude of this was a study produced by the Mandatory government with the cooperation of the Palestine Zionist Executive, entitled *The First Census of Industries: Taken in 1928 by the Trade Section of the Department of Customs, Excise and Trade*. Both entities were interested in the economic development of the country, and the report indicated how much had to be done. Prior to the Mandate, the few existing industries were all related to agriculture such as soap manufacturing, tanning, shoemaking, and so on. The report noted that "Machinery was almost unknown, the only motors in use immediately before the war being in a few flour mills, two or three workshops and orange groves for irrigation purposes." The census went on to credit skilled Jewish immigrants for stimulating industrial activity during the 1920s: "Such industries as the manufacture of bricks and tiles, cement, the extraction and refining of edible oils and essences and flour milling, were firmly established on a large scale, and the number of smaller enterprises employing labour and machinery, and using motor power, increased rapidly." To underscore the innovation brought by these immigrants, the British census noted that 69 percent of all industrial establishments used manual labor, 14 percent used animal power, and only 17 percent used motor power. Most were small: 91 percent employed four workers or fewer. Clearly the establishment of large indus-

6.3. Aerial view of Haifa harbor and city, 1947. Courtesy of the National
Photo Collection, Government Press Office. Photo by Zoltan Kluger.

tries in Haifa was revolutionary in the Palestinian context. It was precisely this kind of change that Zionist entrepreneurs, investors, and
planners envisioned and for which they began to plan in detail (Figure 6.3).

In anticipation of Haifa's development, Zionist organizations made
practical preparations by purchasing land, which they provided to Jewish industries at moderate rental rates. The Jewish National Fund made
several purchases in the area, a rare departure from its bias in favor of
agricultural settlement. The Bayside Land Corporation, a subsidiary of
the New York–based and Zionist-sponsored Palestine Economic Corporation, bought land as well as advanced credits for factory construction
and industrial projects. The total expenditure by the JNF and Bayside
Land Corporation amounted to about £1 million. This was a very large
sum even when compared with that of the British government and private companies, which together invested about £5 or £6 million for the
petroleum industry and the city's infrastructure during the 1930s. Zion-

ist organizations and Jewish immigrants attached themselves to British initiatives and injected capital that stimulated additional growth.[17]

By 1940, Jewish land holdings in the Haifa Bay area constituted 60,000 dunams, of which the Jewish National Fund and Bayside Land owned 80 percent. To plan this large area, the JNF and Bayside Land sought the advice of Patrick Abercrombie of Liverpool University, one of Britain's leading planners, and A. Klein of the Technion, one of the Yishuv's leading architect/planners who had recently emigrated from Europe. Together they proposed a regional plan in which Haifa Bay was divided into three main consecutive zones extending from Haifa toward Acre, across the bay: an industrial zone covering about 14,000 dunams along both banks of the Kishon River; a residential zone of about 20,000 dunams, separated from the industrial zone by a 1,000-foot-wide green-belt; and an agricultural zone linked to the northern section of the residential zone. This plan is an obvious adaptation of the most advanced European thinking on organizing land within a regional framework.[18]

This regional approach influenced the way the British developed the city's infrastructure. They drained the Kishon River, constructed a channel in the harbor, leveled sand dunes, built a highway from Haifa to Acre, reclaimed land near the bay, built an airport, and so on. Zionist organizations took the lead in building the proposed road because it shortened the distance from the Haifa port to the Haifa Bay Jewish residential area by about 2.5 miles, thereby facilitating access for Jewish workers and Jewish industries that might develop nearby.[19]

Richard Kauffmann, the World Zionist Organization's leading planner in Palestine, was also invited to propose a regional plan. A disciple of Ebenezer Howard, he viewed the problem of planning Haifa in a regional frame of reference based on the garden city idea. In particular, he thought in comprehensive terms of the region bounded by the Carmel range down to the site of the future harbor and north along the shore to the ancient port of Acre and then into the plain stretching eastward from the shore. Across this area he envisioned "a network of linked green belts" that would intersect the region with the area subdivided into functional "zones" for residence, industry, parks, agriculture, and recreation. Kauffmann integrated within this plan the port and the related air, rail, and road connections.[20]

He suggested that housing estates fill the plain between Acre and Haifa. This was translated by the end of the 1930s into the largest con-

6.4. Prospect from the new Jewish workers housing estates across the bay toward Mount Carmel, 1938. The total population of Jews on both sides of Haifa Bay enabled Zionist advocates to claim that Jews had a majority in the area and that the expanded city should be within a Jewish state. Courtesy of the National Photo Collection, Government Press Office. Photo by Zoltan Kluger.

centration of workers' housing estates built in the country until after Independence (Figure 6.4). Kauffmann urged that Mount Carmel be devoted largely to housing for health and aesthetic reasons. The location was far removed from malarial areas around the river basin spilling into the Mediterranean, and residents could take advantage of the sea breezes as well as the spectacular views available on Mount Carmel overlooking the Mediterranean and where the Valley of Jezreel meets the ocean.[21]

The underlying conceptions of Abercrombie, Klein, and Kauffmann were similar. They reflected the most sophisticated thinking current in Europe. Abercrombie's influence was felt in many places in England and the British Empire. He is perhaps best remembered for his plans for Greater London, which became a model of metropolitan and regional planning after the Second World War. We have already encountered

Kauffmann as the designer of Nahalal, an aspect of his career that provides further evidence of his contribution to Zionist planning. The fact that his plan for Haifa was published in the prestigious *Town Planning Review* in London indicates his international standing and the interest his work commanded abroad.

Unfortunately, many of the details of these plans were never carried out. The primary problem was that the British government concentrated on establishing the port and serving the oil industry. It did not invest enough money or pay sufficient attention to the relationship between the port and the city that was developing around it. Such integration was fundamental to the conceptions of planners. Many of Haifa's current problems stem from the failure of the British to assert their authority and commit the necessary resources. Nevertheless, the basic objective of creating an industrial and commercial center was realized in a very short time.

It is entirely possible that had the British Mandate not ended in 1948, Haifa would have overtaken Tel Aviv as the premier city in the eastern Mediterranean. Because Israeli Independence ended with armistice lines and closed borders rather than a peace treaty, the Jewish state as well as Haifa were cut off from their natural hinterland. The offices and agencies established in the 1930s by Zionist organizations in Cairo, Baghdad, Damascus, Beirut, and elsewhere in the Middle East were closed. The rail routes from Haifa up the coast to Beirut and eastward across the Jezreel Valley to Jordan and on to Syria and Iraq as well as the route south down the coast to Cairo were all severed. The flow of Iraqi oil also stopped. The promise of Haifa as a great port acting as an intermediary between the Middle East and Europe was no longer realizable.

In the Israeli context, Haifa remained an important city and the center of the nation's industry. Unlike in Herzl's vision, it did not become the cultural and political capital of the country. Instead, Tel Aviv was the preeminent locale of the renaissance of a modern Hebrew culture and the prime magnet for artists, writers, actors, musicians, and publishers. It was also the center for Zionist politics and finance. For all the advantages that Haifa enjoyed, Tel Aviv benefited more from the energies and opportunities generated by the Zionist movement. Nevertheless, both Haifa and Tel Aviv became dynamic "European" cities on the Mediterranean coast, a fulfillment of Zionist aspirations that encompassed far more than returning as peasants to the land of their forefathers. Even as Zionists turned eastward to revitalize Jewish society, they were intent on maintaining their connection with the modern west and were determined to be part of it.

Company Town at the Dead Sea

Zionist industrial colonization extended well beyond the coastal cities where commerce, industry, and the new Hebrew culture developed.[22] Industry was located where there were raw materials or other special assets such the Jordan River, where a hydroelectric plant was established. Perhaps the most extraordinary setting for Zionist colonization was on the northern shore of the Dead Sea, where two settlements were planted. One was a kibbutz, Beit Ha'aravah, established in 1939 by hardy pioneers who literally made a most inhospitable desert bloom with bananas, tomatoes, grapes, and potatoes that they marketed primarily in Jerusalem. The lowest farming village in the world, it was located at 1,253 feet below sea level in a spot that had almost no rain. It had to draw water from the nearby Jordan for human consumption and to bleach the land of chemicals to make agriculture possible. It is not this story, however, that is the subject of this section. It is of Kalia, a neighboring settlement primarily for workers of the Palestine Potash Company's installations at the Dead Sea. Closer to the Dead Sea than even Beit Ha'aravah, this community was at 1,286 feet below sea level, the lowest settlement on earth.

There are few recorded instances of attempts to live in this desolate, arid, and forbidding environment. The best known is the one in Genesis that recounts the destruction of Sodom and Gomorrah, towns at the southern end of the Dead Sea in the days of Abraham about 3,700 years ago. In this isolated and bleak spot, Zionists imagined and built a modern and technologically sophisticated industry together with a company town for its workers. It should be added that the town, industrial installations, and unusual beauty of the site were so attractive that a forty-room hotel and restaurant were built to accommodate visitors, who included Winston Churchill and David Ben-Gurion. Foreign visitors, traveling on sea planes, anchored near the hotel on the route from Europe to India, Syria, and Egypt. This unusual company town was the product of a complicated and tense partnership between Moshe Novomeysky, a visionary industrialist, and the "workers' brigade" of socialist pioneers who could not find employment on a kibbutz as farmers.

Company towns were established in many places in Europe and

America particularly during the latter part of the nineteenth and early twentieth century. The forerunner of this kind of settlement is New Lanark, founded in 1792, which Robert Owen developed in lower Scotland as a textile manufacturing center. More contemporaneous with Herzlian Zionism and the actors in this episode are the following towns: Krupp, built for manufacturing steel in Germany; Bourneville, which the confectionary magnate Cadbury built in the English midlands; Hershey, established by a chocolate manufacturer of that name in the dairy country of Pennsylvania; and Pullman, another town named by an industrialist for himself, for the manufacture of railway cars on a site to the south of Chicago along the shore of Lake Michigan. This is but a small sampling of a widespread phenomenon. Often such endeavors were undertaken by an entrepreneur/industrialist to solve problems related to large-scale industrialization, particularly ensuring a secure supply of labor either where land costs were high or where no labor had yet settled. This involved building outside established cities and on frontiers. Some farsighted and philanthropic industrialists used the occasion to establish a superior if not utopian community. In such instances, philanthropy was joined to enlightened business calculations.

Jewish industrialists in Palestine also attempted to accommodate workers in plants built distant from centers of population. There are two outstanding examples. Pinchas Ruttenberg, who founded the Palestine Electric Corporation and built a hydroelectric dam on the Jordan River, established housing for workers to maintain the installation in two settlements: Tel Or for company workers and Naharayim and a moshav for growing produce.[23] At the same time, Moshe Novomeysky founded the Palestine Potash Company to extract chemicals from the Dead Sea and in the course of this project also constructed worker colonies at the northern end of the Dead Sea.

Ruttenberg and Novomeysky exemplify the drive for a modern European-like transformation of the country. Both ventured into the interior to build industry rather than engage in agriculture. Both realized different aspects of Herzl's vision of a society extensively employing electricity, a relatively new source of energy when he wrote *Altneuland,* and producing wealth from the Dead Sea, a body of water whose very name stimulated and challenged the imagination of European explorers, scientists· and entrepreneurs. Both also grew up in Czarist Russia and became politically active in an attempt to change it. Their politics led them to support revolution against the Czar as well as anti-Bolshevik positions. With the victory of the Bolsheviks, they fled Russia and arrived in Palestine where both organized Zionist-sponsored industrial enterprises of regional importance. They shared similar perspectives on the politics appropriate to large-scale industry in Palestine and neighboring countries.

The more inventive and original of the two was Novomeysky. His company, Palestine Potash Limited, was the largest nonpetroleum-related industry in the Middle East. At Israeli Independence it employed about 1,500 Arabs and Jews. Novomeysky claimed in 1950 that between 10,000 and 15,000 additional people depended on the company for their livelihood.[24] The Dead Sea Works, the successor company established in the early 1950s, is today one of the largest industrial concerns in Israel, employing thousands of workers and earning hundreds of millions of dollars annually from exports and services that span the world. The base for this industry is still extracting minerals by evaporating the waters of the Dead Sea in a series of shallow pools built in and around its natural borders.

The Dead Sea did not become an object of systematic scientific exploration until the beginning of the nineteenth century. The first explorer was a German physician and convert to Islam, Ulrich Seetzen, who reported on his discoveries after walking the shores of the Dead Sea. Not since the Crusades had a European written about travels into this area. His reports served as a guide for others and initiated a process of exploration that excited the interests of Europeans seeking raw materials for their modern, industrial economy.

In 1837, two English scientists transported a boat overland from Jaffa up to Jerusalem and then down to Jericho to near where the Jordan enters the Dead Sea. In the course of their explorations, among the first ever to be made on that body of water rather than along the shore and adjoining territory, they came to the conclusion that the Dead Sea was below sea level. They noticed that water boiled at less than the 100 degrees Celsius normally required and postulated that this was a consequence of air pressure greater than that found at sea level. On receiving their report in 1839, the Royal Geographic Society established a competition to ascertain the exact depth of the Dead Sea (the Hebrew for "Dead Sea," *Yam Ha'melach*, means "Salt Sea"). The puzzle was solved around 1850.

Other scientists and explorers began looking for uses of the chemical-laden waters. The most important of these was Max Blanckenhorn, a German natural scientist who studied the area methodically from 1894 to 1908. His work came to the attention of Zionists, including

Herzl, and provided the inspiration for much of the prosperity outlined in *Altneuland*. Herzl envisioned a chemist as one of the novel's heroes and described him as directing an industry based on extracting minerals from the Dead Sea. Novomeysky first read Herzl in Siberia, where he grew up along the shores of another "salt sea," Lake Baikal. While he was on a trip to Germany in 1905, Otto Warburg, the Zionist leader, presented him with a personal copy of Blanckenhorn's report to Herzl. This reading firmly planted in Novomeysky's mind the idea for his enterprise.

Novomeysky made his first exploration of the area in 1911 but soon returned to Russia. Only after the success of the Bolshevik revolution, which forced him into exile, did he return to Palestine with the intention of developing the technology necessary for commercially extracting potash, bromine, and various other compounds. He spent much of the 1920s in this effort, in attracting international investors, most of whom were British and American Jewish financiers involved with the development of the Yishuv, and in obtaining a concession from the British government to establish the company. During the 1930s and 1940s, he set up laboratories at the Hebrew University and the plant at the Dead Sea in which recent European immigrant scientists further refined his methods and programmatically developed new ways to exploit the chemicals commercially. They could be used in fertilizers and were valuable in pharmaceuticals and cosmetics, for refining aviation fuel, in numerous industrial processes, and in the manufacture of munitions. Potash and bromine became essential to the British particularly during the Second World War for munitions and fuel when they were cut off from normal supplies from Europe and came to rely heavily on Novomeysky's company. It was during this period that Palestine Potash rapidly expanded and reached high levels of profitability (Figure 6.5).

This development would have been impossible without workers willing to spend extensive periods or, indeed, raise their families at the Dead Sea. To house them in the most attractive conditions possible and construct other necessary buildings, in 1929 Novomeysky invited Richard Kauffmann, the Yishuv's premier architect/planner, to plan some of the buildings for the project (Figure 6.6). By then, Kauffmann had already designed ideal communities for workers in Germany and Norway as well as Nahalal, garden suburbs, portions of Jerusalem, Tel Aviv, and Haifa. Other architects and planners who were active in spreading modern design principles, notably Alexander Klein, were engaged to build buildings and plan the town. The results are remarkable examples

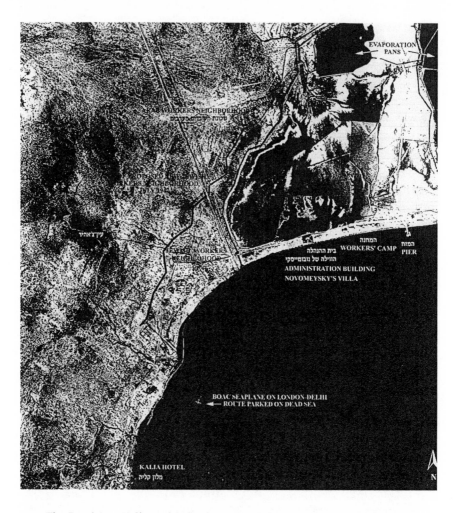

EVAPORATION
PANS

KALIA WORKERS NEIGHBORHOOD
שכונת יהודים (כליה)

עין ג'אהיר

JEWISH NEIGHBORHOOD
פניבת...

המחנה
WORKERS' CAMP
בית התנהלה
ADMINISTRATION BUILDING
הווילה של נובומייסקי
NOVOMEYSKY'S VILLA

המזח
PIER

ARAB WORKERS
NEIGHBOROHOOD

BOAC SEAPLANE ON LONDON-DELHI
◄— ROUTE PARKED ON DEAD SEA

KALIA HOTEL
מלון קליה

N

6.5. The Dead Sea: Kalia and Palestine Potash Company, 1945. Much of the
complex as the company emerged from the Second World War is shown
here. Near the center is the beginning of the feeder canal withdrawing waters into the network of evaporation pans that are partially shown in the upper right corner of the photo. At the bottom left is an indication for the
nearby Kalia Hotel, which offered superior accommodations for passengers
on regularly scheduled BOAC flights that anchored nearby while on the
route between London and India. Separate areas are marked for Jewish and
Arab workers. Courtesy of Dr. Dov Gavish, Aerial Photography Archives, Department of Geography, Hebrew University of Jerusalem.

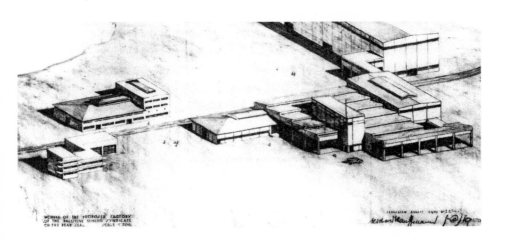

6.6. Richard Kauffmann's plan for the Palestine Potash Company's administration building and plant, 1929. The same aesthetic that marked architecture in Tel Aviv and Haifa was brought to the Dead Sea. One distinguishing adaptation was ensuring that as many work areas as possible were covered as a shield from a blazing sun and that roofs were raised to encourage ventilation. Courtesy of Yad Ben-Zvi.

of Bauhaus architecture adapted to the lowest place on earth, a tribute to the sources and ambitions of the Zionist imagination. Many designs remained on the drawing boards, but the community was real and became a source of enormous pride among those who lived, worked, or visited at the site. Belying the realities of actual conditions, most accepted that it was certain to become a "utopian" community. The constant pressure for expansion of plant and workers' residences was so great that in July 1947 the Mandatory government approved a "regional plan" for Kalia. It would have tripled the number of apartments for Jewish workers resident at the site and still would not have satisfied the demand for accommodations. The outbreak of violence after the UN vote on partition in November 1947 put an end to imagining the ideal community.

As noted above, about half the workers were Arabs—Bedouins, Druze, and others from the hill towns and villages of the West Bank and Transjordan. The other half were Jews who were organized into "labor brigades." It was they who inhabited the town. Such workers identified themselves as *halutzim,* or pioneers, and spoke in terms of *"harosheth"* ("industrial" pioneering). They had a radical ideology and were actively engaged in the Histadrut, which represented them before Novomeysky's company.[25]

As in most company towns, there were clashes between organized workers and capitalistic owners. In this case, the bitterness of dispute was mitigated by a common commitment to ensuring the success of the project. This is a variation of the tension and conflict found in the politics of the working-class versus bourgeois inhabitants of Tel Aviv. At the Dead Sea, neither owners nor managers regarded themselves as mere seekers of profit or of a livelihood. There were competing and yet complementary champions of the daring idea of bringing industry to Palestine's frontier.

Workers and company officers cooperated in advancing the interests of the Yishuv, in much the same way as agricultural villages did on other borders. As elsewhere, the colony necessarily became an armed, frontier camp that staked out and defended Jewish interests on Palestine's eastern border. It also became a clandestine locus for the manufacture and testing of armaments for the Haganah because of access to necessary chemicals and the technical skills of company workers and scientists. For example, the "Davidka," an artillery piece that created more noise than effective fire power and has been credited with the Haganah's victory in Safed in 1948, was designed, manufactured, and tested at the plant. As in the case of the kibbutzim, there was a partnership in defense matters between the Haganah, the settlers, a capitalistic company, the kibbutz movement, and the Histadrut.

The development of this settlement came to an abrupt end. Kalia, Beit Ha'aravah, and the industrial installations were destroyed soon after independence in May 1948, first by the settlers themselves and then by the Jordanian Arab Legion and local Arabs. Situated near one of the strategic entry points into Palestine, the Allenby Bridge, which crosses the southern end of the Jordan River, the Jewish settlements constituted a potential threat to the Jordanian ability to secure lines to their forces engaged in the battle for Jerusalem and the West Bank. The settlements became obvious and immediate targets when the Arab Legion crossed the bridge on May 15, the day after Israel was declared an independent Jewish state. The leadership of the Yishuv appreciated their vulnerability and reluctantly gave the order to abandon and destroy the indefensible outpost. The conflict between Arabs and Jews resulted in the destruction of the entire residential and industrial complex.

This was not the only instance of retreat from outlying settlements and their destruction, but as in other cases, this episode still arouses recrimination over exactly "who gave the order" and whether the settlement had to be abandoned. Settlements, whether based on industry or agriculture, that could not be defended because they were far removed from defensible lines, were abandoned no matter how inspirational the social and political intentions that brought them into being and how valuable they were. Indeed, Novomeysky and other industrialists anticipated this outcome. A dedicated Zionist who was close to Ben-Gurion and the centers of power in the Yishuv, Novomeysky was in New York in the fall of 1947 arguing against partition before the United Nations. He correctly predicted that his enterprise as well as Pinchas Ruttenberg's Palestine Electric Company would become casualties of interethnic/national strife with the end of the Mandate. Both enterprises came to the same end within two weeks after Transjordan and other Arab states invaded the country.[26]

The fate of these enterprises demonstrates the possibilities and limits of Zionist settlement in Palestine. Like Avraham Granovsky and other agricultural economists and planners, Novomeysky and Ruttenberg believed their ambitious plans and technologies could facilitate peaceful cooperation among Jews and Arabs and benefit the region as a whole. Both had been active in "peace movements" since the mid-1930s and were members of a group that sought to establish a binational entity in Palestine. Their company towns and industries were established with the expectation that Zionism would bring prosperity to all and that prosperity was indivisible. Their large-scale power and chemical enterprises were by nature regional in scope. Indeed, the Dead Sea, a very modest body of water in extent, now has the prospect of three distinct and sometimes competing entities on its shores: Israel, Jordan, and the Palestinian Authority. Novomeysky argued that competing nationalisms had to be subordinated to regional, supranational frameworks that served the common good.

This kind of "utopianism" has roots in Herzlian Zionism. Prior to the War of Independence, the Jewish Agency maintained commercial offices in Damascus, Beirut, Cairo, and elsewhere in the Middle East. Herzl, Novomeysky, and others thought that Zionism should and would bring the benefits of science, technology, and industry to all. They believed economic self-interest, when successfully pursued, could mitigate human conflict and that the spread of European civilization would confer benefits on those it reached. Instead, at the conclusion of the 1948 war, Israel was artificially severed from the region in which it desired integration. In terms of Zionist thought and policy, this isolation was wholly unexpected.

Several years after the war, the extraction plant and evaporation pools were reconstructed at the southern and western shores of the Dead Sea because the northern end had fallen into Jordanian hands. Successor companies in both Jordan and Israel carefully partitioned the Dead Sea and established commuter communities in the desert for workers who descended to the processing plants on the opposite shores of a shared body of water. Israeli workers and officials are housed in new towns distributed across the northern Negev such as Arad, Beer-Sheva, and Dimona. The orientation of the company turned toward the Negev rather than Jerusalem, thereby anchoring an orphan population in Israel's sparsely settled southern frontier. After Independence, the idea of establishing settlements to secure borders and frontier regions shifted in direction rather than in method. Industry as well as agriculture remained essential components in defining the economy as well as the borders of Zionist society.

Afula: Garden City

A common way to ridicule a locale in Israel as hopelessly lethargic and boring has been to call it the "Afula of the Future." One reporter commented in an article on the city's fiftieth anniversary: "Since the thirties, Afula has been considered a retarded child among the veteran settlements, a butt for derision. Young people born there were ashamed to admit where they hailed from." He noted that kibbutz members look down upon the town: "They have come to regard Afula as an overgrown Egged bus stop and public convenience on the way home, with kiosks and a cold drink, falafel and an afternoon paper."[27] The historical root of the insult is in the 1920s. At that time Afula enjoyed the kind of reputation boosters lavished on a town they claimed would be a bustling, model city that would attract people and commerce and become a center of culture and social services. Established and touted first by the Histadrut and then by an American-based land development company, Afula was designed by the ubiquitous Richard Kauffmann. Despite the promise, it never lived up to its billing. The reasons for its failure are instructive (Figure 6.7).

The idea for Afula first appeared in the early twenties when Histadrut leaders began to plan the colonization of the Jezreel Valley. Some assumed that a town with educational, health, and cultural facilities would be welcomed by immigrant pioneers who would settle in

6.7. Aerial view of Afula, 1937. Afula was but a town on the road without the promised opera house or other amenities and with but few residents. The straight highway in the upper portion leads directly to Nazareth in the hills, with the cultivated fields of moshavim and kibbutzim on either side. Courtesy of the National Photo Collection, Government Press Office. Photo by Zoltan Kruger.

the region's agricultural colonies. Moreover, it was assumed that even as rural settlements were to be organized on a cooperative basis, so would the urban counterparts. Officials imagined cooperative industries, workshops, and stores. The Kupat Holim, the workers' Sick Fund, was expected to establish a hospital. Kauffmann, who was to plan the moshav Nahalal to the east in the valley, was also called upon to plan a garden city near its center.

The idea appeared sound in theory. The site was at the intersection of important road and rail lines. It was connected by train from Haifa to Zemach, which, south of the Sea of Galilee near the present Israel/Jordanian border, was the gateway to Syria and Iraq. Highways linked Afula to the Mediterranean coast in two places, Haifa and Hadera. Another led to Nahalal, and still others into the mountains of the Galilee to the north and to Jerusalem to the south. By the eve of Independence in 1947, about 100 Egged buses daily entered and left the city with more than 3,000 travelers. At the same time, there were 55 kibbutzim and moshavim on about a quarter million dunams around the city. It was even possible to imagine that the number of settlements would double and that their population could triple to perhaps 60,000, based on an average of 600 people for each of the expected 100 agricultural settlements.[28]

Critics argued that existing cities, especially Haifa and Nazareth, could readily perform the functions envisioned for Afula and that investing in a regional, garden city was unnecessary. Nevertheless, circumstances in the mid-1920s made it possible to inaugurate the project. Wealthy absentee Arab landowners were willing to sell land cheaply. Funds came initially from wealthy Jews from Warsaw and when the Polish economy declined around 1925, American Jews took their place. At a time when many Americans were investing in the distant swamps of Florida in a land boom that would soon go bust, it did not appear so far-fetched to invest in the Jezreel Valley. As in the case of Florida, few investors had ever visited or even knew precisely in what they had invested. Some imagined building homes for themselves and were even enticed to purchase plots within walking distance of the opera house that was never built. Others purchased land solely for speculation.

From these beginnings, the possibility of adhering to an ideal garden city plan became increasingly remote. Land in the future city was hastily parceled without thought of future public needs. The town was honeycombed with plots for agriculture, leaving little space for the public domain. No provision was made on the fringes for an industrial zone. Most important, most owners never came. By the Second World War, Polish Jews were caught in Europe. Through years of depression and then prosperity, American Jews forgot about or ignored their investments. It had been a mistake to accelerate artificially the city's growth by the sale of land to so many absentee property owners. Even as absentee Arab landowners did not contribute to the prosperity of the *fellahin* who originally worked the land, absentee Jewish purchasers did not play an active part in the growth of their city. By Independence, Afula looked from the air like a butterfly with two large, slight wings—Afula and Upper Afula—connected by a narrow ribbon of road. In a park to the south stood the Kupat Holim hospital. In the northern section, the most prominent feature was a swimming pool. Most of the land around and between these wings was cultivated by members of the moshav Balfouria and the kibbutz Merchavia.

The experience of Afula foreshadows the experience of post-Independence Israel when local farming colonies bypassed regional cities, termed "development towns" (discussed in Chapter 9). Afula's problems were formidable. Moshavim and kibbutzim sought essential services in Haifa or even Tel Aviv. Without a proximate border, there was also no compelling strategic justification for the city. The town stagnated. Aesthetic and ideological conceptions could not overcome the lack of economic justification or strategic purpose. Afula became a well-designed irrelevancy in the course of Zionist colonization.

The story of Afula can be counterposed to that of literally thousands of American "ghost towns" between the Civil War and the First World War in such Midwestern states as Kansas, Iowa, and Nebraska.[29] Determining where cities and towns would actually take hold and prosper was risky. In free enterprise, laissez-faire, and individualistic frontier societies unsuccessful settlements are simply deserted. In the case of Zionist colonization, this rarely happened. Almost the only cause for abandoning a Zionist settlement has been destruction by war or changes in political boundaries. That was the fate of Kalia and Beit Ha'aravah as well as other settlements in the course of the War of Independence. The same occurred when Israel evacuated the Sinai as part of a treaty with Egypt and might yet happen again on the West Bank and Gaza through negotiations with the Palestinian Authority. Otherwise, the practice of the Zionist leadership was to invest human and financial resources in maintaining a settlement if it fitted into a grand design. Zionist institutions tended to generate conceptions for organized colonization and to adhere to them despite evidence contradicting the validity of their assumptions. As noted in the analysis of Zionist villages, settlements were often supported for decades despite their lack of economic viability.

Afula continued to languish even after the establishment of Israel. During the state's crucial early years neither the government nor a large company was willing to invest as did the British in Haifa or Palestine Potash in Kalia. During the 1950s, Israel directed immigrants to Afula but supported them with only modest investments in industries unrelated to the agricultural hinterland. The initial design of a city integrated into an agricultural region, and serving the needs of adjacent farms, never materialized.

Kauffmann, the Histadrut, and American sponsors imagined a garden city, but Zionist colonizers had not yet created the garden. Only about 6,000 pioneers were working in the Jezreel Valley when the city was founded. Unlike in Europe where regional and garden cities had great utility, such conceptions were difficult to transfer to Palestine. The European idea was based on a long historical experience wherein villages evolved into towns, which, in turn, developed into cities. This historic process took place even as the countryside was gradually built up. Growth was organic as the urban center matured in tandem with its hinterland. Planting a city in an underdeveloped valley with the expectation that it would immediately become a flourishing settlement was an act of romantic imagination and practical folly. Not all European models and ideas could be transplanted. Zionist planners succeeded in creating a vital community in such an unlikely location as the Dead Sea. They failed in the Jezreel Valley.

These sketches of Haifa, Kalia, and Afula as well as the two distinctive conceptions for Tel Aviv suggest the diversity of Zionism's urban ambitions. Palestine appeared as a frontier of great potential. One could find in the Yishuv much of the inventory of contemporary European design, from the housing estates for workers and the bourgeois to garden suburbs and garden cities, regional towns, company towns, modern cities, and world metropolises. Palestine was a laboratory for all manner of projects. Transplanted Europeans could flex their imaginations and dream and plan. Actual experience proved the limitations of imported concepts. Throughout these histories, I have emphasized the significance of the European background. However, the Zionist imagination was not only involved in imitation and adaptation. The ultimate goal was to create something other than what existed in Europe. As we shall see, it consciously and programmatically achieved distinctiveness and originality.

CHAPTER 7

"Imagined Communities"
The Zionist Variation

I N the modern period, Europeans fixed many of the physical boundaries and much of the social, cultural, and institutional character
of future nation-states. The colonies outside Europe were often
"imagined communities," to use the current phrase of Benedict Anderson, a leading scholar of this phenomenon, and Europeans and European ideas were crucial in shaping them. The European imagination
also clearly contributed to determining the form of Palestine's Zionist
cities and villages and the societies they contained.[1] But the Zionist
imagination was different from that of other European colonizers. In
telling the story of Zionist settlement I have detailed the extent to
which models for organizing and developing Palestine were borrowed
from the European experience. These models were not simply transplanted. What makes the case of Jewish Palestine distinctive is that,
unlike in the experience of most other non-European countries, Zionists
imposed European ideas and forms on themselves. A kind of partnership emerged in which Zionist planners and architects cooperated fully
with European professionals in shaping the country. Often the immigrant professionals initiated contact. But even more significant, the end
result of the process was not so much to transplant or reform a known

culture as to produce an avowedly nontraditional and non-European society.

Imagining Forms and Style

That Zionists took an active role in imagining the society they were attempting to create in Palestine is not surprising. It is also not surprising that Zionists drew on European models, because Zionism was itself a product of European Jewry and European culture. What makes this case so unusual is that there was no Zionist "mother country" in the sense of a state imposing control on its colony. Zionist officials and enthusiasts and the settlers themselves transplanted and transformed the best they knew of Europe into Palestine. Moreover, in making Palestine conform to the policies of the British Empire, the Mandatory government readily absorbed Zionist experts into its imperial professional culture. The impact of European influences was large and immediately visible. Because Palestine was a relatively poor and underpopulated country, it was dramatically transformed by the infusion of Jewish experts and capital.

In 1920, for example, Tel Aviv was scarcely a small town, with a population of only 2,086. By 1937, it had more than 2,000 industrial enterprises in addition to 16 power stations, 40 banks, 3,000 shops, 15,000 dwellings, 100 hotels and pensions, and—as a proof of the new town's urbanity—200 restaurants and coffeehouses. In the words of one contemporary foreign observer, Tel Aviv was "a lively, bustling, developing town of steadily increasing significance in the economic life of Palestine and of the entire Near East."[2] Moreover, Tel Aviv in the 1930s was widely acclaimed as an architectural delight and the best example of the Bauhaus or the "international style" anywhere in the world. Architects pronounced Tel Aviv "beautiful," and the national poet, Natan Alterman, affectionately described the striking modern buildings that emerged from the sand dunes on the Mediterranean shore as the "White City."[3] Haifa, too, was built according to western standards and tastes, even as were the lesser towns and suburbs of the Jewish portion of Mandatory Palestine.

The visual quality of the new Jewish cities and towns was in large measure due to the influence of a coterie of nineteen disciples of the Bauhaus architectural movement who emigrated to Palestine during the 1920s and 1930s. Their presence, together with the large immigration of a Central European middle class with the means to build, the desire to remain in cities, and a taste for architecture, made Palestine in the 1930s a prime location for architectural innovation. It should be pointed out that during most of that decade of worldwide depression and of increasingly powerful fascism, Palestine had both the highest absolute as well as relative rates of immigration in the world. It was the most important refuge for Jews, who more than any other people were necessarily on the move.[4] The local economy and some of the affluent immigrants themselves supported one of the few urban booms of the period. For the professionals trained at the Bauhaus and their local followers, there was much to build—workers' housing, suburbs, hospitals, bus stations, stores, factories, public buildings, and even the residences of wealthy patrons.[5]

One of the leading architects and planners of this time was Arieh Sharon (1900–1980). He helped organize local architects, engineers, and planners into an increasingly important professional group that not only protected the privileges of its members but also educated the public at large concerning ideas that were in the forefront of western planning. In his own career, he was a pioneer in the design of housing complexes for workers and large public building projects as well as private dwellings. Much of his work still stands today in Israel's cities. Because of his training and interest, Sharon also brought the modern concepts of zoning, regional planning, and garden cities to his work in Palestine. Thus, when after the establishment of the state the time came for comprehensive national planning, there was a significant corps of professionals who could be involved and Sharon was invited to head the project.[6]

Two others whose work is especially relevant here are Eric Mendelsohn and Richard Kauffmann. Mendelsohn's (1887–1953) career spanned over four countries. He first achieved fame for his construction of the widely admired Schocken department stores in Stuttgart (1926) and Chemnitz (1928). Seeking a new home outside Germany, he worked in England with architect Serge Chermayeff. In Palestine, Mendelsohn designed homes for Schocken, who left Germany, and for Chaim Weizmann as well as scientific laboratories, university buildings, a power station, hospitals, banks, a hotel, a business center, and garden suburbs. After the Second World War he moved to the United States, where he utilized his talents largely in the design of synagogues. His distinguished work earned him the friendship and respect of such leaders of modern design as Walter Gropius, Mies Van der Rohe, Louis Garnier, and Frank Lloyd Wright.[7]

Richard Kauffmann (1887–1954), who worked on Nahalal, Kalia, and Haifa, began his career in Germany planning garden cities for the workers of Krupp. He next spent several years planning new towns around Oslo, Bergen, and Stavanger in Norway before arriving in Palestine for the remainder of a very productive career (1920–1954). Although Kauffmann has to his credit a long list of private and public buildings, the most important locus of his work was community design. Influenced like so many of his generation by the English and German garden city movement, he applied its principles to farming settlements, most notably in his radial plan for Nahalal, to new garden suburbs including Jerusalem's Talpioth and Beit Hakarem, and to regional development especially in the areas of Haifa and Afula. As a planner, he shared in an international professional culture imbued with the belief that through physical design one could contribute to the shaping of society. There was, then, in Jewish Palestine a cadre of professionals with a common frame of reference and experience who actively took responsibility for conceiving and executing Zionism's settlement projects.[8]

Because both transplanted Europeans and Jews born in Palestine trained in Europe, they found the working environment and framework the British government had established through the Mandate compatible with their professional understandings and interests. The British imprint was due chiefly to leading British planners and civil servants who played an active role in designing institutions, towns, and regions. As the successor-state to a portion of the British Empire, Israel became the beneficiary of the ferment in social and physical planning that had shaped Britain and Europe.[9]

The guiding hand of British planning was felt directly not long after the announcement of the Balfour Declaration in 1917. The World Zionist Organization understood that experts were required in such fields as agriculture, electrical power, law and government, sanitation and health, civil engineering, and architecture and building. By the spring of 1919, the files of the Zionist organization were replete with discussions and memoranda on establishing proper planning procedures. In the excitement about the rebuilding of the country, there was no lack of candidates. Certainly one of the most interesting and influential characters was Patrick Geddes, who became the first official town planner for the Zionist movement as well as an adviser to the Mandatory government.[10]

The choice of Geddes is instructive. By 1919 he was one of the premier British planners. Among many other of his accomplishments, he had been involved in about fifty town planning projects in another part of the empire, in India. Geddes responded to the challenge of planning Palestine and waxed enthusiastic about participating in the Zionist enterprise. In August 1921, before leaving London for Palestine, he outlined in public meetings his plans for building the "New Jerusalem." He proclaimed that "the great scheme of Zion was to create a great Jewish university, not merely for the peoples of the country, but to attract students from all parts of the world." He thought that Albert Einstein might settle in Jerusalem as a professor of physics and that adjacent to the university would be a "garden village" of the kind Ebenezer Howard and his followers were proposing for the English countryside. In other lectures he discussed the future Jaffa, Tel Aviv, and Haifa. His lectures, amply illustrated with plans and drawings, were intended to demonstrate that Palestine could become a showcase for realizing the most advanced ideas for shaping an ideal social and physical environment.[11]

In fact, Geddes achieved a great deal, although not as much as he had intended. In addition to working in Jerusalem, where he sited the campus of the Hebrew University on Mount Scopus and designed some of its buildings, he provided some of the basic designs for the Mount Carmel area of Haifa. During the 1920s he prepared the master plan of Tel Aviv as a modern, large-scale garden city on the Mediterranean. He drafted the fundamental urban planning codes for the Mandatory authorities during the 1920s, and disseminated the idea of comprehensive, regional development. His partner and son-in-law, Captain Frank Mears, carried on his work in Palestine. In this very direct and manifest way, Geddes exported the best in British planning to what had been until only recently an underdeveloped backwater of the Ottoman Empire.[12]

As the Mandatory government became established, the panoply of British governmental offices and institutions were imposed on Palestine as they were elsewhere in the realm. During the quarter century of the Mandate these planning bodies were continually reorganized and their regulations recodified to conform to the latest in British planning practices. Similarly throughout this period, there was an ongoing effort to raise standards and tighten control over the development of the country in accordance with the models current in England: comprehensive planning, regional planning, zoning, public health, civic amenities, aesthetics, and surveys to provide the data for ensuring a proper scientific approach. By the end of the Mandate, the process of building a house or of laying out a suburban development was much the same in Palestine as in England.[13]

British civil servants were essential to creating this uniformity. Many who served in the various departments of the Mandatory government had spent their careers in other colonies and would depart from Palestine to yet other destinations within the British imperial system. The most important of these was Henry Kendall, who, as the chief town planning official in Palestine from the mid-thirties until the end of the Mandate, superintended the transfer of British planning codes and concepts and contributed much to their implementation. It was through his good offices that future Zionist planners were trained and learned to appreciate the advances in planning that were effecting important changes in the British countryside after the First World War. As a colonial official who practiced in Malta, Gibraltar, Kenya, and other African countries and as a member of the Royal Institute of British Architects, Kendall conscientiously and diligently put into practice the latest British concepts and codes. He was responsible, for example, for the regulation for the "Prevention of Erection of Unsightly Buildings" in Jerusalem and other cities. He established and served on many town planning boards; drafted the "Town Planning Ordinance" for numerous towns; reviewed proposals for creating Tel Aviv's suburban towns like Kfar Saba; and enforced regulations to segregate land into zones for industry, commerce, residence, nature reserves, and open spaces. From Kendall's point of view there was nothing exceptional in all this. He was a colonial civil servant and he practiced his profession in the same manner whether in Malta, Kenya, or Palestine.[14]

Kendall also had important relationships with Zionist planners and was in a personal way instrumental in disseminating British planning practices. Geddes, too, influenced local professionals. Upon arrival in Palestine, Kauffmann, a follower of Geddes's planning philosophy, was asked to complete Geddes's design for Jerusalem's Talpioth as a garden suburb. For applying this original British concept in Talpioth and in other projects throughout the country he was made a member of the Town Planning Institute in London in 1927.[15] Another important planner and Zionist official who underwent acculturation into British professional societies was Ya'acov Ben-Sira, the municipal engineer of Tel Aviv from 1929 to 1951. He was initiated into the Royal Town Planning Institute by a follower of Geddes, Patrick Abercrombie, who was engaged in planning Haifa. Ben-Sira was also licensed as an engineer and surveyor by the appropriate British societies. This became the pattern for other Palestinian architects and engineers, who, like Kauffman and Ben-Sira, became members of British professional organizations. Zionist planners, usually Eastern or Central European by birth and certainly European in training, were thus integrated into an international culture that supported their belief that through physical design they could contribute to shaping a more perfect society.[16] Independent of the politics and the tensions that afflicted the relations between Zionism and the British government, European planning ideas were welcomed and readily adopted.[17]

This cooperation between Zionist architects and planners and British civil servants was unusual in nonwestern societies. The typical pattern was that architects from the mother country designed cities or, at a minimum, the special quarters of colonial residents. In Palestine a local corps of superbly trained architects played a leading role and the local population supported their work. Even after Independence the connections with Britain were maintained, and a new generation of planners was sent to Great Britain at the expense of the Israeli government for professional training and experience. In time, Israeli planners themselves became agents for the diffusion of European ideas. Sharon, for example, spent the latter part of his career designing cities and large public projects in the new nations of Africa.

The Europeanness of Zionist planners is wonderfully illustrated in an anecdote concerning a conscious effort to discover an indigenous style that could be used in planning Jewish Palestine. The problem of defining what was uniquely appropriate to the county often occupied local planners and architects. Writing during the great boom years of the 1930s, Yochanan (Eugen) Ratner, then dean of the Technion's architecture faculty, speculated on the possibility of defining and developing concepts that were genuinely rooted in the local environment. He posed the question in terms of discovering "a purely Hebrew style" that was completely appropriate to Jews who returned to their ancient homeland. He concluded that the search was futile and that enlightened imitation and adaptation were the only real possibilities.[18]

An attempt to draw inspiration from the past revealed that the earliest buildings extant in Palestine dated from the Hellenistic period and that there was nothing uniquely Hebrew about them. Moreover, examination of textual descriptions of buildings from as long ago as Solomon's kingdom "lead only to the one conclusion, that they were entirely lacking in any distinctive national style." A possible recourse was to try to develop a semblance of Hebrew nationalism by employing symbolic decorations or ornaments. Some architects therefore used the Star of David or the seven-branched *menorah* (candelabrum) to embellish otherwise universal or non-Hebrew buildings. Ultimately, Ratner noted, this was an unsatisfying solution: "Ornaments may enhance or spoil the effect of a building; they cannot create a style. The Tel-Aviv water tower, notwithstanding the fact that it bears the traditional seven-branched *menorah,* is not Hebrew in style."[19]

Another alternative was to seek something indigenously authentic in Arab architecture: "These buildings, pleasing in appearance and singularly adapted to the climate and the landscape, stimulated a desire to recreate a similar style today." Some expected that from these sources a new, Hebrew style could emerge. In practice some architects engaged in rank imitation of features of local architecture or made slight modifications. But, as Ratner noted, "Palestine architects soon forsook the sterile field of imitation." Among the few noteworthy examples of this pattern were the YMCA building in Jerusalem and a building on the campus of the Hebrew University of Jerusalem. The result was disappointing to Ratner because of the apparent superficiality of the attempts. Ratner observed: "In the majority of cases architecture of this type is singularly devoid of character and these buildings approach as near to an Eastern style as does Hollywood."[20]

A more serious approach was taken by architect Alexander Baerwald (1890–1972), who used not only ornamentation, pillars, and arches but the layout of Arab architecture. The problem was that these features were not in accordance with the "functional needs of the normal modern building" such as a hotel, factory, and other structures required by modern society. Ratner concluded Zionist professionals had a serious dilemma if there were no traditional Hebrew style, if the local traditional style had little to offer, and if it was inappropriate to transfer forms associated with foreign cultures. In the absence of a clearly articulated set of principles, undisciplined eclecticism would inevitably result. If something new emerged, he predicted, it would be "little more than a Levantine mixture of European and American architectural influences." In fact, something quite different happened.[21]

Ratner and his generation adopted and then adapted the "international style." They found satisfaction and inspiration in its "rational" approach to design. Declaring that "modernism" had universal value, they ignored the fact that it was but another "western" import. In effect, this transplanted form became the most important and most deeply rooted transfer from Europe.[22]

This transplantation of techniques, ideas and values was accomplished swiftly and pervasively through the cumulative decisions of émigré professionals. With the establishment of Israel they remained in positions of authority in private practice, in the service of national institutions, and in the schools that trained architects. Because building the state after independence was highly centralized, these planners had an effective instrument for perpetuating the transfer of their ideas and institutionalizing them. This explains the considerable homogeneity of Israeli cities and towns. Viewed from the ground, the abundance of mass-produced public housing evidences the rational and machine-like approach inherent in modernism. Viewed from the air, neighborhoods and communities often exhibit organization features derived from a garden city plan.

Form and Substance in Zionist Design

Although externally there was much about the Yishuv that was familiar to European observers, the content and purposes were highly particular. Zionist planners imported techniques and styles and invested them with meaning that was specific to Jewish Palestine. Although Ratner and his colleagues could not discover a uniquely Hebrew decoration, style, and form, their work consciously and explicitly made manifest the Jewish presence. Indeed, scholars concerned with the sources of the Arab/Jewish conflict contend that Zionism succeeded in endowing the land with an explicitly Jewish character by ignoring and setting aside markers of the Arab presence.[23]

This phenomenon is particularly evident after 1948 in the aftermath of war. With the flight of most of Palestine's Arabs beginning in December 1947 and through the following year, hundreds of Arab towns and villages were razed or occupied by Jews, particularly immigrants who streamed into the country after Independence. Israeli officials renamed the towns and villages and much of the physical landscape. In fact, this process was an essential part of Zionist colonization from the very beginning, when the first Zionist villages were established.

Reclaiming Eretz Israel and repossessing the land meant a denial of Palestine's past under Ottoman rule as well as a denial of the European exile they left behind. Giving new names to the land and its settlements became a visible and significant part in this process. Secular Zionists tried to recover the names found in traditional, sacred texts—particularly the Bible—and often used the Talmud. They also celebrated leaders who had helped the Jewish people persevere in the long exile and those who lead them in the return home. Metaphorically, perhaps, but not merely figuratively, names became the true decorations and an inseparable part of the style that emerged in these decades of frantic building. Rules and principles for selecting names existed in a diffused and informal form from the 1880s and became institutionalized during the Mandate. The demographic and political change that resulted from the War of Independence gave much wider scope for a process that continues wherever new settlements are established.

Renaming Palestine began in Europe in anticipation of actual colonization. As we have seen, Zionist societies across Europe organized from the 1880s to establish villages and cities in the Holy Land. Their covenants and regulations often inscribed the name of the community they intended to establish in the masthead or preamble. In all cases, these names reflected their intent to reshape the land in terms derived from Jewish texts, history, and traditions.[24] For example:

- *Rosh Pina,* one of the first settlements founded in 1882 at the base of the upper Galilee, means "cornerstone." The name derives from a verse that is frequently recited in prayers that metaphorically celebrate national salvation: "The stone that the builders rejected has become the chief cornerstone" (*Psalms* 118:22).
- *Rishon le-Zion,* "a harbinger to Zion," was founded in 1882 on the coastal plain. Its name, too, is based on a Biblical verse: "The things once predicted to Zion—Behold, here they are! And to Jerusalem a messenger of good tidings" (*Isaiah* 41:27).
- *Rehovoth* is the name of a Biblical site in the central part of the coastal plain assumed to be near the location of the new settlement.
- *Sde Eliahu,* a kibbutz in Beit She'an founded in 1939, was named for Rabbi Eliahu Guttmacher, an early Zionist leader in Germany in the nineteenth century. Guttmacher stood against fellow Orthodox rabbis in defending Zionism's position that Jews ought to take the initiative in solving their problems rather than await the Messiah.
- *Kalia* is a town founded in 1930 for workers at the Palestine Potash Company on the shores of the Dead Sea. The original meaning, which derives from *Kalium* (potassium in Latin, whose symbol is therefore K), was preserved in the Arabic name for the site in recognition of the abundant quantities of the chemical found in nearby waters. Zionist colonists reinterpreted the name as a Hebrew acronym whose letters stand for *"Kam Lit'chiyat Yam Hamelach,"* or "Established to revitalize the Salt Sea." More recently the acronym was reduced to

a regular word that refers to a regional plant recorded in the Talmud (*Eruvin* 4:3).

- *Zichron Ya'acov* (Jacob's Memorial) was founded in 1882 on the slopes of Mount Carmel by Romanian immigrants who named it Zamrim after a nearby deserted Arab village. Within two years the settlement failed and was rescued by Baron de Rothschild. The moshava was then renamed in memory of his father, Jacob (Ya'acov).
- *Ha'Ogen* (The Anchor), a kibbutz on the coastal plain, was founded in 1947 by Holocaust survivors who wished to indicate that after their suffering and wandering they had come home and were to be anchored in this land.
- *Ramat Rachel* (The High Place of Rachel) was founded in 1926 as a kibbutz south of Jerusalem. It overlooks the city of Bethlehem and the traditional burial site of the matriarch Rachel.

Other settlements memorialized Zionist leaders such as Haim Arlosoroff (*Givat Haim*, 1932), Berl or Dov Beer Kaznelson (*Be'eri*, 1946), and Hebrew writer Yosef Haim Brenner (*Givat Brenner*, 1928). Perhaps 300 cities, towns, and villages were placed across the map of Palestine prior to the establishment of Israel with new or recovered Hebrew names. The landscape, too, was renamed with reference, whenever possible, to the original Biblical place-name. Thus, the Sea of Galilee became the Kinnereth, and a kibbutz of that name was established on its banks.

There was no interest in preserving Arabic place-names. These were treated as corruptions of Hebrew and were replaced with what was taken to be the original. This practice was first established by generations of Christian Biblical archaeologists who, since at least the 1840s, tried to recover Palestine's Biblical—that is, Hebrew—past, which they expected lay just beneath the ruins of a land they viewed as desolate. They tended to view Arabs as primitive guardians of a country with a glorious past.[25] Discovery of the Biblical place-name appeared to verify their understanding of their sacred and historical texts.

As Jews returned to Eretz Israel, they also felt impelled to rediscover the former grandeur with which they wanted to identify. Recovering the past outside Europe was a unique experience among European-born colonizers. The usual pattern was to blend native or aborigine names with European ones. The resulting maps thereby reflect a synthesis between the old and the new. Zionists did not attempt to recall Europe or the Diaspora in this process. In Israel there is no New Vilna, New Bialystock, New Warsaw, New Minsk, New Pinsk, or New Plonsk, unlike in former European colonies that recalled the "old country" in New

England, New York, New Orleans, New Madrid. Nor is there an Oxford, Cambridge, Paris, Berlin, and so on.

With the arrival of the British after the First World War, naming also became part of the contest for asserting control over Palestine. During the 1920s, Jewish advisers to the Mandate counseled on giving official recognition to Hebrew names. Approving and assigning names in Palestine as well as throughout the British Empire was supervised by the Royal Geographical Society's Geographical Committee for Names. The British made maps that constituted clear political statements. In 1920, for example, Jewish representatives to the committee objected to labeling Biblical "Shechem" as Arab "Nablus." The British decided otherwise and inscribed the Arab name on its maps. After the 1967 conquest of the West Bank, Israel rectified what it saw as a historical injustice and replaced Nablus with Shechem on its own maps.

However, during the Ottoman period, Jews were not hindered in assigning names to new moshavoth or to the new city of Tel Aviv. The practice continued throughout the development of the Yishuv. Hundreds of names were given to settlements, large and small, to their streets, public squares, and the landscape. Signs in Hebrew signaling the return of Jews to Eretz Israel were everywhere—at the entrance to communities, at the corners of streets, and on the blueprints of planners. They also appeared on maps and in official documents, newspaper stories, literature, and song. When Israel was established, it set up its own committee for naming settlements, streets, and the landscape. Two of its members had served in a similar capacity as representatives of the Zionist authorities during the Mandate and brought that experience to the new state. While the assignment of names had preceded the establishment of Israel, a sovereign Jewish state gave unprecendented latitude and authority.[26] The committee named nearly eight hundred places in the first fifty years of the state.[27] The total effect invited residents and foreign observers to appreciate that Zionist settlements were the concrete manifestation of national revival in the homeland.

The meaning of this large-scale enterprise of physical construction and spiritual renewal was also captured in other cultural forms—music, art, and literature.

Writing songs was a popular and pervasive method for affirming the meaning of settlement. Since the 1880s, genres of songs were written in Hebrew celebrating in detail the building of the country and the transformation of pioneers and their society. As with architecture, the forms were imported. That is, the melodies were European, particularly

Eastern European, but the words were in the old/new language of the old/new land.

Popular songs included: *Mi yivneh hagalil?* (Who will build the Galilee?) and *Mi Yivneh Bayit be-Tel Aviv?* (Who will build a house in Tel Aviv?). A tradition of composing songs for new settlements began with the First Aliyah and was carried on for decades.[28] The common meaning expressed by such songs was epitomized in a favorite, *Anu banu artza livnot u'lehibanot ba* (We have come to the land to build it and to be rebuilt in it).

Numerous songs expressed love of country through celebration of landscape such as Shaul Tschernichowsky's *Hoy Artzi, Moladati* (Oh my land, my birthplace) and those of the poetess Rachel. Although place and nature were celebrated, so was the idea of transforming them through building the country and the redeeming power of hard work and self-sacrifice. In Europe in 1904 on the eve of the Second Aliyah, Chaim Bialik composed *Birkhat Am* (Benediction of the people), which became an unofficial anthem of Zionist pioneering:

> May your arms, our brothers, be blessed and strong
> Dust of the land, wherever you are
> May your spirits never fall—come now with joyful song
> To the aid of our people, one and all.
>
> For we cherish your arriving
> And the flow of sweat and tears upon the land
> Like dewdrops reviving
> The weary soul of Israel in your hand.
>
> Each tear will be forever saved
> In the sea unfathomed of our nation's
> Sacrifice, with the drops of sweat that paved
> God's road—the blood and fat of our offering.[29]

Although many songs were connected with rural, agricultural settlements, there was no less a repertoire connected with the building of the modern "White City" of Tel Aviv. Poets and musicians in this center of nascent national culture celebrated what was taking place around them. These included not only Bialik but Tschernichowsky, Natan Alterman, Alexander Pen, and Avraham Shlonsky. They sang of hammers, crushing stones, whitewash, steel, and concrete.[30] Some, like Shlonsky, actually engaged in construction work and composed songs to imitate

7.1. Workers dancing the hora at Tel Aviv's new port, 1936. Courtesy of the Photo Archive–Jewish National Fund–K.K.L.

the rhythm of work in paving roads or working on buildings. Another favorite theme was the building of the port of Tel Aviv under the rubric of the "conquest of the sea" even as land-based pioneers in the interiors sang of the "conquest of labor" in the "redeeming of the land" or "making the desert bloom." Here, too, there was a sense of collective rejuvenation through turning the sand dunes into a thriving city and in mastering the proximate sea so that it would serve the new Jewish city (Figure 7.1). Lyrics written by Shimshon Meltzer to the music of Tzadok Ben Menachem (Kugel) capture the exultation of the first day the port of Tel Aviv opened. The song, "Tel Aviv Shore," was first sung as workers joined arms and danced in the water alongside the newly opened pier. The refrain declares: "With strength and song we are here, we are here, / As we turned sand into a city, / We shall make the sea into a homeland!"

All these categories are found in one of the first motion pictures of the Yishuv: *To a New Life* (*Le-chaim chadashim*). Commissioned by the Keren Hayesod (Palestine Foundation Fund) in 1934 together with Fox movie studios, Natan Alterman, then a young poet of twenty-five, wrote the lyrics to four songs by Daniel Sambursky that became immediate sensations. The songs covered much of the range of subjects that were part of the pioneering discourse and images of self during that generation. They were *Song of the Valley* (of Jezreel), with the words "And rest comes to the weary [pioneer]"; *Song of the Morning,* which includes words "We love you, our native land, with joy, with song and with labor"; *Song of the Hammer,* with the refrain "Pound hammer, rise and fall"; and *Tel Aviv,* which sang of redemption to "a land humiliated, a land of our birth . . . rise up, hold back your tears, we have begun and we shall finish the work." The film and its songs that celebrated redeeming the land through the "conquest of labor" won first prize in the Venice film festival of 1935 as the best documentary of the year, recognition that enhanced the songs' popularity.

One could almost consider the collective work of modern Hebrew poets and songwriters of that generation a contemporary, secular version of the *Song of Songs.* This book's very expressive and sensual language describes lovers amid the fauna and flora of Eretz Israel. In Jewish tradition, it has been interpreted as a metaphor for the love that exists between God and the Children of Israel. God is symbolized by the bridegroom, and his people are the bride. In fact, verses and phrases from the *Song of Songs* have entered into the repertoire of secular, modern Hebrew songs with the same intimate love relationship carried on by the people and the land. The intimacy of this connection is reflected in the school texts of the Yishuv in a subject termed *yediat ha'aretz* (knowing the land) where the Biblical word for "knowing" refers to deep and intimate knowledge rather than mere information.[31]

The culture of creating such songs stemmed from a conscious effort to establish a repertoire of "folk music." The roots of this invented folk music can be found in pre-Czarist Russia with the Society for Jewish Folk Music, which was founded in St. Petersburg in 1908. Some of its members and ideas then moved to Berlin, the European capital of Hebrew culture during the 1920s. At the same time, the ideas of the society moved with some of its members to Palestine. Until the outbreak of the Second World War, many others followed from Eastern and Central Europe with the avowed purpose of making the Yishuv the center of nonliturgical folk music in secular Hebrew. By 1949, nearly 200 composers had produced more than 4,000 Hebrew folk songs, most of these since the 1920s.[32] While some composed melodies, others, including some of the most important Hebrew poets of the Yishuv, wrote the words to these songs. The schools, the Jewish National Fund, the Histadrut, the kibbutz movement, other institutions, and individuals provided a voracious market for what Eric Hobsbawn has termed the "invented tradition."[33]

This was clearly a paradox. Folk music and folk culture apparently derive from the past, and their authors spring from the people. In this case, the songs were sung by immigrants seeking an authentic and deeply rooted relationship with their homeland. Through ubiquitous choral groups, records, radio broadcasts, and inexpensive sheet music the repertoire became an instant common heritage. Again, some of the form—in terms of melodies and harmonies—derived from Europe, particularly from Russia. Other songs derived from actual or imagined Yemenite traditions.[34] These diverse sources blended to create a shared heritage that reflected love of the land and hope for regeneration.

Different forms served the same function. Song was accompanied by dance. Newly created folk dances became an important feature of celebrations, festivals, and social occasions. The best known, perhaps, was the hora, a spirited circle dance that was a mainstay of Palestinian Jewish culture beginning with the Second Aliyah. Popular in farming settlements, it spread to the cities during the 1920s. These songs and dances were part of an ensemble of elements that proclaimed both rootedness in the land and a collective identity.

Recovery and invention of the Hebrew past is also manifest in the arts allied to architecture. At the Bezalel School of Arts and Crafts in Jerusalem in the decade before and after the First World War, the Bible played a central role in the motifs programmatically emphasized. The name of the school hearkens back to the Biblical master craftsman who designed and executed the Tabernacle: "The Lord spoke to Moses, saying: See, I have singled out by name Bezalel. . . . I have endowed him with divine spirit of skill, ability, and knowledge in every craft" (Exodus 31:1–3). The institution was founded in 1906 explicitly to teach European techniques in the building and decorative arts and to adapt them to Zionist purposes.[35]

Nahum Gutman (1898–1980), a student at Bezalel during the First World War and a preeminent native-born painter, explained the intent of its instructional program: "In everything we saw the Bible. We were truly Zionists. We wanted . . . to get through the Bible to a deeprootedness greater than that of life in the Diaspora *shtetl*."[36] The Biblical motifs Gutman encountered at Bezalel were not mournful or tragic, as was often the case in Diaspora art. Instead, the avowedly Zionist art of Bezalel artists dwelt on heroes, agriculture, and the celebration of festivals in the natural setting of the country. In this way, Boris Schatz, the founder-director of Bezalel, believed he could stimulate a Jewish art that could emerge only from the soil of Eretz Israel.[37]

A variation of this "rootedness" is evident in Gutman's own work, which drew on the Jewish human and physcial landscape of Palestine as prime themes. For example, Gutman often portrayed scences of urban life in early Tel Aviv with citrus orchards spreading over the adjacent countryside. Other artists such as Tsiona Taggar—native-born, like Gutman—sought out different themes, whether depictions of the rough and uncultivated harshness of the land or urban structures and cityscapes. In this art are influences of cubism, fauvism, futurism, expressionism, and other styles current in Paris, Berlin, and elsewhere in Europe. However, for all the technique Gutman, Taggar, and their colleagues learned from contemporary Europe, the themes, colors, light, and results were unmistakably the consequence of a search for something new and nationally authentic. The local products were explicitly and intentionally rooted in the landscape of the Yishuv. Poets and painters developed a native vernacular related to, but different from, European models.[38] An interesting foreshadowing of the appreciation for the dramatic austerity and roughness of landscape rather than an imported and superimposed romantic view is reflected in Taggar's illustration of *Kimshonim* (Thistles), a book of poetry of another native, Esther Raab (Figure 7.2).

The rediscovery of the land, the rejection of Europe, and the creation of a new, modern Hebrew were captured in the term applied by the end of the 1930s to native-born Jewish youth: "sabra." Ironically, the cactus, and its fruit, also termed "prickly pear," was native to America and arrived in Palestine around the seventeenth century, but it has been popularly considered indigenous to Palestine. The sabra, different in culture and language from Diaspora ancestors, was the "new Jew" fostered by the Zionist movement. At one extreme, perceived and hoped-for differences led to a total rejection of Europe and the Diaspora experience as in the "Canaanite" movement that appeared in the 1940s. More commonly, a process of more or less radical adaptation of European Jewish culture was advocated. Whatever the specific form or the result, Zionism challenged itself with the task of creating Hebrew-speaking individuals in a distinctive society that would be differentiated from the Diaspora and Europe.[39] Ironically, they may have succeeded too well. After the creation of the state, when the leaders of the Yishuv came to evaluate what they had achieved, they often lamented the culture of the sabra. For example, a national program for "Jewish Consciousness"

7.2. Illustration by Tsiona Taggar in Esther Raab's book of poetry, *Kimshonim* [thistles] (Hebrew) (Tel Aviv, 1930). Courtesy of the Taggar family.

was instituted by Zalman Aranne, an influential Minister of Education, to combat the extreme extent to which sabra youth had become cut off from the European roots of Zionist culture.[40]

This theme of adaptation and even rejection of Europe reverberated throughout the intellectual and cultural reality in which Zionist planners worked. It was patently clear that Zionism was engaging in neither mere imitation nor direct transplantation. Rather, Zionists strove to imagine and renew a distinctive form of national life, and to imbue physical forms that might appear "universal" to contemporary observers with new content. The Jewish economic and social "bubble" also had unique cultural and aesthetic characteristics.

This analysis suggests that fundamentally Zionists did not see themselves as foreigners or conquerors. For centuries, in the Diaspora they had been strangers. In Eretz Israel they expended enormous creative energy to feel quickly and easily at home. The imaginings that animated the first generation of Zionists at the end of the nineteenth century found full expression in the Yishuv well before Independence. The authentic Hebrew style Ratner sought was manifest after all, if not in architecture, then in language, names, music, literature, and art as they cultivated and reshaped the rural and urban landscape. It was also this rejuvenation that impressed a large portion of the world community with the vitality and reality of the Zionist entity. Two-thirds of the members of the United Nations voted for the partition of Palestine into independent Jewish and Arab states on November 29, 1947. Jews had successfully made the case that they were entitled to independence within that portion of the country they had so distinctively and effectively marked. In the phrase that resonated in the debates over Palestine and that became part of the formal and legal recognition of the Zionist enterprise, Jews had come to the country to "reconstitute" themselves as a people.[41] There was the widespread recognition that they were not strangers to the land. Rather, they had reconstituted themselves as natives by successfully redefining themselves in that land. The historic tragedy is that Arabs did not recognize the authenticity and legitimacy of this movement and of what it had accomplished.

It was certainly not any visible natural wealth that attracted Jews to Palestine. As I shall discuss in Chapter 8, Jews consciously came to a land that was economically underdeveloped and sparsely populated, with large areas of semiarid wilderness. Its colonization attracted insignificant numbers of other Europeans. For Zionists, it was precisely the relative desolation of the country that provided an energizing challenge. Their collective memory of having once been a people in a land that had flowed with "milk and honey" drove their determination to resettle in the Land of Israel. They would come to transform themselves by transforming the land—"to build it and to be rebuilt in it."

Part III
Post-Independence Opportunities and Necessities

CHAPTER 8

The Science and Politics of National Development

I must studiously and faithfully unlearn a great many things I have somehow absorbed concerning Palestine. I must begin a system of reduction. . . . The word Palestine always brought to my mind a vague suggestion of a country as large as the United States. I do not know why, but such was the case. I suppose it was because I could not conceive of a small country having so large a history.
—MARK TWAIN, *Innocents Abroad or the New Pilgrim's Progress*

Jewish research into Land and Book is still in its infancy. It requires the help of all branches of learning, the natural sciences and the humanities, history, philology, botany, mineralogy, hydrology, the sciences of ocean and air and all the rest. The unearthing of antiquities here takes on an especial place. We are grateful to the archaeologists from all over the world who inaugurated antiquarian research in our Land: the British, French, Americans and Germans . . . although it was not always the purest scientific motives that prompted their excavations.
—DAVID BEN-GURION, *Like Stars and Dust: Essays from Israel's Government Year Book*

O N November 29, 1947, the United Nations resolved to replace the British Mandate with two independent states, Arab and Jewish, in most of Palestine. The area around Jerusalem was to remain a *corpus separatum* and become internationalized under United Nations control. It was believed that only in this way could a violent civil conflict be averted. According to this plan, the Jewish state was not exclusively Jewish. Nearly 40 percent of the population was to be Palestinian Arab. The Jewish Agency accepted the plan. The Arabs inside and outside Palestine rejected it and immediately inaugurated a campaign of violence to stifle the Jewish state and ensure it would be still-born. When the State of Israel was declared on May 14, 1948, the Yishuv had already been under attack for five and a half months largely by local Arabs within Palestine.

The initial phase of the War of Independence did not bode well for the Zionist cause. The situation was sufficiently precarious that by March the United States was calling for a review of the UN decision. Israeli leaders were also not certain of the outcome. Accordingly, the Haganah formulated a strategy, Plan D, that underscored that a successful defense would have to be mounted beyond the very narrow confines of the land allotted the Jewish state. It is clear only in retrospect that Israel would survive the initial civil war and the invasion of regular Arab armies on May 15.[1]

When the conflict ended in 1949, Israel had extended its boundaries beyond the UN partition plan. There were also significant changes in demography. Many Arabs from within the designated Jewish state and in the areas incorporated in the course of the war had become refugees, reducing Israel's Arab population to 13 percent of the total. Some left to evade conflict and others did so because they were forced to leave. Few were permitted to return. Had the policy that evolved toward the end of the war been different, those who returned might have become reconciled to the Jewish state and have become a bridge to peace. Concerned over a potential fifth column, and eager to increase the lands available for Jewish settlement, the Israeli government chose permanent exclusion. An immediate consequence was recruiting Jewish immigrants to settle along the country's borders.

Zionist planners had imagined a Jewish state as part of the Middle East enjoying normal relations with its neighbors. Instead, after the war, Israel was confined within armistice lines rather than recognized borders. To address these unanticipated realities, new plans were drafted for developing the country. These included officially redefining the concept of a Jewish state. Shortly after Independence, Israel declared it would become a modern industrial state rather than an agricultural society.

The visions of Theodor Herzl and of Meir Dizengoff became the foundation for national policy. This transformation was foreshadowed by the struggle to enlarge the "economic absorptive capacity" of Palestine by revising the calculations of how many people the land could support at a reasonable standard of living. This issue had direct consequences

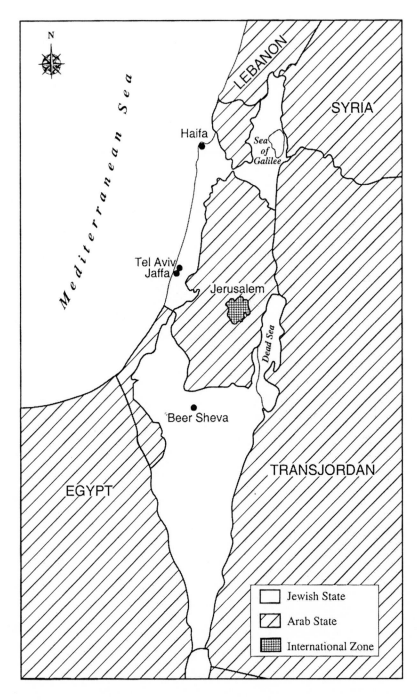

Map 8.1. United Nations partition plan for Palestine, November 29, 1947.

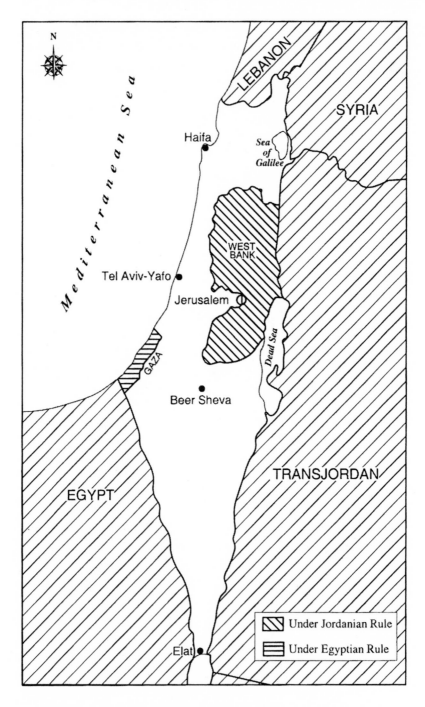

Map 8.2. Armistice lines after War of Independence, 1949.

for Jews who wanted to immigrate prior to the Second World War but were denied entry because of a narrow and limited reading of the country's potential. It also had implications for how post-Independence immigrants were absorbed into Zionist society.

In 1950, the newly established State of Israel radically departed from its established ideology and practice of investing in agricultural and communitarian settlements. Israel's first Master Plan (also known as the Sharon Plan), produced by a team of social scientists and other experts headed by Arieh Sharon, advocated an ambitious construction program. It created a hierarchical national urban network that included several metropolitan areas, regional cities, development towns, and villages set in the countryside. The plan assumed that the majority of Israel's population, approximately 80 percent, would live in towns and cities. Its adoption signified that the initial Zionist dream of renaissance in a physiocratic utopia of Jewish peasants had been supplanted by a vision of a modern, urban, technologically advanced society modeled on Western Europe and Japan. In large measure, the face of Israel at the beginning of the twenty-first century has been determined by this plan.[2]

The 1950 plan is an Israeli variant of the national programming that was becoming characteristic of modern states. With Europe recovering from the destruction and dislocation of the Second World War and with decolonization that created new states in the Third World, large-scale plans for reconstruction and development were not exceptional. Nevertheless, the Israeli plan was one of the most closely examined. It appeared to show the way for other new nations because it employed the language and the techniques of the best in western planning and applied them to an emerging, developing nation. Through the wide appreciation accorded the kibbutz, Israel already enjoyed a reputation for originality in planning. Achievements in organizing agricultural settlements would be followed, after Independence, by innovations in urban planning. The paths to utopia led through the city as well as the countryside.[3]

Students of Israeli planning invariably comment on the radical nature of the 1950 program. Looking at the plan from the perspective of Zionist history, they tend to fault the pre-state Zionist movement and the rural and agricultural biases of Zionist ideology for the apparent delay in adopting a comprehensive urban plan. Such criticism is misleading. The mandatory formula for governing immigration, based on the "economic absorptive capacity of Palestine," was calculated by the Zionist leadership in largely agricultural terms in the 1920s. By the end of the Mandate, however, the leadership came before the international community to announce that the Jewish homeland would have a modern economy and a decidedly urban character. In so doing, they acknowledged the fact that since the mid-1920s and despite the rural orientation in classical Zionist thought, most immigrants had chosen to live in Tel Aviv, Haifa, and Jerusalem and to work in commercial and manufacturing enterprises. As we have seen, Jewish Palestine had become largely urban well before the state was established and before official policy or ideology sanctioned this transformation.[5]

Urban planning in Israel developed on solid foundations. Nevertheless, the Master Plan of 1950 did not merely reflect the preferences and practices of immigrants who came to Palestine. It was a product of extreme and painful historical circumstances: European anti-Semitism and the rise of Nazism that culminated in the Holocaust, and an increasingly bitter conflict with Arabs over the right of Jews to live in the country. In response to these circumstances, Zionist planners devised expansive models of development to demonstrate how Palestine could absorb the growing number of Jewish refugees and immigrants who needed or wanted to come.

Recalculating the Economic Absorptive Capacity of Palestine

With the promulgation of the first immigration ordinance of the British mandatory authorities on September 1, 1920, the way seemed open for the rapid colonization of Palestine by Jewish immigrants. This first ordinance was extremely liberal, admitting any Jew who was healthy in body and mind and assured of a livelihood, provided he or she did not pose any political or criminal threat. Based on the Balfour Declaration of November 1917, it was intended to contribute to the fulfillment of the promise that Palestine would be transformed into the Jewish National Homeland.[4]

The anticipated influx of Jewish pioneers did not occur for a variety of reasons: there were more attractive destinations; the paths of alternative emigration were well-organized; and Palestine was economically unattractive and lacked the physical comforts that could be found elsewhere. Concerned lest they could not cope with a mass immigration, Zionist authorities did not attempt to recruit large numbers for immediate aliyah. At the same time, Arabs hostile to the creation of a Jewish majority in Palestine demonstrated and lobbied against it.[5]

Given this context, the British quickly retreated from an open-door policy. First officially presented in a *White Paper* in June 1922, they defined the concept of the "economic absorptive capacity" with far-reaching consequences for immigration. This phrase became the key element in the formula that was thenceforth employed in limiting Jewish immigration, which, as the *White Paper* stipulated: "cannot be so great in volume as to exceed whatever may be the economic capacity of the country at the time to absorb new arrivals. It is essential to ensure that the immigrants should not be a burden upon the people of Palestine as a whole, and that they should not deprive any section of the present population of their employment."[6]

This declaration meant that Zionists could not merely claim Jewish rights to Palestine in terms of history or any other form of legal justification. The burden of proof was on them to show that they could support the entry of Jews. The debate that would determine the demography of Palestinian society was bolstered by the calculations of social scientists from disciplines as disparate as archaeology, economics, sociology, geography, and civil engineering. Some scholarship was independently conducted, though the practical implications were often as apparent to the academic audience as to the politicians. Other research was consciously created or directed with a view to uncovering desired results. Whoever sponsored the research, it was well understood that it was not merely academic. The conclusions were vital to the debate over Palestine's future.

The crux of controversy in the various British *White Papers*, international commissions, and policy statements from the 1920s through the establishment of Israel in 1948 was this: Precisely how many people could Palestine support, and how many of them ought to be Jews? The restrictions imposed after the Hope Simpson *Report on Immigration, Land Settlement and Development* and the *White Paper* of 1930 at a time of growing pressure for refuge from a fascist and anti-Semitic Europe meant that the interpretation of absorptive capacity was critical. A wide range of scientific disciplines were mobilized to engage in the debate that raged in the scientific literature of specialized journals, reports, and books as well as in political arenas.

Archaeology and Politics

The findings of archaeological research provided the initial corpus of evidence used to ascertain Palestine's absorptive capacity. Although archaeologists became interested in charting and understanding fluctuations in the size of populations long before the Balfour Declaration and quite apart from it, conflicts over immigration policy did significantly encourage using interpretations of the past to draw conclusions about the future. This exercise was facilitated by Palestine's extraordinarily rich documentation in written materials and physical remains. The historical record was used to generate two conflicting interpretations: one school blamed people, particularly the Arabs, for failing to maintain the fertility of the Holy Land; the other argued that climatic change was responsible for the country's poverty. From this historical debate a fierce moral-political argument emerged. If people rather than climate were responsible for a decline in the country's productivity, then other people could claim the land if they could make it prosper.

The precursors of modern archaeology arrived in Palestine in the mid-nineteenth century and initially engaged in identifying places associated with Biblical events. Among the first and most important was Edward Robinson, a teacher of Hebrew at Andover Theological Seminary in Massachusetts, who came to the Holy Land in 1838. Defining himself as a "Biblical geographer," he pioneered the development of Biblical topography, or the identification of sites mentioned in the Bible. With the establishment of the British-sponsored Palestine Exploration Fund (PEF) in 1865, Robinson's field of inquiry was substantially expanded. Particularly noteworthy are the early PEF-sponsored maps of Palestine and volumes on topography, place-names, fauna, and flora based on the surveys carried out by Lieutenants Claude R. Conder and Horatio Kitchener (later Lord Kitchener of Khartoum). Together with the work of another soldier-scholar, Lieutenant (and later Sir) Charles Warren, who undertook a similar study of Jerusalem, these PEF studies constitute an impressive body of data on the ancient history of the Holy Land. Such research, in fact, continued through the British Mandate so that in the *Statistical Abstract of Palestine, 1944–45*, the mandatory government was able to identify 2,048 abandoned sites.[7]

With the introduction of new analytical techniques at the end of the nineteenth century came new interpretations of the growing mass of data that was being accumulated. In 1890, British archaeologist Sir Flinders Petrie introduced a method for evaluating the physical remains of archaeological sites in order to establish chronologies. This analytical breakthrough made it possible to place numbers and densities in a chronological context and to assess the relative vitality and size of populations during such periods as the Bronze Age, ancient Hebrew, Hellenistic, Roman-Byzantine, and Moslem. Still missing, however, was a conclusive theory to explain the reasons for fluctuations in prosperity and population size from one period to another.

The conventional wisdom was that the depletion of the soil and disrepair of the country could be blamed on the Arab population that had inhabited the land for centuries and on the Ottoman authorities who had neglected it. Lieutenant Conder asserted this in his 1876 report to the Palestine Exploration Fund on "The Fertility of Ancient Palestine": "The curse of the country is bad government and oppression. Justice and security of person and property once established, Palestine would become once more a land of corn, vines and olives, rivaling in fertility and in wealth its ancient condition, as deduced from careful study of such notices as remain to us in the Bible and in the later Jewish writings."[8] At the same time, Sir Charles Warren wrote in *The Land of Promise* (1875): "Give Palestine a good government and increase the commercial life of the people, and they may increase tenfold and yet there is room. Its [the land's] productiveness will increase in proportion to labour bestowed on the soil until a population of 15 million may be accomodated [sic] there."[9] This perception supported the Zionist view that the land could be made far more bountiful if only the most efficient modern techniques were used to cultivate it.

The most important challenge to this view was made by a Yale professor of geography, Ellsworth Huntington, a leader of a controversial approach that applied determinism to the study of geography. His work was brought to public attention in *Palestine and Its Transformation* (1911), which was widely quoted by Arab proponents of a very restrictive interpretation of the economic absorptive capacity. Supported by a fund administered by Yale president Arthur T. Hadley and by the Palestine Exploration Fund, Huntington was interested in "the effect of physical environment upon the distribution of living beings and upon man's mode of life and thought" and wanted to investigate whether man or nature were responsible for the country's decline. Like most visitors and researchers, he noted that in the past the population of the country had been far more dense: "Something has clearly changed. Has it been the type of inhabitant? Is the present state of the country worse than that of the past because the idle Arab has displaced the industrious Jew, and the vacillating Turk the strong Roman? Has the substitution of misrule and oppression for a just, firm government caused the physical deterioration of the country? Or has nature herself suffered a change which has brought in its train depopulation, and all the miseries of the present unsettled conditions?"[10]

Huntington's answer was that the climate had changed. Higher temperatures and less rain caused desert. Lower temperatures and more rain created an environment that could sustain a more substantial agriculture. Thus, in the Roman-Byzantine period when the climate was more favorable, the population had reached perhaps the greatest numbers in its recorded history. Drought and heat, not people, caused the decline of civilizations: "Rain is the missing element. . . . Irrigation is necessary to insure against famine in bad years, but no more water can be obtained. The supply appears to have decreased permanently."[11]

Two young Zionist leaders, David Ben-Gurion and Yitzhak Ben-Zvi, recognized the political implications of Huntington's analysis and quickly responded with their best-selling book on the means for colonizing Palestine, *Eretz Israel in the Past and in the Present* (1918).[12] Living as exiles from Turkish Palestine in New York, Ben-Gurion and Ben-Zvi spent much of their time at the New York Public Library reading assiduously everything they could find in English, German, French, and Hebrew relevant to country's past and potential. Emulating Conder, whom they described as "the greatest authority in all that pertains to Eretz Israel," they argued that a population of 10 million could live in historic Eretz Yisrael or the Palestine of both sides of the Jordan River.[13]

Ben-Gurion and Ben-Zvi well understood the political and moral value of blaming Arabs rather than climate for the devastation of the Holy Land. The conclusion of the two volumes of the best evidence they could gather had a distinctly Zionist political message that directly challenged Huntington's claims with their own reading of archaeological and textual evidence: modern Palestine was "a land without a people"; the land could be redeemed by industrious Jews, who were "a people without a land."[14]

Support for the Ben-Gurion and Ben-Zvi approach was provided after the First World War when American and European archaeologists and scholars of the ancient Near East organized in a systematic and institutionalized effort to re-create the social and economic history of the Middle East. Operating through the Rockefeller-funded American Schools of Oriental Research throughout the region, these scholars blended philology, linguistics, critical textual analysis, the study of material culture, and whatever else was available into an instrument of great analytic power. It became their objective not only to engage in religious and Biblical scholarship but to write the social and economic history of the area.

Of the accomplished scholars attracted to the study of Palestine, William F. Albright of Johns Hopkins University and the American School of Oriental Research in Jerusalem emerged as the central figure. In a popular series of lectures published in 1931 he synthesized a picture of ancient Palestinian society that went beyond validation or illumination of the Bible. It offered a reconstruction of the culture, demography, and economy of the peoples who had inhabited the land. Without making explicit reference to contemporary politics, he provided evidence that Palestine was indeed capable of supporting millions more inhabitants. He painted a picture of a Palestine in which dense populations dwelled in some areas as early as the Iron Age. However, together with most scholars, he singled out the Roman-Byzantine period as having a peak population of 4 or more million—three times as many inhabitants as were present in Palestine during the interwar period. It appeared that historic Palestine enjoyed a flourishing agriculture, considerable international trade, large towns throughout the country, even in the Negev desert, and large cities on the coast. Among the lessons drawn from this was that if the entire country prospered and supported high densities in the distant past, then it should be able to do so again in the present, particularly if modern technology were placed in the hands of those who knew how to use it.[15]

The political implications of this work were never far from the surface and echoed continually in the literature of archaeology. Nelson Glueck, a follower of Albright and the foremost scholar of Negev archaeology, repeatedly unearthed evidence that people, not climate, were responsible for success in settling the country's deserts. Like Ben-Gurion and Ben-Zvi, he explicitly countered Huntington's argument by placing blame for desertification on nomadic Bedouins, Arabs, inferior government, and wars "rather than drastic changes in the weather." Indeed, from his studies on the Negev he concluded: "Never in historical times had radical and permanent changes in climate placed it [the Negev] beyond the pale of settlement."[16]

The findings of Glueck and others were succinctly summarized at an international conference sponsored by the Research Council of Israel shortly after the establishment of the state. Although the battle for a state was over and Israel could now decide for itself at what rate it should take in immigrants, the old themes persisted. As Adolf Reifenberg, a Hebrew University archaeologist, proclaimed: "The Israel we see today is but the ruin of a once flourishing country. . . . It is human mismanagement, which has brought about a continuing deterioration in the natural conditions." Placing Palestine in an international context, other scholars from Western Europe, the United States, and North Africa concurred that in Palestine as well as in other desert areas in the world, it was people rather than climate that was the major factor in what was termed the struggle between the "Desert and the Sown." Organization and social values were held to be the key to national development.[17]

It is only recently that this interpretation of Palestine's past has again been questioned. Israeli archaeologist Magen Broshi has reviewed all the archaeological evidence and finds that Albright and his disciples miscalculated by a factor of up to three the number of people who could have been supported in Palestine during the Roman-Byzantine period. In addition, recent geological research has lead to speculation that there may be substance to Huntington's claims. For example, it has been suggested that a worldwide minor ice age coincided with the Roman-Byzantine period. This caused lower temperatures and higher rainfall, which benefited agriculture. Based on analysis of rocks, sediments, and other geological remains, it has been proposed that this period of prosperity terminated when temperatures rose and rainfall was diminished. These changes coincided with the incursion of the Arabs from expanding desert areas and their conquest of a Palestine that was far less favored climatically.[18]

Nevertheless, during the crucial pre-state period when Zionism was pressing it claims before the international community, archaeological research played an important, one-sided, and unambiguous role in the debate over the scope of Jewish immigration. Usually cited at least in the introductions to reports by the various international commissions on the Arab-Zionist conflict, it lent moral force by virtue of providing historical evidence for the Zionist demand that Palestine open its doors to multitudes of Jewish refugees who would work to reclaim the land.[19]

Foreign Experts and Absorptive Capacity

Experts first came to Palestine in significant numbers and on an organized basis soon after the Balfour Declaration. It was widely believed in Europe and the United States that the rejuvenation of Palestine was imminent, since Jerusalem and the Holy Land were once again in competent hands. In addition to the British, who were now charged through the Mandate with superintending the development of the country, the international Zionist network began organizing for the task of transforming Palestine into the Jewish National Homeland. Monetary resources were few, the conditions harsh, and the task immense. It was clear that developing Palestine into a home for the Jews required informed and detailed planning.

By the spring of 1919, the London office of the World Zionist Organization became actively engaged in recruiting professionals. Experts with practical experience as well as academic researchers including engineers, geographers, economists, and social planners interested in the problems of development became involved with the effort to prepare the country for the absorption of immigrants. Many of these experts were foreigners who viewed the issues of developing Palestine in a comparative framework. With experience in the dry lands of the American West, the Far East, particularly China, and the deserts of North Africa, they were dedicated to enhancing the economic absorptive capacity of land wherever they were invited to research and advise. In effect, the prejudice that societies themselves are responsible for success or failure in mastering the environment was inherent in their outlooks and justified their intervention. Invited by Zionist organizations, they used their expertise to address the many problems attendant on transforming the country into the promised Jewish National Homeland. It is not surprising that individually and collectively they produced data that supported the view that the country was far from exploiting its potential and that it could become a home for a significantly larger population. We have discussed the involvement of Elwood Mead and William T. Cory as well as the 1928 *Report of the Experts,* who were sent by American Zionists to support and shape the development of Zionist villages. Patrick Geddes, Patrick Abercrombie, and other urban and regional planners were also part of this large influx of experts from various fields. Many became directly involved in debates over the "economic absorptive capacity" of the country.

Walter Lowdermilk was perhaps the most important engineer who not only manifestly contributed to the development of the country but, as a non-Jew, supported the Zionist position that Jewish pioneers should be entrusted with the task of making the land flourish again. Assistant chief of the U.S. Soil Conservation Service, he was an expert with extensive international experience including work in China in a region that contained loess soil similar to that found in many parts of Palestine. He first came to Palestine in 1939 to consult on ways in which the country's agricultural productivity might be increased. Not surprisingly, he proposed a local adaptation of one of the great engineering, political, and social enterprises of the New Deal. That is, he suggested a massive land reclamation project, which he labeled the Jordan Valley Authority (JVA). As with the Tennessee Valley Authority (TVA) in the United States, the scheme was expected to increase the yield from the soil, augment the acreage available for agriculture, and provide hydroelectric power. Specifically, Lowdermilk argued that if the JVA were implemented, up to 4 million Jewish immigrants could be absorbed in addition to Palestine's current population of 1.5 million. The explicit political message was that the economic absorptive capacity of the country was a dynamic phenomenon that depended on people organizing themselves to apply the appropriate technology. Throughout the 1940s, Lowdermilk's ideas were the basis of Zionist settlement programs and the staple of Zionist argumentation in all sorts of forums. He also taught for many years at the Technion, producing a generation of local experts who spread his technical ideas and his public and political message.[20]

Another scientist who contributed to the Zionist side of the debate was Jean Gottmann, one of the leading geographers of his generation. Perhaps best known for his work on Western Europe and North America and especially for his study *Megalopolis*, Gottmann focused his earliest work on Palestine, and he maintained a continuing interest in it.[21] Born in Kharkov in 1915 to a well-established family that often hosted the leader of Revisionist Zionism, Vladimir Jabotinsky, he was exposed to Zionist politics early in life. In the aftermath of upheavals of the Russian Revolution, his family left the Soviet Union and he went to Paris, where he studied geography at the Sorbonne. Gottmann's doctoral dissertation was a reaction to the British *White Paper* of 1930, which, based on a restricted evaluation of Palestine's economic absorptive capacity, drastically curtailed Jewish immigration. Active in Zionist politics, Gottmann applied his scientific skills on behalf of the Zionist position by arguing in conferences and published papers that through proper cultivation and irrigation, the arid and neglected areas of Palestine could be made fruitful. His collection of essays, *Etudes sur L'état d'Isräel et le Moyen Orient (1935–1958)*, bears testimony to a twenty-year effort to demonstrate that Palestine could be a productive home for a large population. Directly and through the work of local geographers on whom he exerted considerable influence Gottmann helped create a body of scholarship and research that propagated an expansive conception of development.[22]

Because the economic absorptive capacity was at issue, it was economics that inevitably became the key discipline among the social sciences called upon to address the problem. The most important and comprehensive study undertaken was by a team of American economists— Robert Nathan, Oscar Gass, and Daniel Creamer. Together, they produced *Palestine: Problems and Promise, An Economic Study* in 1946. Their work quickly became the standard piece of literature used to persuade international forums in the critical period before the United Nations vote on partition. Nathan, the chief author, brought particular prestige to this volume because of his prominence as a leading practicing economist. Trained by economist Simon Kuznets, he had already earned a large reputation as one of the bright young men of the New Deal through his work as Director of the National Income Division of the U.S. Department of Commerce and Chairman of the Central Planning Division of the War Production Board.

The focus of the research was made explicit at the outset of the study. It was undertaken to fill "the need for an authoritative and objective appraisal of the economic potentialities of Palestine." The study was funded by "the American Palestine Institute, a nonpartisan research organization," which raised about $100,000, probably the largest sum theretofore committed to study an issue of public policy through social science research. In keeping with the scientific and objective approach, the organizers of the project set the policy that "the cost of the study was borne by individuals and organizations of varied, even divergent, views with regard to Zionism." They accepted funds from those who were identified on a "range from ardent Zionism through what may be called neutrality to a position of opposition to political Zionism." What bound everyone together was an agreement on "the need for this objective study."[23]

Palestine: Problem and Promise examined natural resources; agricultural prospects; manufacturing possibilities in a variety of industries; construction requirements, particularly in housing; the amount of capital necessary for development; and the possible sources of such funds. In sum, the experts produced a comprehensive analysis of how the country could be developed in order to accommodate the more than 1 million immigrants who might want or need to come during the following decade. They argued that despite limited natural resources, Palestine could be made productive because it possessed an enormous asset in the talent and dynamism of the Jewish population. Thus, findings of economists corroborated the view held by archaeologists and geographers. As founding director of one of the most active economic consulting firms in the postwar decades, Nathan was to claim later that the results of research in Palestine were confirmed by research into more than fifty other countries in the period following the Second World War. Reflecting recently on what he learned from his experience in Palestine, Nathan concluded that human resources are even more important than natural ones because people with talent are the key to development. This scientifically based point of view became an important part of the political arsenal of supporters of a Jewish state as they pleaded their cause before the great powers and the United Nations.[24]

Institutionalized Zionist Research in Palestine

As the political debate over the economic capacity of the country intensified, the accumulation of data and its analysis necessarily became a major occupation of Jews and Arabs as well as the British. Systematic official research on Palestine's economy had begun in the 1920s with attempts to create regular and standardized statistics on society and the economy. Early important contributions were made by the British with the publication of data in the *Palestine Blue Book* beginning in 1926 and a *Census of Industry* in 1928. Also significant were the data collected for the variety of commissions established by the British and that resulted in reports and *White Papers*.

Those responsible for Zionist colonization had been aware of the value of research for the success of their efforts before the Mandate and continued to create their own data independently of the British. As early as 1907, the World Zionist Organization sent Dr. Arthur Ruppin from Germany to investigate conditions in the country and to superintend development programs. To this task Ruppin brought scientific training in sociology, demography and social statistics, law, and business as well as the backing of Germany's wealthiest and most powerful Zionists. After publishing a prize-winning book on the sociology of the Jews through the centuries, he focused increasingly on the problems of resettling Jews in their own land. Appointed lecturer in sociology soon after the establishment of the Hebrew University in Jerusalem, he was throughout his life in Palestine (1907–1943) one of the central figures engaged in research into Palestinian society and its economy. At the same time, he was among the key Zionist officials responsible for charting and implementing settlement policy. Significantly, soon after his arrival in Palestine he undertook to establish the first census of Jerusalem in perhaps two thousand years.[25]

Prior to the 1930 *White Paper* and Nazi control in Germany, Ruppin did not press for large-scale immigration. On the contrary, as in his 1919 essay, "The Selection of the Fittest," he argued that Zionist authorities should carefully screen candidates for pioneering and give preference to those who were able and willing to work the land. Here, and elsewhere, he advanced the idea that a gradual approach was required to develop a backward, neglected, and resource-poor country.[26] Even in 1933, in the face of the threat from Nazism, Ruppin claimed in an address before the Zionist Congress in Prague that only some tens of thousands of German Jews could be absorbed. His analysis was based on a "scientific" formula that for every Jew settled on the land, only another two to three could be located in towns. In this view, the Jewish population of Palestine was necessarily limited because Jews owned a modest amount of land and more was hard to acquire. Thus Ruppin, one of the key Zionist officials responsible for Jewish settlement in Palestine, advised that the primary solution to the immediate dangers facing German Jewry was to organize the transit of Jews to the United States, Latin America, and other countries. At most, he envisaged "that Palestine can absorb a considerable population—a quarter, a third, and perhaps even a half—of the 200,000 German Jews who will leave their native land in the next five, eight or ten years."[27]

Political pressures and the plight of European Jewry demanded a more aggressive program. Ruppin's diary records an exchange with Ben-Gurion in February 1941 that reflects the pressure on experts to supply politically useful data. In response to Ben-Gurion's request that he travel to the United States to raise funds, Ruppin explained that he had to remain in order to engage in "the preparation of facts and suggestions for the future peace conference." He pointed out that "The Jews would show up very badly at this conference if they did not appear with a wealth of factual material and well-considered plans; nobody else will think of them for us." Ben-Gurion, Ruppin's superior as Chairman of the Jewish Agency, welcomed Ruppin's idea but, at the same time, gave him a mandate: "I hope that you will show that there is a way of bringing five million Jews to Palestine." Ruppin refused to commit himself to a particular figure, noting that "the investigation would have to show what the largest possible number could be." Ruppin's cautious approach and projections were not altered by the flow of information concerning the annihilation of European Jewry and the adamant British refusal to permit significant Jewish immigration. With Ruppin's death two years later, Ben-Gurion, the political leader of Palestinian Zionism, turned to other experts to provide a different response. Clearly it would be necessary to move beyond Ruppin's relatively static formula of absorption, which was based on the limited capacity for agricultural expansion.[28]

Ruppin had appreciated that necessary preconditions for greater absorption were the establishment of a stronger local economy, the purchase of more land, and the development of better markets. It was, in part, this understanding that led to the establishment in 1935 of the Economic Research Institute of the Jewish Agency. Founded with a grant provided by wealthy British Jews, it brought together "a number of young economists of high standing" who had come to the country "largely as the result of the immigration from Germany." The mandate given the institute was the collection of "existing material and the creation of material not yet in existence through original research." Not only was the group to develop plans for expanding the economy, but it was also to provide data to the Executive of the Jewish Agency "on which they can base their decisions."[29]

One of the Central European economists Ruppin brought into the department, Alfred Bonné, came to direct the institute after Ruppin's death in 1943. It was during Bonné's tenure that the institute developed its expansive conception of the Palestinian economy, a formula no longer based on two or three settlers in towns for every one on the land. Bonné's model was that of a developing urban and industrial economy. Writing in the midst of the war against the Axis Powers, he claimed that Zionist planners could learn a great deal from the way in which other societies, particularly Japan, had successfully made the transition from a traditional agrarian economy to a modern, industrial one. If Palestine could not offer a sufficiently high standard of living, on a par with Western European nations, he warned, Jews who came to Palestine would not remain: "The implications of this new concept may not be very welcome to those who regard agriculture as the basis of economic life. But it is no use shutting one's eyes to realities. Even the ideal of bringing an urbanised people back to the soil should not delude us into ignoring the fact that it is far easier for the new immigrant to obtain a decent livelihood in congenial surroundings in urban occupations than in agriculture."[30]

Between 1943 and 1948, Bonné's institute became the center of the campaign waged by Jewish Agency researchers to develop plans for an expanded Jewish Palestine and to counter British restrictions and Arab claims. Much of this work was conducted discretely in a subcommittee called the Planning Committee (Va'adat Tikon), established and chaired by Ben-Gurion.[31] The occasion for creating this group was an announcement on March 22, 1943, by the British High Commissioner that the Mandatory government was appointing a committee on the postwar reconstruction of Palestine. This in itself was unexceptional, as similar committees had been formed throughout the British Empire, in Britain itself, and even by refugee groups from Poland, France, Belgium, and Norway. However, in establishing the Palestine committee, the High Commissioner maintained that, despite its recent industrial and urban growth, "Palestine is essentially an agricultural country."[32] For Zionism, the implications were extremely dangerous. Ben-Gurion understood that if such a definition went unchallenged, it would prohibit the immigration of masses of Jews. The Planning Committee was Ben-Gurion's answer to this threat.

During the course of the next five years, until the creation of the State of Israel, architects, engineers, economists, sociologists, and people with experience in government, banking, industry, and agriculture from within the Jewish community in Palestine as well as from abroad submitted studies or came to testify before the committee's experts in sessions that Ben-Gurion often chaired personally. The committee accumulated plans, many of them quite elaborate and detailed, for absorbing the masses of immigrants who would come to the state in its first decade. They called for national construction projects and industries that could provide employment and generate wealth; for situating agricultural settlements; for building roads and establishing a transportation system; for designing the location of parks and other recreational facilities; and for building cities. Well before the end of the Second World War studies dealt with how these projects were to be funded, and included an outline of the taxes that the future Jewish state would levy, the loans it would need from the world community, and even the reparations the Germans would be asked to pay. It was, in part, based on the work of the Planning Committee. Chaim Weizmann could claim in 1945, in a letter to President Truman, that "Palestine, for its size, is probably the most investigated country in the world."[33]

Committee documents were circulated among and commented on by scientists and politicians who were to play crucial roles in the founding of the state and in determining its shape and priorities. They included, in addition to leading sociologists, engineers, and planners:

Ben-Gurion, the first Prime Minister; Bonné, the founding Dean of Social Sciences at the Hebrew University; David Horowitz, the first Director General of the Finance Ministry and first Governor of the Bank of Israel; Eliezer Kaplan, the first Minister of Finance; Eliezer Hoofien, director of the country's largest bank and first chairman of the Advisory Committee of the Bank of Israel; and Richard Kauffmann, architect and planner. In effect, the Planning Committee was a seminar in nation-building for the future leaders of Israel and its professional planners. However, its first assignment was to provide materials for the ongoing public debate concerning the future of Palestine.[34]

While much of the research was in the form of internal documents with restricted circulation, some studies found their way to the public through popular and scientific journals and books. Still others formed the basis for the argument that was made before the various international commissions that deliberated on the possibility of creating a Jewish state. A significant illustration of the often indirect impact of the committee is Nathan, Gass, and Creamer's "objective" study. Nathan has reported that among his chief informants were Bonné, Horowitz, and Kaplan. Gass and Creamer also derived their information from the best sources available, which meant, in effect, the Jewish Agency's economists and planners. Indeed, a careful reading of their *Palestine: Problems and Promise* offers no surprises to a reader of the Planning Committee's reports and files. In the crucial period between the end of the Second World War and Israel's War for Independence, social scientists within Palestine and without developed a common base of scientific data and came to similar conclusions about the means for rapidly increasing the country's economic absorptive capacity.

Toward the Law of Return

From the Balfour Declaration to the establishment of Israel, there was a marked shift of Zionist attitudes toward the "economic absorptive capacity" of Palestine. In the early years of the Mandate, many Zionists did not adopt an unrestricted definition of how many Jews could live in Palestine. On the contrary, leaders like Ruppin felt it could be disastrous for Zionism if too many pioneers came, only to be disappointed by what they found. Although it was anticipated that the country could absorb millions, it was generally assumed that this process would require time. Thus, the initial Zionist response to the British formula was to collaborate in restricting numbers in accordance with a gradual approach to the colonization of Palestine rather than take issue with the principle.

Changed political circumstances forced a change in attitude. By the 1930s the Arab pressure on the British to restrict Jewish immigration and the Nazi pressure on Jews to leave Europe forced a rethinking of the Zionist settlement program. Models for development had to allow for immediate absorption of large numbers of refugees. This led to the shift from conceiving of Palestine essentially as an agricultural country to envisioning it as an urban and industrial society. Development towns and cities were added to the moshav and the kibbutz in the inventory of official planning programs. Absorbing immigrants and increasing national and individual prosperity at the most rapid rate possible became issues of supreme political importance and required the marshaling of intellectual resources from a wide range of academic disciplines. In the course of this work, the imagining of Palestinian society came to be dominated by the statistics and modeling of social scientists. Experts and professionals gained primacy over philosophers and idealogues.

By 1948, the Planning Committee had produced a model of an Israel that would be 80 percent urban and only 20 percent rural. Sharon's Master Plan of 1950 was the distillation of this work of collaborative research and became the basis for the physical, social, and economic development of Israel through the 1960s.[35] This conception of the country also proved decisive in the discussions over how many Jews Israel could absorb upon independence. While still at war and then under pressure from hostile neighbors, the young state had to decide whether to undertake the absorption of the large numbers seeking admission from Cyprus and Europe as well as from Yemen, Iraq, and the Middle East. Ben-Gurion chose mass rather than selective immigration and carried the government with him. This historic decision, which has shaped Israel's history and society, was not based solely on sentiment or ideology. It was the product of an extended scientific discussion carried on by the country's best researchers and by prominent analysts from abroad. Together, they had produced a body of data that enabled them to make projections and detailed plans for organizing the new state. As a consequence, Israel would be based on a policy of encouraging immigration at all times and from wherever it might come. When the government enacted the Law of Return in 1950, Israel ended the debate over the economic absorptive capacity of the country and took responsibility for a liberal and open-ended conception of Zionist settlement.

CHAPTER 9

From New Towns to Development Towns

I SRAEL'S national Master Plan of 1950 is considered an outstanding example of post–Second World War national planning.[1] This thoughtful and carefully formulated document situates physical planning in relation to the development of a national economy, the integration of a multitude of immigrants from diverse cultures, and the possibility that the War of Independence might not be Israel's final conflict. The plan also reflects new opportunities once the British no longer limited settlement. Blaming the Mandatory authorities for "restrictive political conditions" that inhibited a normal distribution of the Jewish population throughout the country, it called for a radical alteration of the distorted pattern of settlement that had characterized the Yishuv prior to Independence. The British policy of obstructing land purchases outside of designated zones resulted in excessive concentration of the Jewish population in large cities, especially Tel Aviv. Sharon repeatedly noted that the proportion of Israelis living in Tel Aviv as opposed to the rest of the country constituted a world record with 43 percent while Vienna had 33 percent and London 22 percent. This abnormal situation gave rise to unwelcome pathologies and dangers. Excessive population density not only made for reduced standards for public health and amenities and costly services, but it also constituted a compact, vulnerable target in the event of future hostilities.[2]

The massive influx of immigrants coupled with centralized governmental control over most of the country's land as a consequence of independence seemed to provide an unparalleled opportunity for redressing demographic imbalances and achieving social and economic objectives. Sharon's plan was based on the premise that the state had to "guide" immigrants in a manner that would advance national goals. Accordingly, the team of experts assembled in Sharon's office divided the country into twenty-four planning districts and established target populations for different areas. On a national level, they foresaw an agricultural population of no more than 20 percent. To reach this quota, they envisaged an immediate and extraordinary expansion of the Zionist practice of organizing modest villages of approximately a hundred families in the form of a kibbutz or a moshav. Nearly three hundred such communities were planted within the first five years of statehood. In keeping with a regional approach, special efforts were made to establish these villages in the Negev and Galilee, the Jerusalem corridor, and other locations, most important along the country's long and underpopulated border areas. Israel's farmland also burgeoned beyond the limited boundaries for agricultural settlement that had been fixed by Arab hostility to Jewish land acquisition as expressed in the British *White Papers*. After Independence approximately 13 percent of the new immigrants were directed to agricultural villages, many of which were in areas that had only recently become available for Jewish settlement.[3]

A far larger proportion of the new state's projected population of 2,650,000 was directed to new towns. Of the 80 percent who were expected to remain urbanites, the plan provided that 45 percent would continue to reside in existing large cities—Tel Aviv, Haifa, and Jerusalem—and 55 percent in proposed medium-sized cities of between 40,000 and 60,000 inhabitants and towns with populations of 6,000 to 12,000. This meant that well over 1 million residents, most of whom would be drawn from the pool of new immigrants, would be directed to the new urban centers. The need for redistributing the population was not merely the subject of bureaucratic and technical discussion. It was brought to the public. The poster shown in Figure 9.1 was but one of a series of publications attempting to persuade Israelis to settle the interior of the country. It reads: "75% of the population is crowded in only three cities." They are, from top to bottom, Jerusalem, Tel Aviv, and Haifa, which are shown in three different years: 1924, 1936, and 1948.

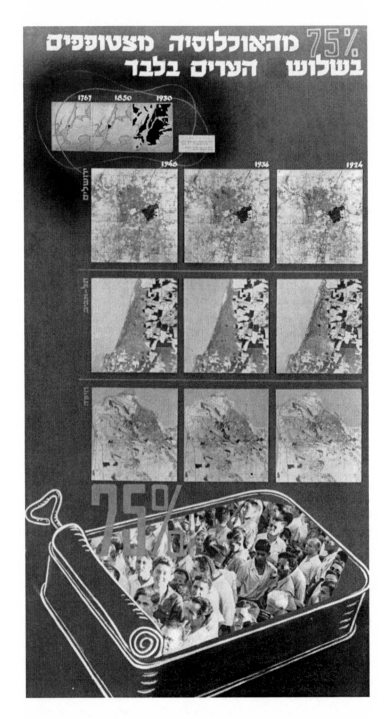

9.1. Poster advocating population dispersal, 1950. Courtesy of the National Photo Collection, Government Press Office.

The boxes at the upper left show how congestion spread in New York City from 1767 to 1850 to 1930. Emphasizing the point even further is the can of sardines filled with people, where the viewer is again warned of the "75%." Less visual but still constant and ubiquitous exhortations were articulated in the period's public rhetoric.

For any country, population dispersal, particularly through the building of settlements, would be an ambitious program. For a new state—poor in resources, attempting to recover from war, and doubling its population from immigration within its first four years—this was an immense, self-imposed challenge. It is not surprising that implementation was fraught with miscalculations and shortcomings or that there were numerous disappointments and misguided assumptions. Yet, for better and for worse, the national Master Plan profoundly transformed the Yishuv and has had a lasting impact on shaping the demographic and economic distribution of the country. Perhaps the most significant innovation of Israeli national planning in the first years of the state was the new town. How and why Zionist planners incorporated the new town idea, and the problems they encountered in trying to implement it, are the subjects of this chapter.[4]

The International Context

Israel's new town policy was part of an international movement that began in Great Britain and spread to Europe and beyond. Called *ayarot pituach,* or "development towns" in Israel, new towns have been variously named in different cultures: *neustadt, villeneuve, novgorod,* and *novigrad.* New towns are said to provide an alternative and a "corrective to city overgrowth and congestion on the one hand and unduly scattered human settlement on the other hand." These twin purposes reflect a widespread analysis of severe social and economic problems that afflict modern industrial societies. Appalled by the squalor and deviancy in the slums of the modern metropolis, critics at the beginning of the twentieth century proposed establishing new communities of a modest size outside of existing population concentrations where less expensive land was available for residential and industrial development. At the same time they recognized that the industrial and agricultural revolutions had led to a marked deterioration in the quality of life for rural populations. Through the new towns they sought to bring a renewed vitality to the countryside. Towns of limited size would stabilize rural populations while restricting metropolitan growth. They were expected to reduce the unhealthy crowding associated with metropolitan life and to ameliorate the quality of life in the countryside.[5]

These conceptions were forcefully and clearly articulated in 1898 by Ebenezer Howard's *Tomorrow: A Peaceful Path to Reform*. This book stimulated the organization of the garden city movement, which soon produced several experimental communities. It also provided a focus for reformers and professionals who incorporated and developed Howard's ideas into proposals advanced by a host of local, national, and international organizations. Translating these concepts into large-scale programs proved difficult. Implementation of the new town idea was gradual and sporadic until the end of the Second World War, when, in response to a pressing need for postwar reconstruction, states undertook and carried out on a large scale the ideas crystallized by Howard.

It is precisely in this international context that the Israeli new town policy has been most widely appreciated. In a standard British survey of new town accomplishments in the postwar period, Frederic Osborn and Arnold Whittick observe: "Israel, being a new state, has perhaps pursued more logically than any other the planned location of population and industry. Before the 1939–45 War too large a proportion had been massed in three cities. Later the effort was made to restrain their growth, and the national plan was for the creation of 24 regional centers of 10,000 to 60,000, with many smaller towns and villages. There is now a reaction towards somewhat larger urban units, but the principle of control of size is intelligently retained."[6] Similarly, in a methodical analysis of Israel's new towns, German critic Erika Spiegel commented that while Israeli new town planning had some unique characteristics, it could be readily identified as an instance of a general phenomenon. She noted that Israel's new towns "were revolutionary or reformatory only in the sense that they were definitely and decisively opposed to the previous trends of Jewish settlement in Palestine, and to the contemporary influx into big cities in general, noticeable nearly all over the world."[7]

Ann Louise Strong, an American, also considered the Israeli experience to be part of a larger international movement and compared it to the postwar experience in Sweden, Finland, the Netherlands, and France. Her interest in all these examples, however, was to exhort her countrymen to imitation. Of all the case studies, she concluded, Israel was in many ways the most important, for it could point the way to the future. In comparing the United States with Israel, she writes:

Israel's people have many of the better attributes of our pioneers: optimism, vitality, courage, and strength. Their confident belief in their country and its future is reminiscent of a spirit we have lost. The analogy to an earlier America ends there. The Israelis are builders, not plunderers. . . . They have taken a barren and inhospitable, backward and lightly populated land and, with the resources of brains and money, have transformed it into a productive and, absent war, almost self-supporting economy for more than 2.5 million people. Israel has a national physical master plan and, under it, has shaped the settlement of people, the allocation of land to agriculture or development, and the management of scarce resources, particularly water. To an even greater extent than Great Britain (given their comparative population bases), Israel has built and populated a hierarchy of new towns from Ashdod, with an anticipated population of 350,000, down to scores of farm villages. In the process, Israel has learned much about new town size and structure.

Strong concluded that Israel, which "started with a relatively simple theoretical structure[, had] built a country as rapidly as possible (substituting pragmatism for theory in many instances), and now is reconsidering theory in light of experience."[8]

Israeli planners enjoyed this acclaim. They, too, viewed what they had done from a comparative and international perspective. When important Israeli planners did find fault, which happened only rarely in the early years, they employed an international point of reference in evaluating the plans of colleagues. Self-congratulations subsided and finally turned to harsh self-criticism in the 1960s when it became apparent that many towns remained islands of poverty in a larger society that was steadily emerging from the trials of post-Independence economic stringency. However, rather than criticizing the original conception, advocates of the new town approach blamed faulty execution of a grand design that was still found to be inspiring.

Exploring the international perspective is useful, for it suggests several important features of Israeli planning. As noted earlier, most planners were either transplanted Europeans or European-trained, and their conceptions were fundamentally derived from the European experience. Although they lived in a developing country, their frame of reference was the experience of modern, industrial societies. They were, in effect, anticipating the excesses and problems of a society and economic order that did not yet exist in Israel. In so doing, they themselves were contributing to the enduring social problems of cities on the country's periphery.

New Town Policy among Zionist Planners

Perhaps the first voice that consistently called for an urban colonization policy was that of engineer and planner Eliezer Brutzkus. Shortly before the outbreak of the Second World War, Brutzkus criticized the national Zionist institutions for focusing excessively on agricultural settlement. By the end of the war, his early criticisms had developed into a well-articulated rationale, and he vigorously advocated a revolutionary change in the priorities of traditional Zionist planning.[9]

In a 1945 essay in the leading journal of Zionist architects and engineers, *Handasa Ve'adrichalut* (Engineering and Architecture), Brutzkus complained that Zionist planning was biased toward the agricultural sector and that the time had come for a radical departure. He explained what he saw as a historical failure largely in terms of a misdirected and limiting ideology: "First of all we must state that the urban settlement was a kind of exception to our colonization effort. The Zionist movement always preferred the agricultural settlement. One always prefers that which one lacks. The Jewish people lacked an agricultural class and consequently preferred agricultural settlement." He went on to describe how Jewish Agency settlement experts, despite ideological preferences, continually reduced the proportion of the Jewish population expected to work in the agricultural sector. While after the First World War the majority of settlers were expected to be farmers, the experts dropped this proportion to a half, then to a third, and, finally, after the Second World War, to no more than 20 percent. The expanding role assigned to the urban sector was not, however, accompanied by an interest in town planning. Brutzkus charged that Zionist planning had left urban development to the vagaries of the marketplace.[10]

The danger with neglect was that an unwanted pattern of national development could result. In viewing the possible alternatives, Brutzkus considered the example of other frontier societies such as Australia, Argentina, Canada, and the United States and measured their experience against that of Europe. The Australian model, despite the enormous difference in scale, was the one most frequently cited because it represented one end of the spectrum of what Israel could look like. In 1945, after a century and a half of development, 92 percent of Australia's nonagricultural work force was concentrated in large cities. This proportion was similar to that found in other frontiers settled by large numbers of transplanted Europeans, as in Argentina or on the west coasts of the United States and Canada. Such population distribution was termed "polar," reflecting the sharp dichotomy in population densities between the large cities and outlying areas. This polar model is characterized by few major urban centers, even fewer or no medium-sized centers, and a dispersed agricultural population that depends directly on the metropolis for services and supplies. These metropolises are typically located on the coast and are connected with the international market. In fact, this was how the Yishuv had developed. The Jewish national institutions scattered moshavim and kibbutzim throughout the country, while the majority of the population, together with industry and commerce, was concentrated in the coastal cities of Tel Aviv and Haifa.

The other model, termed "hierarchical," which Brutzkus championed, derived from the European experience with which he was personally familiar and that he knew also from the writings of the European scholar Walter Christaller. A hierarchical spatial organization developed naturally over the centuries. Populations were more evenly distributed over large territories, and there was a full range of types of settlement from the farm to the village through local towns, regional cities, and the national metropolis. An important characteristic of the hierarchical model was the observed division of the country into regions that all had more or less the same pattern of hierarchical organization. In advocating centralized control in shaping the country in the European model, planners such as Brutzkus had in mind the development of small and medium-sized cities scattered throughout the country in a predetermined, comprehensive regional design.[11] Writing from the vantage point of the 1960s, Brutzkus observed that the polar model was characteristic of the primary or pioneering period in national history. A more mature Zionist society would emulate the European "hierarchical" model.[12] Here, as in many other places, Zionist planners imagined that Palestine was malleable and that it could readily be shaped by professionals and settlement agencies.

By 1945, leading Yishuv professionals had come to share Brutzkus's views. During the latter part of 1943, a formal and systematic discussion of the economic and physical organization of the Yishuv had been inaugurated under the auspices of the Jewish Agency. As David Ben-Gurion's Planning Committee attempted to devise a strategy for mass immigration in the aftermath of the Second World War, it became clear that agricultural colonies would be incapable of absorbing significant numbers. Zionist planners therefore turned for the first time to consider how the Yishuv's cities and industries could be employed in a comprehensive program of national development.

Anticipating the rapid absorption of very large numbers, perhaps up to 1 million in only a few years, Zionist planners faced an unprecedented challenge and began to explore new areas and models of settlement. Whereas prewar immigrants from Poland and Central Europe found work and housing largely on their own or through the organizations of the Labor movement, the overwhelming majority of postwar refugees would be totally dependent on the national institutions. This projected dependency inevitably increased the urgency and enhanced the prospect of controlling development through planning. A far-reaching new town policy involving the planned settlement of hundreds of thousands of people appeared to be both necessary and attainable.[13]

Thinking along these lines took place simultaneously in two important forums, one private and the other public. As noted above, Ben-Gurion organized a group of experts to work out detailed plans for postwar mass immigration. At the same time, the Association of Engineers and Architects in Palestine (AEAP), which served as a meeting place for Jewish and British officials and professionals, conducted an ongoing program of seminars on professional issues including postwar reconstruction. There was, in fact, a convergence of discussions in these two groups. In November 1943, for example, the AEAP held a "Symposium on Planning and Development Problems" with the participation of leading Yishuv economists and planners including Eliezer Hoofien (director of the Yishuv's largest bank), Eliezer Kaplan (an economist and senior Jewish Agency official), David Horowitz (a senior Jewish Agency economist), Alfred Bonné (an economist and director of planning for the Jewish Agency), Ya'acov Ben-Sira (Tel Aviv's Municipal Engineer), and Eliezer Brutzkus. The common theme of the economic experts was the industrialization of the Yishuv, which they viewed as the only answer to accommodating up to 50,000 demobilized soldiers and war workers and an influx of an undetermined but large number of immigrants. The planners envisaged a much larger population residing and working in new towns of 10,000 and of 50,000. Ben-Sira thought no Palestinian city should exceed 300,000 (presumably Tel Aviv) and that a 200,000 ceiling would be preferable for a few larger towns. Numbers varied in different proposals, but common to all was the conception of small, medium, and large communities with the upper limit in the range of several hundred thousand.[14] This physical model echoed an earlier report to the association by a British expert who described population dispersal proposals in Great Britain.[15]

These fashionable ideas, widely circulated in lectures and articles, became the standard features of internal Jewish Agency proposals by mid-1945. Throughout these discussions, there is repeated reference to the 1940 Barlow Report (*Royal Commission on the Geographical Distribution of Industrial Population in England*) and Patrick Abercrombie's *Greater London Plan* (1944), an outgrowth of the earlier work. The Barlow Report was widely read, and Abercrombie's ideas were also communicated personally during his visits to Palestine. Indeed, because he was the most important national and town planner in the postwar period, Sharon conferred with him in England before submitting Israel's Master Plan.[16]

As we have seen, the intellectual, professional, and personal ties between Zionist and British planners were close and productive. Public attention to British planning was substantially increased by the visible impact of the Second World War on Britain. The economic, social, and aesthetic ideas previously associated with proposals for decentralization were not new to experts. However, the aerial attacks on London gave this principle a manifest and unprecedented urgency that was readily appreciated by both professionals and the public at large. To the social and economic motivations for decentralization as expressed in variations of the garden city concept was added the value of decentralization of population and industry to national security. This lesson was not lost on Zionist planners, and they incorporated it in the Master Plan. Security considerations were particularly relevant in the territory of a small Jewish state that might yet be carved out of Palestine.

National planning with a new town orientation, based largely on the British experience, had thus moved to the center of discussion in the half-decade prior to Independence. At that time Zionist planners still lacked legal authority, financial resources, and the power a state could provide. Missing, too, were essential data on the territory and the borders of the Jewish state so that exact and explicit locations of new towns and, indeed, all settlements could be fixed. Independence provided the necessary institutional arrangements and the necessary physical and political data. With Independence, planning moved from the office of David Ben-Gurion, the Chairman of the Jewish Agency, to that of the Prime Minister Ben-Gurion. Some personnel moved along with the function. Others, like Sharon, joined them. With the principles already well-established, Sharon's Planning Department provided the details and finishing touches.

Map 9.1. Post-Independence development towns.

The Sharon Plan has logic, elegance, and clarity. The national scale and the manifesto of economic and social principles are ambitious and inspiring. As we have seen, the reputation of the plan was immediate and enduring. However, analysis of its implementation suggests a very different assessment of Israeli national planning. Sampling the history of several new towns illustrates the disparity between theory and its implementation. Some succeeded and others failed, but regardless of who went to them, what they did there, and how they fared, a wide gulf existed between the blueprints of professionals and the actual experience of many residents.

Beit She'an

The development of Beit She'an should have been a textbook case of a new town related to a regional plan. Built at the site of one of the oldest cities in the country, from the stone age through the pre-Biblical period it was a trading center with strategic value at the junction of two important axes: north–south along the Jordan River and east–west to the lands on both sides of the Jordan. Egyptians, Canaanites, Philistines, Israelites, and Romans maintained cities at the site. In the days of Imperial Rome, it was the largest city in the Jordan Valley, a thriving commercial center in one of the Middle East's most fertile areas. In the Talmud, it was called the "gate to the Garden of Eden." A long decline set in after the Muslim conquests, and the Ottomans did not attempt to revitalize the town. According to archaeological remains, twenty-eight cities preceded modern Beit She'an.[17]

The population of the town grew slowly as the population in Palestine as a whole increased. In 1900 Beit She'an was a slowly growing Arab town with no Jewish residents. By 1922, there were 41 Kurdish Jews. As a consequence of Arab violence in 1929, even this small community left. By the War of Independence there were approximately 5,000 Arab inhabitants and no Jews. In the course of the conflict, residents quit the town, the last leaving on May 13, 1948, the day before Israeli Independence was declared. At Independence, Beit She'an was a ghost town.[18]

Zionist planners established their first settlements in the area around Beit She'an in 1936. They did so in the context of the growing struggle between Arabs and Jews for control over Palestine. The first settlements were characteristically agricultural—kibbutzim and moshavim. As noted earlier, it was here, in the valley along the Jordan River, that planners placed the first stockade and tower settlements. Acting in accordance with a decision of the Nineteenth Zionist Congress meeting in Lucerne, Switzerland, the World Zionist Organization directed the Jewish Agency to settle the Beit She'an Valley on a planned, regional basis. In early 1936 the first kibbutz, Tel Amal, was established. The outbreak of Arab riots in April 1936 made it difficult to maintain the colony, and the site was temporarily abandoned. Reestablished in December 1936, Tel Amal became the first kibbutz designed as a military outpost according to the principles of stockade and tower. By 1938, the Arab town of Beit She'an was ringed by Beit Yosef (1937) to the north; Maoz Haim (1937), and Kfar Ruppin (1938) to the east; Tirat Zvi (1937) to the south; and Nir David (1937) to the west. The total number of Jewish residents by the time of Independence was fewer than 2,000. In the case of Beit She'an, the perception of the region as the fundamental unit of planning anticipated the Master Plan, although the reasons for this were security and strategic concerns rather than a concept of population dispersal derived from the social sciences.[19]

After Independence, in accordance with the declared need to decentralize populations and find housing for new immigrants who were pouring into the country, the abandoned Arab town was designated for settlement. At the same time, Israeli policy did not allow for the return of Arab refugees, thereby ensuring an absence of competition for place. In was not until May 1949, a year after Independence and just before the final armistice lines were formalized, that the first immigrants, largely from Czechoslovakia, Poland, and Bulgaria, were placed in homes refurbished by the Absorption Department of the Jewish Agency. Surrounding kibbutzim and moshavim pressed to establish an urban cooperative that would serve the proximate rural settlements and forestall the possibility that the future city would become a dumping ground for new immigrants. They proposed that the city adopt the same kind of social and economic form that was found in their societies. That is, they requested that the immigrants be chosen with care and the community organized cooperatively, in accordance with ideological principles. Indeed, the first sixty families to arrive were organized as a cooperative to make clothes and small artifacts and to provide services for the region's settlements. The cooperative failed, but immigrants continued to arrive.[20]

Beit She'an became, in fact, a large transit camp, in an isolated, economically undeveloped valley distant from the country's center and proximate to a hostile border. The vacant Arab residences were of poor quality and too few to satisfactorily house the stream of immigrants, so two transit camps (*ma'abarot*) with tents and other temporary structures were added. The newcomers lacked the financial resources that might have enabled them to develop the city, and the government invested little. Some work was available in government-supported projects such as afforestation or in the region's settlements as agricultural laborers, but there was widespread unemployment. Those with skills in carpentry, construction, and metal-working soon left for profitable employment elsewhere, especially in the center of the country. With few services, limited employment, and no hope of advancement, Beit She'an became a community of dependent immigrants located and maintained on the periphery by government policy.[21]

In 1954, five years after the town had been "resettled," the first significant injection of resources occurred through a decision of the Labor Ministry to construct 450 housing units. However, this had little impact on the town, which by then had 4,500 residents, mostly from Persia and Iraq. Not one factory existed. The town still lacked paved sidewalks or streets, and only a few blocks were connected to electricity. There was no public transportation and only such minimal services as an infirmary and a post office. There was no ambulance and no fire station. No restaurants, bookstores, or amusement centers for adults or youth. One survey showed that only 100 daily newspapers were distributed among the population of 4,500. Only one school, the town's largest, went up to only the eighth grade. In the understated words of one report: "A discouraging situation has been created with regard to attracting people with skills and with culture which are essential for the development of Beit She'an."[22]

Reports typically blamed authorities: "Instead of sending to Beit She'an intellectual and vocational forces necessary like air for breathing, the Jewish Agency sent over this past year, without consulting any local authorities, welfare cases that have yet to become accustomed to the city and who have become a burden for the impoverished local population." The Regional Council, which was primarily concerned with agricultural settlements, offered little assistance to the town. Instead, as farming became increasingly mechanized, the need for Beit She'an's laborers diminished. Rather than developing, the town was sinking further into hopelessness and depression. The Master Plan notwithstanding, the report charged that Israel had produced not a new town but "a backward Levantine city."[23]

Kiryat Shemona

At about the time Beit She'an was resettled, Kiryat Shemona was founded in the Upper Galilee. In September 1949, 100 immigrant families from Yemen were placed in the vacated Arab village of Khalsa. Located on a mountainside near the Lebanese border, the site never had the historical importance of Beit She'an, nor did it possess natural advantages or resources. It was a backwater community that over the past century had gained notoriety as a breeding ground of Moslem violence, first against Christian Arabs and later against Jewish settlers. Khalsa's new, Hebrew name, Kiryat Shemona, recalls the martyrdom of eight members of the neighboring settlement of Tel Hai, where Josef Trumpeldor, a heroic figure in the history of Zionist settlement, and seven comrades were killed by a band from Khalsa.[24]

The initial plan called for a rural village where each family would have five dunams for a house, vegetable garden, and orchard. Additional income would be earned from employment in public works or agricultural labor in the settlements of the Upper Galilee. This conception derived from the satellite cities for workers, like Shchunat Borochov, built near Tel Aviv in the early 1920s. As happened in Shchunat Borochov, it was soon discovered that there was insufficient land to go around, so the allotments were reduced from five to two dunams. Even this smaller area seemed excessive when they considered the densities required for a city of thousands. Planners decided that a city of up to 25,000 based on industry and on service to the region's agriculture would be more appropriate. On this basis, 5,000 additional immigrants were brought to Khalsa during the course of 1950–51 and the city's name was changed to Kiryat Yosef (Trumpeldor) and finally to Kiryat Shemona.

Immigration continued to create enormous pressure for housing, work, and services. The first step was to create a small-scale and highly unstable cottage industry among the Yemenites who wove textiles for a Tel Aviv entrepreneur. The first factory, a textile plant, was opened only at the end of the town's first decade, in 1958. As in Beit She'an, Kiryat Shemona's residents were dependent on government or Histadrut (Jewish Federation of Labor) initiative and investment. Here, too, there was enormous movement in and out of the town. It has been estimated that during the first 25 years approximately 75,000 entered and left Kiryat Shemona. This was hardly the fulfillment of a 1950 declaration that "Here will rise the city of the North."[25]

Kiryat Malachi

Similar situations existed throughout the country. Kiryat Malachi, for example, was established in 1951 at the crossroads of ancient highways leading from Beer-Sheva to Jaffa and the coast and from the Mediterranean at Gaza to Jerusalem. Indeed, it is between 31 and 37 miles from all these points. From the perspective of national planning, the site was naturally suited for a future city. Beginning as a transit camp composed of tents, it grew only as a consequence of external decisions to channel immigrants to the location. Dependent on decisions of the settlement authorities, its growth was erratic, and it took seven years before it was considered sufficiently stable and permanent for status as a "local authority"—that is, an independent governing unit.[26]

The problems of Kiryat Malachi were apparent from its beginning. As with many new towns, Kiryat Malachi's founding was intimately related to an anticipated relationship with an agricultural hinterland. After the War of Independence, the new state had considerable territories in the southern region of the country but very few settlements. Decentralization was the proposed corrective. The idea for Kiryat Malachi originated in an attempt to create a town that would meet the needs of this region's agricultural settlements. The driving force was a local leader of the moshav movement, Mordechai Gruber of the moshav Beer Tuvia, who urged that immigrants be sent to colonize the countryside. Gruber recognized that these colonies would require both local services and a proximate source of seasonal labor. Here, again, there was an echo of Shchunat Borochov. Also, new venues for receiving immigrants had to be created. A deserted British army base and vacant land at the historic crossroads appeared to be a suitable site for accomplishing Gruber's objective. Levi Eshkol, the Jewish Agency official responsible for rural settlement, agreed and authorized sending the first thirty families.

The projections of those responsible for establishing the town corresponded to the expectations of the first settlers. The following testimony is typical:

> I made aliyah on 15/8/1950 from Iraq. I remained for more than a month in the "Sh'ar Ha'aliyah" (Gate of Immigration) Camp near Haifa. They considered transferring us to a transit camp. At that time there were no transit camps available anywhere. Afterwards it became known that there was a place called Kastina near Beer Tuvia. Instructors from the Jewish Agency persuaded us to settle there promising that each family would be given a house and a plot of land of from three to four dunams

with which to establish a truck garden and a hen house. Trees would be planted so that, as it is written, each man could sit "under his vine and under his fig tree.". . . The settling agency knew that the area was suited for agriculture and that there was ample work during the summer and during the rainy season. During other periods the settler could attend to his garden in order to supplement his income.[27]

The reality turned out to be different. On October, 27, 1950, fifty families and their belongings were loaded on trucks together with food for a day or two "until things would be sorted out." In fact the trucks lost their way and the settlers arrived in the middle of the night not knowing where they were. In the morning they went out to explore their surroundings and discovered that they had been dropped in "a sea of weeds and thorns." In the distance they found a deserted and run-down former British army camp and a small village with a poorly provisioned store that received occasional supplies of bread, margarine, and the like but had insufficient supplies for the newest arrivals. A few days later additional immigrants came from Romania and Poland. Some time later, they found a contractor who was widening a road in the area, and they signed on for manual work in moving asphalt.[28]

In the years to come most residents of Kiryat Malachi continued to encounter difficulties in finding employment. There were proposals for factories, machine shops for producing agricultural equipment, wholesale warehouses, and the like in order to fulfill the original idea that the community should serve the region's farmers. Nothing came of these ideas through the 1950s. In 1957, with a population of 5,000, Kiryat Malachi could not support doctors, mechanics, merchants, pharmacists, or even shoemakers. Perhaps the largest, external, private investment was for a primitive movie theater, which provided the town's only entertainment. Change came only in 1962, when the government assisted in establishing 20 factories and 130 workshops in the context of a program to settle yet another wave of immigrants. Government neglect had resulted in a legacy of more than a decade of poverty and suffering. Kiryat Malachi hardly fit the image of the new town celebrated by experts.[29]

Ashkelon

Examples of successful new town development do exist. Ashkelon, on the Mediterranean coast just above the Gaza strip, was built on the *via maris* (sea road) leading to Egypt. It had been the location of important and vital cities at different times in history. With the flight of the local Arab population during the war, settlement authorities urgently planned for a Jewish presence in an area that the United Nations had designated in the 1947 partition plan as beyond the future Jewish state's boundaries. With the signing of an armistice agreement with Egypt in February 1949, the first settlers were brought into the region and located at the former Arab town of Madjdal. Here, as in Beit She'an, planners expected to develop an urban cooperative. Two hundred immigrant families were brought to Madjdal, but the effort failed within six months. In early 1950, a new attempt at urban settlement was undertaken outside Madjdal, with most of the initial inhabitants drawn from the Madjdal cooperative.[30]

This time, planners prepared to establish a new town. Over the next two years, they made detailed plans. In addition to government and Histadrut assistance, they sought foreign investment. The South African Zionist Federation adopted the project and became an active participant in the town's development. Billed as a "scientifically planned modeltown," Ashkelon was to be supported by tourism and manufacturing rather than agriculture. They initially projected hotels near the beach and a Histadrut-sponsored irrigation-pipe factory with 600 workers. A 1952 brochure produced by the development company, Afridar, describes the town's immediate past and its prospects: "Here [Madjdal] the Arabs lived their simple, nomad, Bedouin life without striving for any civilization. They ate oranges and the many different sub-tropical fruits which grew around them, and they raised sheep and hens. They grew wheat to make their own bread, pittah, and they bought rice as an additional accompaniment to their roasted lamb. This, then, was the atmosphere [of the site] chosen for a future garden city."[31] This pastoral scene was to be replaced by "Anglo Saxon–style" single-family homes and ways of living. To a considerable degree this did come about, although the process was slower than planners envisioned and the benefits were unevenly distributed. A large tourist industry did not take root, but the town did develop industry from the beginning. In addition to the pipe factory, within a decade Ashkelon's immigrants worked in the manufacture of insecticides, wires and cables, cement, and plastics, as well as food processing. Within two decades, it was no longer classified as a development town. It became a medium-sized, relatively prosperous city that brought Israel's Jewish population to a previously underpopulated and largely Arab border area.

Beer-Sheva

Beer-Sheva is also a success story of the new town movement and is so featured in the standard accounts of Israel's development. Its history can be briefly sketched.[32]

Beer-Sheva is situated on historic crossroads from Africa and Egypt in the south to the Judean Hills and Jerusalem to the north and from the Mediterranean in the west to the Dead Sea and beyond in the east. The city is often described in the Bible as defining the southern border of the Hebrew kingdoms. Even more than Beit She'an, it suffered a long decline. In 1900, there was no permanent structure at the site. Just prior to the First World War, the Ottomans decided to develop it as a regional administrative center and a military outpost for controlling the Bedouins. While a small number of Jews participated in its development, Arab uprisings left the town without Jewish residents from 1929. Here, too, the war resulted in a ghost town that planners sought to resettle in accordance with national development policy.

Beer-Sheva became a "boom town" soon after Independence. Set in the desert 84 miles from Tel Aviv, it required the creation of a host of local services including governmental, mercantile, and medical. Various industries were added to this base. Within two years after Independence, the population had reached 14,000. In some months as many as 1,000 newcomers arrived. As in so many similar new towns, the first immigrants lived in tents with minimal services. However, in Beer-Sheva, unlike in so many other cases, government assistance was substantial. The treasury, for example, allocated funds in 1950 to ensure that the city was connected to the national electrical grid. The Histadrut also made significant investments. It supported the building of a regional hospital; located maintenance shops for vehicles connected with Histadrut companies; built factories to manufacture ceramics, fireproof building materials, and chemicals; and erected Beer-Sheva's movie theater, the Keren, which was the country's largest.

The pace of growth was sufficiently rapid and steady that early plans had to be revised. Within twenty years, Beer-Sheva grew beyond projections of 30,000 and 50,000 to become a regional center of approximately 100,000. By 2000, it had nearly 200,000 and about another 200,000 in a metropolitan area that had once been a sparsely populated desert inhabited by nomadic Bedouins. Organizing its physical development with zoned areas and neighborhoods of controlled size, the city won wide recognition by the early 1960s as a singularly successful adapta-

9.2. Beer-Sheva in 2000. View of western edge of Beer-Sheva expanding north into desert. Courtesy of Albatross Aerial Photography. Photo by Dubi Tal.

tion of garden city concepts to a desert environment. For foreign experts interested in an example of how the new town idea was exported to distant places, Beer-Sheva provided an excellent case study (Figure 9.2).

Comparative Success and Failure

These sketches suggest some significant differences in the way the new town idea, as expressed in the Sharon Plan, was implemented in Israel. Ashkelon and Beer-Sheva were successful. The former fulfilled the expectations of planners, and the latter far exceeded them. Yet, most towns failed to achieve the goals established for them. Rather than becoming centers of population and industry, they became impoverished settlements on the country's periphery, offering few prospects of either social or economic integration for a largely immigrant population. Israeli planners wanted to achieve more and had the technical competence to do so. However, their program far outstripped available resources, and it also did not adequately address the status and needs of the immigrants who were sent to realize these plans. Indeed, Israel's new town policy, which sought to establish twenty-four regional centers with 10,000 to 60,000 inhabitants each, would have been too ambitious for even more established countries. By way of comparison, Great Britain's New Towns Act of 1946 fixed a target of only twenty new towns. In a far better organized and richer country, even this comparatively modest objective was not achieved. Between 1947 and 1950 only fourteen were started—twelve in England and Wales and two in Scotland. Few were added after this period of initial enthusiasm. Building new towns is expensive. New towns were initially proposed for mature industrial societies that had considerable infrastructure and resources; making them the centerpiece of a poor, underdeveloped country challenged the limits of rationality and good intentions. It was often a cruel and disastrous imposition on expectant and trusting immigrants to send them to such locations. The scars from that experience erupted a generation later as immigrants and their children took to the ballot box in the 1970s and changed the face of Israeli politics by deposing Labor from its traditional place as Israel's undisputed leading party.

There is some irony in targeting the Labor establishment. In Israel, local investors looked to Tel Aviv and the more established areas of the country where they were more likely to achieve a quick and secure return for their money. Only the government and the Histadrut were willing and able to invest in new towns. Typically only Bank Hapoalim (The Workers' Bank), associated with the Histadrut, was willing to establish a branch in outlying regions. It did so despite the likelihood that it would take a financial loss. The challenge of simultaneously absorbing immigrants and building the country pushed the government's and the private sector's means to the limits. As a consequence, those towns that had access to the center of power and external resources had a chance of overcoming at least some of the difficulties of the early years. Without such access, most towns languished.

Private capital did not become an important factor until after the mid-1950s when the government began to provide incentives to foreigners who invested in new town industrialization. In effect, a conscious if unspoken policy of weaning the country from centralistic and socialistic traditions had characterized urban pioneering. Private investments transformed post-Independence towns and gave a healthier start to those founded after the mid-1950s. Problems of unemployment were alleviated by labor-intensive industries such as textiles and food processing. However, by the end of the 1960s towns on the periphery once again experienced social and economic difficulties as the center of the country progressed into a more advanced stage of industrialization. In the mid-1970s, the crisis became so severe that many towns were made the focus of a national program of urban renewal.[33]

Even as failure requires explanation, so does success. A key variable is the politics of allocation. For example, David Tuviyahu, Beer-Sheva's first and longest-serving mayor, was the director of the Negev division of Sollel Boneh, the large Histadrut building company. Private contractors did not venture as far south as Beer-Sheva, so the responsibility for building the town and its industries became almost exclusively that of the Histadrut and the government. From this position of power, Tuviyahu moved to the mayor's office. His connections with the Labor Party establishment both in the government and in the Histadrut proved to be an invaluable asset to the city. Such political stability and power were rare in new towns, and there were justified complaints of favoritism. Clearly, the political connections of Beer-Sheva's early leaders contributed to the comparatively greater share of resources appropriated to the city.

Politics also had important consequences for the place of the planner in Israeli society. In the pre-state period, planning was centralized within the office of the Chairman of the Jewish Agency, David Ben-Gurion. It was here that ideas were generated, sifted, and crystallized.

Because the Chairman also had great influence over disbursing funds, the work of Jewish Agency planners translated directly into projects. Planners hoped this pattern would continue after Independence. Ben-Gurion did initially take the planners with him to the office of Prime Minister. The politics of coalition-building, however, fragmented responsibility for policy and its execution: the Ministry of Labor engaged in the construction of development towns; the Ministry of Agriculture controlled land and water; the Settlement Department of the Jewish Agency was the prime mover in agricultural settlements. In addition, the transfer of responsibility for national planning from the Prime Minister's office to the Ministry of the Interior resulted in planners functioning as regulators rather than as innovators building the country.[34]

The Ministry of Defense was also actively involved in planning even as the Haganah had been during the British Mandate. Continuing the cooperation with the military that preceded the state, planners used agricultural settlements to define areas under Jewish control and to consolidate territorial gains won in the war. At the same time, town planning was first employed for strategic purposes. Throughout the following decade, the location and number of new towns reflected not only the calculations of social scientists but also strategic needs as defined by the military, which undoubtedly had priority in determining the location of cities. The most dramatic case may be the background to the establishment of Ashdod as Israel's southern port. Tel Aviv, which built a small jetty into the Mediterranean to serve as a harbor during the 1930s, wanted the facility expanded. Economists and other experts and local politicians thought a port would be appropriate for Israel's largest city. The military first calculated the range of artillery from the Jordanian army positions in the Judean Hills and the angle at which shells might come in from enemy ships along the coast. Both dictated that the area behind the relatively high dunes of what would be Ashdod would make a more secure port and reduce the potential national damage from a bombardment from land or sea on densely populated Tel Aviv. Similarly, the siting of Eilat, Ashkelon, and, indeed, any other town required army approval. The use of agricultural settlements by planners in establishing and maintaining frontiers is widely appreciated. The same logic was applied to urban development.

Finally, new town policy did succeed in contributing to the present pattern of population distribution. Israel has become a highly urbanized society, with its population spread beyond Jerusalem and coastal megalopolises. It is unlikely a free market system would have brought many immigrants to peripheral areas. Few had the ideological commitment, financial resources, or skills to engage in pioneering Israel's agricultural or urban frontiers. Directing immigrants to new towns may have been the only possible way of bringing substantial populations to distant and underpopulated or even vacant areas. Although a rational planning policy based solely on economics did not justify so many new towns, Israel's planners operated within a framework that gave primacy to collective needs. In so doing they continued a tradition originating with the first Zionist agricultural colonies, whose location was perceived in terms of national requirements rather than benefits for individuals.

While decentralization through new towns was rooted in European conceptions, its realization in Israel also reflects particular local conditions. In Europe, new towns were a response to long-term social and economic problems characteristic of modern industrial society. In Israel, new towns were actually planted well in advance of industrialization. Israeli towns seemed to provide a practical solution to an immediate problem: the sudden influx of largely destitute immigrants, many of whom were refugees in flight from Arab lands or from the Displaced Persons' Camps in post-Holocaust Europe, who might otherwise have congregated solely in coastal cities. In many cases the short-term solution led to negative long-term results. Finally, the dispersal of new towns served the need to settle a contested country. Zionist planners had always been concerned with placing a stable and productive population on frontiers. Together with defense strategists, they preferred civilian settlements to fortresses for securing borders. New towns proved to be a useful concept in realizing that objective. In Israel, then, new towns were a response to a unique combination of factors: an anticipated, planned industrialization, mass immigration, and potential threats to national security.

CHAPTER 10

Israeli Villages
Transforming the Countryside

N parallel with the post-Independence emphasis on developing cities, Zionist planners continued to be active in the countryside. Indeed, about 400 villages were established in Israel's first decade; more than at any other period during the first century of Zionist colonization. Statehood provided planners with legal powers, bureaucracies, land reserves, and financial resources. Moreover, the strategic concerns of the new state gave priority to massive settlement of frontiers. From the Lebanese and Syrian borders in the Upper Galilee southward into the Negev, graduates of youth movements, ex-soldiers, and new immigrants established kibbutzim and moshavim. In terms of numbers and pioneers, this first decade was the apogee in Zionism's aspiration to return Jews to villages where they would farm their own land. Yet this rush was not without problems, and in the search for solutions, new models of village settlement replaced older models. In the first decade of statehood, the moshav replaced the kibbutz as the preferred village, particularly in areas not immediately adjacent to borders. A decade later, in the mid-1960s, both the moshav and kibbutz were eclipsed by a new construct—the "rurban" village.

In devising these new models of rural colonization, planners were contending with familiar ideological, cultural, and economic issues. However the main problem they confronted, as in the decade prior to Independence, was that the state was not yet secure. Where only armistice lines separated Israel from neighboring Arab states, settlements were used to delineate borders. These villages also laid claim to Arab lands vacated during the war and reinforced the "Jewish presence" (*nochachut yehudit*) in areas where Jews remained the minority. Colonization thus continued to be shaped by security and political considerations and the army remained an active partner in locating and designing settlements.

By the early 1960s, however, agricultural colonization had reached its limits. There were not enough recruits, whether ideologically motivated cadres from youth movements or new immigrants who wanted to establish kibbutzim or moshavim. Further expansion would have to be in cities or in villages integrated with Israel's modern, industrial economy. In an effort to establish a significant "Jewish presence" in outlying areas, in the mid-1960s planners invented the rurban village, a nonagricultural community set in the countryside. This innovation was originally designed to "Judaize" (*le-yaheyd*) predominantly Arab sections of the Galilee where an agricultural economy was impractical. The most extensive use of rurban villages has been in Judea and Samaria, the areas of the West Bank captured from the Jordanians in the 1967 Six-Day War. Most such settlements are neither secular nor based on totally cooperative let alone collectivist ideologies. They are intentionally bourgeois communities based on white-collar occupations and usually driven by religious-nationalist imperatives. In the course of a century of settlement, the Zionist village completed a circle. At the start of the twenty-first century, most rural colonization has been by traditional and religious Jews who, like the first pioneers on the moshavoth, are engaged in building small communities with a high quotient of shared values. But unlike the founders of the moshavoth or of the moshav or kibbutz, rurban settlers are no longer farmers.

The War of Independence and Planning

When the United Nations voted for partition of Palestine into a Jewish and an Arab state, local Arabs immediately initiated attacks against Jews, focusing initially on the country's transportation arteries. Between December 1947 and May 1948 the range of targets widened to include cities with mixed Jewish/Arab populations and outlying settlements. The Yishuv responded in kind, and the country became enmeshed in a nearly ubiquitous and bloody civil war. At midnight between May 14 and 15, regular armies from neighboring Arab states invaded Jewish-held territories, transforming the struggle into a larger conflict. By the same date, the last of the British forces departed Palestine, leaving Arabs and Jews to contend with one another for control over Palestine.

Until April 1948, Jewish forces were largely on the defensive. Indeed, in March more than 1,200 Jewish soldiers and civilians were killed, fully one-fifth of the total casualties in the entire year and a half conflict. So dark were Jewish prospects that the United States proposed delaying partition and suggested that the United Nations institute a trusteeship to replace the Mandate. During April 1948, Jewish forces undertook a series of initiatives, and on May 14 David Ben-Gurion publicly read the Declaration of Independence, which effectively ended the prospects of freezing the situation. By July, the Israeli army had beaten back the attackers on most fronts, and it had begun to expand the territory allotted by the United Nations. Continuing Israeli successes further extended the areas controlled by the new Jewish state, and these were fixed in separate armistice agreements signed with Egypt, Jordan, Lebanon, and Syria through July 1949.

An important consequence of the war was a radical change in the political geography and demography of Palestine. Approximately 77,000 Jews were forced to leave their homes during the fighting. Most were residents of cities with mixed populations such as Jaffa, Tiberias, and Jerusalem. No return was possible in several outlying areas, particularly in the region proximate to Jerusalem where entire neighborhoods came under Jordanian control, the settlements of the Etzion Block to the south of the city, and the workers' colonies at the Palestine Potash Company settlements on the Dead Sea. Most Jews, however, could eventually reclaim their homes.[1]

The situation of Palestine's Arabs was immeasurably more serious, even catastrophic. Indeed, in the collective memory of Palestinian Arabs the period is termed the *nakba* (catastrophe). At the end of the war, upward of 600,000 were displaced and beyond Israel's borders. This left Israel with a much smaller proportion of Arab residents than provided for by the UN partition plan and, at the same time, greatly increased territory. By November 1948, Israel decided that Arabs would not be permitted to return, irrespective of whether they had wanted to get out of harm's way, had anticipated return after an Arab victory, or had been forced out by Israeli troops.[2]

In order to convert front lines into armistice lines and then transform these into de facto borders, vacant areas had to be populated with the greatest possible speed. The settlement policy initiated during the struggle for land in the pre-state period and coordinated by World Zionist Organization agencies, the Jewish Agency, and the Haganah was maintained after Independence. Although the government replaced the Jewish Agency and the Israel Defense Forces (IDF) supplanted the Haganah, continuities in conception and policy were ensured because the personnel remained largely the same. As we have seen, generals, architects, settlement officials, and politicians continued to play similar roles after Independence and operated in comparable ways. Ben-Gurion's double role as Prime Minister and Minister of Defense further facilitated the uninterrupted coordination between civil and military bureaucracies that had characterized Zionist institutions prior to the state.[3]

About a decade was required to consolidate gains on the ground. During the course of the war, thirty-seven settlements, twenty-six of which were kibbutzim, had been established. By July 1948, the military and civilian settlement authorities had begun planning the first new settlements that would use Arab lands. This was a new departure. From the settlements of the First Aliyah through the end of the Mandate, all lands on which Jews created colonies had been purchased. It was assumed that compensation had to be provided and that additional, public lands would become available to a Jewish state as the successor to the British Mandate and the Ottoman Empire.

The war created circumstances where force was used to expand Jewish holdings. Within the community of planners, the chief advocate of exploiting the war to achieve national objectives was Josef Weitz, the longtime head of the Jewish National Fund. Weitz had advocated the transfer of Arab populations out of Jewish areas prior to the formation of the state. The outbreak of war convinced him that the opportunity for effecting such a far-reaching solution had finally and fortuitously arrived. His models for population transfer were based on international precedents set largely in the period that coincided with the Mandate, when there were massive population movements and exchanges of Armenians, Greeks, Germans, Czechs, Indians, and Pakistanis. Further, Weitz and his generation had witnessed the transfer of millions of Germans and Poles, among others, out of areas in which they had long resided during years immediately following the Second World War. Ir-reconcilable national differences, in his view, led to either civil war or transfer. With unabashed rectitude, he publicly and privately advocated population transfer in historical, comparative, moral, and practical terms as the best option for Palestine.

The actual weight of Weitz's argument in government councils is open to question. What is clear is that circumstances contributed to the partial realization of Weitz's solution. In a war punctuated by repeated armistices that the warring parties used for strengthening their posi-tions in the next round, Israeli policy became increasingly committed to clearing Arab populations from strategically valuable and contested areas. As this policy evolved, villages were razed both to prevent their use as a base for hostile operations and to enable the establishment of Jewish settlements.[4]

In the early stages of the war, settlements were planted solely on lands purchased by Zionist entities. By July 1948 the Israeli government was leasing vacated land, particularly in the Jezreel Valley, to nearby kibbutzim. It was not yet determined that these lands would become permanently Jewish. However, as Israeli forces captured additional terri-tory distant from existing settlements, colonies were established so the new lands could be controlled and utilized. By August, there were plans for sixty-one new settlements in such strategic places as the Jerusalem corridor, sections of the Galilee, and routes to the Negev. Through the fall, plans were made for even larger numbers.[5]

The turning point came at the end of the year. Israel refused to abide by UN Resolution 194 of December 11, 1948, which called for the return of Arab refugees to their lands. The Israelis argued that the conflict had made the original UN partition plan unworkable and that Arab violence had abrogated it. Perhaps most important, the conflict had produced widespread agreement that the presence of a large and potentially hos-tile minority was intolerable in a small Jewish country set in the pre-dominantly Arab Middle East. Consequently, at the end of December, the government sold about a million acres of "abandoned" Arab lands to the Jewish National Fund for the purposes of Jewish settlement.

Ironically, despite the availability of land and the powers of the state, planners encountered unanticipated difficulties in carrying out a massive settlement program. During the first four months of 1948, not one new Jewish settlement was established. Potential settlers were still engaged in military service. Five settlements were established after the state was proclaimed, during the last two weeks of May and during

June. Only after the first victories and the armistice in June, when the immediate threat to the new state's existence was allayed, did settlement activity resume on a larger scale. In June, plans were laid for founding nineteen settlements. In July, planners called for twenty-one and another thirty-two in August. Arab lands were still not used throughout this period.

This changed in the fall and early winter when the army began the systematic razing of abandoned Arab villages. The dwellings were considered unsuitable, and the sites were appropriated to forestall the return of the original owners.[6] From the end of the war through the spring of 1950, planners marked out 190 new settlements. They added even more in the following months as mass immigration radically increased Israel's population. Indeed, immigration itself became a prime reason for large-scale rural settlement. Israel's greatly augmented population needed to be fed. All economic plans of the period emphasize increasing food production lest precious foreign currency be diverted to purchase food from external sources.[7]

The cardinal questions were where villages would be placed and who would settle in them. The issue of location readily enjoyed consensus. Once Israel's leadership decided to defend the armistice lines and convert them into borders, it followed that Jewish settlers should be placed on vacated Arab lands. Moreover, there were large, empty territories in which neither Jews nor Arabs had established villages. This was true in difficult hill terrain as well as on the arid plain that separated Jordanian-held Hebron and Egyptian-held Gaza, the area that became the Lakhish region, with Kiryat Gat as its central development town. The ability to plan on such a scale gave further impetus to thinking in regional terms. From clusters of colonies, the scope of rural planning became ever wider and more directed, controlled, and rationalized.

Post-Independence Pioneers

The colonization of the countryside, even of the most sensitive border areas, proceeded far more slowly than expected. The fundamental problem appeared early in the war. Planners could not build the number of new colonies projected for the summer and fall of 1948. The preferred village form, particularly in areas of conflict, was the kibbutz, whose members traditionally came from youth movements and elite groups such as Palmach, so the first call for settlers went to these sources. This group was engaged in combat, however, and few had been released from service. Because military as well as farming skills were required, settlement officials then turned to veterans who had served in the Allied armies during the Second World War. There were not enough recruits from this source or any other. Consequently, many kibbutzim remained mere blueprints, and borders were only sparsely settled. This problem became acute in the postwar period, when there were continual incursions by irregular armed fighters, and by thieves as well as civilians wanting to return to their former homes and reclaim property.[8]

For the first time there was land but not enough settlers. This was an entirely novel situation in the Zionist settlement experience. It was the reverse of the pattern that had bedeviled planners and that had sometimes forced idealistic youth to turn to the cities or even leave the country in frustration. In the search for the solution to the recruitment problem two novel and quite different paths changed the face of settlement.

The first was the creation of the Nahal, which stands for No'ar Halutzi Lochem (Fighting Pioneer Youth). These regular army units, trained for both farming and soldiering, were sent out to settle critical sites along the borders. The Nahal insignia, a sickle crossing a rifle, reflects the purpose of these units. It was expected that after a period of development and stabilization, these paramilitary outposts would become civilian settlements, probably kibbutzim. The first Nahal outpost, Nahal Oz, was established in 1951 near the border of the Gaza strip. Others followed along the long border with Jordan, the Jerusalem corridor, and the borders with Syria and Lebanon in the Galilee. Some Nahal soldiers joined established kibbutzim in order to supplement and strengthen the founding group. Map 10.1 shows how Nahal units were deployed from 1951 through 1967. This widespread effort was significant, but it was still inadequate to the challenge at hand.[9]

The creation of this corps reflects how intimate, open, and official agricultural pioneering and soldiering had become. In an essay in the *Government Year Book*, Ben-Gurion declared that the Israeli army was "unique" and that there "is nothing like it in any other Army; but for us it is a categorical imperative of our security and existence." He went on to describe in graphic terms the peculiar characteristics of such agricultural outposts: "The frontier villages will not be cantonments of soldiers, but farm settlements like any other, in which a man will live his own life, raise his family and bring up sons. We need men and women pioneers in equal measure. The inhabitants of these settle-

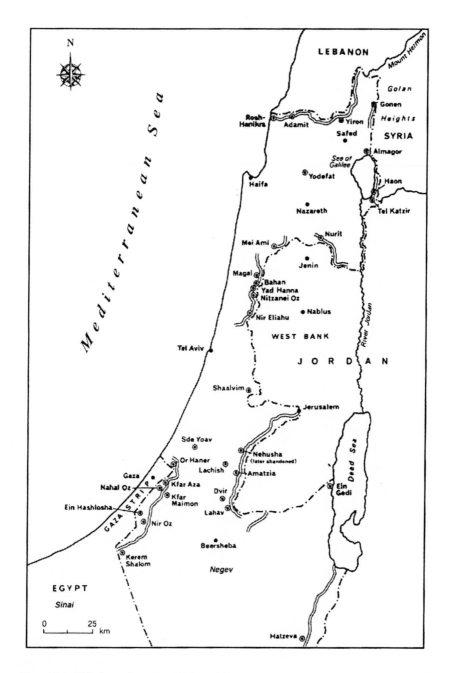

Map 10.1. Nahal settlements, 1951–1967.

ments, likely to be among the first attacked in any invasion by regular troops or bands of irregulars, must know how to carry and how to use firearms."[10]

The second path was to recruit new immigrants, who were arriving in unprecedented numbers. At Independence there were about 650,000 Jews in the country. In less than four years, from May 15, 1948, through the end of 1951, 687,000 entered Israel. To accommodate more than a doubled population, radical and far-reaching changes were made in the Zionist village.

During the Mandate, Zionist authorities could often be selective about colonists because there were far fewer certificates than applicants. The British *White Papers* set the terms of Jewish immigration and involved the Jewish Agency in a process of choosing among applicants that began in Europe. Zionist bodies could use their discretion in giving preference to youth who had undergone training and ideological preparation.[11] Most post-Independence immigrants had experienced neither agricultural work nor ideological indoctrination. A majority were Holocaust survivors who had spent a large portion of the postwar period in Displaced Persons Camps or had found other forms of temporary shelter in various parts of Europe. Most Oriental Jews from North Africa or the Middle East came as members of whole communities that were uprooted as a consequence of persecution in the Arab world. Few in either stream had undergone the kind of extensive training that had characterized members of Hechalutz, the leading youth movement that had established numerous kibbutzim since the 1920s.

The kibbutz movement, always highly selective in admitting new members, did not act differently in the face of post-Independence immigration. The literal meaning of *halutz*, derived from the *Book of Joshua*, is "pioneer" in the sense of an avant-garde that "went before the host."[12] The kibbutz was by design an elitist form of settlement predicated on a high degree of internal egalitarianism among its members. Efforts to integrate Oriental Jews, who constituted an increasingly large proportion of the immigrant population, were limited. Little common ground was assumed with the newcomers who were unfamiliar with kibbutz ideologies. Giving priority to the commitment to shared ideological principles, kibbutzim were reluctant to enlarge membership and increase settlements. This reluctance to reach out was abetted by negative stereotypes of the new immigrants often held by European-born kibbutz members.[13] As one kibbutz brochure designed for visitors explained, entry into the membership ranks was a "process of gradual selection." A period of probation of at least a year was generally required. A large proportion of applicants dropped out, and even many who were accepted left after a short period. By self-definition and in practice, the kibbutz proved unsuitable as an instrument of mass absorption and large-scale colonization.[14]

The failure of the kibbutz movement to take an active role in what was defined as a national mission brought it into open conflict with Ben-Gurion. From his early days in the country through his years as the preeminent leader of the Yishuv and Israel, he identified with the kibbutz even though his offices were in Tel Aviv, where he maintained a home, and in Jerusalem. In 1953, he dramatically retired from the offices of Prime Minister and Minister of Defense to a modest dwelling, termed a *tzrif*, or "hut," at a newly founded kibbutz at Sede Boker in the heart of the Negev. When the "Old Man" joined Sede Boker, an independent and unaffiliated kibbutz, his rupture with the kibbutz movement was a matter of public controversy. In a searing speech in the Knesseth (Parliament) in January 1950, the Prime Minister proclaimed that he was "utterly ashamed" (*bosh venichlam*) of the kibbutzim for failing to play their role in absorbing more immigrants. Identifying himself as one who would "even prefer to milk cows than be Minister of Defense," he declared that "I have the bitter obligation to make several observations not as a member of the Government but as a *halutz*":

> Our great pioneering movement that so esteems *haltuziut* [pioneering] has never so disappointed as in this great and difficult moment. Where is the pioneering movement in the absorption of immigrants? Thousands of *halutzim* have performed great deeds in the farms and kibbutzim—[but] what have they done for this mass immigration? . . . but what have they done for the 300,000 immigrants? I am utterly ashamed. In these two years we have witnessed the failure of the pioneering movement. The greatest event in our history is taking place. The exodus from Egypt has begun. The ingathering of the exiles has begun—but what have our pioneers done? Have the kibbutzim mobilized for this?[15]

The use of the phrase "utterly ashamed" was not accidental. He returned to it again as he castigated Zionism's elitist pioneers for their indifference to the waves of immigrants entering the country. He claimed things could be different, noting that the moshav was receptive to the mass immigration.

Party politics, no less than ideology and sentiment, played a role in this confrontation. The various groupings of kibbutzim were associated

Table 10.1 Establishing settlements 1943–1967 (by 5-year periods)

Period	Kibbutz	Moshav	Total
1943–47	56	24	80
1948–52	79	213	292
1953–57	15	66	81
1958–62	3	17	20
1963–67	2	8	10
Total:	155	328	483

Note: Calculations derive from Alex Bein, *Immigration and Settlement in the State of Israel* (Hebrew) (Tel Aviv, 1982), 260–98. 1967 extends only until June, when the war broke out.

with political parties to the left of Ben-Gurion's party.[16] The moshav movements, on the other hand, had closer political ties to Ben-Gurion.[17] However, Ben-Gurion's overriding commitment was to *mamlachtiyut* (statism or étatism). On occasion he was willing to undercut the interests of his own party and the organizations associated with it by supporting institutions whose loyalty was to the state and the fulfillment of national purposes rather than particularistic political interests. In a well-known and long-disputed incident, he had disbanded the Palmach and all other politically related military organizations and built up instead a *mamlachti*, or state-controlled army. A similar process took place in public education when, prior to Independence, he supported a state-sponsored school system rather than one associated with the Labor movement. His disappointment with the kibbtuz movement drove him to distance himself from longtime allies. With his approval, the new state shifted resources to the moshav.

During the 1950s, the moshav replaced the kibbutz as the most dynamic form of colonization and became the most common form of rural settlement. In the first five years after Independence, 213 moshavim were established and only 79 kibbutzim. From 1953 until the 1967 war only another 20 kibbutzim were added, in contrast to the 91 moshavim that were founded (Table 10.1). The kibbutz, unlike the moshav, reached its limits in the early 1950s.

In comparing the kibbutz with the moshav, planning authorities concluded that the latter could more readily accommodate family-oriented, nonideological immigrants. While the moshav shared the values of mutual help and cooperation that characterized the kibbutz, it also accommodated a strong tendency for individualism. In the kibbutz, the group was paramount; in the moshav the family was the prime unit of production, consumption, and social organization. It was conveniently assumed that the flood of Jews from North African and Asian communities would prefer the moshav because they would not want to be socialized into the socialistic, communitarian, and secular ethic upon which most kibbutzim were based. Even European immigrants demonstrated a lack of enthusiasm for these values. Religious kibbutzim were too small a factor to make a difference and also had limited appeal.[18]

It has been well documented that many immigrants did not choose moshavim but were channeled there by planners who were using the state's resources to direct the flow and dispersal of population. Indeed, the indifference or antipathy to the cooperative principles underlying the moshav movement was so pervasive among immigrants that a principal scholar of the moshav has termed them "reluctant pioneers." While settlers were forced to adapt to life on an agricultural cooperative, the moshav, in turn, was transformed by the values and traditions of the newcomers in a process of mutual accommodation.[19]

Economic Pressures in Village Transformation
The Moshav

By 1967, nearly a generation after the founding of numerous post-Independence moshavim, it had become apparent that however flexible the moshav was socially, it was problematic as an economic system. The major contributing factor was the family, the cornerstone of both the social and economic systems, and the fundamental problem was the future of the children who had grown up on moshavim. There was simply not enough work for them. By moshav regulations, the land could not be subdivided and could be passed on only to one member, usually the oldest son. The demand for more land necessarily became acute as families grew larger and a second generation began their own families. Moreover, as Israeli agriculture became more mechanized and less reliant on field labor, there was not enough employment to absorb additional hands on the family farm, in the local community, or in the neighboring area. Indeed, the kind and quantity of labor required by increasingly sophisticated and productive family farms permitted heads of families to organize the work so that their wives and children could manage the farm while they brought in additional income from nonagricultural work away from the moshav.[20]

Planners used two strategies in their attempt to address the problem of finding employment for the second generation. The first and by far the more extensive was through the development towns that were established to disperse industry and thereby to ensure the dispersal of population. These development towns, located from the Upper Galilee in the north through the Negev desert in the south, served to anchor a significant population outside the traditional urban centers, particularly Jerusalem and the coastal cities of Tel Aviv and Haifa. They provided employment opportunities for the residents of these new towns, and for many residents of the moshavim as well.[21] The second strategy was to integrate industry with the moshav pattern of settlement. This latter concept, first applied in the Galilee before 1967, ultimately contributed to the concept of the "rurban" village that spread throughout the West Bank after the Six-Day War.

The problem of the second generation was especially pressing in the Galilee, where 43 moshavim with a population of 10,000 had been established between 1949 and 1967. About a third of this population were children under age fourteen in households that averaged just under 5 members. The typical moshav had 60 families, and only 15 had as many as 100 or more. Because land in the region was characterized by rocky hills and there was limited water, the number of agricultural moshavim was severely restricted. Also, Galilee settlements were remote from the centers of Jewish population, and inadequate roads made them relatively inaccessible. Consequently, there were few opportunities for work outside the community. Concern for the economic plight of the next generation was aggravated by the political consequences of failing to keep them on the land. If the young people left and additional moshavim were not built, then Arabs in the Galilee would significantly outnumber Jews and a Jewish presence would be jeopardized.[22]

The Kibbutz

Advocates of the kibbutz anticipated the economic problems of the purely agricultural moshav. Perhaps the most interesting entry point into the ongoing discussions of Zionist villages is a conference held at the Hebrew University of Jerusalem in 1945 and chaired by Martin Buber. Present were leading intellectuals, political figures, and planners. At issue were the prospects of the Zionist village, especially the kibbutz.

Buber, one of the most distinguished philosophers of his day and an intellectual leader of the Yishuv, had just published a powerful and succinct book, *Pathways in Utopia*. Like other European-born intellectuals, Buber had witnessed the ravages of war in Europe. In the forefront of his thinking were the social and political pathologies of modern societies. Like many former Europeans in the Yishuv, Buber was reconsidering models for building ideal societies. His classic work can be read as a comparative study of national planning in which several contemporary doxies—notably fascism and communism—are examined and found lacking. His work was complemented by that of Hebrew University historian Jacob Talmon, a commanding figure in the study of national ideologies and totalitarianism in particular, who, like Buber, critiqued European ideologies that promised better societies. In this context, social planning was an immediate concern. The topic imposed itself on the intellectual imagination of European scholars, including émigrés, in the mid-twentieth century. Ideological claims contended in the academy and on the battlefield, and Jews had frequently been victims of both forms of combat.

Buber's survey viewed the kibbutz as "the experiment that has not failed." Whatever flaws he found, they were far outweighed by the apparently successful quest of small communities whose members invested their minds, energies, and lives in the pursuit of more just and humane societies. Importantly, they did so while tilling the soil. Buber called attention to the relatedness of the words *adam* (man) and *adama* (land), arguing that the connection between the settlers and the land must be ethical. Without appreciating or at least commenting on the uses to which the kibbutz was put within the grand scheme of Zionist colonization, he claimed that the kibbutz was as ideal a society as then existed anywhere.

Although most symposium participants concentrated on the kibbutz in their remarks, the title given the proceedings was more inclusive: "The Social Character of the Hebrew Village in Eretz Israel." Indeed, even if the kibbutz was the ideal form of settlement, the participants had come together to question the viability of the Zionist village.

Yitzhak Ben-Zvi, a veteran Zionist leader and future President of Israel with considerable scholarly interests in Jewish history, typically applauded the return to the land and the reestablishment of an agricultural vocation as the best expression of the quest for renewal, innovation, and radical change among modern Jews. Hugo Bergmann, a professor of philosophy at the Hebrew University, echoed the conviction that re-creating Jewish villages was the most original act of the Zionist colonization effort. He repeated what were by then classic themes: Jews, as farmers, would not be economic parasites; working the land was morally redemptive; agriculture was a necessary base in the creation of a healthy national economy and would root a wandering people firmly in the land. He concluded, characteristically, that no matter how significant or numerous Jews may be in commerce and industry, they would be suspect without a peasantry. The proper mode of becoming full citizens in any country was to share in working the land. This was as true in the Diaspora as in the homeland.

Such observations had become received truths. The occasion for voicing them again was the first glimmer of doubt that social scientists and planners brought to bear. Alfred Bonné, who at that time was the leading social scientist in the Yishuv and engaged in formulating an urban/industrial model for establishing the economic absorptive capacity of Palestine, was also present. He, too, observed that "The original creation of the Zionist movement in Eretz Israel is the Hebrew village."[23] But, he predicted, the village had achieved a kind of stability and was unlikely to play a larger role as the country developed. He contended that "it would be a big mistake to see the Eretz-Israel world as one unto itself, isolated and protected from the great social processes that are taking place outside our borders." Mechanization and industrialization would affect the Yishuv and populations would move into the towns in Palestine as elsewhere. He held that "The ideology of the fathers of Zionism derived from hopes that are no longer valid." Change had come because there were now other occupations that were no less moral and useful for society. Although Sharon's Master Plan of 1950 would later identify 20 percent as the target for rural population, Bonné concluded that only 10 or 12 percent was more realistic. Even this smaller percentage could be reached only if Palestine's cities would grow substantially. A large urban population was necessary for the economic success of farmers, who would provide city folk with food and raw materials.[24]

In retrospect it is clear that even Bonné's prediction of 10 or 12 percent was overly generous. At the close of the twentieth century, in keeping with modern, industrial countries like the United States and Germany, fewer than 5 percent of Israelis were farmers. Even had all the members of the Palmach, veterans of the Second World War, and a large proportion of the immigrants chosen to live on the land, few could have remained. After having removed the political and territorial obstacles to its expansion, the Zionist village had to retract in the face of inexorable physical and economic realities.

There was a spurt of extraordinary expansion in the decade after

Table 10.2. **Key agricultural indicators, 1949–1985**

Year	Cultivated domestic area*	Irrigated crops*	Field crops*	Emloyed in agriculture	Tractors	Net product**
1949	1,650	300	955		1,300	
1950	2,480	375	1,640		2,600	
1955	3,590	890	2,370	102,000	4,100	31
1960	4,075	1,305	2,451	121,000	7,400	59
1965	4,130	1,510	2,633	114,400	11,100	85
1970	4,105	1,720	2,518	89,800	16,300	109
1975	4,325	1,800	2,695	80,400	19,300	158
1980	4,386	2,003	2,593	87,700	26,800	205
1985	4,336	2,327	2,417	87,000	26,300	293

Note: *In thousands of dunams (4 dunams = 1 acre); **Agricultural account (quantity index with 1967/8 = 100)

Independence, but by around 1960, Israeli agriculture had reached a plateau of about 4 million dunams, or 1 million acres, of cultivated land. In the following quarter century, from 1960 to 1985, there was only a very modest increase in area used for farming whether for field crops or through irrigation. At the same time, on approximately the same amount of land, Israeli agriculture became more than four times as productive (Table 10.2).

Israeli agriculture, in a departure from Yitzhak Elazari-Volcani's medieval model, formulated in the conditions of the 1920s, achieved extraordinary success through mechanization, the introduction of new technologies, substantial financial investment, and careful selection of economically advantageous crops. In 1985, for example, approximately three and a half times more tractors worked the same amount of land as in 1960. Mechanization contributed not only to far greater productivity, as Volcani predicted, but to a decline in labor requirements, from a peak of 127,600 workers in 1961 to 87,000 in 1985. In addition, the widespread introduction of irrigation not only substantially increased yields but made possible a new range of profitable crops. While the amount of land under irrigation nearly doubled between 1960 and 1985, dry farming of field crops declined slightly. As Israeli farmers increasingly adopted irrigation, they discovered that they had as much land as their dwindling population needed. In effect, a decreasing number of farmers achieved higher levels of production while consuming ever greater quantities of water. Israeli agriculture required more water, not additional territory or labor.

After 1967, the extension of Israeli control to Judea and Samaria added rocky hills and desert but only limited territory with fertile land, most of which was under cultivation by the Arab population. It did not bring new water resources. Israel already enjoyed access to the Jordan River and to the subterranean sources that were shared with the West Bank. Analysts pointed out that the supply could be stretched to support a growing urban population, not agriculture. Thus, Israeli planners had to recognize that an attempt to colonize the territories with Jewish farmers would not only place the new settlements in competition with Arab neighbors but also diminish the supply of water available to established farms inside the old borders.[25]

A further reason for placing limits on agricultural expansion was that only the export of industrial goods could provide the needed earnings of foreign exchange. Since 1949, despite absolute increases on the order of 12 percent per year in their value, agricultural exports declined dramatically and steadily in relation to total exports, from 64 percent in 1949 to only 10 percent in 1980. At the same time industrial exports grew from only $10 million to $5 billion. As Bonné and his colleagues anticipated, it became clear that industry was the key to economic independence and national power and, as such, had to be given priority. In the course of industrialization not only was the national economy transformed but also the social and economic structure of the agricultural sector, in particular the organization of the kibbutz and the moshav.[26]

Industrialization of Zionist Villages

The most instructive illustration of the inexorable shift away from agriculture is found in the experience of the kibbutz. This archetypal form of Zionist agricultural colonization, like the economy in general, was necessarily changed by the pervasive tendency to industrialize.

The process of restructuring the kibbutz economy toward nonagricultural activities accelerated in the 1950s, although there had previously been some slight movement in that direction. In the 1930s, for example, kibbutzim were fairly isolated and had little contact with urban centers both because their ideology shunned bourgeois values and because poor transportation limited access to cities. As a consequence, many developed their own workshops. A few opened guest houses and embarked on modest agriculture-related industries such as packaging, canning, and food processing. Orders from the British army during the

Second World War stimulated the development of modest manufacturing enterprises. However, during these war years even the largest kibbutz enterprise had fewer than 100 workers, and the 15 largest kibbutz manufactories together employed under 1,000 workers. Until the early 1950s, the cooperative settlements that characterized the kibbutz movement were overwhelmingly committed to farming.

Significant change occurred during the 1950s as an increasing proportion of kibbutz members shifted from farming to working in modest, kibbutz-operated manufacturing enterprises. In 1954, only about 25 percent of the kibbutzim had even one factory. Within ten years that proportion doubled, and another 25 percent was added within the following decade. By the early 1970s, fully one-third of the nonservice workforce had left the fields for the settlement factory. As the leading economic historian of the kibbutz has observed, the kibbutz sector achieved "industrial take-off" by 1960, and by the early 1970s the kibbutz had "already moved a long way towards a versatile industrial structure in which manufacturing is of substantial importance."[27] Several kibbutzim developed large-scale enterprises, but the overwhelming majority preferred, if only for ideological reasons, plants employing from forty to sixty workers. Such enterprises manufactured plastics, precision tools, and electronics. Despite a few examples of labor-intensive factories that, because of scale, depended on salaried outsiders, the industrialization of the kibbutz featured skill-intensive manufacturing largely if not entirely based on the work of the collective's membership. In effect, the kibbutz experience indicated the potential to develop semi-industrialized and relatively autonomous colonies, dispersed throughout the countryside, largely divorced economically and socially from neighboring communities. The success of this experience significantly influenced post-1967 plans for building small, independent, economically viable villages in the occupied territories of Judea and Samaria.

While the internal transformations of the kibbutz economy were significant for positing the rurban village, kibbutz society could not be replicated easily. Numbering slightly more than 200 settlements in the early 1950s, with approximately 4 percent of the country's total Jewish population, the kibbutz remained at these levels for the next twenty years. As both advocates and critics have noted, this elite form of settlement typically prefers a membership in the several hundreds. Only very few kibbutzim have grown to as many as several thousand members. Unfettered expansion, it was held, would dilute and compromise the community's value system.

The Post-1967 Rurban Village

The moshav reached the limits of growth about a decade after the kibbutz because the problems inherent in its economic design kept incomes depressed for at least the second and subsequent generations. It became clear to planners during the 1960s that as the village form adapted to the modern age, members would have to work outside agriculture. Rather than attempt to transform the kibbutz and moshav, planners decided to establish new villages, from the beginning, on a nonagricultural basis. The need to do so was driven by political and security considerations.

Raanan Weitz (1913–1998), Josef Weitz's son and the leading figure in the Settlement Department of the Jewish Agency after Independence, played an important role in designing the solution. He implemented his plan within the pre-1967 borders, and beyond them in the aftermath of the 1967 war. His first proposals called for placing Jews on the high ground in sections of the Lower Galilee so that the settlements could control the region militarily. These settlements were to be established in clusters together with nearby industrial zones. Although each village would have its own center for basic services, there was to be convenient access to a larger regional center. Employment would be provided in agriculturally related industries such as packing plants and in military-related factories such as the manufacture of spare parts or metal fabrication. Not only had such settlements been planned but portions of the infrastructure had been built by the time the 1967 war broke out. However, the 1967 war and then the redirection of resources to Judea and Samaria delayed and diminished implementation. Weitz's program was reactivated between 1977 and 1984 with the establishment of thirty *mitzpim*, or mountaintop rurban communities, in the Galilee and the Golan Heights. At the same time, sixty rurban villages were built in Judea and Samaria.[28] In effect, planners were grafting the small-scale kind of industrialization developed by the kibbutz onto the more individualistic social and economic system of the moshav.

In determining the form of settlement suitable for the regions acquired by the 1967 war, planners had a wide range of choice. The experience of nearly a century of colonization in the agricultural sector had led to colonies of independent farmers, the moshava, and various forms of collectives, the kibbutz and the moshav; in the nonagricultural sector there were garden cities and garden suburbs, workers' suburbs and inner-city workers' estates, and development towns. In choosing be-

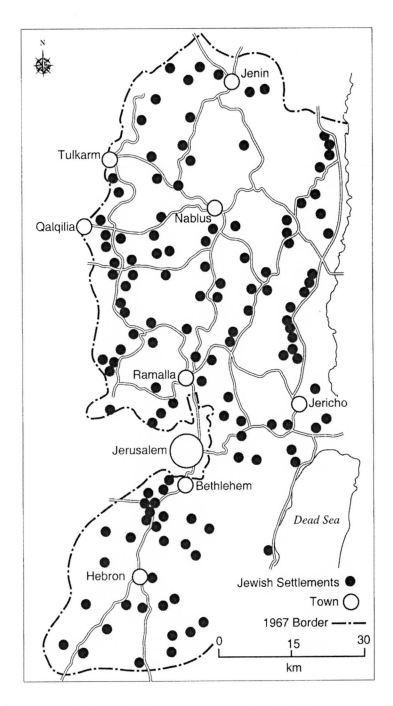

Map 10.2. Jewish settlements in Judea and Samaria, 1990.

tween models, they had to take into account the economic factors in community structure and physical design. Also, as in all settlement plans, they had to address strategic and defense issues that dictated the location of settlements and contributed to physical design as well. To meet both economic and strategic requirements, planners drew primarily on their experience with the kibbutz and the moshav. The rurban village was the result. As with the moshav, the social structure of the rurban village could accommodate the individualistic preferences of the target population. Tied to the urban economy inside the former borders rather than to the existing Arab cities nearby, rurban villages were expected, like many kibbutzim, to leapfrog proximate, regional centers in favor of Israel's major cities. In fact, many residents of Judea and Samaria's rurban villages commute to Jerusalem or Tel Aviv for work while others remain at home providing services or producing a large variety of products from plastics to electronics, or writing software for computers or texts on parchments for international markets.

An explicit and evocative description of these villages can be found in the many brochures disseminated to attract settlers.[29] In typical fashion, the pamphlet designed for potential immigrants from English-speaking countries advertises one new settlement on the West Bank as "a rural settlement whose economy is based exclusively on industrial plants owned and operated by the village residents." Residents are advised that they can "walk to work in minutes instead of commuting up to an hour in traffic." "You can own your own house and garden in a country of apartment dwellers," they are promised, and "can share ownership of a high level technology manufacturing enterprise." The settlement is described as "a community where you know and cooperate with your neighbors, instead of a large, anonymous apartment complex." In keeping with this idyllic image, the master plan provides for a community of 1,000 families in four distinct but interrelated villages that are "not in the form of neat rows of tract houses." The brochure invites the reader to admire "a sophisticated physical plan combining the amenities of a house and garden with the high level of community services usually available only in a medium size city." Appropriately, the illustrations show unattached single-family homes set in a garden in a beautifully landscaped community that features many recreational services including a swimming pool, tennis courts, a track, a day-care center, and a community center, and further boasts "a modern school-shopping-business center."

The brochure, couched in terms designed to appeal to educated,

10.1. Ariel, a city on the West Bank, 2000. Courtesy of the National Photo Collection, Government Press Office. Photo by Moshe Milner.

white-collar western immigrants, promises to replicate the best and most familiar features of middle class, West European or American society. It also appeals to Israelis who aspire to enjoy that "life-style" in their own country. For all, it blends opportunities for individual ownership and advancement with communitarian values such as consumer cooperatives and the democratically organized public life of a small and intimate society as cultivated by the moshav and the kibbutz or a New England town. However, for others, larger urban settlements set in the landscape were more appealing. Ariel, a satellite commuter town on the periphery of Tel Aviv was particularly popular (Figure 10.1). Whether small or larger, settlements on the West Bank were manifestly urban, attracting settlers with amenities instead of ideology.

Changes in the economy and sociology of the rurban village have transfigured the military attributes of the pioneer. The original and traditional identification of the pioneering farmer with soldiering has undergone an embourgeoisement. Cincinnatus on the Israeli frontier is no longer the citizen/soldier/farmer. He is an urbanized, white-collar worker, who like most men and women in Israel, has had military train-ing. The romantically conceived frontiersman or -woman who works the land and defends it has been replaced by a new breed of pioneer, often academically trained, who views land in terms of landscape rather than as a means of livelihood. The fact that many rurban villagers com-mute to work was seen by most strategists through the mid-1980s as an added advantage, for their presence on the roads apparently made a vital contribution to controlling transportation routes that had long been a prime area of contention in the Jewish/Arab conflict. Only with the outbreak of the *intifadas* in the late 1980s and again in 2000 did it become clear that there were great risks as well. In particular, the need to protect isolated and distant settlements and their access roads has raised questions as to their strategic value. Some claim it makes them a military and political liability. These doubts coexist with the convic-tion that rurban villages are a necessary addition to military camps and installations. Echoing the earliest commitments of Labor Zionism and the experience of other peoples who have tried to assert control in the Holy Land, one politician and general observed: "Whoever has properly learned the lessons of the Crusader kingdom in Jerusalem knows that the setting up of strongholds and army camps is not a guarantee for control over territory. One must settle on the land and strike roots in it."[30]

These rurban villages have become the subject of intense contro-versy within Israeli society and among the military. The settlement model is well-suited to right wing groups, particularly the religious/ nationalist Gush Emunim movement.[31] Critics oppose these settlements on several grounds. It is claimed that they are uneconomical. Rurban villages require such a heavy investment in infrastructure and mainte-nance that they draw away funds required for social and development investments within the pre-1967 borders. Opponents also claim that these settlements have become obstacles to peace because they deprive Arabs of their lands and the territory required to build their own state. Maintaining these settlements may make the conflict irreconcilable. Furthermore, because the settlements need protection in a period of protracted violence as occasioned by the intifada, it is argued they are a constant drain on military resources and are likely to be a strategic liability rather than an asset, especially in an age of missiles that reduce the defensive value of territory.

These economic and military arguments as well as moral and legal issues have engendered among Israeli Jews an opposition that is unprecedented in the history of Zionist colonization. The controversy extends well beyond potentially quantifiable costs and benefits and the professional skills of planners. It concerns assessments of the rights and obligations of Jews in relation to the rights of the Palestinian Arabs. It also concerns the real or perhaps imagined dangers Jews face in an area of the world that has been chronically unstable and largely hostile to the idea of a Jewish state within any agreed borders. In sum, how necessary are these settlements for security, and how weighty is ideology when measured against the pragmatic need for compromise?

Advocates of these settlements have interpreted their efforts within a tradition of colonization that has been central to the struggle to reestablish an independent Jewish state. In little more than a century, the Jewish population of Palestine grew two hundred–fold, from a maximum of about 25,000 in 1880 to almost 5 million at the close of the twentieth century. With the continuing influx of Jews, largely from the former Soviet Union and natural population growth, Israel's Jewish population is likely to continue to grow at a considerable rate. By definition, planners do not merely target an existing population but integrate settlement politics with long-range projections. Degania was intended as a forerunner of future Jewish colonization around the Sea of Galilee before the First World War; the "stockade and tower" settlements were similarly conceived for other frontiers before the Second World War; and the Master Plan of 1950 quickly established what was hoped would be an efficient and effective framework on which to build a far more populous and secure state within the 1949 armistice lines. In this tradition rurban villages were planned as spearheads on yet another frontier.

Many argue that these villages are likely to fail in their long-term purposes. In addition to objections on political and moral grounds, some critics warn that there are too few settlers in relation to the large and growing Palestinian Arab population.[32] In their view the unfavorable demographic imbalance will likely continue and may become even more severe. The costs of investing in such settlements will necessarily be proportionately far higher than for fellow citizens within the 1967 borders. Such demographic and economic arguments have not deterred proponents. The master plans for Judea and Samaria continually enlarged their projections. The *1983 Master Plan for Settlement of Judea and Samaria,* for example, was based on a forecast of 1.3 million Jews together with 1.8 million Arabs within thirty years or by 2010. Although it is clear that the Jewish population will not reach its target, hopes for its continuing growth and permanence remain among supporters.[33]

With the interest in finding an accommodation with Palestinian Arabs after the Oslo Accords and the widespread acceptance of an independent Arab state in most of the West Bank, there is a declining commitment to this earlier view. Prime Minister Ehud Barak, in particular, by the end of 2000, expressed willingness for an extensive exchange of "land for peace" in the West Bank, thereby agreeing to withdraw from many settlements. At the time of this writing, the outcome is far from clear. As I suggest in Chapter 12, the most likely scenario is retrenchment into the large blocks of settlements around Jerusalem, which would accommodate about 80 percent of those who built their homes in the rurban settlements and the urban extensions of metropolitan Jerusalem. Outlying, poorly populated, and isolated settlements are likely to be evacuated in the event of a peace agreement. Many Israeli Jews would support such a pragmatic compromise if it established borders that were accepted as legitimate and binding by the Palestinians and the Arab states. Such an outcome would also ensure that Israel would continue to maintain a decisively Jewish majority rather than possibly become, owing to the extraordinarily high birthrate among Palestinian Arabs, a minority confronting a restive and even openly hostile majority within an entity lacking internationally recognized borders. Such a potential outcome has already led to the widespread consensus that Gaza, with its very small Jewish population, must necessarily become part of a Palestinian state.

It has become clear that the technical ingenuity of planners alone cannot determine the outcome of this debate over the West Bank. Their expertise shaped the discourse of the future of the Zionist village and provided an original contribution to contemporary planning theory and practice. This Israeli experiment is also a response to the challenge of designing and dispersing small communities in modern societies, an issue with which modern planners have wrestled since confronting the negative and harmful consequences of urban congestion in the mid-nineteenth century.[34] However, their ultimate significance for Israelis has become distinctive in the unique context of Zionist colonization. Supporters primarily view them as heroic successors to the rugged farming villages on the first frontiers of Zionist settlement even as detractors consider them a misguided and dangerous application of inventive but overly ambitious planning.

CHAPTER 11

Establishing a Capital
Jerusalem, 1948–1967

If I forget thee, O Jerusalem, let my right hand wither! Let my tongue cleave to the roof of my mouth if I remember thee not, if I set not Jerusalem above my chiefest joy!
—*Psalms* 137:6

> *From the Summit of Mount Scopus*
> I will prostrate myself.
> From the summit of Mount Scopus,
> Peace to you Jerusalem!
> I have dreamed of you for a hundred generations,
> To be privileged to view, by the light of your face.
> Jerusalem, Jerusalem,
> Let your countenance shine on your children.
> Jerusalem, Jerusalem,
> I shall build you from your ruins!
> —AVIGDOR HA'MEIRI

JERUSALEM has been exceptional not only in the history of Zionist planning and but also in twentieth-century urban planning. In setting forth the anomalies of this city, I begin with what it is not: it is not the product of the informed insights of well-trained professionals acting in accordance with modern planning theory; nor is it a consequence of the energizing forces of contemporary finance, commerce, or industry. Rather, it is an ancient city that has undergone a rapid and extensive renaissance for many of the same reasons that brought it into existence 3,000 years ago. Jerusalem is again the center of national rituals, conceived in religious and secular terms, and of political authority. Moreover, like premodern cities, it is designed with many of the characteristics of a fortress because it is the object of intense and deeply rooted rivalries. Guided by political and military objectives, Jerusalem's professional planners have given primacy to two major concerns: ensuring the strategic viability of the city, and shaping it as a cultural, spiritual, and historical symbol. One can readily imagine David, Solomon, Hasmonean rulers, Herod, the Crusaders, and Suleiman the Magnificent exercising their powers to similar ends.

Israel declared Jerusalem its capital on December 13, 1949. The city entered history as a capital approximately 3,000 years earlier when King David sought to build a political and religious center for his expanding kingdom. Over the next millennium, Jerusalem remained the capital and religious center of the various Hebrew political entities that succeeded his kingdom. After the Romans destroyed the Temple and captured the city in 70 A.D., Jerusalem's fortunes declined. Particularly during the Ottoman period (1517–1917), the city receded into a provincial backwater of no political or material significance. Indeed, from the Roman and Byzantine periods through the various Muslim conquests, the country was governed from Ramla and Caeserea or proximate imperial centers such as Cairo and Damascus.

At the beginning of the twentieth century, Jerusalem's population was small enough to be enclosed within the confines of what is now referred to as "the Old City" and several modest suburbs beyond its western walls. Adrien Bonfils, a photographer in Beirut, captured how the city looked in the 1870s on the eve of Zionist settlement (Figure 11.1). He recorded a small, walled city with a desolate appearance set in a barren countryside. On the opposite side, to the west, beyond the walls, is Jerusalem expanding largely through Jewish suburbs. One hundred years later, the city has burst beyond the walls and spread across the mountainous landscape to become a metropolis of more than 600,000. Nevertheless, Jerusalem has long been a capital in the collective imaginations of Jews, Christians, and Moslems. Jerusalem, as the Heavenly City, reigned in these religions as a place of unique and transcendental significance even if the Earthly City became an unimportant and impoverished shadow of its more resplendent celestial and ancient self. The story that interests me here is Israel's attempt to implant the splendor of the Heavenly City in the mundane one.[1]

Although the first tentative steps in Jerusalem's transformation

11.1. Jerusalem, 1870s. Courtesy of Nadav Mann of Merhavia and Yad Yitzhak Ben-Zvi. Photo by Adrien Bonfils of Beirut.

were visible in the last years of the Ottoman Empire, significant and sustained change commenced under the British Mandate (1922–1948), and it is therefore with the British impact on Jerusalem that I begin, and with Jerusalem's conversion into the capital of modern Israel in the half-century following 1948. The first decade after Independence deserves particular attention, because this is when dramatic changes in Jerusalem's population and size take place. It is also in this period that the now familiar characteristics of the plans for Israel become clearly defined and discernible.

British Jerusalem

Jerusalem reemerges as a city of consequence beginning with the British conquest of the Holy Land toward the end of the First World War.[2] Freed from Ottoman neglect, Palestine prospered with the security and opportunities provided under the British Mandate and the incorporation of the country within the British imperial system. Jewish interests fared very well in this new context. On the eve of the First World War 65,000 Jews constituted only 10 percent of Palestine's total population; when the state was proclaimed little more than three decades later, the Jewish population had grown tenfold to about 650,000, or about a third of the country's population.

Jerusalem participated in this prosperity, although proportionately less than the rest of the country. Jewish immigrants brought about the most far-reaching changes to the city. During the Mandate (1922–1948), Jerusalem's Jewish population more than doubled and provided the economic and demographic engine for the city's growth as it did elsewhere in Palestine. On a micro level, the nature of the city's physical expansion continued much the same as it had under Ottoman rule. The Jewish sector developed, as did the Moslem and Christian sectors, based on the traditional pattern of group initiative rather than by private speculation, so that highly differentiated neighborhoods or quarters continued to characterize the city. Even within the Jewish community, building was organized along political, class, and religious lines. Typically, projects were sponsored by middle-class or working-class associations or by orthodox religious groups. Dwellings in this primarily residential city ranged from groups of villas inspired by the garden city idea to multistory housing estates usually built around a shared compound. During the Mandate growth was so substantial that development had to take place well outside the Old City, which, until the end of the nineteenth century, had housed the majority of Jerusalem's population. Only 2 percent of Jerusalem's Jews, who had formed the city's majority since 1840, still lived in the Old City by the end of the Mandate.[3]

As Jerusalem's Jewish population pushed the city westward, it attracted essential urban services. The incipient transformation since Bonfils's photograph of the 1870s is captured in an extraordinary photograph taken by a German air force officer, Rudolf Holzhausen, on November 2, 1917—the day the Balfour Declaration was announced, presaging the change to British rule and the extraordinary expansion of the Yishuv under the Mandate (Figure 11.2). Although the crowded Old City was the focus of the photographer's attention, the scope of the aerial photograph records the directions in which twentieth-century Jerusalem would eventually grow. By the 1920s, retail shops were concentrated around Zion Square, food at Machane Yehuda, textiles around Mamilla, and religious artifacts for sale at Mea She'arim. Jewish political and administrative institutions that followed attracted additional

11.2. Jerusalem, November 2, 1917. Courtesy of Central Zionist Archives, Jerusalem. Photo by Rudolf Holzhausen of the German air force.

population, thus effectively creating a Jewish administrative center outside the walls of the Old City. The major exception to this westward movement was the Hebrew University and the Hadassah Medical Center located on Mount Scopus; they faced the Old City from the East.

Until the arrival of the British, there were no guidelines or legal limits on construction outside the historic Old City. The Turkish administration had no overall regulations to govern the housing schemes of foreign groups interested in settling in the city. The first comprehensive plans for Jerusalem were initiated by the British. Although they recognized that neighborhoods would have distinctive religious and national characteristics, they endeavored to place the separate parts within an intelligible and well-designed whole. They applied traditional British planning principles, using them primarily to preserve the core of the ancient city. Although they paid some attention to urban transportation flows, this was not a central concern because there was no thought that Jerusalem might develop into a modern metropolis of any significant size. (The same was true of Patrick Geddes's plans for Tel Aviv.) The British plan was based on their perception of the historic role of Jerusalem and its place in the imagination of adherents of the three related monotheistic religions. This focus did not require imagining extensive zones for industry or commerce. On the contrary, the British were intent on creating an attractive, living museum.

At the same time, the British elevated Jerusalem's position in the modern period by making it their administrative and military head-quarters for the Holy Land, and they attempted to shape the city in accordance with this status. Under Turkish rule the city had been nothing more than an insignificant provincial center. When the British and French divided the Middle East in the aftermath of the First World War, Palestine emerged as a distinct entity that required an administrative center. For the British, the conquest of Jerusalem echoed with the return of Christianity to the Holy Land a millennium after the Crusades, and it was under the spell of this historic event that their approach to Jerusalem took shape. Indeed, Gen. Edmund Allenby, the first of the modern conquerors, gave expression to these sentiments by entering the city as a pedestrian, like an ordinary pilgrim, in a dramatic demonstration of homage to the traditional status of the city. As one long-time American Christian resident who observed the event wrote: "We thought then we were witnessing the triumph of the last crusade. A Christian nation had conquered Palestine!" For Allenby and his colleagues, the planning of modern Jerusalem was to be a product of their religious imagination and their imperial sense of responsibility.[4]

It is pertinent and instructive to compare the planning of Jerusalem with that of the two other cities that were also products of the twentieth-century development of Palestine: Haifa and Tel Aviv. Although Jerusalem certainly benefited from the Mandate, and the same authorities, professionals, and interested parties engaged in developing all three major cities, Haifa and Tel Aviv enjoyed far greater prosperity. The uniqueness of the approach to developing Jerusalem stems from the way both the British and Zionists envisaged the future role of the city.

Haifa was an inconsequential village across the bay from the ancient city of Acre until the British transformed it to serve imperial military and economic interests. The story of Haifa has already been told and need not detain us except to recall that such leading British planners as Geddes, Clifford Holliday, and Patrick Abercrombie all left their mark on the city both in the design of individual neighborhoods and, most important, in terms of comprehensive planning. All of them envisioned Haifa as a twentieth-century commercial and industrial city. This vision was shared by Jews in Britain and the World Zionist Organization who invested significant material resources in the economy and directed population to the city. They also built the Technion to provide the skilled scientific and technical personnel necessary for modern industry. Had the British continued to control Palestine and the Middle East, particularly the pipeline to the Haifa port from Jordan and the Mosul oil fields, Haifa would most likely have become the most important city in the region. Nothing remotely comparable in terms of conception, energy, and finance was invested in Jerusalem by British or Zionist entities.

Tel Aviv, too, was a twentieth-century city planned from its beginnings on the basis of modern design concepts. Founded in 1909, Tel Aviv had a population of 15,000 by the beginning of the Mandate. British professionals such as Geddes, Abercrombie, and Holliday played a role in planning Tel Aviv even as they did in Haifa. The city was conceived by Jews as the commercial, industrial, and cultural center of the Zionist enterprise. Until Independence it was also the Zionist movement's effective administrative capital. Even today, various ministries maintain offices in the city, which is now less than an hour's drive from the official capital in Jerusalem. Significantly, the Ministry of Defense, the largest government department in the country, is located in Tel Aviv. Only in 1995 did the General Federation of Labor move its offices to Jerusalem. Tel Aviv is also where most of the Hebrew secular literature is published. Tel Aviv, "the city that never stops," is the political, cultural, and economic center of the country. Jerusalem is the traditional, spiritual, and religious capital.

In both a symbolic and, indeed, concrete manner, the differences between Jerusalem and its secular counterparts on the Mediterranean coast are visible in the physical aspects of these cities. Tel Aviv and Haifa are leading exemplars of Bauhaus architecture. Concrete structures in the international style and, more recently, glass skyscrapers are dominant features of their landscape. Jerusalem, in large measure thanks to a British planning regulation, continues to be built of hewn stone blocks or stone facing. These complement the still visible walls of the Old City as well as much of what is contained therein.

During the Mandate, there were practical reasons for Jews to prefer investing their creative energies on the coast and particularly in Tel Aviv, the first totally new city built and governed by Jews for nearly

2,000 years. Its development offered latitude and freedom economically and culturally. In contrast, Jerusalem was governed by a powerful empire that intended to continue governing the city by itself or in concert with other nations. Between 1936 and 1947, British and UN plans for the partition of Palestine into Jewish and Arab states conspicuously left Jerusalem as extraterritorial to both groups. Jerusalem was to have been internationalized. That is, European or western powers intended to maintain a presence through the manipulations of diplomacy even though it was apparent that fewer Christians would be part of the resident population. That negotiations might eventually change this status was never seriously contemplated.

Until 1948 Zionists acted on existing political and economic realities. Theodor Herzl's prediction that the country's major metropolis would be on the coast was fundamentally correct although that city was Tel Aviv rather than Haifa. As a European utopian writer fascinated by the possibilities of modern technologies, he naturally envisioned a modern city where it ought to be—on a harbor surrounded by modern industries. Jerusalem, for Herzl, as for later British planners, was destined to remain a kind of museum and a spiritual center. In sum, neither Zionists nor the British imagined Jerusalem as a twentieth-century commercial/industrial metropolis during the Mandate. The 1948 war, which partitioned Palestine and divided Jerusalem, ended the prospect of internationalization. Only then did it become possible to challenge the policies of the western powers and to imagine Jerusalem as the capital of a modern sovereign state.

Nevertheless, British planners did have an impact on Jerusalem, and their concern for its future actually antedated their conquest of the city. In anticipation of British control, General Allenby called for Sir William MacLean, the City Engineer of Alexandria, to prepare what became the first modern town plan for Jerusalem. In significant ways, the MacLean proposal affected all subsequent British planning. It reflected an overriding concern with preservation, not development. It was meant to protect and maintain primarily the wall surrounding the Old City, its ecclesiastical buildings, the decaying if colorful neighborhoods, and the skyline. This same concern with preservation accounts for the logic behind the well-known ordinance that buildings in Jerusalem be constructed of stone or at least stone facing rather than the more modern materials, particularly concrete, that were being introduced extensively throughout Palestine by Jewish settlers and the British.

The primary feature of MacLean's 1918 plan was that it imposed the

European concept of zoning to control urban development. The plan defined four distinctive areas and was intended:

1. To preserve the district of the Old City circumscribed by its walls. No new building was to be permitted except under special conditions and with official approval. This ancient core, which housed sites sacred to Judaism, Christianity, and Islam, was to be maintained as it existed and was intended to serve as the focal point for the city as a whole. The plan was to preserve the "natural state" and the "Mediaeval aspect" of Jerusalem as it appeared on picture postcards that pilgrims brought home.
2. To create a permanent belt around the walls and extending to the adjacent Mount of Olives. In this belt, existing structures were to be taken down and no new ones erected. Such a ring would enhance the visual prominence of the Old City.
3. To restrict building in the north and northeast so that only structures judged to be in harmony with the existing skyline of the city were permitted.
4. To direct development largely to sectors to the west that were intended for Jerusalem's future growth. An outline of a road system was also sketched.

Even in the zone marked for development there were restrictions that preserved the character of the city. In order to maintain the skyline the height of buildings was limited to 36 feet. Roofs were to be covered with stone or tile. Perhaps most significantly, no industrial buildings were to be erected. The city was to be kept "postcard perfect."

The fundamental guidelines of the 1918 plan were followed throughout the Mandate. Geddes's proposals in 1919 adhered to the same criteria outlined in MacLean's design. In subsequent years a variety of commissions and other proposals attempted to control Jerusalem's growth. The last of the British plans was the 1944 scheme prepared by Henry Kendall, the most important British official in Palestinian planning from the mid-1930s until the end of the Mandate. Familiar with planning in other parts of the empire, he imported the best of British thinking and adapted it to the fundamental preservation objectives of his predecessors. He elaborated on Jerusalem's road network, introducing "arterial roads" to ensure good communication in the rapidly growing city. Remaining faithful to the principle of zoning, he planned finely articulated areas for residence and commerce as well as industry, and modulated heights and land usage so as to ensure an attractive skyline as well as modest densities.[5]

The last High Commissioner, Gen. Sir Alan Gordon Cunningham, succinctly articulated the overall intent of British planning in his introduction to Kendall's proposal: "In these pages will be found an important part of the story of the discharge of that trust, of the efforts made to conserve the old, while adding the new in keeping with it, of the process of marrying modern progress with treasured antiquity. . . . Let old Jerusalem stand firm, and new Jerusalem grow in grace."[6] These were the same principles that had guided British MacLean and Geddes. This was the legacy the British left their successors—the Jordanians and Israelis—when they departed in May 1948.

Partition and the War of Independence shattered the notion that Jerusalem could be internationalized. Jerusalem had often been a battleground in the ancient world but had been relatively free of conflict for about five centuries. With the end of the Mandate it again became a major battlefield between contending peoples. Both Jews and Muslims held firmly to their gains in a very bloody and difficult conflict. Jordanian forces held the Old City and proximate sections in the east of the city. Israel controlled the western sectors. As happened with Berlin, an unanticipated interlude of division created a differential in development that posed challenges for planners upon reunification.[7]

The division of Jerusalem confirmed the British conception of the city in several ways. As foreseen by MacLean and his successors, the east that bordered on the desert remained relatively far less developed than the west. It could have been otherwise, but the Hashemite Kingdom decided to entrench Amman, on the other side of the Jordan River, as their capital and neglected East Jerusalem. Significant elements of the Palestinian leadership who had resided in Jerusalem naturally gravitated to the center of power, which was in Amman. Others left for greater opportunities in the Middle East and elsewhere. This was particularly true of the Christian population, which was caught in a conflict between Jewish and Islamic nationalism. The only industry that flourished was tourism, which capitalized on the drawing power of preservation rather than change and growth.

Kendall, who continued his role in Jerusalem as an advisor to the Jordanians, contributed to maintaining the character of the city as he understood it. Most residential areas were located on the ridges that were accessible to main roads. Terraced agriculture was encouraged in valleys and wadis. Thus the British preference for building on the hilltops and preserving valleys as open spaces was maintained. An area north of the city, Anata, was set aside for heavy industry, but in the absence of investment it developed poorly. Despite these and several other modest changes such as the development of a shopping area outside the Damascus Gate, East Jerusalem would have been entirely recognizable to a visitor who had left the city in May 1948 and returned after the June 1967 war.

Israeli Jerusalem

A very different process took place on the Israeli side of West Jerusalem. Jewish Jerusalem grew to the west as anticipated in MacLean's 1918 plan. Although this process began during the Mandate, the greatest catalyst for westward expansion was the new state's decision to transfer its capital from Tel Aviv to Jerusalem. Government offices were moved, heavy investments were made in infrastructure, and new immigrants were directed to the city. These policies changed the city's western neighborhoods and the hinterland that adjoined them as well as the region leading up to Jerusalem from the coastal plane. Thus peculiar features that came to characterize metropolitan Jerusalem during the decade after Israeli Independence foreshadow the contemporary pattern. Indeed, the patterns of growth that occurred after the 1967 war and again after the Likud Party (right wing, lead by Menachem Begin) defeated Labor in the 1977 elections were elaborations and intensifications of the decisions taken and rationales developed in the decade following Independence.

It is important to observe that although foreign consultants gave advice, Jerusalem was transformed into a metropolis by Israeli planners. This group included not only architects and other planning professionals but also, significantly, politicians and military strategists. The special characteristics of Jerusalem's development, if not its uniqueness, may be explained by the unconventional composition of these planning groups, particularly the overriding importance of political and military professionals whose judgments were paramount in decision-making. In taking account of this unusual balance in modern planning, I treat the analysis of Jerusalem's post-1948 transformation in three parts: economic, symbolic, and strategic.

The Economic Challenge

Even at present, Jerusalem presents a particularly formidable challenge to contemporary economic planners who aim at making the city self-sufficient.[8] The city is located in a mountainous, semi-arid zone with inadequate water resources. It is far from modern trade routes, and it lacks a profitable agricultural hinterland or adjacent natural resources. It also lacks a well-trained workforce with industrial skills. Under these circumstances, it is not surprising that private investors before and after the establishment of the state preferred Tel Aviv and Haifa. The state had to allocate the resources to sustain and develop Jerusalem. This may not be unusual for capital cities elsewhere when the selection of the site is dictated by political considerations rather than economic logic. King David chose this site some three thousand years ago because it was at the divide of the tribes that became part of the northern Kingdom and those that made up the southern Kingdom. In the case of modern Israel, Jerusalem was not between anything. It was at the edge of a spearhead implanted in territory held by hostile Jordanian forces on three sides.

The economic problem of developing Jerusalem also has a moral dimension. Depending on external support to sustain settlements was the antithesis of Zionist ideology. Largely in response to anti-Semitic accusations made in Europe on the allegedly unproductive and even parasitic role of Jews in the economy, Zionist planning policy was based on the economic logic and moral value of making Jews self-sufficient and productive in agriculture and, later, industry. Living off charity was viewed as a phenomenon characteristic of pre-Zionist Palestine. The worst case of such "corrupt" behavior was, in fact, Jerusalem, where for centuries the Jewish inhabitants engaged almost entirely in study and religious activities while living off the philanthropy of distant co-religionists. Post-Independence realities, however, were more powerful than ideological intentions.

After the state was proclaimed, Jerusalem endured a traumatic siege and became isolated from the main body of the country along the coast so that the first government had to be set up in Tel Aviv. Nearly one-third of the slightly more than 100,000 Jewish residents left the embattled and battered city during and immediately after the war. By January 1950, a population of 100,000 had been restored; within another year, West Jerusalem reached 150,000. Such rapid growth was affected by the kind of political decisions that had characterized Zionist planning since its beginnings: people were settled in designated locations as a means of establishing and defending borders. However, Zionist planners had also learned that such settlements had to be supported by public funds—termed "the national wealth"—because they were rarely able to achieve economic independence quickly. Israeli planners had much experience supporting rural border settlements such as a kibbutz that numbered several scores of settlers, but the challenge of sustaining a border "settlement" the size of Jerusalem was unprecedented.

It was apparent that unless the economy of the city was systematically developed, Jerusalem would relapse into its pre-Zionist situation as a community dependent on outside support. Throughout the post-Independence period, a succession of commissions, agencies, and experts advised on how to bring industry to the city. All acknowledged that government workers and those employed in educational, cultural, and religious institutions could not by themselves generate self-sustaining prosperity. Jerusalem's roles as a historic relic, living museum, tourist attraction, government center, and seat of learning were not sufficient for sustaining a vital, economically independent metropolis.[9]

The primary economic problem of the new state during its first four years was to absorb the massive immigration that doubled Israel's population. With its resources overcommitted, Israel had limited resources to allocate to its new capital. Even the process of transferring the entire governmental machinery was stretched out over a period of years while offices, adequate housing for employees, and infrastructure were built. It was equally unfeasible to establish industries and businesses before transport, housing, water, light, and power facilities were provided.

Outlining the process of building Jerusalem suggests the magnitude of the challenge and the means adopted to meet it. For example, perhaps the first project was a Loan Fund operated through the Ministry of War Sufferers to assist families in repairing the 2,000 homes damaged by the shelling. In 1949, only the Supreme Court and portions of the ministries of Religious Affairs, Treasury, Justice, and the Post Office had been installed in the city. A year later, the Knesseth—Israel's parliament—was meeting in the city. In the course of the following years still other government functions were gradually moved. During the first half of the 1950s, the government invested in relocating the Hebrew University and the Hadassah Medical Center in western Jerusalem.[10] Because Mount Scopus, although legally in Israeli hands, was now deep in the eastern or Jordanian zone and therefore inaccessible, a new university campus and medical center had to be erected in western Jerusalem. Moreover, it required several years and substantial government expenditure to repair old roads and construct new ones as well as other parts of the city's infrastructure. The path of the armistice lines with Jordan, for example, necessitated constructing a new route to the city from the coast because important parts of the original highway were in enemy hands. Similarly large-scale projects for supplying water and electricity were undertaken and required intensive investment in time and resources. Implementing these plans required organizing an independent and functional municipality. However, while all these projects were beneficial to the residents and also employed large numbers of people over many years, they did not produce foreign exchange. In effect, Jerusalem was built with a massive national subsidy that put large numbers of its citizens to work.

In a real way, Jerusalem was the largest development town of all. The investment in the city was made at the expense of other parts of the country. A useful way to understand the consequences of this differential is to place the building of Jerusalem within the context of Israel's national plan. Curiously, the Master Plan of 1950 has very little to say about Jerusalem. It does, however, discuss at length the establishment of new towns in the context of regional development. Yet, most of these efforts, as celebrated as they were in the professional literature until the early 1960s, actually suffered because of an unequal allocation of national resources. Like other new towns, Jerusalem was meant to develop a strategically important frontier and distribute population away from the coast. In this sense, it succeeded. From the point of view of economics, however, it was only marginally more rational than, say, Kiryat Shemona, on the Lebanese border; Beit She'an, near the Jordan River; or Ofakim, in the Negev desert. Unlike these examples of relative failure, Jerusalem was given preferential treatment. The possibility of finding employment in Jerusalem was significantly greater than in other settlements that depended on government largesse. Dependence on public resources still differentiates Jerusalem from other major Israeli cities. Despite massive transfer of payments to a portion of the city's population, largely to religious Jews, it has the largest population of poor in the country. Without continuing support, modern Jerusalem as it is cannot exist.

New Symbols

Why such a heavy investment has been made in Jerusalem appears obvious. The city clearly has great appeal to the historical imagination of Jews and, indeed, to the world at large. This historic connection was systematically cultivated and developed. As is often the case with modern nation-states, capitals are employed to evoke and shape public memory, to build allegiance, and to define national purpose. Jerusalem's ancient monuments and topography rich in historical associations proved fertile ground for Israeli planners, who have added considerably to the large inventory of symbols and memorials that crowd the local landscape.

It is possible that if Jerusalem had not been divided or if Israel had not been denied access to the Old City with its Temple Mount, the Wailing or Western Wall, and the Jewish Quarter, it would not have invested so much in endowing western Jerusalem with significance relevant to the new Jewish state. However, following partition, most significant traditional sites were in the hands of Jordanians and inaccessible to Jews. In the face of this loss, planners had to find ways to transform what were essentially European-type suburbs, with their many examples of international-style architecture, into a Jewish capital rooted in the parochial history of the Holy Land and reflecting the universal history of the Jewish people. Both the local connection with the Land of Israel and the long history of the Jewish people in exile had to find some expression in the modern Jewish capital. These tasks resonate in Israel's Proclamation of Independence and in the public rhetoric of the period of regained national independence. It was this twin historical justification that provided the rationale for the ingathering of Jews from around the world and for reestablishing them in the ancient homeland. In realizing these historic tasks the western portion of Jerusalem was the most natural choice to become not only the political capital but the spiritual center of a new civil religion and the national culture.

Jerusalem's new status and national functions were instituted and implanted by making the desired meanings of nationhood visible. This was accomplished by naming parts of the city including the avenues, the streets, and even the alleys according to a new order that reverberates with the historic meaning and mission of the state, and by inventing a modern sacred topography that reflects Israel's ideology.

Memorializing through Names

Street names were used to call attention to the Jewish past and present. For example, in the Baka Quarter, streets are named for the twelve tribes until one reaches the major thoroughfares named for the matriarchs. Rehavia's streets are named for Jewish sages of the Middle Ages such as Maimonides, Nachmonides, Alfasi, Ibn Ezra, and Ibn Gabirol. In yet another section, street names resonate with the institutions and individuals who struggled to create the state such as the Jewish National Fund and Zionist settlement agencies. The names of important individuals in the history of Zionist thought and action are used. So, too, events in the battle for Jerusalem are celebrated through the names of military units and fallen soldiers. Jewish life in the Diaspora is also incorporated in the city through the names of individuals known for their religious and secular learning as well as community leaders and philanthropists.[11]

Unlike the United States, where streets are typically named for trees (Walnut, Cherry, and Oak, for example) or functions (Broad, Front, and Market) or numbers that provide order (First and Second) or Presidents and other significant individuals, the routes of the new city of Jerusalem provide a visible and manifest interpretation of the history of the Jewish people from the ancient period and their long exile in different lands through the still fresh struggle for the long-awaited return. These evocations invite the pedestrian—of whatever origin and culture—to appreciate the historic significance of the capital and its relation to the Jewish people through the ages. This is crucial because, unlike other ancient cities whose growth was evolutionary and incremental, Jewish Jerusalem is a new creation that sprang up relatively quickly on the Judean Hills. Street names declared, in an orderly and programmed fashion, the version of history that Zionism wished to convey. One part of this process was translating Arab place-names back to the Biblical Hebrew names on which they were based. Thus after 1967, the Arab "Beit Jalla" became the Israeli "Gilo." The message was that descendants of the ancient Hebrews had returned to establish a modern presence. In so doing they systematically replaced the modified or corrupted versions of ancient names with the Hebrew originals. This mixing of past and present in the creation of a new collective memory is found throughout Israel. In Jerusalem, it is particularly salient because of the special functions that a national capital performs.

Consecrating the Landscape: The National Cemetery

To fulfill another special function of a capital, Jerusalem had to have a national cemetery in which the nation's greats would be buried. This is an ancient as well as a modern custom. Memories of leaders are concretized in magnificent memorials in the capitals of nations that heroes have created or shaped—witness the mausoleums devoted to Lenin in the USSR, Ataturk in Turkey, Mao Tse Tung in China, or Ho Chi Minh in Vietnam. Washington, D.C., too, has memorials to its most revered presidents. Modern national cemeteries are designed to fuse myth and landscape in the way in which they celebrate a specific historical interpretation or construction. In fact, cemeteries can become a prime text of a national narrative. Even the spatial organization of gravesites can produce historic texts with hierarchies of meanings. In Israel, because burials could not take place on the Mount of Olives, the traditional cemetery that had served Jews through the centuries and was located in the Jordanian sector, a new cemetery was established to accommodate the remains of Zionism's founder, Theodor Herzl.

On August 17, 1949, Herzl's remains were transferred to Jerusalem from Vienna and reinterred on a commanding hill on the northwestern outskirts of the city. The ceremony gave fitting expression to the symbolic place Jerusalem holds in the national rebirth of the Jewish people. Although Herzl had been buried in Vienna, where he worked and died, the new state chose to celebrate its history by bringing his remains to Israel for reburial. This was perhaps the first step in marking out a sacred topography of Israeli nationhood. It also delineated in a symbolic and visible way the continuity between the new, secular state and the traditional, religiously based Diaspora communities that preceded it. That is, for innumerable generations, beginning with Jacob and Joseph, religious leaders had their remains transferred to the Holy Land. Herzl, the visionary who foresaw a new Jewish state and the secular founder of a modern national political movement, was viewed as an appropriate successor to the more traditional leadership that had served the people in the past. As such, he, too, had to be returned to Zion (Figure 11.3).[12]

Planning for the reinterment of Herzl began immediately after Independence. The chosen site was inaugurated just a few months after the end of the war in the first state funeral in Israel's history. Because the site had no Hebrew name, it was officially designated "Mount Herzl." This heretofore unknown hill became the epicenter of the new Israeli nationhood, as representatives of settlements throughout the country were invited to pour bags of earth from their lands into the open grave. This ritual transformed the site into a figurative focal point of modern Jewish colonization, and demonstrated that Herzl's vision, the Zionist vision, was being realized.

11.3. Herzl's tomb on Mount Herzl, 1977. Courtesy of the National Photo Collection, Government Press Office. Photo by Moshe Milner.

Great care was given to invest transcendent meaning in the choice of trees (the cedar), the shape of the tombstone, and the construction of a small museum so that the site would engender devotion to the Zionist idea. The division of the mountain reflected ideological needs. Gravesites are thematically organized according to historical events, especially military actions, and affiliation with institutions of the state and the Zionist Organization. One section memorializes "The Greats of the Nation," where many major political figures from the right and the left as well as Israel's presidents are buried. The sad and impressive gathering of world leaders who came to pay their respects to the assassinated Prime Minister of Israel, Yitzhak Rabin, took place here. Approximately one and a quarter million Israelis visited his gravesite in the course of the week following his burial in 1995, engaging in an act of pilgrimage and carrying out traditional rituals including the lighting of candles and the leaving of written messages, as is done at the Western Wall. Rabin's grave on Mount Herzl has become a national shrine (Figure 11.4).

The other major section on Mount Herzl is a military cemetery,

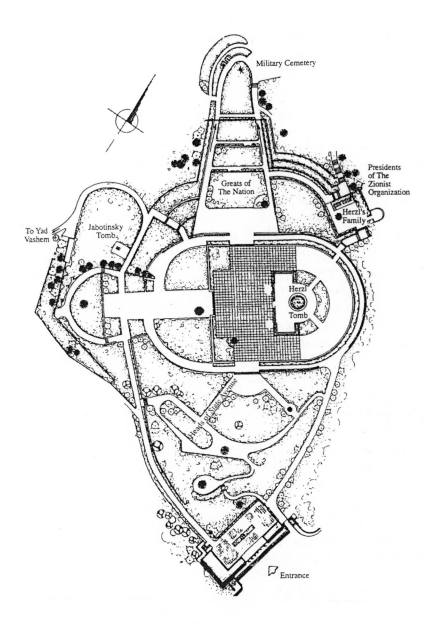

Military Cemetery

Presidents
of The
Zionist
Organization

Greats of
The Nation

Herzl's
Family

To Yad
Vashem

Jabotinsky
Tomb

Herzl
Tomb

Heads of State Avenue

Entrance

11.4. Mount Herzl: the civilian portion. Courtesy of the Department for the
Commemoration of Fallen Soldiers, Ministry of Defense.

where some of those who fell in the struggles from before Independence to the present are buried. This part of the mountain is a veritable history of the Zionist struggle and the price paid for achieving and maintaining Jewish independence. It is Israel's equivalent to Arlington National Cemetery, which is so much a part of the landscape of Washington, D.C., and to similar sites elsewhere in new nations.

There is interesting anecdotal testimony of how this mountain has contributed through ritual and ceremony to transforming Jerusalem into the national capital. In December 1949, for example, a mass demonstration was organized in response to a UN resolution to separate Jerusalem from the main body of Israel and to internationalize the city. The climax of the ceremony was held during Hannukah, the Festival of Lights, which celebrates the victory of the Maccabees more than 2,000 years ago. The demonstration consisted of an assembly of representatives of Israeli youth who carried torches from the various ancient and modern battlefields from throughout Israel to Mount Herzl. With great pageantry they held a festival with a dramatic text celebrating Jewish heroism, the national revival, and the rebuilding of Jerusalem.

Through such highly ritualized public events, Mount Herzl has become a central focus for an emerging civil religion that, as the planners envisaged nearly fifty years ago, has further anchored Jerusalem in the collective national memory and thereby gives meaning and purpose to a modern, secular Jewish state. It has become a counterpart to the Temple Mount, which was the focus of traditional Judaism. Put another way, Mount Herzl has become the secular/national complement to the Western Wall of the Temple, which symbolizes the religious/eschatological tradition in Judaism. As such, the Western Wall and Mount Herzl represent complementary visions of Israel's collective national identity.

This kind of topographical consecration took place at other elevated sites. Physically related to Mount Herzl is a hilltop that has become the site of Yad Vashem, Israel's Holocaust memorial. The proximity of the location and its relationship were expected to affirm the message that out of the ashes of the Jewish tragedy of the Second World War, the nation was reborn as an independent Jewish state. Also, as a memorial to European Jews it affirmed the traditional connection between Diaspora Jewry and the new state.[13]

Other prominent locations have been chosen to emphasize particular messages. Near the entrance to Jerusalem a national convention center, named the Buildings of the People (*binyanei ha-ooma*), was built. Central government buildings were located not far away, also on a hilltop.

The national university was developed close to this complex. Nearby, too, is a network of national museums, the Israel Museum, that celebrate the long cultural history of the Jewish people both in the Diaspora and in the Holy Land. One prominent building in the complex, the Shrine of the Book, houses a display of ancient texts discovered at Qumran near the Dead Sea during the War of Independence; others exhibit archaeological finds from throughout Eretz Israel; still others present ritual objects and artifacts of Jewish life in the Diaspora.

Names were given and sites were made prominent in order to create a Jerusalem that manifestly transcended a particular moment and place to become the political capital of the contemporary sovereign Jewish state. At the same time, Jerusalem became the spiritual and cultural center of a people long dispersed, a people who even as they returned to their ancient homeland understood themselves as a universal community that extends across time and over numerous locales. Jerusalem was consciously constructed to convey this symbolic message and to represent in its physical design the rationale for Israel's establishment as a home for the Jewish people.

Strategic Problems

Particularly during the early years of the state, certainly up to the 1956 Sinai Campaign, Israel operated under a deeply felt sense of vulnerability and concern over the tentativeness of the armistice lines. Begin's negotiation's with Sadat of Egypt and then Rabin's with Hussein of Jordan contributed to changing this. After Independence both the walls of the Old City (lying to the east in Jordanian hands or in no-man's-land) and the wreck-strewn road up from Bab-el-Wad to the entrance of western Jerusalem where convoys had tried to break the siege of the city were a constant and poignant reminder that economic development and memorials were insufficient to ensure that Jerusalem would remain Israel's capital. Today it appears that defining the borders of this city may well prove to be even more difficult than establishing those of the country. It is not surprising, then, that planners have been directed to pay keen attention to Jerusalem's defense.

It is undoubtedly strange for scholars and practitioners of modern planning to consider walls and other defensive devices as germane to planning a contemporary metropolis. The idea of the city as fortress was diminished by the development of modern artillery and made obsolete by air power. Nevertheless, perhaps the most striking feature of post-1948 construction in Jerusalem is the way planners have incorporated premodern military concepts and adapted conventional design ideas for strategic purposes. Jerusalem's modern walls are unconventional. Some take the form of concrete apartment buildings organized into neighborhoods that are spread out in a line atop the hills that ring the Old City. The design of the new campus of the Hebrew University on Mount Scopus after 1967 was consistent with this approach. It is a concrete fortress spreading over the mountain's highest ridge, with corridors reputedly wide enough to permit the passage of armored vehicles.

The apparent logic of such planning and building techniques derives from the experience of the 1948 war, in which the battle for Jerusalem raged from neighborhood to neighborhood. In that conflict, Jews lost the Old City's Jewish Quarter and the Western Wall. Mount Scopus became an isolated and unusable enclave behind Jordanian lines. The city's fragmentation as well as the traumatic experience of siege, the capture of soldiers as well as civilians, and the loss of important strategic and sacred ground required a response from Israel's planners. In accordance with the well-known saying about generals planning for the next war as if they were still fighting the last, Jerusalem's planners were obliged to address the possibility the city might again be the center of conflict. Indeed, although the Jordanian attack in June 1967 had a happier outcome than did the 1948 war, from the Israeli point of view, the city did become an urban battleground, with contending sides fighting at close range in populated areas. This occurred more recently during the intifada that began on September 28, 2000, at the Temple Mount. In the following months stones, Molotov cocktails, and live ammunition have echoed through the city, turning neighborhoods such as Gilo into battlegrounds.

There are many examples of the pervasive impact of war on urban planning. With the end of the War of Independence, several neighborhoods went unprotected in the southern part of the city facing Arab Bethlehem and Beit Jala. New immigrants were quickly brought into this section, the Katamon Quarter, and settled in relatively low-rise apartment buildings. Their maximum building height was set not for aesthetic reasons but by the army, which needed an unrestricted line of fire to cover the high ground in enemy hands facing them from the north. Typically, the buildings themselves were not fortified. Their purpose was to establish an active Israeli presence right up to the border. As

11.5. A street in the border zone of Jerusalem, 1955. Proximate to the downtown center of West Jerusalem, these buildings housing immigrant families literally form part of the border in a divided city. The large concrete wall to the right is designed to protect against sniper fire. Courtesy of the National Photo Collection, Government Press Office. Photo by Hans Pinn.

had been the case since the beginnings of Zionist colonization, planners applied the principle that people create borders and hold territory. This principle was extended from the kibbutz on the rural frontier to the defense of a city (Figure 11.5).

Even such a typically mundane issue as positioning the entrances to buildings had strategic implications. The new Israeli government established some of its main buildings little more than a mile behind the Katamon "shield" on the ridge of Giv'at Ram. The Knesseth building, originally planned with its entrance facing south toward Mar Elias, a Jordanian-controlled area, was turned around at the request of the then Deputy Chief of Staff, Yitzhak Rabin, so that people arriving at Israel's parliament would not be vulnerable to Jordanian fire. Rabin's directive was based in reality. In 1956, machine guns from Mar Elias fired into a group of archaeologists and students examining excavations at Ramat Rachel, killing four and wounding seventeen.[14]

Strategic concepts were also applied to the development of Jerusalem's metropolitan region. The need for this was popularly understood and part of the public discourse. For example, in an extensive survey conducted in the fall of 1949 on how to defend the city, Israel's leading newspaper, *Davar*, tried to analyze what had gone wrong in the battle for Jerusalem when such brilliant victories had been achieved elsewhere. One far-reaching conclusion was that traditional settlement concepts were inadequate for defending the city. *Davar* not only urged the strategic placement of buildings within Jerusalem but claimed that there needed to be "a continuous string of settlements on the entire route connecting the city with the coastal plain."[15] In time, this idea became part of the strategic planning doctrine termed "thickening" (*'ibuiy*) of the settlements. Indeed, within three years after the War for Independence, the number of such settlements that were strategically placed down the land corridor linking the city with the coastal plain quadrupled.[16]

The idea of "thickening" was related to the concept that the defense of the city must begin as far away from the main city as possible. In effect, this led to providing Jerusalem with a metropolitan plan. The anomalous origin of imagining and planning Jerusalem's metropolitan region needs to be underscored. Regional and metropolitan planning originated in nineteenth-century industrial Europe, which viewed decentralization as a means of mitigating the problems of a noxious, inefficient, and congested urban core. In Jerusalem, the development of a rural hinterland with villages and satellite cities was related to the need to control and defend the countryside so as to provide better protection for a city that had yet to be fully developed.

As I explain in Chapter 12, the principles of control and defense have extended over a far larger area since the 1967 war when Israel took control of the West Bank. Prior to 1967, the metropolitan region could expand only in a westerly direction toward the coast. Contemporary Jerusalem has moved to all the other points on the compass. It is important to emphasize once again that the newly acquired areas proximate to Jerusalem are not organically related to the city in conventional terms. The city's remarkable metropolitan development in the past thirty years has been anchored in political and strategic objectives rather than economic reality. Among the consequences of this situation is perhaps the most innovative contribution to planning design to come out of the recent Israeli experience. As we have already seen, the "rurban" village that developed as a substitute for the moshav and kibbutz is, in fact, an urban community set in the countryside. It does not grow organically out of the local rural economy. Rather, the settlement is composed of white-collar "pioneers" who are economically tied to the urban or international market. In addition to several satellite residential cities, scores of these rurban villages fan out from Jerusalem, creating a new political map in a greatly enlarged metropolitan area.

After 1967, Israel annexed land on the West Bank as part of the process of urban and metropolitan development. Between 1967 and 1970 Jerusalem's municipal boundaries tripled. This growth was managed in a selective manner to establish strategic advantage within the Old City and ring Jerusalem with suburbs. New communities were located with a view to controlling the major access routes to the city. At the same time, annexation was designed to incorporate as little of the area's Arab population as possible. Within a decade of the 1967 war, 60,000 Jews were living in these annexed areas, in addition to about 100,000 Arabs. The pace of Jewish settlement accelerated greatly under the Likud government from 1977 so that there is now a Jewish majority across the "Green Line," the old armistice lines of 1948–1967, as well as in Jerusalem as a whole. By 1980, one informed observer described Likud policy: "It aimed, in effect, at creating a new wall to defend the expanded city. This wall of housing could stake out the city's boundaries in stone, and—if the worse came to the worst—could even play a military role."[17]

This kind of "siege mentality" is not new. It has informed the Israeli approach to Jerusalem since the first days of Jewish rule in the city. On December 1, 1948, the first President of Israel, Chaim Weizmann, made a grand entry into the city. In his speech he reiterated Jewish claims to Jerusalem and noted that historic ties had been strengthened further by the blood shed in the War of Independence. He told his audience that "With your blood you have renewed the covenant" with the city. He concluded by quoting the final refrain from "Hatikvah," the Zionist song that became Israel's national anthem: "To be a free people in our land, in the land of Zion and Jerusalem." In so doing he was reaffirming a dream of the ages that had at last been realized. This peroration gave voice to a long and deeply felt connection of the Jewish people to Jerusalem. It was enthusiastically received at the time by people still engaged in battle, and it continues to resonate with the overwhelming proportion of Israel's Jewish population. The approach of Israel's leaders and most of its citizens to Jerusalem cannot be understood apart from the exhilaration occasioned by this new reality—the reestablishment of Jerusalem as the capital after a hiatus of nearly two millennia.[18]

In retrospect, the extent of enthusiasm and energy invested in West Jerusalem is remarkable given that this portion of the city lacked the sites that had been sacred to Jews for approximately 3,000 years. Even without holy territory, however, so great was the yearning—reiterated several times a day in prayers over the nineteen centuries after the destruction of the Second Temple by the Romans in 70 A.D.—that secular Zionists committed themselves to building, sustaining, and protecting the portion Israel retained after the disasters and defeat in the War of Independence. When Israel recovered its losses and gained control over the entire eastern portion of Jerusalem in 1967, it invested great energy and resources to reestablish its capital in the reunified city. After 1967, secular Zionists were joined by traditional religious Jews in building and transforming the eastern parts of Jerusalem and in ensuring Israel's control over the whole. This effort became the largest single project ever undertaken in the first century of the Zionist settlement experience.

Israel's Jerusalem is not typical of how contemporary cities have been planned. The city was intended to serve religious and political purposes, as it did when it was first established by King David 3,000 years ago. With the city's function so defined, the economic irrationality of developing a modern metropolis in the Judean mountains was a problem that had to be overcome. In the ancient world as in the modern one, the Mediterrean coast is where great cities developed far more naturally. Centers of ritual and political capitals were removed from the coast and thereby from the dangers of attack from the sea. Such was the case with Athens and Piraeus, Rome and Ostia. In the case of modern Jerusalem, the Arab/Israeli conflict is not bound by such limitations. This often violent rivalry has made contemporary Israeli planners as sensitive to fortifying their mountain capital and securing its hinterland as were their ancient predecessors. The planning principles that guide the design of cities elsewhere could not be applied to Jerusalem without radical change in the political context. Paradoxically, if a political compromise were reached, there would be little economic justification for maintaining Jerusalem as a modern metropolis. The exceptional aspects of Jerusalem, so characteristic of the city since Independence, became even more pronounced in the aftermath of the Six-Day War.

CHAPTER 12

Contested Metropolis
Jerusalem After the 1967 War

Jerusalem united in its entirety is the capital of Israel.
—Basic Law: Jerusalem, Capital of Israel, 5740–1980
Passed by the Knesseth, July 30, 1980

> And I will rejoice in Jerusalem and delight in her people;
> never again shall be heard there the sound of weeping and wailing.
> And they shall build houses, and inhabit them;
> and they shall plant vineyards, and eat the fruit of them.
> —*Isaiah* 65:19, 21

THE Six-Day War of June 5 through 10, 1967, both deepened and transformed the strategies employed in developing Jerusalem.[1] If Jordan's King Hussein had not launched an attack on the Jewish section of the city, it is possible that in time Israelis might have resigned themselves to the loss of the Old City and accepted the new Jerusalem they had created to the west of the historic Old City as a spiritual as well as a political capital.[2] There was always resentment over Jordan's noncompliance with the armistice agreement that had promised access to the Israeli enclave on Mount Scopus, where the Hadassah Hospital and the original campus of the Hebrew University were located. Israelis were also bitter about the fact that Arabs had abused Jewish property and institutions such as the ancient cemetery on the Mount of Olives, whose monument stones they used in construction or otherwise desecrated. But the public did not demand conquest of the Arab part of Jerusalem or of the captured Jewish Quarter in the Old City. An apparent fait accompli had been created since 1948. Jerusalem was a divided city, and there was no open policy of irredentism.

In the generation since the battles of 1948, the new western portion of Jerusalem had become a worthy, impressive, aesthetic, and functional capital. Also, the new Jerusalem readily allowed for growth toward the west, as had been the case since Jewish settlements first expanded beyond the walls in the mid-nineteenth century. Perhaps partition seemed unavoidable in the context of similar conflicts that occurred elsewhere after the Second World War. Berlin was the outstanding example of another recently divided city on a continent where an iron curtain and hostile borders separated former neighbors. The same occurred elsewhere at the same time on the Indian subcontinent and the Korean peninsula. In Jerusalem, too, postwar ethnic, communal, and ideological conflicts had created new and unaccustomed borders.

The Six-Day War resulted in dramatically new circumstances and opportunities. After a period of threats and an illegal blockade in the Straits of Tiran by Egypt in the spring of 1967, Israel responded with an air attack on Egyptian air bases and an invasion of the Sinai on June 5, 1967. The Syrians soon joined in the conflict, and a second front developed in Israel's north. Although Israel urged Hussein to stay out of the conflict, he entered the war on June 5 after receiving inaccurate information from Egypt's president Gamal Nasser, who masked the extent of Egypt's catastrophic losses early that morning.[3]

The Jordanians launched their attack with a bombardment of Tel Aviv and Jewish Jerusalem. The latter caused the greatest concern because Israeli enclaves on Mount Scopus were particularly vulnerable. Manned only by a token force of 120 soldiers as mandated by the armistice agreements, Mount Scopus was in danger of being overwhelmed and then lost should the United Nations call for a cease-fire. The Jordanian offensive in Jerusalem was destructive, with about 250 Israeli civilians wounded and 20 killed. Israel was unable to retaliate immediately with full strength because its forces were committed to the Egyptian sector. However, as the campaign became increasingly successful in the south, forces were redirected to the West Bank and particularly Jerusalem. Observing the collapse of the Egyptians and the disintegration of his own army, by the evening of June 7 Hussein was anxious for a cease-fire superintended by the United Nations. Unexpectedly, in less than three days, Israeli forces controlled all of Palestine west of the Jordan River.

The aftermath of the war presented Israel with the opportunity to achieve far-reaching changes, and inaugurated a period of internal debate on what those changes might be and how they could be achieved. Nevertheless, even as a consensus emerged that called for exchanging most of the newly conquered territories of the West Bank for recognition and peace, Jerusalem was a prize few were willing to relinquish. More than a third of Israel's casualties fell in the battle for Jerusalem. It was this hard-won victory that became most immediately enshrined in the national consciousness and engendered collective relief and wonder at a triumph many held to be miraculous.

The sudden turn of events brought control over Jewish holy sites whose symbolic significance, affirmed in daily prayers, had been central in the Jewish imagination over centuries of exile. The conquest of the Old City and the newly won access to the Western Wall profoundly moved secular as well as religious Jews and found immediate expression in public culture and in political thinking. Naomi Shemer's song, "Jerusalem of Gold," first composed in May 1967 and revised after the war, speaks prophetically of undiminished yearning for connection with the historic city. "Jerusalem of Gold" became an anthem, an emblem of the war and the liberated city that had been held captive for so long:

> We have returned to the cisterns
> To the marketplace and the square
> The shofar calls from the Temple Mount
> In the Old City,
> And in the caverns in the stone cliff
> A thousand suns are shining
> We shall go down to the Dead Sea again
> By the Road to Jericho.

Another revealing expression of the pervasive euphoria is to be found in the diary of David Ben-Gurion. Although no longer Prime Minister, he remained close to the center of power. Continually informed of events, he regularly offered advice to the inner circle of decision makers. Prior to the outbreak of war, he consistently counseled caution and was even occasionally overcome by apprehension and anxiety over a possible catastrophe. On June 5 he was brought to the "situation room" of the General Staff, where he was briefed on the extraordinarily successful air attacks on Egyptian airfields and on the advance of Israeli forces toward the Suez Canal. The transformation from deep anxiety to celebration began with the first glimmer of victory.

Although in private and in public Ben-Gurion reflected on a host of issues confronting Israel after the war, it was the fate of Jerusalem that became his primary focus. He was obsessed with the immediate need to populate the Old City with as many Jews as possible in order to solidify and confirm Israeli control. He warned that Jerusalem would not remain in Jewish hands unless the government initiated energetic programs of directed settlement and construction. For Ben-Gurion, this new situation offered an opportunity for rectifying one of the failures of Israel's War of Independence: the forced transfer of Jews from the city's historic core and the total denial of access to Jewish religious sites.

Iconic representations reflect the widespread support for reestablishing a Jewish presence. Generals and soldiers were photographed in reverential poses at the Western (Wailing) Wall, which was the most prominent remaining part of the Second Temple, destroyed in 70 A.D. by the Romans. Secular Jews made pilgrimages to the wall even though they were unaccustomed to prayer. Many partook of the tradition of inserting notes with wishes or prayers in the cracks of the wall, and others were content simply to touch its stones. Regaining the wall symbolized the requited yearnings of the Jewish people and a triumphant vindication of their right to reclaim the sacred property that had first been wrested from them by the Romans nearly 2,000 years earlier. It was as if the centuries of physical and spiritual exile were finally, unexpectedly, ended. A reporter tried to capture the moment with words: "The hands that had just held weapons and ammunition now caress with love and unending yearning the most precious stones of the wall. Generals and soldiers congregated at the wall and prayed the Afternoon Service, The chief Rabbi of the army, Rabbi Shlomo Goren, blew the shofar. The Kaddish and the Memorial Service for the Dead was then recited. The ceremony was at an end."[4]

It is not surprising, then, that the first planning decision regarding Jerusalem was the order to clear the area adjacent to the wall of all structures so that a plaza could be created to accommodate large-scale prayer and public celebrations. The site, deemed sacred by secular as well as religious Jews, achieved a centrality in the national imagination that surpassed what might have been anticipated only a short time earlier. This attachment has deepened over the years. When Israel and the Palestinian Authority came to negotiate over the Temple Mount (Haram al-Sharif, in Arabic) more than three decades later, there was widespread consensus that the wall had to remain an integral part of Israel—

12.1. The Western [Wailing] Wall, 1910. This was the only visible remnant of the Temple and, as such, a place where the pious prayed and inserted notes in the crevices. This narrow street was widened in June 1967 by removing proximate houses in order to accommodate large-scale religious and secular functions. Courtesy of the National Photo Collection, Government Press Office. Photo by Eric Matson.

although the wisdom of insisting on control of the top of the Temple Mount, the site of two mosques, was disputed.[5]

The decision to incorporate the site and its environs was acted on even prior to the conclusion of hostilities on all fronts. On June 8, accompanied by air force generals Ezer Weizman and Mordechai Hod, Ben-Gurion noted that "All the way to Jerusalem and in the New City soldiers cheered us. We entered the Old City and headed straight for the Western Wall. I noticed that since the Old City has been closed to us [since 1948], buildings were erected next to the Wall. I was surprised that an order hasn't been given to knock these constructions down." He went on to observe that "the international struggle will begin immediately" and that Israel's position must be clear and firm: "On Jerusalem we must not budge. We have to quickly establish a large Jewish settlement there." The area near the wall was almost immediately cleared, but the process of reestablishing a Jewish presence in the Old City took longer (Figure 12.1).[6]

The logic of asserting Jewish control was soon extended beyond the confines of the walled Old City to all of East Jerusalem. The means for doing so were far more sophisticated than removing buildings and establishing Jewish occupancy in existing structures. They involved redrawing the city's map. Perhaps the most important and ambitious plans required redefining the extent of Jerusalem so that it could contain new chains of neighborhoods inside the existing municipality as well as settlements to be located adjacent to it. In effect, in order to maintain control over the Old City, Israeli authorities moved to create a new Jerusalem in a metropolitan and regional framework. Israel's modern Jerusalem would extend far beyond the city imagined by British planners for the modest hill town they encountered earlier in the century or, for that matter, by any of the city's rulers in the ancient past. Important parts of Israel within the 1967 borders as well as in the West Bank were incorporated into the city, and other large areas were tied to it.[7]

New Municipal Borders

The process of reconstructing Jerusalem as a united city under Israeli control commenced even before the end of hostilities, with the removal of border signs, barbed wire, concrete barricades, and other obstacles between the eastern and western sections. This act declared in a vivid and practical way that the nineteen years of Jerusalem's division were an unnatural interlude much in the same way that tearing down the wall that separated the former Soviet sector from the western sectors in Berlin proclaimed the restoration of a united city.[8]

The removal of these barriers occasioned enthusiastic public approval. It was especially significant for Israelis who had known the pre-1948 united city, had lived in or frequented its eastern portions, and even had Arab friends there. For them, unification represented a restoration of normality and a final healing of the scars of war. With the removal of the barbed wire, anti-tank devices, and other obstructions, both Arab and Jewish residents of the city moved across the former dangerous no-man's-lands in relative freedom and security. There appeared to be good reason and general support for the conviction that unified Jerusalem was a matter of fact.

Erasing divisions also required construction. As Ben-Gurion urged, a program for reestablishing a Jewish "presence" was undertaken. The patterns of Zionist colonization of rural Palestine were now adapted to Jerusalem. An urban colonization program was required. The first step was to reestablish the Jewish Quarter in the Old City, whether in homes previously occupied by Jews or in new structures built to replicate traditional architecture. This was an arduous and slow task because the area of the Old City was built up and already overcrowded, and massive expropriations or expulsions were politically unacceptable. Nevertheless, the reconstitution of a small community in the Jewish Quarter, like the clearing of space to make the Western Wall visible, was an act of great symbolic importance and was accomplished with energy.

The only opportunity for large-scale settlement was outside the Old City and beyond the built-up portions of the eastern sector. New neighborhoods required recovering lands owned by Jews prior to 1948, purchasing lands from Arabs, laying claim to public property controlled by the Jordanian government as well as expropriation of private Arab land. These areas were then incorporated into the expanded city limits of post-1967 Jerusalem. In this way, the Jewish population of an enlarged city was significantly augmented. In effect, redrawing the municipal borders assured an overwhelming Jewish majority, and political control depended on this. That was at the heart of Ben-Gurion's advocacy of immediate Jewish settlement in the city. In keeping with what had been learned during the Yishuv, Jewish settlement would define borders and assert de facto control over contested land.

The first major expansion was undertaken within three weeks after

the end of the war. Seventy thousand dunams were added to the municipality by government directive on June 28, 1967. At the same time, the
Knesseth extended Israel's law, jurisdiction, and administration to
these areas. A far more modest expansion was carried out on March 10,
1985, on the city's eastern and southern borders around Talpioth and
Ramat Rachel. A more significant expansion began to take shape in August 1988, when a committee headed by Haim Kaberski, Director General of the Ministry of the Interior, announced the intention to move
westward. The Kaberski Committee shifted attention from the Arab
West Bank to lands that were populated largely by Jews within the
Green Line, or the pre-1967, borders. Like growing cities elsewhere, Jerusalem planned to absorb its suburbs, but unlike such moves elsewhere,
the justification was not mainly in terms of efficiency or rationality. The
motivations were manifestly geopolitical and derived from the terms
established by generations of conflict with Palestine's Arabs. The settlement policy that redefined Jerusalem was primarily determined by considerations of security and political strategy.

The anomaly of this last expansion is reflected in the public discourse it occasioned. It was unlike earlier expansions into the Arab West
Bank, where protests were only rarely heard in Israeli public discourse
and seldom interfered with planning decisions. The Kaberski Committee's plan excited very vocal and organized resistance that was expressed in a public campaign against incorporation. The effort was partially successful and delayed implementation by several years. This
public debate illuminates the motives for the progressive redefinition
of Jerusalem's borders.[9]

Jerusalem's suburbanites opposed incorporation in terms common
in other developed countries. They claimed they had left Jerusalem's
inner city to improve their quality of life and to escape onerous taxation
for inferior services. Their prime concern was that the municipal authorities would encourage builders to develop housing estates and possibly industrial zones that would compromise the intimacies and spa-
ciousness for which they had left the city. Moreover, they felt they
would lose control over their schools, whose quality could be diminished by incorporation into the municipal system. In sum, independence from the city was a necessary form of protection to preserve the
kind of communities they sought to create. One expert consultant to
the Kaberski Committee agreed, urging Israel to create the kind of
county system of government found in the United States, where large
inner cities and independent suburbs function within a regional gov-

ernment framework that encourages autonomy as well as cooperation in essential, shared services.[10]

Government officials countered with familiar arguments. They invoked the international practice that views divisions between the central city and its suburbs as injurious to proper government. They claimed a unitary metropolitan approach to governance would produce improvements in transportation, infrastructure, employment, housing, and so on. They observed that governments in Europe and the United States had made similar choices for the same reasons. In sum, defenders and opponents of Jerusalem's expansion played out a well-known scenario.

From the point of view of planning, this debate hinged on the uniqueness of the Jerusalem case. Both government officials and invited experts acknowledged without embarrassment that political and demographic considerations were primary. It was their intention to ensure that Jews would remain an overwhelming majority of Jerusalem's population. Achieving this goal required a redefinition of the city's boundaries in order to include Jewish suburbs while excluding proximate Arab communities. This was well understood by all, including Jerusalem's Arab leadership, since the first redefinition of the city in 1967. Many areas with large Arab populations with historic ties to the city, such as Kalandia and 'Al-'Azaryah, were excluded even as they were bounded by Jerusalem's Jewish neighborhoods. Anwar Nusseibah, an Arab notable from East Jerusalem, described the feeling among Arabs as one of "strangulation" and "suffocation."[11] It was clear that fixing Jerusalem's borders involved gerrymandering. The results were irregular municipal lines that could not be explained away by mountainous topography. The debate over the western suburbs ended in 1993 with most of those targeted by the Kaberski Committee incorporated into the municipality.[12]

The relative proportion of Jews to Arabs had been a source of intense concern since 1967. Statistics were regularly used to demonstrate a historic process that had long prefigured the divisions of the War of Independence. They showed that Jews were the city's largest minority from around 1840 in a community composed of Jews, Christians, and Muslims (Table 12.1). From approximately 1860 onward, Jews constituted an absolute majority and maintained this position under Ottoman and British rule. The intended conclusion is clear: undivided Jerusalem had long been a Jewish city, and it was fitting that the Jewish state govern it as an undivided city. Viewed in this context, the expansion of the city

Table 12.1. Jerusalem's population in historical perspective

Year	Jews	Non-Jews	Total	% Jews
1844	7,120	8,390	15,510	45.9
1896	28,112	17,308	45,420	61.9
1922	33,971	18,110	52,081	65.2
1948	100,000	65,000	165,000	60.6
1967	195,700	67,509	263,209	74.4
1990	378,200	146,200	524,400	72.1
2000	450,000	200,000	650,000	69.2

Source: Israel Central Bureau of Statistics; *Israel Yearbook and Almanac;* "Jerusalem's population reaches 650,000," *Israel Line,* February 6, 2000. *(ISRAEL@Pankow.Inter.net.il)*

in 1993 was a means to buttress the Jewish majority. The additional 15,000 dunams were expected to increase Jerusalem's Jewish population by 100,000.[13]

The concern over demographic preponderance stemmed from the more rapid rate of increase of Arabs. Both natural increase and the influx of Arabs from the West Bank, particularly from Hebron and its environs, steadily if slowly increased the Arab proportion at a slightly faster rate than the Jewish. Even a fraction of a percentage point per annum could be viewed with alarm when extrapolated to decades. Ironically, the movement of Arabs into the city was a consequence of the building boom set off by Israeli construction policies and the prosperity it generated. Recognizing these trends and anxious to validate Jewish claims to the city in the face of Arab as well as international criticism, Israeli planners set targets wherein the Jewish population would constitute at least 70 to 72 percent of the total. In achieving this goal, repopulating the Jewish Quarter of the Old City had only symbolic value. Building Jewish neighborhoods in Jordanian Jerusalem was also insufficient. The only effective strategy was to redefine Jerusalem's historic boundaries and fill them with new Jewish neighborhoods inside and beyond the 1967 limits.[14]

Security

Defense considerations were paramount in reshaping Jerusalem as a regional metropolis. Demographic preponderance could have been achieved by building high-rises within existing or slightly modified borders. That is, the city could have grown vertically rather than horizontally. Instead, a limit on building height was set even for commercial buildings at around ten stories, a regulation that has been largely observed. Skyscrapers of several times that height now mark the skyline of the coastal cities and can be found even on top of Haifa's Mount Carmel. In contrast, in Jerusalem's new neighborhoods apartment houses of about four stories coexist with single-family homes and cottages typically built in rows but often also with modest gardens in a way that limits density. Thus the politics of expansion pushed the city to the north, east, and south into the West Bank and west into Israel proper. Strategic value no less than availability determined which lands would be appropriated for Jewish settlement.

The first indication of the strategic factor in settlement policy was revealed in the weeks following the 1967 war. Israel moved quickly to construct neighborhoods linking West Jerusalem to Mount Scopus, thereby ending its isolation of the previous two decades. This was the logic behind constructing Ramat Eshkol, Giv'at Shapira, French Hill, and Giv'at Ha-mivtar. This "land bridge" of concrete and stone apartments was further strengthened through the expansion of the Sanhedria neighborhood and the construction of Ma'aloth Dafna. Nearly all this construction took place without expropriating Arab landowners and by appropriating land under state control and Jewish ownership. This first project was substantially completed by 1969. The vulnerability of Mount Scopus and its important national institutions, the original Hebrew University campus, and the Hadassah Hospital was significantly reduced. The new neighborhoods not only created a strategic contiguity between Jewish areas but also acted as a divide between Arab neighborhoods in the north of the city and those at its core. This was an important step in asserting Israeli control over East Jerusalem.[15]

The visit in December 1969 by U.S. Secretary of State William Rogers marked a new point of departure for Israeli settlement policy.[16] Rogers's comprehensive plan for establishing peace agreements between Israel and its neighbors sought to remove the causes of the 1967 war. On the one hand, this entailed ensuring Israel's right of passage in international waterways leading to the southern port of Eilat as well as Arab recognition of Israel and peace treaties with it. On the other hand, Rogers advocated returning territories conquered in the war. This could have meant a return of some form of Jordanian presence and authority over Jerusalem. The possibility was met with alarm by the Israeli leadership, who opposed dividing the city again and returning sacred Jewish sites to foreign control. Israel's response was quick and far-reaching.

12.2. Gilo, 1986. The form of building established at Gilo was replicated throughout the new sections of Jerusalem. Buildings are of stone facing and concrete and placed in rows so that they suggest a series of walls. Construction began at the top and gradually moved down. Courtesy of the National Photo Collection, Government Press Office. Photo by Nati Harnik.

Large-scale building projects, inaugurated to inject as large a Jewish population as possible into the city's expanded borders, were endorsed by a large consensus from across the political spectrum.

A prime method for carrying out this policy was to establish large communities in the eastern sector in order to ring the Old City core. These communities were Ramot, Neveh Ya'acov, Eastern Talpioth, and Gilo (Figure 12.2). Each was planned as a self-contained community of from 30,000 to 45,000 inhabitants. Although shops, schools, community centers, and, of course, housing would be built in the new section, residents were expected to work downtown or in nearby industrial areas. In effect, these new sites were internal bedroom suburbs within the enlarged municipality. The daily commute to work would display the magnitude of the Jewish presence throughout the metropolis. Finally, unlike conventional suburbs, most new neighborhoods were made heterogeneous in class through the construction of different types of dwellings, from a variety of condominium apartments to private homes on modest lots. This was to encourage and reflect solidarity among the Jewish community in an important national project.

Construction was comprehensive. It required establishing a new internal network of roads in belts around the central city and access roads from outlying communities to the core. Jewish suburbs typically were placed on the heights of the area's hills, and main roads traversed the valleys. Where there was vacant land, the Jewish National Fund planted forests of conifers on land claimed for Jews. Arabs staked their own claims by planting olive trees. Competition in planting different types of trees reflected the larger conflict.[17]

This immense effort involved a massive investment that was far beyond the capabilities of the municipality. Jerusalem lacked an adequate tax-base because it contained the country's largest concentration of poor and did not have sufficient industry and other revenue-producing assets. Moreover, the incorporation of a large Arab population substantially increased costs because they were eligible for social welfare benefits and other entitlements.[18] Thus, the direct and indirect costs of expansion were an enormous burden. In practice, the national government paid the bills at the expense of other national projects, including slowing down the development of other parts of the country. Nevertheless, despite the infusion of funds, Jerusalem, unlike most capital cities, remained poor. This was not a new situation. Political and strategic objectives continued to override economic considerations.[19]

The Yom Kippur War of October 1973 initiated the next stage in the city's expansion. While this time the Jordanians did not enter the war, security concerns generated by the conflict deepened the commitment to providing improved defenses. A consequence was the establishment of "blocks" (*Gush*) of settlements in the West Bank beyond the new limits of the expanded city.

The first was Gush Etzion. South of Jerusalem and not far from Bethlehem, the area was actually first settled prior to the state by religious Zionists. In one of the most traumatic disasters of the 1948 war and on the eve of the declaration of Israel's independence, its residents were either taken captive or killed, and attempts to save the settlement ended in the massacre of the would-be rescuers. The entire incident was engraved in the national memory. In the aftermath of the 1967 war there was widespread sentiment favoring the return of descendants of the Etzion Block's first settlers to rebuild their community. This was initially done on a modest scale through the reestablishment of Kfar

Etzion (Etzion village). The original concept included creating two additional settlements oriented toward the descent from the Judean Hills toward the Lakhish region on the coastal plain. All building was to be accomplished on land owned by Jews.

After the Yom Kippur War, the orientation of the Eztion Block changed toward Jerusalem with the establishment of Alon Shevut, Rosh Tsurim, and Elazar. The latter was intended as an enlarged "rurban" community. A far more significant initiative was the decision to build Efrata, a city with an intended population of 10,000. The expanded Gush Etzion was also planned to include additional communities—Tekoah, Migdal Oz, Kfar Daniel, and Midgal Adar. The consequence was a substantial extension of metropolitan Jerusalem to the south into the Judean Hills.

The same pattern occurred to the east, which was new ground for Zionist settlement. This region is particularly arid and its soil and topography do not lend themselves easily to agriculture. Indeed, the designated territory blends into a desert that terminates only as the Judean Hills join the plain leading to the Jordan River. On the slope descending from the city, planners established Ma'aleh Adumim and projected a population of upward of 40,000 at a distance of 4.5 miles from the city's new borders. Smaller satellite communities were developed, as was a regional industrial zone. As with most Zionist settlement since the 1960s, colonization was urban and industrial.

This initiative was actively and forcefully supported by Gush Emunim (Block of the Faithful), an extremist branch of religious Zionists who viewed settlement in the West Bank from an ideological perspective rooted in religious faith. The project, however, also enjoyed wide support including from the Labor Party. Ma'aleh Adumim, which commands the road leading up from the Jordan River near Jericho, can be viewed as a strategic asset because it overlooks an approach to the city from the east. In fact, its establishment fits within a strategic concept first proposed by Yigal Allon, a general and Labor leader, in a well-circulated article in *Foreign Affairs* whose principles still resonate among secular Zionists. In this article Allon argued for security settlements across the West Bank and along the Jordan River. Situated along the Samarian massif, Ma'aleh Adumim fits within this concept.[20] Its formal linkage to Jerusalem was initially proposed under Labor rule when Yitzhak Rabin was Prime Minister and finally approved in 1999 under Likud's Prime Minister Binyamin Netanyahu. Sentiment for sacred or historic territory does not alone explain a continuing investment in establishing Ma'aleh Adumim or strengthening the connection to Jerusalem proper. A wide consensus continues to see these areas as vital to defense and supports retaining them within Israel's borders even after a compromise with the Palestinian Authority.[21]

Finally, a major suburb designated as Giv'at Ze'ev was constructed to the northwest in the Evron Block. This collection of settlements is considerably smaller in scale than those to the east and south, yet they are also substantial enough to expand the metropolitan definition of the city. As in Gush Etzion prior to 1948, Jews had owned property that was lost in the war, and their retreat from the area compromised the position of those who lived in Jerusalem's central areas. In the light of this experience, Giv'at Ze'ev appeared to be strategic ground.

New settlements were also built within the pre-1967 armistice lines. The most significant were located in the corridor leading up from the Mediterranean coast through the hills to Jerusalem. Har Adar, north of the old Jewish settlement of Kiryat Anavim, was built inside a now secure border, as was Beitar Illit, a community of ultra-Orthodox Jews, established along the corridor's southern line. These settlements were, of course, within boundaries Israelis could readily imagine as a final consequence of a peace agreement with the Arabs. Other settlements outside the former borders were criticized as excessively expensive, preemptive of a possible compromise, or at least creating points of friction that would complicate if not preclude a resolution of the Jewish/Arab conflict.

The decision to build many of these settlements within and outside the 1967 borders was taken by Yitzhak Rabin, a member of the Labor Party, and Prime Minister following Golda Meir's resignation after the 1973 Yom Kippur War. When Menachem Begin, the leader of the rightist Revisionist Party, assumed office in 1977, he could readily build on conceptual and actual foundations established by his predecessor. The pattern and methodology of Zionist colonization were firmly established and understood. Only the decision of where and when to expand settlements was subject to challenge.[22]

Begin's government inaugurated a far more ambitious program that drew substantial opposition within Israel and from abroad. Representing supporters of the concept of "The Greater Land of Israel," he chose to press forward Jewish claims to all of Eretz Israel. That is, he encouraged colonization at locations distant from Jerusalem. The peace agreements signed with Anwar Sadat of Egypt in March 1979 gave added and practical impetus to a settlement program throughout the West Bank. Since Israel had fulfilled the post-1967 pledge of returning territories for peace by painfully dismantling settlements established along the coasts of the Sinai, the new settlement program forcefully demonstrated that withdrawal from the Sinai was not a precedent for the West Bank.

Post-1977 initiatives ensured that the outer rings Rabin had established after the Yom Kippur War would be more firmly connected to the expanding core of Jewish settlement in the city. The most distant and fragile connections were with Pisgat Ze'ev to the north. In order to secure linkage with this block, the government built highways and established condominiums that it offered to Jewish settlers on very generous terms. By acquiring the land of individual Arabs through purchase and expropriation, Israel built a new ribbon of settlements leading from the French Hill, near Mount Scopus, to Neveh Ya'acov, near Pisgat Ze'ev. The intention was to ensure contiguity between Jewish areas in metropolitan Jerusalem and to sever connections between Arab areas. As with the neighborhoods built to link West Jerusalem and Mount Scopus, planners created Arab enclaves within a Jewish capital.[23]

Other ambitious projects further entrenched the Jewish presence in the eastern part of the city. A sure way to increase the Jewish population as well as imprint a manifest Jewish character on the city was to build apartments and other community facilities for ultra-Orthodox Jews, who typically had exceptionally large families and a distinctive appearance. Another method was building government offices and transferring ministries. Even though the decentralization of government activities in the western part of the city brought some inefficiencies in administration, it made manifest the intention to ensure that all Jerusalem be brought under Israeli aegis. The enhanced Jewish presence was also carried to the Old City although necessarily at a much slower pace. Renovations took place on buildings owned by Jews, and additional properties were sought. Expropriation here would have raised a public storm that no Israeli government would have wanted to confront. Instead, various societies were formed with the purpose of purchasing properties from Muslims and Christian Arabs. In many cases the sales were conducted through "straw" or fictitious intermediaries so as to insulate Arab sellers from criticism or even actual harm.[24] With the help of the Israeli government, the Jewish National Fund, and individual Jews in Israel and abroad, real estate was acquired and transferred to Jewish owners. Christian Arabs tended to be more willing to sell, and some properties were acquired from churches.[25] The new owners were often ultra-Orthodox associations that established institutions for the study of Torah as well as domiciles for students and families. As a result, the Jewish population within the Old City increased slowly but steadily. Through all these means, the Jewish presence was progressively and systematically reinforced from Jerusalem's outer suburbs through the inner ring of new neighborhoods and to the Old City and nearby neighborhoods.

Reality of a Divided City

On July 30, 1980, the Knesseth passed the "Basic Law—Jerusalem" (*Khok Yerushalayim*), which proclaimed that reunited Jerusalem is the eternal capital of Israel and that the city is the seat of the President, the Knesseth, the government, and the Supreme Court. As we have seen, that claim was supported by more than three decades of settlement during which Jews constituted approximately 70 percent of the city's population.[26] Despite demographic competition, this majority is reasonably secure for at least the near future. Given the strategic physical distribution of this population and the strength of the government that supports it, it is possible to give some credence to the oft-repeated claim that Jerusalem is a Jewish city and will not again be divided. Nevertheless, there are powerful counterforces and counterfacts that seriously challenge such declarations. The conditions on the ground suggest a more complex reality and a more cautious view.

Numerous academic studies and the media have long pointed out that Jerusalem has remained not only a "mosaic" of clearly defined communities but a "City of Strangers."[27] Maps of the religious and national character of Jerusalem's neighborhoods graphically confirm this reality. Observers have noted that the social borders have been so resistant to integration that a political division of the city is inevitable. Thus, the Jewish Agency could readily identify and accept the city's partition by the Peel Commission of 1937 into a "Hebrew Jerusalem" while forgoing claims to the whole.[28] In fact, then as now, the *eruv* (the legal partition that defines Jewish residence for ritual purposes on the Sabbath) does not include major sections of East Jerusalem and some outlying areas that have been incorporated in the expanded and "united" city. In a city such as Jerusalem, the eruv has been a traditional indicator of where Jews live and may be taken as a communal delineator.[29]

Unlike during the War of Independence when many Arabs throughout Palestine left their homes, after the 1967 war in Jerusalem most remained. As noted above, their numbers even increased as they benefited from the employment and social service opportunities in Israel. For example, pre-1967 East Jerusalem suffered from such severe chronic unemployment that up to a quarter of the adult workforce was forced to seek work elsewhere on the West Bank or abroad.[30] Post-1967 Jerusalem attracted Arab workers. The growth of the city's Arab population meant some neighborhoods retained their distinctive Arab identity. In sum, Jerusalem continued to be a city of neighborhoods or quarters after 1967. Israeli planners built on this characteristic form in devising new neighborhoods that were exclusively Jewish even as they skirted neighborhoods and villages that were entirely Arab. There never has been a western or particularly American ideal of an open city where residence is determined purely by individual preference, and with little reference to a national or religious community. Nor are there calls from either Jews or Arabs to integrate the city's peoples in heterogeneous, undifferentiated quarters.[31]

The traditional mosaic character of Jerusalem, anchored for centuries throughout the Middle East in the social system of Muslim culture, goes far in explaining the social divides in a city Israelis claimed had become unified.[32] In most areas of life, Jews and Arabs live separately.[33] However, the issue goes well beyond residence. Jews and Arabs also purchase their food in different shops, worship in different places, and work in different establishments or, if they have the same employer, have different jobs and responsibilities. Segregation also extends to education. Children attend different schools and study distinct and even contradictory curricula either in Arabic or in Hebrew. The textbooks of Jerusalem's Arab children are imported from Jordan or Egypt, while Israeli children are taught the course of study established by the Ministry of Education with headquarters in Jerusalem.[34] One more revealing example is the two separate bus companies that carry Jews and Arabs: one operates in Arab neighborhoods and the other in Jewish ones, although their routes occasionally overlap.

Segregation usually reflects and encourages inequality. While Israeli control greatly improved the standard of living among Jerusalem's Arabs as compared with the period prior to reunification, the income of Jews remained substantially higher. This can be readily explained, but the fact remains. Although there was considerable improvement in the quality of life as in health and social services as compared with the period prior to 1967, this mitigated neither the alienation of the Arab population nor their animosity toward the city's government. Perhaps the most symbolically significant change was that the primary language of the city became Hebrew.

Political disparities were built in from the beginning of unification in 1967. Israel offered citizenship to the city's Arab residents, but very few accepted. Instead, they maintained exceptional status. Israel offered them the status of "resident" (*toshav*), with the right to enjoy social benefits and services and the obligation to pay taxes like other Jerusalemites. Although they could hold Jordanian passports, they could also obtain Israeli identity cards and vote in municipal elections though not in national ones. Moreover, they alone among the Arab population of Israel could travel to Mecca on pilgrimage using Israeli papers on the western side of the Jordan River and Jordanian papers on the eastern side.

The fact that within the unified city there was a fundamental and apparently unbridgeable divide was not well recognized in the first years after 1967. Few appreciated the depth of the gulf and understood its permanence and potential volatility. Teddy Kollek, Jerusalem's long-term mayor, proposed shortly after unification that some form of borough or quarter plan could be instituted to address the needs and sense of exclusion among many of the city's Arabs. His model was London, which provides for considerable autonomy, rather than New York, which does not. Kollek's goal was "practical yet harmonious coexistence."[35] Sensitive to charges of cooption, Arabs did not embrace his idea nor did Israeli officials endorse a plan that might suggest any form of political redivision. Over the years, numerous institutes, foundations, and individuals have floated ideas on how the reality of the city's partition might be channeled into political structures that would both retain Israel's sovereignty without compromising the city's functioning and address the dissatisfactions and alienation of the Arab population. Reconciling the ambitions of both peoples has been a frustrating and extraordinarily demanding challenge.[36]

Friction has increased over the years. Even as Israel apparently deepened its hold through the construction of neighborhoods and settlements, Arab protests increased. The intifadas that began in 1987 and again in 2000 reflect opposition to and perhaps even desperation with Israeli rule.

Postscript

Refusal to accept Jewish rule in Jerusalem, or elsewhere in Palestine, is not new nor exceptional in the history of relations between Jews and Arabs. So long as the Ottomans governed the country, there was no opportunity to upset the established order. Arabs had long challenged the legitimacy of Jewish equality let alone independence and sovereignty in a land defined as a significant part of the *Dār a' Islām*—"the House of Islam where Muslims rule and the law of Islam prevails."[37] Given the religious importance attached to Jerusalem, resistance to Jewish control over the city and particularly over the Temple Mount has been adamant and intense. Despite the long-term presence of a Jewish majority, repeated attempts have been made to keep Jews in a secondary if not subservient position that is consistent with Moslem theology and experience. Muslims have long objected to Jews using the Western Wall as a place of prayer and have repeatedly employed violence to assert their position. Indeed, the history of this past century's Arab/Jewish conflict has been punctuated by Arab-initiated riots that began at this site and then spread to other parts of the country. Both the 1929 riots and the intifada of 2000 began in Jerusalem with an attack on Jews at the wall.

In retrospect, it was well for the successful progress of Zionist settlement that the main venues for development were far from the Old City. It was Jewish settlement in the Galilee, the Jezreel Valley, and the coast that had been the focus of Zionist activity and provided the basis for establishing a state. Only when Israel was more secure could it undertake to stake out its claim to Jerusalem with its contentious holy places.

In a sense, the intensity and scope of efforts to redefine the city reflect an awareness of the attitudes of Arabs in Palestine and of the Moslem world at large. Anticipating opposition, there was a need to "create facts" as quickly as possible. This need also informed the diplomatic strategy of Israeli peacemakers over the past generation. With the initiation of peace talks with the Palestinian Authority in Oslo, an agenda was established in which Jerusalem was reserved for the end of negotiations. The claims of both sides were potentially so inflammatory and perhaps irreconcilable that it seemed wise to deal first with items that could be more readily resolved. It was hoped that "confidence-building" through successive agreements would ultimately make compromise over Jerusalem possible. At the same time, Israel never yielded in claiming the right to develop and defend its historic and new capital.

By 2000, under the leadership of Prime Minister Ehud Barak, Chairman Yasser Arafat, and President Bill Clinton, the two sides ventured to take the last steps in resolving the conflict. Clinton's proposals, with Barak's assent, provided a framework for the final partition of Palestine into two sovereign states. It denied the "right of return" of Arabs to the

Israeli portion of Palestine; provided for the division of Jerusalem into two capitals for two states; and suggested possible formulas to navigate the problem of sovereignty over the Temple Mount.

All issues have provoked bitter dispute, but controversy over the Temple Mount has proved particularly explosive. It is an issue that has involved supporters living beyond the borders of Israel and Palestine as co-religionists have rallied to the side of the rival local parties. Indeed, the dispute over the Temple Mount escalated into a conflict over symbols that resonate with an historic confrontation between contending religious civilizations. Even as Muslims in the Middle East and elsewhere proclaimed exclusive rights to the Temple Mount, so did rabbis and Jewish lay leaders in the Diaspora. For all, the same area became an evocative icon inviting the steadfast loyalty of the faithful.[38]

Whatever agreement is finally reached, it will be extraordinarily difficult to divide and disentangle modern Jerusalem. Maps can be drawn based on national predominance, but they will carry both ironies and problems. For the Israelis, gerrymandering has produced unwanted results. For example, in 2000 there were 70,000 Jewish residents in the northern neighborhoods of Pisgat Ze'ev and Neveh Ya'acov. As projections into the heavily populated Palestinian areas of Shu'afat, Beit Hanina, Hizme, and Anata, they are effectively enclosed by these communities. As the intifada of 2000 has demonstrated, commuters whose presence on the roads was to signal Jewish control have fallen victim to hostile marksmen. It is no wonder that the Jewish residents of this northern block of communities fear that the city's division would place them in jeopardy. Appreciating this, they have organized protests under the theme "Warning Before the Cut-Off." Arabs in their neighborhoods share similar concerns. Both Israelis and Palestinians believe they need to achieve contiguity and strategic advantage. It is difficult to imagine a plan that could simultaneously address the requirements and apprehensions of both communities.[39]

At the same time, real municipal housekeeping problems confront proponents of division. Water supply, electricity, sewage, transportation, and zoning regulations are but a few of the areas for which Jerusalem's redivision would create a technical nightmare. For example, outside a farce, it is difficult to imagine two different police forces attempting to patrol the opposing sides of the same street or control its traffic. The Palestinians' call for partition might satisfy emotional aspirations but could seriously damage practical interests. Nearly half of East Jerusalem's Arabs work in Jewish West Jerusalem, and the prosperity of the city as a whole depends on the Israeli economy. It would be difficult and injurious to disentangle relationships that have been built up over more than three decades.[40] Finally, any technical solution to establishing boundaries would necessarily be temporary. In an open and thriving city in which residents do not carry passports, boundaries must be fluid and permeable. Borders inevitably would become unrealistic if not irrelevant from one generation to the next, rendering any plan for partition obsolescent.

In the absence of a political compromise achieved in good faith, it is difficult to foresee partition of Jerusalem into competing sovereignties. So long as an agreed resolution is not achieved, Israel is likely to further entrench its settlements rather than endure a division that would be practically inefficient and would pose security risks even more formidable than managing a city rife with tension. In effect, the problem of Jerusalem reflects a dilemma that has confronted the Zionist movement over the past century. In the face of challenges to its legitimacy and physical threats, it emphasizes security over the uncertainties of an elusive accommodation. Until a solution is found to the conflict between Jews and Arabs, Israel is likely to continue to pursue policies that protect the permanence and security of a Jewish presence in a city so central to Jewish history and experience.

Israel into the Twenty-First Century

> But you
> Have no fear, My servant Jacob,
> Be not dismayed, O Israel!
> I will deliver you from far away,
> Your fold from their land of captivity;
> And Jacob again shall have calm
> And quiet, with none to trouble him.
> —*Jeremiah* 46:2

FROM the founding of the first Zionist agricultural colonies more than a century ago, Jewish settlement in Palestine and in the State of Israel has been shaped by a shifting balance between ideology, economics, and defense strategy. The configuration of these three factors transformed a variety of imported European ideas and theories as they were adapted to local circumstances. Nearly 700 communities including the kibbutzim and moshavim, garden cities, garden suburbs, new towns, and cities intended as metropolises were established within the rubric of regional, metropolitan, and national plans. With a keen sense that the country might be at a historic turning point, Israel in the 1990s began preparing for the next century with a new national plan entitled "Israel 2020." As in the past, the guiding concepts are familiar to students of western planning, especially the sensitivity to ecological problems and the attempt to find an appropriate mix between public responsibility and private initiative.[1]

"Israel 2020" exposes three significant changes in Israeli society that affect the interplay of ideology, economics, and defense. The Jewish state is beginning to incorporate elements of a civil society; the economy is well on the way to privatization; and there is the possibility of movement toward resolving a century of conflict with Arabs inside and outside Israel's borders.

The Primacy of Security

Beginning in the 1930s, defense considerations dominated design and settlement choices, superseding economic and ideological considerations. During the 1920s discussions over potential borders had focused on the future economic needs of the Yishuv rather than on securing Jewish areas in a hostile environment.[2] Zionists were convinced they could live in harmony with their neighbors. However, Arab attacks on Jewish settlements during the riots of 1929 and particularly the disturbances of 1936–1939 shifted this emphasis.

A prime indicator of change was the preference given the kibbutz over the moshav. While pioneers enthusiastically endorsed the kibbutz in ideological terms as the highest form of social organization in the 1920s, it was only from the mid-1930s that planners and Zionist authorities gave priority to this previously secondary and disputed form of colonization. Planned as a frontier fortress with walls and a watchtower, and located even in areas unsuitable for farming, the kibbutz was used to penetrate and hold difficult terrain in hostile territory. In the decade and a half prior to Independence, it was the prime instrument in establishing a Jewish presence and marking boundaries in a land that Zionists anticipated might be partitioned into Jewish and Arab states. At this time, the kibbutz became an icon of heroic virtues with appeal beyond the limited circle of pioneers.

Security needs also led a growing number of planners and other experts to reconsider strategies. They argued that only a modern urban-industrial economy could support an expansive immigration policy and ensure the successful settlement of large numbers of potential refugees who were essential for establishing a Jewish state. Economic considerations alone might have channeled investments to Haifa and Tel Aviv on the Mediterranean coast. However, the damage done by the V-2 (a German rocket) to London and by modern artillery and aircraft to other urban centers during the Second World War prompted adoption of European plans to decentralize population and industry. With the control over territory and resources provided by Independence, the new Jewish state embarked on a massive program to create new towns in border areas and underpopulated regions.

The same drive to consolidate and protect vulnerable areas led in the 1960s to the establishment of hilltop "rurban" villages in the Galilee overlooking valleys heavily populated by Arabs. Their purpose was to ensure a Jewish presence and control in regions where Israel's hold was fragile. By then, too, agriculture was approaching its natural limits because water resources were reaching their maximum utilization. These urban settlements, set in the countryside but divorced from the agricultural economy, came into their own after the 1967 war. Although Labor-led governments inaugurated their planting on the West Bank, their expanded use by rightist Likud governments, beginning in 1977, reflected their commitment to a permanent extension of Israel's borders beyond the 1967 armistice lines. A debate has ensued over whether they are a security asset or a liability, but there was wide consensus through the 1980s that they would consolidate Jewish control in areas deemed vital in Judea and Samaria.

As we have seen, the most costly and sustained campaign of strategic planning has focused on Jerusalem and its environs. The enormous investment in this project was a response to the fact that Jerusalem was a battleground in 1948 and in 1967. At the time of this writing, in the aftermath of the 'Al-'Aksa intifada, which began in September 2000, Jerusalem is again under attack from Arab villages outside the city and from terrorist actions inside. Strategically positioned Jewish enclaves in a newly created metropolitan area make it unlikely that Jewish Jerusalem will fall again to siege or suffer serious damage. Nevertheless, the pressure on the government to provide security is unabated.

As a society carrying out national development under repeated wars and terrorist attacks, Israel is probably unique in the twentieth and twenty-first centuries. Unlike other contemporary societies where ideology, social values, and economic rationality determine planning choices, in Israel these have generally been secondary. Attempts to break out of this anomalous situation have been repeatedly rebuffed. Offers for division of the country and peaceful relations were spurned by Arabs in 1937, 1948, and 1967. In the aftermath of the 1967 war, for example, Israel offered the exchange of conquered land for a peace treaty. Had the Arab response been positive, Jewish settlement beyond the 1967 armistice lines would have been substantially inhibited or totally arrested. Instead, the Arab League responded at their meeting in Khartoum in September 1967 with three notorious negatives: no peace with Israel, no negotiations with Israel, and no recognition of Israel. The hope that the Arab/Jewish conflict might be resolved through diplomatic processes then appeared delusory and remote.

By the beginning of the 1990s, changing international political circumstances contributed to the possibility of historic change in Arab/Israeli relations. Beginning with the international peace conference in Madrid in November 1991, it appeared that negotiations could produce recognition and peace in return for territorial concessions. That impression was confirmed by the "Declaration of Principles," or the Oslo Accords, signed at the White House in September 1993, when Israel and the Palestine Liberation Organization entered into negotiations on this basis. Much, in fact, was achieved through the end of the decade in repeated American-brokered agreements, usually captured in other impressive ceremonies on the lawn of the White House. Israeli negotiators expected that declarations of good intentions could be cemented through mutual economic self-interest and implementation of the land-for-peace formula. It is within this framework of the promise of the end of conflict, mutual recognition, and shared gains that Israelis could begin to imagine a new future. It is this radically different context that gave rise to "Israel 2020" and the systematic reconsideration of Zionism's prospects and programs for the twenty-first century.

It is not yet possible to know if a new departure is possible. The rejection by PLO Chairman Yasser Arafat of compromises put forward by Israeli Prime Minister Ehud Barak and endorsed by President Bill Clinton in July 2000 indicated that the termination of the conflict might not be imminent after all. The outbreak of sustained violence in the 'Al-'Aksa intifada has further diminished confidence that normalization of relations is close at hand. Still, it is possible that Madrid and Oslo will have a more enduring impact and that the current violence may be the final outbreak of hostility before a permanent settlement is reached. The hope engendered by the negotiations of the previous decade is reflected in the "normal" future envisaged in "Israel 2020." Even if this perspective proves to be misguided, the exercise throws into relief how different Israel could become under conditions of peace.

The Second Century

A fundamental shift from collective, national goals is perhaps the salient feature in Israel's proposed new national Master Plan, "Israel

2020." It is an extraordinarily ambitious, systematic analysis of Israel in the twenty-first century that replaces the primacy of security with ideology and economics. Since 1993, when the first projections were published, more than 250 experts from a wide variety of academic disciplines as well as professionals and public officials have produced more than 200 overviews, scenarios, and specific plans. The urgency behind this remarkable effort is that much of Israel (with the exception of the lightly populated Negev and Galilee) is already the fifth most densely populated country in the world (after Singapore, Malta, Bangladesh, and Bahrain) and could become the most densely populated by 2020. At the same time, Israel's rapidly expanding, high value-added, and increasingly hi-tech economy could push its per capita wealth to the levels of advanced Western European countries. Future plans must incorporate and confront the problem of an advanced, industrial state organized on a modern capitalistic basis in the turbulent Middle East.

"Israel 2020" postulates that there will be two political entities between the Jordan River and the Mediterranean: a Jewish one and a Palestinian one. Moreover, it anticipates that the Palestinian entity may federate or confederate with Jordan, that it will be autonomous, and that it will conduct its own affairs with the exception of military and security matters. The borders with the Palestinian entity as well as with the neighboring Arab states are expected to be open for the controlled movement of people and goods but closed to migration into Israeli territory. This also implies that the demand of the PLO for a return to pre-1967 Israel will be rejected and lapse. While acknowledging that this scenario will take time to accomplish and that there will be numerous setbacks, planners predict that the principles outlined here will be achieved by people of goodwill on all sides and through the pressure of the world community. In sum, they expect the military conflict to be defused and a regional framework for economic cooperation to be established. With this prospect, there is much that national planners can do.

The "Israel 2020" planners give this optimistic view far more attention than the extreme, negative alternative. Perhaps such optimism is necessary because in a doomsday scenario with an all-out attack using unconventional weapons, planning is pointless. The only counsel "Israel 2020" offers in the event of catastrophic scenarios is investing in infrastructure, improving building codes for civilian structures, and providing multiple centers for "redundancy" in order to enhance "survivability." Only when conventional warfare was a constant threat did it make sense to disperse population along borders and at other strategic locations and to subordinate economic rationality and preferred social philosophies to defense. Unlike in the past, contemporary military planners do not propose novel settlement types. The prime actors shaping the context in which Israeli physical planners will work in the future are diplomats, politicians, and economists rather than the military.[3]

The scenario for Israel's future is one of unprecedented concentrations of population and industry. Tel Aviv will continue to develop as Israel's primary city, with a population of millions. Haifa, farther north on the Mediterranean coast, will be closely related to Tel Aviv and the country's second metropolis. Jerusalem is expected to radiate out particularly toward the coastal plain and the Tel Aviv region. As anyone who has driven from Jerusalem to Haifa knows, it is possible to view all three metropolises as essentially contiguous and forming one large megalopolis. Only Beer-Sheva, in the Negev, will be separated from this conurbation by open land. It will stand alone as a metropolis of perhaps a million or more residents in Israel's desert to the south.

Contemporary planners find this blueprint attractive because of its economic advantages and appropriateness to a new moment in the evolution of Zionist thought. The new, national economic ethos no longer requires planners to invest irrationally, from a strict economic perspective, in frontier regions. Support previously provided to unskilled populations, particularly immigrants from nonwestern countries in labor-intensive and unprofitable industries such as textiles, is now associated with the historic necessities of state-building. Instead, "Israel 2020" planners endorse a rational approach of bringing skilled labor and high value-added industries, such as those associated with advanced technologies, in close proximity to one another. They willingly submit to the power of large cities to attract population. Competition and free choice are viewed as the most serviceable and efficient methods of advancing the prosperity of individuals and society. These concepts are familiar in Western Europe where experts advocate enhancing a few selected metropolitan nodes rather than artificially supporting diffusion.

This development assumes differentiation in economic activity between Israel and its Arab neighbors. According to "Israel 2020," the Jewish and Arab sectors will be integrated economically but characterized by distinctive activities. Skilled labor and high-tech jobs will abound in Israel. Palestinian Arabs will continue to be more heavily concentrated in agriculture and unskilled labor. The authors of "Israel 2020" view such asymmetry with equanimity. They predict a high-tech and highly prosper-

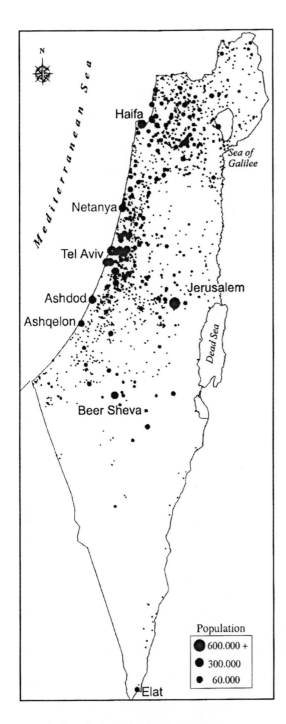

Map E1. Population distribution, 2000.

ous Israeli city-state enjoying harmonious reciprocal relations with thriving but, certainly in the near future, less advanced and less affluent Arab neighbors. This extraordinary hypothesis assumes that economic interdependence and self-interest will provide sufficient motivation for the movement to peace in all camps, and that ethnic and national rivalries will be subordinated to material gain. "Separate and unequal" is posited as acceptable in a context of overall abundance. This prospect has been endorsed and disseminated by former Prime Minister Shimon Peres in his call for a "New Middle East." It is an elaboration of a perspective consistently maintained by Zionist planners since they first responded in the 1930s to Palestinian Arab claims for exclusive rights to Palestine and the inability of the country to support more than one people.

This rose-tinted vision also represents a significant change from the ideologies that shaped the first century of Zionist planning, which placed the collective rather than the individual at the center of its purposes and value system. Israel was established as the "Jewish State" to serve the needs and interests of the Jewish people. All settlement models were ultimately justified in terms of fulfilling national purposes. They were not designed to further an individual's right to the pursuit of happiness. The widespread appreciation of socialist values rather those of an individualistic capitalism also contributed to a commitment to defining and supporting the common good.[4]

An interesting and revealing index of this change is the emergence of a new attitude toward control over land. Unlike in many western societies where access to land is identified with *individual* liberty, in Zionist thought land has been identified with *national* independence and freedom.[5] The centrality of collective rights to territory has also been true for Palestinian nationalists who have threatened and even murdered Arabs who have sold their land to Jews. Altering the rules to liberalize the acquisition of land is therefore a prime indicator of how far Israel has moved or can move to a civil and perhaps nonethnic state. Should it do so, Israel would be an even greater anomaly in a region where states and societies are rooted in ethnic, national, and religious identities rather than in the primacy of the individual.

Nevertheless, in recent years, some Israelis have argued that the prohibition of land sales on the basis of nationality or religion represents an unacceptable limitation of the rights of individuals—that is, restrictions on non-Jewish citizens. Such controls have become issues of public debate and legal action. In particular, the demands of Israeli Arabs for equal access to the lands of the "Jewish State" can now be raised with great power and effect. As a 1998 editorial in *Ha'aretz* noted concerning the suit of an Israeli Arab family for the right to purchase a home in an all-Jewish community established by Jewish settlement agencies: "After fifty years of statehood can there be a moral justification for designating lands exclusively to Jews while consciously discriminating against Arab citizens of the state that suffer from severe housing problems? Are concepts such as 'the conquest' (*kiboosh*) of the land or 'the redemption' (*ge'ulaht*) of the land or the 'Judaization' (*yehud*) of the land, which were of significance in the period prior to independence, still valid in a state that pretends to equality in its relations with its citizens?"[6]

The policy of the Supreme Court, under the leadership of the liberal Chief Justice Aharon Barak, had been to urge the opposing sides to work out a solution on their own.[7] While citizens' rights groups may find this lamentable, the Court's delay of four years in intervening in such a sensitive and defining issue is noteworthy. It is unlikely that the Court would have hesitated to favor security and national interests over individual rights in the past. In this instance, Barak ruled in favor of the Arab family but very carefully noted that this was not to be a precedent for cases involving national security interests, nor did it prejudice the right of specialized, homogeneous communities, such as the kibbutz or religious neighborhoods, to exclude dissimilar individuals.

The Court's reluctance to decide reflects a growing tendency to place individual rights alongside the state's obligation to defend collective Jewish interests. American legal theory has clearly affected Israeli judicial thought in this and in a host of other issues related to civil liberties. If the possibility of peaceful coexistence with Arab neighbors somewhat alleviates security anxieties, the state will likely come under increasing pressure to acknowledge the rights of individual citizens without reference to the community with which they are associated. This is an indication that Israel is redefining itself according to the attributes of a civil society. It is a significant step taken in a society that is apparently still consciously struggling to become "normal" within a rubric associated with western democracies.[8]

Movement in this direction will be cautious and within the particular context of the Jewish historical experience. The justices explained that democratic and egalitarian principles are deeply rooted within Judaism and noted that Jews were in the forefront of movements for civil rights and justice. Thus, when they finally decided in favor of the Arab family's petition, all declared that Israel can be both a Jewish and a democratic state, yet they sought a remedy to a particular situation rather than a precedent for fundamental reform. In this spirit, although much of the judges' opinion was based on American precedents, particularly those rooted in civil rights litigation, none claimed that Israel should become a "state of all its citizens" or an imitation of a deethnicized and individualistic American civil society. The covenantal and collective base of Israel as a Jewish state remained intact. Indeed, they emphasized that democracy can be and must be derived from Jewish sources and historical experience. For the foreseeable future, there is likely to be considerable residual power in the founding collective ideals and traditions even among secular and outward-looking Jewish intellectuals.

The split between the majority and minority opinion (Justice Kedmi) touches on the salience of "security" as a crucial determinant and a warning against establishing an unwanted precedent. It has been suggested that had the defense argued for exclusion of the Arab family on grounds of security requirements, a majority would have been in favor of maintaining the exclusive Jewish character of the settlement. In other words, Oslo and the promise of peaceful coexistence entailed in the ongoing negotiations provided a context to support the majority decision in favor of the Arab petitioner.

The easing of security pressures also had an impact on how planners related to ecological issues. What once passed for ecology was only nature preservation. This coincided with a romantic nationalism that sought to rediscover the country as it had been in the ancient world and the need to familiarize an essentially immigrant population with the ancient homeland and to nurture a sense of rootedness in it. Generations of Israeli youth have hiked across the country, becoming intimately familiar with the natural and historic treasures present in the landscape. This nurtured intimacy with the land was expected to enhance the willingness and ability to defend it.[9]

As in other countries that have undergone rapid development and pursued a higher standard of living, in Israel, too, much of the natural environment has been abused. Affluence and industry place enormous demands on the scarce resources of a small country. The tenfold increase in population over this past century has resulted in growing competition among agricultural, industrial, and residential needs and between these and the need to preserve the country's landscape, air, and water. Struggles loom over choices of means of transportation and land and water usage. So, too, there are debates over whether to encourage private-home ownership through suburban development or to maintain land reserves by allowing for greater urban densities. Still other points of dispute concern the disposition of Israel's very limited littoral areas and the few remaining vacant interior lands. The terms of debate in these and a host of other issues emphasize the public interest versus the private interest. This challenge by individual citizens and nongovernmental organizations against the "official" version of the public good is a striking new phenomenon.[10]

A host of citizens' organizations are springing up to advocate interests and positions as they have done in the United States, which provides models for many activists of patterns of organization and identification of issues. In the debates over Israel's future a cacophony of voices clamors for attention. The efflorescence of issues and parties to controversy so reminiscent of debates in the United States and other modern societies reflects the new way in which Zionist planners define "normalization." The erosion of exceptionalism, particularly the salience of state-building and national security in shaping policy, is clearly part of this trend. This may presage a shift from planning by a centralized bureaucracy that is invested with the authority to determine the best interests of a nation under siege.

I have outlined above a trend that is obviously growing. However, it is far from certain how radical and far-reaching the transformation may be. While these changes are taking place, traditional planning practices continue. In early 1998, for example, the Israel Lands Authority announced a plan to establish 62,000 dwelling units. The apportionment is suggestive for this moment in Israel's history. About half, or 30,000, are planned for the area behind Haifa Bay in response to pent-up demand for housing in the expanding coastal megalopolis. This action accurately reflects Israel's projected choices and needs as 2020 approaches. The other 32,000 units, which will house approximately 140,000, are for the frontier within the Israeli side of the pre-1967 Six-Day War armistice lines. They are intended to strengthen a kind of human Maginot line that has been under construction for most of the past century. The units are designed to shore up the boundaries that may separate Israel from a potential Palestinian state and to block the expansion of Hebron, the major Palestinian city in the Judean Hills south of Jerusalem. It is still an open question whether this type of planning is among the last in a practice that characterized Zionist settlement for so much of the twentieth century.[11]

It is far from certain that the scenarios of "Israel 2020" will come to pass. The forces among Palestinians and in the Arab world against reconciliation with Israel are powerful. On the Israeli side, many now doubt that the essential component of "Israel 2020," a permanent accommodation with the Palestinians, can be achieved. "Israel 2020" may be written off as an interesting exercise in wish fulfillment. Implementing its scenarios will become complicated or perhaps compromised.

"Israel 2020," then, was drafted at a moment in Israel's history when, after a century of sustained effort, enterprise, and strife, planners began to see a way out of the past and believed the future could and should be different. The differences it projects go beyond the end of conflict. The plan assumes a new national ideology that favors privatism and the capitalism that usually accompanies it. Such a course is not without irony. "Normal" societies, where individuals and their needs enjoy priority, often impede planners. Experts naturally prefer situations in which they not only have responsibility for defining common problems but enjoy the power to solve them. Until recently, at least, such optimal conditions existed for those engaged in planning Zion. The hostile environment reduced the range of choice even as it endowed planners with legal and moral authority.

Should Israel be able to imagine its future in an environment of peace, it would do so, for the first time, without the burdens of organizing a fortress society. "Israel 2020" ultimately tries to imagine scenarios of rational decisions based on values shared with advanced and progressive societies that enjoy prestige and admiration. Barak's July 2000 offer of a Palestinian state in virtually all of the West Bank and Gaza, territorial compensation for land Israel would retain for settlements, a redivided Jerusalem, and restitution for refugees of the War of Independence was made in the spirit of "Israel 2020" and is a consequence of the process set in motion by the Oslo Accords. That proposal was rejected, and the Palestinian Authority embarked on a campaign of violence and terror.[12] It is not now possible to know how this new conflict will end. In this, as in the UN resolution of November 1947, peace and prosperity would come through the establishment of two states that would live together in harmony. Then, as now, much depends on whether the terms for partition can be successfully negotiated. Whatever the actual future, it is significant and hopeful that, after a century of energetic settlement and a long period of conflict, the Zionist imagination looks forward to such an alternative.

Notes

Chapter 1. Covenantal Communities

Epigraph: Yitzhak Elazari-Volcani, *The communistic settlements in the Jewish colonisation of Palestine* (Tel Aviv, 1927), 10–11.

1. Calculations on number and type of settlements derive from the standard work on the history of rural settlement through the establishment of the state: Alex Bein, *Immigration and settlement in the State of Israel* (Hebrew) (Tel Aviv, 1982), 260–98. Also useful for this period are Shalom Reichman, *From foothold to settled territory: The Jewish settlement, 1918–1948: A geographical interpretation and documentation* (Hebrew) (Jerusalem, 1979); Zvi Shilony, *Jewish National Fund and settlement in Eretz Israel, 1903–1914* (Jerusalem, 1998); Yossi Katz, *The "business" of settlement: Private entrepreneurship in the Jewish settlement of Palestine, 1900–1914* (Jerusalem, 1994); Dov Weintraub, Moshe Lissak, and Yael Azmon, *Moshava, kibbutz and moshav: Patterns of Jewish rural settlements and development in Palestine* (Ithaca, N.Y., 1969).

2. Richard I. Cohen, ed., *Conflict in the Holy Land* (Jerusalem, 1985), 141–62.

3. There is a large literature on the moshavoth. The anniversary or jubilee volumes on each of the settlements is an excellent place to begin. They were often issued on the fifth, tenth, twentieth, twenty-fifth, fiftieth, etc., anniversary of the founding. For example, see D. Yudelovitz, *Rishon Le-Zion: 1882–1941* (Hebrew) (Rishon le-Zion, 1941). The Kressel Collection at the Oxford Centre for Hebrew and Jewish Studies in Yarnton, Oxford, has an outstanding collection of books, pamphlets and newspaper clippings on most settlements over the past century.

4. The literature of the New England town is extensive. Three works have direct relevance to the themes outlined here. First, Kenneth A. Lockridge, *A New England town: The first hundred years; Dedham, Massachusetts, 1636–1736* (New York, 1970), is a model for analyzing the relationship between environment and avowed purposes. A larger and more synthetic study that echoes with the issues raised by observing how European settlers developed strategies for accommodating themselves and their principles to the frontier is found in Daniel J. Boorstin, *The Americans: The colonial experience* (New York, 1958). Finally, the intellectual history of the process of accommodation is emphasized in Perry Miller, *Errand into the wilderness* (New York, 1964).

5. The debate over the primary orientation of Zionist colonists has recently erupted again with great vehemence. Zeev Sternhell finds that the pioneers of the Second and Third Aliyahs favored nationalism over socialism. See Zeev Sternhell, *The founding myths of Israel,* trans. D. Maisel (Princeton, N.J., 1998). I fully accept that national solidarity was the overwhelming ethos that motivated settlers, even those who held to socialism. For a critical view of Sternhell, see Yosef Gorny, "The historical reality of constructive socialism," *Israel Studies* 1: 1 (Spring 1996): 295–305.

6. Tudor Parfitt, *The Jews in Palestine 1800–1882* (London, 1987).

7. See Menachem Elon, *Hebrew law: Its history, sources, and principles* (Hebrew) (Jerusalem, 1973), III, 1278–80. For the application of Jewish law in the organization of communities in Palestine, see Ruth Kark, *Jerusalem neighborhoods: Planning and by-laws (1855–1930)* (Jerusalem, 1991).

8. *Documents on the history of Hibbat-Zion and the settlement of Eretz Israel* (Hebrew), comp. and ed. Alter Druyanov, rev. ed. Shulamit Laskov, 7 vols. (Tel Aviv, 1982–1993).

9. Droyanov and Laskov, *Documents on the history of Hibbat-Zion and the settlement of Eretz Israel,* 1, 339–41.

10. Moshe Smilansky, *Rehovoth: Sixty years of her life, 1890–1950* (Hebrew) (Rehovoth, 1950), 195–200.

11. Droyanov and Laskov, *Documents on the history of Hibbat-Zion and the settlement of Eretz Israel,* 2, 172–78.

12. Idem.

13. *Writings on the history of Hibbat Zion and of the Settlement of Eretz Israel* (Hebrew) (Tel Aviv, 1932), 911–16.

14. Shmuel Yavnieli, ed., *The book of Zionism: The period of Hibbat-Zion* (Hebrew) (Tel Aviv, 1961), vol. 2, 202–6.

15. *Writings on the history of Hibbat Zion,* 915. The significance of Shabbath Nachamu is explained in a history of another moshava. See Moshe Smilansky, *Ness Ziona: 70 years of its existence* (Hebrew) (Ness Ziona, 1953), 60–62.

16. In Rosh Pina, for example, the colonists assembled to formulate their takanoth on *Shabbath Shuva*, the Sabbath that falls between the New Year and the Day of Atonement. Yavnieli, *The book of Zionism*, 2, 202–6.

17. For a general treatment see Shlomo Dov Goitein, *Jews and Arabs, their contacts through the ages* (New York, 1964). For the relationship in Palestine see Neville Mandel, *The Arabs and Zionism before World War I* (Berkeley, 1976); Yosef Gorny, *Zionism and the Arabs, 1882–1948: A study of ideology* (New York, 1987); and Shabtai Teveth, *Ben-Gurion and the Palestinian Arabs: From peace to war* (New York, 1985).

18. Palestine Census Office, *Census of Palestine, 1931* (Jerusalem, 1931), is a typical example, as are the various *White Papers* on Palestine. The "partition" of Palestine is to be found throughout the international literature. As one significant example, see Esco Foundation for Palestine, *Palestine: A study of Jewish, Arab, and British policies* (New Haven, 1947), 2 vols. The division of Palestine into two national communities is explored in Chapter 3 of this book.

19. The patterns of Jewish self-government have been extensively examined by Daniel Elazar, *People and polity: The organizational dynamics of world Jewry* (Detroit, 1989), and Alan Dowty, *The Jewish state: A century later* (Berkeley, 1998).

20. Mandel and Menashe Mayerovitz, *The Hebrew colonies in Eretz Israel until the World War* (Cairo, 1919), 39–45.

Chapter 2. Trial and Error in the Village Economy

1. This lack of immediate return was understood quite early. The early classic essay on this topic is Ahad Ha-Am (Asher Ginzberg), "The wrong way" (1889), trans. Leon Simon, *Ten essays on Zionism and Judaism* (London, 1922), 1–24. Ahad Ha-Am faulted the Hovevei-Zion (Lovers of Zion) for not being steadfast and patient in the face of obvious difficulties. He also criticized the "individualistic" character of some would-be pioneers. A willingness to sacrifice for the sake of the whole and over a long term would be necessary. He termed this quality "nationalistic."

2. The conscious, economic irrationality of Zionist settlement is analyzed in Baruch Kimmerling, *Zionism and economy* (Cambridge, Mass., 1983) and *Socio-territorial dimensions of Zionist politics* (Berkeley, 1983).

3. For a good overview see Dov Weintraub, Moshe Lissak, and Yael Azmon, *Moshava, kibbutz and moshav: Patterns of Jewish rural settlement and development in Palestine* (Ithaca, N.Y., 1969). The ideological perspectives of labor are in Israel Kolatt, *Ideology and reality in the labor movement in Eretz Israel* (Hebrew) (Jerusalem, 1964); Yosef Gorny, *Achdut ha-Avodah 1919–1930: Ideological foundations and political methods* (Hebrew) (Tel Aviv, 1973); and Anita Shapira, *The futile struggle: The Jewish labor controversy 1929–1939* (Hebrew) (Tel Aviv, 1977).

4. See Emmanuel Yalan, *The design of agricultural settlements: Technological aspects of rural community development* (Jerusalem, 1975).

5. Peter J. Schmitt in *Back to nature: The arcadian myth in urban America* (New York, 1969), describes the attempt to recapture a rural past as a reaction to the apparently inexorable drift toward urban/industrial society throughout Europe and the United States at the turn of the twentieth century.

6. Simon Schama, *Two Rothschilds and the Land of Israel* (London, 1978); Ran

Aaronsohn, *Baron Rothschild and the colonies: The beginnings of Jewish colonization in Eretz Israel—1882–1890* (Hebrew) (Jerusalem, 1990); Yossi Ben-Artzi, *Early Jewish settlement patterns in Palestine, 1882–1914* (Jerusalem, 1997).

7. Adolf Boehm, *The Jewish National Fund: Its history, function and activity* (Jerusalem, 1932); Derek J. Penslar, *Zionism and technocracy: The engineering of Jewish settlement in Palestine, 1870–1918* (Bloomington, Ind., 1991); Zvi Shilony, *Jewish National Fund and settlement in Eretz-Israel, 1903–1914* (Hebrew) (Jerusalem, 1990).

8. Schama, *Two Rothschilds*, 67 ff. As might be expected, Jewish European philanthropists shared the ideas current in nineteenth- and early-twentieth-century Europe, particularly the distinction between the "unworthy" poor and the "worthy" poor, with the objective of nurturing the "worthy" toward economic independence. A good exposition of the history of this approach is Gertrude Himmelfarb, *The idea of poverty: England in the early industrial age* (New York, 1984).

9. Schama, *Two Rothschilds*, 71.

10. Nahum Karlinsky, *Private entrepreneurship in Eretz Yisrael during the period of the British Mandate: The citrus industry: 1920–1939* (Hebrew) (unpublished Ph.D. dissertation, Hebrew University, 1995).

11. Schama, *Two Rothschilds*, 108–9. An interesting parallel can be found in the American experience concerning the problems of settling the colony of Georgia. See Daniel J. Boorstin, *The Americans: The colonial experience* (New York, 1958), 71–96.

12. Schama, *Two Rothschilds*, 122–23.

13. Schama, *Two Rothschilds*, 126.

14. The visit was timed to coincide with a tour by Kaiser Wilhelm. Herzl greeted the Kaiser at the Mikve Israel training farm. He was also received enthusiastically by the settlers at Rishon le-Zion, Ness Tziona, and Rehovoth. See Alex Bein, *Theodor Herzl: A biography*, trans. Maurice Samuel (Cleveland, 1962).

15. Benjamin Jaffe, ed., *A Herzl reader* (Jerusalem, 1960), 158–59.

16. Theodor Herzl, *Old-New land* (*Altneuland*), trans. Lotta Levensohn (New York, 1941), Book Three, 115–85.

17. Herzl, *Old-New land*, 143, 152–53. Herzl had visited moshavoth in Palestine and also appreciated the German Templar villages.

18. Franz Oppenheimer, *Co-operative colonization in Palestine* (The Hague, 1913), and *Merchavia: A Jewish co-operative settlement in Palestine* (New York, 1914). A good review of nineteenth-century European utopian thought can be found in Frank Manuel, *Utopian thought in the western world* (Cambridge, 1979). Edward Bellamy's *Looking backward, 2000–1887* had a particularly important impact on Zionism. First published in Boston in 1888, it was translated into Hebrew by 1902 and into Yiddish by 1900. See S. Ilan Troen, "The Discovery of America in the Israeli University: Historical, Cultural and Methodological Perspectives," *Journal of American History*, vol. 81, no. 1 (June 1994), 164–82. The Rochdale Principles of Co-operation originated in Rochdale, England, in 1844 and were adopted by reformers throughout Europe and America as an essential part of a variety of programs for social change. In Israel, cooperative associations of producers and consumers have had an important place in the economy.

19. Yitzhak Elazari-Volcani, *The communistic settlements in the Jewish colonization of Palestine* (Tel Aviv, 1927). The most significant book of a revisionist caste

on this scholarship is Gershon Shafir, *Land, labor and the origins of the Israeli-Palestinian conflict, 1882–1914* (Berkeley, 1989).

20. Elazari-Volcani, *The communistic settlements,* 32 ff.

21. See note 5 in Chapter 1 for reference to the overriding importance of national goals among pioneers.

22. Elazari-Volcani, *The communistic settlements,* 51 ff.

23. The best study of the Zionist connection to the German experience is Penslar, *Zionism and technocracy.*

24. On the idea of an international culture of planning see Anthony Sutcliffe, *Towards the planned city: Germany, Britain, the United States and France, 1870–1914* (Oxford, 1981); Andrew Lees, *Cities perceived: Urban society in European and American thought, 1820–1920* (New York, 1985); and Selwyn Troen, "The diffusion of an urban social science: France, England and the United States in the nineteenth century," *Comparative Social Research,* 9 (1986): 247–66.

25. Central Zionist Archives in Jerusalem (CZA), File 8002.

26. Elwood Mead et al., *Reports of the experts submitted to the Joint Palestine Survey Commission* (Boston, 1928), 13–15. In addition to Mead, the commission members were Jacob Lipman, director of the Agricultural Experiment Station of the New Jersey College of Agriculture, Arthur Strahorn, soil technologist with the U.S. Department of Agriculture, Frank Adams, an irrigation specialist at the University of California, Knowles Ryerson, an American serving in the Agricultural Experiment Station in Haiti, and Cyril Henriques, irrigation engineer of the Zionist Organization in Palestine.

27. Elwood Mead, *Agricultural development in Palestine: Report to the Zionist Executive* (London, 1924). In an address to the American Palestine Conference in New York on Feb. 17, 1924, by Arthur Ruppin, who was in charge of planning in Palestine for the WZO, Ruppin observed: "Elwood Mead, Professor at the University of California, who is regarded as the best living authority on agricultural colonization has, at the request of the Zionist Organization, inspected the Jewish agricultural settlements in Palestine, a few months ago. Prof. Mead compared Palestine with California." A. Ruppin, "The Economic development of Palestine," *The Zionist Review,* 8 (May 1924): 9–10. For the international context of Mead's work see Ian Tyrrell, *True garden of the Gods: Californian-Australian environmental reform, 1860–1930* (Berkeley, 1999).

28. Mead et al., *Report of the experts,* 28.

29. Ibid., 33.

30. Ibid., 35.

31. Ibid., 36.

32. Idem.

33. Margalit Shilo, *The settlement policy of the Palestine Office 1908–1914* (Hebrew) (Ph.D. dissertation, Hebrew University, 1985).

34. "Organisation Report," *Report of the Executive of the Zionist Organization to the XIIth Zionist Congress,* part 3 (London, July 1921), 72–73. American agriculture had already been brought to Palestine by Aaron Aaronsohn, who grew up in Zichron Ya'acov and became an expert in the Baron's service. In the course of his work, he became a world famous botanist and spent time in the United States under the auspices of the U.S. Department of Agriculture in 1909–10. There, he became familiar with Zionist leaders such as Louis D. Brandeis, Judah Magnes, and Jacob Schiff.

35. Elazari-Volcani, *The communistic settlements,* 59–71.

36. Ibid., 64–65.

37. Ibid., 106–7.

38. For essential studies of the ideologies of Labor Zionism's approach to the land see Gorny, *Ahdut Ha-Avodah 1919–1930,* and Shapira, *The futile struggle.*

39. Ibid., 12.

40. Idem.

41. See Yossi Katz, *The "business" of settlement,* and Nahum Karlinsky, *Citrus blossoms: Jewish entrepreneurship in Palestine, 1890–1939* (Hebrew) (Jerusalem, 2000).

42. Ibid., 74.

43. Yitzhak Elazari-Volcani, *The transition of a dairy industry in Palestine* (Tel Aviv, 1930), 4–5.

44. Volcani, *The communistic settlements,* 88.

45. Ibid., 126.

46. Mead et al., *Report of the experts,* 167.

47. *Key for the settlement of various zones in Palestine: Reports of the Preparatory Commissions,* submitted to the Department of Colonisation of the Palestine Executive Jerusalem/Tel Aviv, May 1929 (Hebrew) (Kressel Collection).

48. *Report of the Executive of the Zionist Organisation to the XIVth Zionist Congress* (London, 1925), 198 ff.

49. *Report of the Joint Palestine Survey Commission* (London, 1928), 66–67.

50. Ibid., 142–43.

51. Ibid., 14–15. There are many foreshadowings of Volcani's position. An early formulation can be found in Moshe Smilanski, "From our moshavoth in Eretz-Israel" (Hebrew) *Hashiloach,* 26 (1912): 59–66. Moreover, Volcani was a professional in the employ of the World Zionist Organization and reflected official policy that was continually reiterated in regular international meetings of that organization throughout the decade. See, for example, *Report of the Executive of the Zionist Organisation to the XIIIth Zionist Congress* (London, 1923), 147–56.

Chapter 3. Economic Basis for Arab/Jewish Accommodation

Epigraphs: Jewish Agency for Palestine, *The Jewish plan for Palestine: Memoranda and statements* (Jerusalem, 1947), 89; Abraham Granovsky, "Land settlement and development in Palestine," *Palestine & Near East Economic Magazine,* 6: 2–3 (1931): 33.

1. A convenient source for the documents cited here is Palestine Government, *A Survey of Palestine,* prepared in December 1945 and January 1946 for the information of the Anglo-American Committee of Inquiry, vols. 1–3 (Jerusalem, 1946). See, too, vol. 1, 4–11.

2. Two essays trace the evolution of the Zionist attitude toward Palestine's Arabs. See Alan Dowty, "Much ado about little: Ahad Ha-Am's 'Truth from Eretz Israel,' " *Israel Studies,* 5: 2 (Fall 2000): 154–81, and " 'A question that outweighs all others': Yitzhak Epstein and Zionist recognition of the Arab issue," *Israel Studies,* 6: 1 (Spring 2001): 34–54.

3. Isaiah Friedman, *The question of Palestine 1914–1918: British-Jewish-Arab relations* (New York, 1973); Leonard Stein, *The Balfour Declaration* (London, 1961).

4. My emphasis.

5. On the internal debate over partition and its dimensions see Yossi Katz,

Partner to partition: The Jewish Agency's partition plan in the Mandate era (London, 1998); Itzhak Galnoor, *Partition of Palestine: Decision crossroads in the Zionist movement* (Albany, 1995). See, too, Baruch Ben-Avram and Henry Near, *Studies in the third aliyah (1919–1924)* (Hebrew) (Jerusalem, 1995), 138–68.

6. A leading proponent of the thesis that "transfer" of the Arab population was a deep and central part of Zionist ideology and praxis has been Benny Morris. A useful way into the controversy is provided by Arieh Naor, in "A Matter of distoriography: Efraim Karsh, the "new historians" of Israel, their methodologies and perspective," *Israel Studies*, 6: 2 (Fall 2001): 139–50.

7. Nahum Karlinsky, *Citrus blossoms: Jewish entrepreneurship in Palestine, 1890–1939* (Hebrew) (Jerusalem, 2000).

8. Esco Foundation for Palestine, *Palestine: A study of Jewish, Arab, and British policies*, vol. 2, 687–92.

9. In the ongoing debate over the character of the Yishuv, I rely on Dan Horowitz and Moshe Lissak, *Origins of the Israeli polity: Palestine under the Mandate* (Chicago, 1978). For a recent discussion of the topic of the "bubble" and the debate it engenders see M. Lissak, " 'Critical' sociology and 'establishment' sociology in the Israeli academic community: ideological struggles or academic discourse," *Israel Studies*, 1: 1 (Spring 1996): 262–69. In the final analysis Palestine was effectively divided into two societies prior to proposals for partition in 1937 of the Mandate into discrete political entities or an Arab and a Jewish state. The explanations and the assessment of responsibility or guilt will continue to be the subject for debate. Here, the important issue is that Zionist planners took as a "given" that discrete communities would necessarily develop.

10. The Palestine Potash Company is the subject of Chapter 7. For the Palestine Electric Company, a parallel company, see Eli She'altiel, *Pinchas Ruttenberg: The rise and fall of a "strong man" in Eretz Israel, 1879–1942* (Hebrew) (Tel Aviv, 1990).

11. Deborah Bernstein, *Constructing boundaries: Jewish and Arab workers in Mandatory Palestine* (Albany, N.Y., 2000), 213.

12. Esco Foundation for Palestine, *Palestine: A study of Jewish, Arab, and British policies*, 697 ff., and David Horowitz, *Industry in Palestine: Achievements and possibilities* (Tel Aviv, 1941).

13. Lissak, " 'Critical' sociology and 'establishment' sociology," 264.

14. Useful indicators have been provided by the economic historian Jacob Metzer, who employed the Human Development Index (HDI), a statistical instrument designed "to measure investments in physical and cultural well-being as a means to achieve the prime development goal of increasing people's overall access to goods and services." According to the HDI, in 1939 the Yishuv ranked ahead of several European countries: Czechoslovakia, Italy, Hungary, and Greece. Together with Thailand, it ranked ahead of non-European countries. Finally, it was far ahead of the Palestinian Arab community. Jacob Metzer, *The divided economy of Mandatory Palestine* (Cambridge, 1998), 55–58. Other useful studies closer to the period include David Horowitz, *Economic trends of Jewish development* (Jerusalem, 1947).

15. For a convenient summary see the Jewish Agency for Palestine, *The Jewish case: Before the Anglo-American Committee of Inquiry on Palestine: Statements and memoranda* (Jerusalem, 1947).

16. Metzer, *The divided economy of Mandatory Palestine*, 12.

17. Ibid., 17.

18. Ibid., 19.

19. Quoted in *The Jewish plan for Palestine: Memoranda and statements presented by the Jewish Agency for Palestine to the United Nations Special Committee on Palestine* (Jerusalem, 1947), 113.

20. A concise summary of these claims can be found in *The Jewish plan for Palestine*, 113–25.

21. Theodor Herzl, *Altneuland*, trans. Paula Arnold (Haifa, 1960), 185.

22. Quoted in Alan Dowty, " 'A question that outweighs all others'," *Israel Studies*.

23. For a general review of Zionist thought concerning the benefits Jewish colonization would bring to Arabs see Anita Shapira, *Land and power: The Zionist resort to force, 1881–1948* (New York, 1992), 40–52.

24. Shimon Peres, with Arye Naor, *The new Middle East* (New York, 1993), 98.

25. *Report to the General Assembly by the U.N. Special Committee on Palestine: Geneva, 31 August 1947*, 53.

26. Rashid Khalidi, *Palestinian identity: The construction of modern national consciousness* (New York, 1997), 9–34. Other pertinent sources are Yehoshua Porath, *The emergence of the Palestinian–Arab national movement, 1918–1929* (London, 1974), and *The Palestinian–Arab national movement: From riots to rebellion, 1929–1939* (London, 1977).

27. Moshe Shemesh, *The Palestinian entity, 1919–1974: Arab politics and the PLO* (London, 1996); Yehoshafat Harkabi, *The Palestinian covenant and its meaning* (London, 1981).

28. Abraham Granovsky, "Land settlement and development in Palestine," *Palestine & Near East Economic Magazine*, 6: 2–3 (1931): 25–62. See, too, Kenneth W. Stein, *The land question in Palestine, 1917–1939* (Chapel Hill, N.C., 1984), chap. 5.

29. Granovsky, "Land settlement and development in Palestine," 32–33, 62.

30. Ibid., 38–49.

31. Ibid., 33.

32. Ibid.

33. On the issue of character of Zionist settlement see Ran Aaronsohn for the noncolonialist argument: "Settlement in Eretz-Israel—a colonialist enterprise: 'Critical' scholarship and historical geography," *Israel Studies*, 1: 2 (Fall 1996): 214–29. The contrary view can be found in Amir Ben-Porat, "They did not lie on the fence: Opportunity, longing and the breakthrough to Palestine" (Hebrew), *Iyunim be'Tekumat Israel*, 4 (1993), 278–98; Gershon Shafir, "Land, labor and population in Zionist colonization: General and specific aspects," in Uri Ram, ed. (Hebrew), *Israeli society: Critical aspects* (Tel Aviv, 1993).

34. Dispossession by force occurred only after the Mandate and during the fierce Arab/Jewish conflict that brought Israel into existence. See Benny Morris, *The birth of the Palestinian refugee problem, 1947–1949* (Cambridge, 1987).

35. Granovsky, "Land settlement and development in Palestine," 54–56.

36. Martin Buber, ed., *Towards the nature of the Hebrew village in Eretz Israel* (Hebrew) (Jerusalem, 1946); *Paths in utopia* (London, 1949).

37. For a succinct analysis of the origins and development of the attempt to blend nationalism and universal humanistic perspectives see George Mosse, "Can nationalism be saved? About Zionism, rightful and unjust nationalism," *Israel Studies*, 2: 1 (Spring 1997): 156–73.

38. This conception in the Ottoman Empire led to the development of the

millet system, which provided an individual with rights that depended on the privileges enjoyed by the religious community or millet to which he belonged. The millet was self-governing in its internal affairs: its head, elected by the community and with the confirmation of the Sultan, had just enough executive power to enable him to collect the taxes imposed on his community by the state.

39. The Palestinian reassessment of the economic absorptive capacity appears in the Palestinian press and in Egypt's *Al Ahram.* "Battle for 'Right of Return' taking shape," *Arutz-7 News,* Wednesday, March 22, 2000 (*http://www.ArutzSheva.org*).

Chapter 4. The Village as Military Outpost

1. Doreen Warriner, *Land reform in principle and practice* (Oxford, 1969), 68.

2. Henry Near, *The kibbutz movement, a history: Origins and growth, 1909–1939,* vol. 1 (Oxford, 1992), 175.

3. Calculations derive from Alex Bein, *Immigration and settlement in the State of Israel* (Hebrew) (Tel Aviv, 1982), 260–98.

4. An excellent collection of papers relating to this phenomenon is to be found in the Ra'anan Weitz Papers at the Central Zionist Archives in Jerusalem (CZA). The Security Principles are in file S/15/9786. For additional materials and correspondence see files 8747; 313610; 15/82461.

5. Emmanuel Yalan, *The design of agricultural settlements: Technological aspects of rural community development* (Jerusalem, 1975), 16 ff. This topic is discussed extensively in Chapter 10.

6. For the original plan see Richard Kauffmann, *Die Begauungsplane der Kleinsiedlungen Kfar-Nahalal und Kfar Yecheskiel* (Jerusalem, 1923). An early indication of intentions is in Jacob Ettinger *The village of Nahalal: How the Keren ha-Yesod builds new villages in Palestine on the land of the Jewish National Fund* (London, 1924). Other important sources are Shmuel Dayan, *Man and the soil: The history of the first four decades of Nahalal* (Tel Aviv, 1965); Samuel Dayan, *Nahalal* (Tel Aviv, 1936); and the Center for the Study of Rural and Urban Settlement, *Not by bread alone: Continuity and change in moshav Nahalal* (Hebrew) (Rehovoth, 1974).

7. See note 5.

8. Near, *The kibbutz movement,* 314 ff.

9. Kenneth W. Stein, *The land question in Palestine, 1917–1939* (Chapel Hill, N.C., 1984), 207, and Elhanan Orren, *Settlement amidst struggles: Settlement strategy prior to the State 1936–1947* (Hebrew) (Jerusalem, 1978), 62–63, 86–89.

10. Moshe Sharett, *Political diary* (Hebrew) (Tel Aviv, 1971), 2, 172–63. For an analysis of Sharett's role in shaping policy during this period see Motti Golani, "Moshe Shertok (Sharett)—The statesman of 'stockade and tower,'" in Mordechai Naor, ed., *The days of stockade and tower, 1936–1939* (Hebrew) (Jerusalem, 1987), 51–60.

11. A pertinent review is found in Kenneth Stein, "One hundred years of social change: The creation of the Palestinian refugee problem," in Laurence Silberstein, ed., *New perspectives on Israeli history: The early years of the state* (New York, 1991), 57–81. See, too, Abraham Granott, *The land system in Palestine: History and structure,* trans. H. Simon (London, 1952).

12. Stein, *The land question,* 211, and Orren, *Settlement amidst struggles,* 22–28.

13. Near, *The kibbutz movement,* 326; and Nachumi Har-Zion, "From the top

of the tower—songs of the days of tower and stockade" (Hebrew), in Naor, *The days of stockade and tower*, 193–204.

14. Joseph Weitz, *The struggle for land* (Hebrew) (Tel Aviv, 1950).

15. Ruth Kark, "The expansive settlement of the Negev in the decade prior to the establishment of the State" (Hebrew) in *Settling the Negev, 1900–1960* (Jerusalem, 1986), 81–99, and Shalom Reichman, *From foothold to settled territory: The Jewish settlement, 1918–1948: A geographical interpretation and documentation* (Hebrew) (Jerusalem, 1979).

16. Orren, *Settlement amidst struggles*.

17. There is a considerable literature on the development of Zionist military organizations and of the Israeli army. See Ze'ev Schiff, *A history of the Israeli army: 1874 to the present* (London, 1987), and Edward Luttwak and Dan Horowitz, *The Israeli army* (London, 1975).

18. Yochanan Ratner, *My life and myself* (Hebrew) (Tel Aviv, 1978), 249–56.

19. Ratner, *My life and myself*, 349 ff. Kisch also wrote an interesting memoir of this period. See Frederick Kisch, *Palestine diary, by Lt.-Colonel F. H. Kisch* (London, 1938), and Norman Bentwich, *Brigadier Frederick Kisch: Soldier and Zionist* (London, 1966).

Chapter 5. Tel Aviv

Epigraphs: Nathan Shaham, *The Rosendorf quartet* (New York, 1987), 273; Nathan Shaham, *The Rosendorf quartet*, 276–77.

1. Theodor Herzl, *Old-New land (Altneuland)*, trans. Lotta Levensohn (New York, 1941), 218.

2. Amos Elon, *Herzl* (New York, 1975), 348.

3. Herzl, *Old-New land*, 175–76.

4. Ibid., 127.

5. Ibid., 128.

6. Ibid., 195.

7. The idea of the booster is developed in Daniel Boorstin, *The Americans: The national experience* (New York, 1965), 113–68. The transnational nature of planning is captured in Anthony Sutcliffe, *Towards the planned city: Germany, Britain, the United States and France, 1870–1914* (Oxford, 1981); Andrew Lees, *Cities perceived: Urban society in European and American thought, 1820–1920* (New York, 1985); Daniel Rodgers, *Atlantic crossings: Social politics in a progressive age* (Cambridge, Mass., 1998); Selwyn Troen, "The diffusion of an urban social science: France, England and the United States in the nineteenth century," *Comparative Social Research*, 9 (1986): 247–66; and Gideon Biger, "European influence on town planning and town building in Palestine, 1850–1920, *Urbanism Past and Present*, 9 (1984): 30–35. The present chapter places Zionist urban development within this western context.

8. Meir Dizengoff (1861–1937) served as one of the leaders of the company that organized in 1906 to build Tel Aviv and then as head of the local council from 1911 to 1921. The office was subsequently transformed into that of Mayor in a reconstituted municipal government. For background see Yossi Katz, "Ideology and urban development: Zionism and the origins of Tel-Aviv, 1906–1914," *Journal of Historical Geography*, 12 (1986): 402–24. See, too, Mordechai Naor, ed., *Tel-Aviv at its beginnings, 1909–1934* (Hebrew) (Jerusalem, 1984).

9. Clifford Holliday, "Town and Country Planning in Palestine," *Palestine & Middle East Economic Magazine*, 7–8 (1933): 290–92.

10. Ibid.

11. For the significance of the Vienna model see Avraham Zaberski, "Basic Problems in Housing Workers" (Hebrew) *Ma'asim u'Magamot* (1942): 169–93; Walter Preuss, "The socialist urban settlement movement in Austria" (Hebrew) *Pinkas*, 3 (1924): 22–24; Iris Graicer "Social architecture in Palestine: Conceptions in working-class housing, 1920–1938," in Ruth Kark, ed., *The land that became Israel: Studies in historical geography* (New Haven, 1989), 287–307. On the European background see Josef Weidenhalzer, "Red Vienna: A new Atlantis?" in Anson Rabinach, ed., *The Austrian socialist experiment—Social democracy and Austro-Marxism 1918–1979* (Boulder, Colo., 1985), 195–99; Charles A. Gulick, *Austria from Habsburg to Hitler* (Berkeley, 1948), 391–400. Middle-class Vienna is examined in Carl Schorske, *Fin-de-siècle Vienna* (New York, 1979). For a more nuanced view of the multitude of models that had an impact on the city see Anat Helman, "East or west: Tel-Aviv in the 1920s and 1930s," in Ezra Mendelsohn, ed., *Studies in contemporary Jewry* (Oxford, 1999), vol. 15, 68–79.

12. Quoted in Ben-Zion Kedar, *Looking twice at the Land of Israel* (Hebrew) (Tel Aviv, 1992), 94.

13. Meir Dizengoff, "Concerning the history of Tel Aviv" (Hebrew), Feb. 13, 1931, Tel Aviv Municipal Archives, IV/1305/14–17.

14. Abraham Yaffa, *The first twenty years: Literature and art in "Little Tel-Aviv" 1909–1929* (Hebrew) (Tel Aviv, 1980); Meir Dizengoff, *And it came to pass on the fiftieth jubilee year* (Hebrew), 1929, Tel Aviv Municipal Archives; Dizengoff, *On the history of Tel-Aviv.*

15. "City advertisement," 1927, Tel Aviv Municipal Archives, IV/14/7.

16. The same theme was expressed in Herzl's *Old-New land.* For example: "We made the New Society not because we were better than others, but simply because we were ordinary men with the ordinary human needs for air and light, health and honor, for the right to acquire property and security of possession" (154); "The vast works of colonization had required a large staff of trained engineers, jurists and administrators. Large opportunities were suddenly opened to educated young men who in the anti-Semitic times had no sphere for the exercise of their skill. Jewish university graduates, men trained in the technological institutes and commercial colleges, used to flounder helplessly; but now there was ample room for them in the public and private undertakings so numerous in Palestine" (177); "The Jews had, as a matter of fact, long been among the most ingenious *entrepreneurs.* . . . We could be no less enterprising in Palestine than elsewhere" (195).

17. "Municipal Matter" (Hebrew) *Yediot Iriyat Tel-Aviv*, vol. 2 (December 1932): 6; Chaim Nachman Bialik, "Tel-Aviv—The Homeland" (Hebrew), *Yediot Iriyat Tel-Aviv*, vol. 4 (January 1933): 97.

18. Meir Dizengoff, *Small housing estates* (Hebrew), Tel Aviv Municipal Archives, n.d., II/6/3. See also Meir Dizengoff, "The Future of Tel-Aviv" (Hebrew), *The city of Tel-Aviv: Its needs and future: A collection of articles for the elections to the fifth city council of the municipality of Tel-Aviv*, 1932, *Dizengoff Papers* (Archives of the Museum of the History of Tel Aviv).

19. This issue is discussed extensively in Chapter 8, which focuses on the "economic absorptive capacity" of Palestine.

20. Vladimir Jabotinsky, "The meaning of Tel-Aviv," *Near East Economic Magazine*, vol. 4 (April 9, 1929): 110.

21. Meir Dizengoff, "Credit help for industry and for a small part of middle industry," 1929, *Dizengoff Papers*, II/6; Meir Dizengoff, "Opportunities for the economic development of Palestine," ca. 1926, *Dizengoff Papers*, II/6; and Avraham Esterman, "Build cheap dwellings for those who live in huts!" from Dizengoff, *The city of Tel-Aviv*, 32.

22. The details and rationale of Dizengoff's voyage to America are extensively described in his diary, "Dizengoff Diary: May 12, 1923–August 16, 1923," *Dizengoff Papers*. See, too, his letter to Mr. Conheim of New York, Dec. 7, 1922 *Dizengoff Papers*, IV, 1/1518. The reaction to Dizengoff's appeal is found in "M. Dizengoff, the Mayor of Tel-Aviv arrived yesterday with an important message to American Jews" (Yiddish) *Der Tog*, May 30, 1923, and "Tel-Aviv" (Yiddish) *Der Tog*, May 31, 1923.

23. Dizengoff-Weizmann correspondence, *Dizengoff Papers*, II/25.

24. Meir Dizengoff, "Election speech, November 18, 1929" (Hebrew), *Dizengoff Papers*.

25. Even as Tel Aviv remained a bastion of middle-class Zionism, it failed to translate that power to control of the national institutions. This problem has led historians to speculate on this failure. See Yigal Drori, "The organization of the middle class in Eretz Yisrael: Attempts at political organization in the 1920's" (Hebrew) *Cathedra*, 44 (June 1987): 116–25; Dan Giladi, "Private initiative, national wealth, and the political crystallization of the right" (Hebrew) *Avanim*, 5 (1965): 90–102; and Baruch Ben-Avram, *Political parties and organization during the British Mandate, 1918–1948* (Hebrew) (Jerusalem, 1978), chap. 3.

26. The standard view of the anti-urban bias of Zionist planning can be found in Erik Cohen, "The city in Zionist ideology," *Jerusalem Urban Studies*, vol. 1 (1970): 1–62; Arieh Schahar, "Israel's development towns: Evaluation of national urbanization policy," *Journal of the American Institute of Planners*, 37 (1971): 362–72; Elisabeth Altman and Betsey Rosenbaum, "Principles of planning and Zionist ideology: The Israeli development town," *Journal of the American Institution of Planners* (1973): 316–25. For the standard agricultural orientation of Zionist settlement history see Yosef Gorny, *From Rosh Pina and Degania to Dimona: A history of constructive Zionism* (Hebrew) (Tel Aviv, 1989); Haim Gvati, *100 Years of settlement: A history of Jewish settlement in Eretz-Yisrael* (Hebrew) (Tel Aviv, 1981); and Alexander Bein, *Immigration and settlement in Eretz Yisrael* (Hebrew) (Tel Aviv, 1982).

27. Avraham Ulitzur, *National capital and upbuilding Palestine: Facts and figures* (Hebrew) (Jerusalem, 1939), 134.

28. For the negative side to these developments, a worthwhile analysis of a leading Labor figure is Shlomo Avineri, *Arlosoroff* (London, 1989), 38–59.

29. As we have seen in Chapter 4, the rationale for rural projects is also strategic. See Elhanan Orren, "Settlement as a basis for independence, 1878–1949" (Hebrew), *Skirah Hodshit* (March–April 1982): 12–33.

30. Gerhard Muenzer, *Jewish labour economy in Palestine: The economic activities of the General Federation of Jewish Labour* (Hebrew) (Jerusalem, 1943), 122–27, 172–80; David Horowitz and Rita Hinden, *Economic survey of Palestine* (Jerusalem, 1938), 111–12.

31. A wealth of information can be found in municipal publications. See, for example, "On the question of rentals in Tel-Aviv: Memorandum by the Tel-

Aviv municipality to the Mandatory government, May 1925" (Hebrew) *Yediot Tel-Aviv,* vol. 2–3, Sept. 15, 1925, 16–20. The Labor movement is the other essential source of statistics and analysis. See General Federation of Labor, *Collection of essays on workers' housing estates* (Hebrew) (Tel Aviv, 1927); Engineers', Architects' and Surveyors' Union of Palestine, *Twenty years of building, settlement, housing and institutions for workers* (Hebrew) (Tel Aviv, 1940); Leo Kauffmann, "Housing urban workers" (Hebrew), *Hameshek HaShitufi,* 1 (1933): 42–45, 60–63, 82–85; A. Eserov, "The housing problem in Palestine," *Palestine and Near East,* 1: 8 (1926): 290–92; General Federation of Labor, *In the thirtieth year: Surveys and summaries* (Hebrew), 52, 256 ff. See, too, Iris Graicer, "Workers' estates: socio-ideological experimentations in shaping the urban scene in Palestine during the British Mandate" (Hebrew) (unpublished Ph.D. thesis, Hebrew University of Jerusalem, 1982).

32. "Memorandum by the Tel-Aviv Municipality on the question of rentals in Tel-Aviv" (Hebrew), 16–18, and Meir Dizengoff, "Proposals for the solution of the barrack housing problems in Tel Aviv" (Hebrew), Tel Aviv Municipal Archives, IV/1/31/AB, 1931.

33. The activities in 1923 are well-recorded and inaugurate the movement for housing reform. See "The third council of Achdut Ha'Avodah" (Hebrew) *Kuntress,* 6 (1923), chap. 3.

34. For the Bauhaus in Israel see Michael Levine, *White city: Architecture in the international style in Israel* (Hebrew) (Tel Aviv, 1984); Michael Levine, "Architects who brought the Bauhaus to Israel" (Hebrew) *Kav,* 2 (1981): 65–72; Arieh Sharon, *Kibbutz + Bauhaus: Arieh Sharon: The way of an architect; an exhibition organized by the Bauhaus Archive together with the Academy of Arts, Berlin* (Stuttgart, 1976); *From planning to reality: An exhibition of plans and photographs representing the work of Richard Kauffmann* (Jerusalem, 1977).

35. In addition to *Kovetz Shchunat Ha-Ovdim,* the Hebrew newspaper associated with the General Federation of Labor, *Davar,* carried important articles discussing the principles of workers' housing estates. See, for example, "How we will build workers' neighborhoods" (Hebrew) *Davar,* Oct. 28, 1925; "The questions of workers neighborhoods" (Hebrew), *Davar,* Feb. 4, 1927; "From the meetings of the organizations for workers' neighborhoods" (Hebrew), *Davar,* April 28, 1927; "The bridge between the city and the village" (Hebrew), *Davar,* June 12, 1927.

36. Arieh Sharon, "Planning of cooperative houses," *Habinyan—A Magazine of Architecture and Town-Planning* (August 1937): 1–3. On the European background see John Mullin, "Ideology, planning theory and the German city in the inter-war years," *Town Planning Review,* 53 (1982): 115–30, 257–72; Peter Marcuse, "The housing policy of social democracy: Determinants and consequences," in Rabinach, ed., *The Austrian socialist experiment,* 201–21. Some excellent detail is contained in L. Orgad, "Workers' Housing Estates" (Hebrew) in *Tel-Aviv, 1931–1937: Conceptions, planning, construction and comparison with popular housing in Europe* (Hebrew) (M.A. thesis in art and art history, Tel Aviv University, 1985).

37. On European background see Mullin, "Ideology, planning theory and the German city," 127; Helmut Gruber, "Socialist party culture and the realities of working-class life in Red Vienna," in Rabinach, ed., *The Austrian socialist experiment,* 223–46. For extension to Palestine see "From the meetings of the organizations for workers' neighborhoods" (Hebrew), *Davar,* April 28, 1927, and "The bridge between the city and the village" (Hebrew), *Davar,* June 12, 1927.

38. Gideon Kressel, *Shchunat Borochov: The history of the first workers' housing estate* (Hebrew) (Tel Aviv, 1961), 19–25. For the continued application of these principles see Zvi Ganin, *Kiryat Hayyim: An experiment in an urban utopia, 1933–1983* (Hebrew) (Tel Aviv, 1984), 44–45.

39. Muenzer, *Jewish labour economy in Palestine*, 180.

40. Two outstanding analyses of the difficulties in perpetuating such societies are Stanley Buder, *Pullman: An experiment in industrial order and community planning, 1880–1930* (New York, 1967), and Rosabeth Kanter, *Commitment and community: Communes and utopias in sociological perspective* (Cambridge, 1972). There have been repeated attempts to adapt the kibbutz to the city. See, for example, Shmuel Gelbatz, *Urban commune* (Hebrew) (Tel Aviv, 1940), and Dan Yahav, *Communes in Tel-Aviv during the thirties and forties* (Hebrew) (Ramat Efal, 1990).

Chapter 6. Urban Alternatives

1. The standard scholarly view is stated in Erik Cohen, "The city in Zionist ideology." An early and important critique of the rural preference can be found in Eliezer Brutzkus, "The question of urban settlement" (Hebrew), *Handasa Ve'adrichalut*, 5 (1944), 13–14, and *Physical planning in Israel: Problems and achievements* (Jerusalem, 1964).

2. Arnon Soffer and Baruch Kipnis, eds., *Atlas of Haifa and Mount Carmel* (Haifa, 1980), 48.

3. S. Ilan Troen, "Higher education in Israel: An historical perspective," *Higher education: The International Journal of Higher Education and Educational Planning*, 23: 1 (January 1992): 45–63.

4. Gilbert Herbert and Silvina Sosnovsky, *Bauhaus on the Carmel and the crossroads of empire* (Jerusalem, 1993), 20–33.

5. Yossi Katz, "The founding and beginning of Herzlia neighborhood—The first Hebrew neighborhood on Mt. Carmel" (Hebrew), *Ofakim*, no. 8 (1983): 49–56.

6. Alex Carmel, "Haifa at the end of the Ottoman period" (Hebrew), in Mordechai Naor and Yossi Ben-Artzi, eds., *The development of Haifa 1918–1948* (Jerusalem, 1977), 2–19.

7. Soffer and Kipnis, eds., *Atlas of Haifa and Mount Carmel*, 52.

8. See FO371/272–73, Jan. 29, 1919 (Public Record Office, London). For an overview of the British role in the development of the city see Yonatan Fein, "The development of the port of Haifa in British policy 1906–1924: Strategic considerations" (Hebrew) *Cathedra*, 89 (October 1998): 127–54.

9. See FO371/272–73, "Confidential Memorandum," by Lt. Col. E. A. Stanton, 24 December 1918 (Public Record Office, London).

10. FO371/12278/63, Dec. 15, 1927 (Public Record Office, London).

11. FO371/13020/p. 154, "Desert Railway: Haifa–Baghdad," note by Brig. General H. O. Mance, 21 September 1927 (Public Record Office, London).

12. FO371/13020/p. 154, "Desert Railway: Haifa—Baghdad note by Brig. General H. O. Mance, 15 September 1927" (Public Record Office, London).

13. David Horowitz, "Economic and Geographic Position," in Sophie Udin, ed., *Palestine year book 5708* (New York, 1947), 113; Herbert Sidebotham, *Great Britain and Palestine* (London, 1937), 120–28.

14. Samuel Tenenbaum, "The future of Palestine: An interview with Harry Sacher of the Zionist Executive," *Jewish Tribune*, Oct. 12, 1928.

15. Ibid.

16. For a discussion of how this policy led to the creation of Israel Bonds, the logical conclusion of the philosophy supported by members of the Palestine Economic Corporation, see S. Ilan Troen, "American experts in the design of Zionist society: The reports of Elwood Mead and Robert Nathan," in Allon Gal, ed., *Envisioning Israel: The changing ideals and images of North American Jews* (Jerusalem, 1996), 204–18.

17. Abraham Granovsky, "Haifa Bay land policy," *Palestine & Near East Economic Magazine*, 4: 4–5 (March 20, 1929), 74–75.

18. *Report of activities of the Palestine Economic Corporation presented to the Palestine Royal Commission* (New York, 1936), 24; Kurt Ruppin, "Haifa Bay Progress: Garden cities and industries arise on reclaimed wasteland," *Palestine & Middle East Economic Magazine*, 12: 23 (1940): 336.

19. Kurt Ruppin, "Haifa Bay progress," 333.

20. Richard Kauffmann, "Preliminary regional scheme for opening up the territory of Haifa Bay, Palestine," *Town Planning Review*, 12: 3 (June 1927): 210; Richard Kauffmann, "Problems of the organic development of Haifa," *Palestine & Near East Economic Magazine*, 4: 4–5 (March 20, 1929): 68–69, 80; Richard Kauffmann, "Fundamental problems of Haifa's future development,"*Palestine & Near East Economic Magazine*, 3: 19 (Oct. 10, 1928): 433–35. Kauffmann's criticisms were complemented by those of a premier British architect-planner, Clifford Holliday, who frequently visited Palestine. See Clifford Holliday, "Town and country planning in Palestine," *Palestine & Middle East Economic Magazine*, 7–8 (1933): 290–92.

21. Kauffmann, "Preliminary regional scheme," 206–11.

22. The information and details in this section derive largely from the archives of the Palestine Potash Company, which have been organized within the David Tuviyahu Archives on the History of the Settlement of the Negev at Ben-Gurion University's Aranne Library in Beer-Sheva. This large collection was organized under my supervision through a grant from the Dead Sea Works, the successor company to Palestine Potash, and the sponsorship of Yad Ben-Zvi. Much secondary literature has been cited in S. Ilan Troen, "The price of partition, 1948: The dissolution of the Palestine Potash Company," *Journal of Israeli History*, 15: 1 (Spring 1994): 53–83. Central items include Moshe Novomeysky, *My Siberian life* (London, 1956), and *Given to salt: The struggle for the Dead Sea concession* (London, 1958); Mordechai Naor, ed., *The Dead Sea and the Judean desert, 1900–1967* (Hebrew) (Jerusalem 1990); Israel Brody, *The true story of Palestine Potash Ltd.* (Jerusalem, 1950).

23. No author, *The light of Abraham, light from fire: The electric company and the Haganah, 1920–1948* (Hebrew) (Tel Aviv, 1994), 42–43. For the history of the company and its founder see Eli She'altiel, *Pinchas Ruttenberg: The rise and fall of a "strong man" in Eretz Israel, 1879–1942* (Hebrew) (Tel Aviv, 1990).

24. Moshe Novomeysky, *The truth about the concession for the Dead Sea* (Hebrew) (Tel Aviv, 1950), 7–8.

25. Yehuda Almog and Ben-Zion Eshel, *The Sodom region* (Hebrew) (Tel Aviv, 1949), 179–80, 270–72, 318–21.

26. Troen, "The price of partition, 1948"; Susan Lee Hattis, *The bi-national idea in Palestine during the Mandate times* (Haifa, 1970).

27. Ya'acov Ardon, "Catching up in Afula," *Jerusalem Post*, Jan. 26, 1973. The history of Afula can be readily accessed through anniversary volumes of its

founding. See, for example, Abraham Mash, ed., *The city of Jezreel—Afula at twenty-five, 1925–1950* (Hebrew) (Afula, 1950).

28. Numerous clippings (in Hebrew) are found in the Afula file at the Kressel Collection in Oxford including Abraham Mash, "Towards the development of Afula: The City of the Valley" *Davar*, Nov. 26, 1947. "Afula; the regional hospital to be established in Afula," *Davar*, Aug. 26, 1952; "The progress of the City of the Valley will be presented," *Davar*, March 31, 1952.

29. Daniel Boorstin, *The Americans: The national experience* (New York, 1965, vol. 2.

Chapter 7. "Imagined Communities"

1. Benedict Anderson, *Imagined communities: Reflections on the origins and spread of nationalism* (New York, 1991).

2. Herbert Sidebotham, *Great Britain and Palestine* (London, 1937), 118; Shalom Reichman, *From foothold to settled territory: The Jewish settlement, 1918–1948: A geographical interpretation and documentation* (Hebrew) (Jerusalem, 1979), 80 ff.

3. Michael Levine, *White city: International style architecture in Israel: Portrait of an era* (Hebrew) (Tel Aviv, 1984).

4. David Horowitz and Rita Hinden, *Economic survey of Palestine; with special reference to the years 1936 and 1937* (Jerusalem, 1938), 35.

5. Michael Levine, "Architects who brought the Bauhaus to Israel" (Hebrew) *Kav*, 2 (1981): 65–72.

6. Arieh Sharon, *Kibbutz + Bauhaus: An architect's way in a new land* (Stuttgart, 1976).

7. Oskar Beyer, *Eric Mendelsohn: Letters of an architect* (London, 1967); Arnold Whittick, *Eric Mendelsohn* (London, 1956).

8. Richard Kauffmann, "Planning of Jewish settlements in Palestine," *Town Planning Review*, 12 (1926): 93–116; Keren Hayesod, *From planning to reality: An exhibition of plans and photographs representing the work of Richard Kauffmann* (Jerusalem, 1977).

9. Gordon Cherry, *The evolution of British town planning* (New York, 1974); John Sheail, "Interwar planning in Britain: The wider context," *Journal of Urban History*, 2 (1985): 335–51.

10. The major sources of information on Geddes and his work in Palestine are the Central Zionist Archives (hereafter, CZA), in Jerusalem, and the *Geddes Papers* in the National Library of Scotland in Edinburgh.

11. August 1 and 21, 1921, *Times* (London). See, too, Patrick Geddes, "The Zionist university," *Sociological Review*, 17 (1925): 223–24; *Geddes Papers*, MS 10574; MS 10573; and *The proposed Hebrew University of Jerusalem: A preliminary report 1919*, in MS 10613. An interesting illustration of the assumed relationship between physical and social forms can be found in Geddes's plans for the Hebrew University. He initially planned the Senate Building in 1919 as a hexagon or the six-pointed Jewish star. The building was to represent the fundamental unity of knowledge while from each of the points a separate faculty building was to have originated. Intensive and often disappointing contacts with university professors and Zionist authorities suggested a different form ten years later: "The fact is that Jews can't or won't work together—the proper plan for their university would be one with an infinite number of dispersed cells each with

a rostrum on the top. They can't bear getting together." *Geddes Papers, MS 10573,*
173.

12. CZA, L18/50/5, ZTP/20/44, Z/54/898, Z4/2790.

13. See for example Patrick Geddes, *Town planning report—Jaffa and Tel Aviv,*
1925 in CZA Z/34 v4459; *Town planning handbook of Palestine, 1930* (Jerusalem,
1930). An excellent source of materials is found in the section "Urban Development" in the periodical *Palestine and Middle East* from the late 1930s through
the mid-1940s.

14. CZA, Z/1/44, Z/Z/44, Z/23/45, and Z/21/1946; Henry Kendall, *Town plan-*
ning in Uganda: A brief description of the efforts made by Government to control de-
velopment of urban areas from 1915 to 1955 (Entebbe, 1955), 19–20. For his work in
Palestine, see Henry Kendall, *Village development in Palestine during the Mandate*
(London, 1949), and *Town planning adviser: Annual report for 1937* (Jerusalem, 1937).

15. Kauffmann, *Planning of Jewish settlements in Palestine;* and Keren Hayesod,
From planning to reality.

16. See Ya'acov Ben-Sira, "My work as the municipal engineer of Tel Aviv
(1929–1951)" (Hebrew) *Gazit,* 33 (1984): 171–74.

17. Among the important British reports that influenced planning in Palestine were the Barlow Report of 1940 (*Royal Commission on the Distribution of the*
Industrial Population) and the Uthwatt Report of 1942 (*Report of the Expert Commit-*
tee on Compensation and Betterment). For local recognition of the British importance to planning see Karl Baruth, *The physical planning of Israel: The legal and*
technical basis (London, 1949). For an overview of the international context of
postwar planning see Leonardo Benevolo, *History of modern architecture* (Cambridge, 1977), vol. 2, chaps. 19 and 20.

18. Eugen Ratner, "Architecture in Palestine," *Palestine & Middle East Eco-*
nomic Magazine, nos. 7–8 (1933): 293–97.

19. Ibid.

20. Ibid.

21. Eugen Ratner, "Architecture in Palestine," 296. See also Eugen Ratner,
"Will Israel have a national style of architecture?" *Technion Year Book* (Haifa,
1950): 234–37.

22. Levin, *White city.*

23. Meron Benvenisti, *Sacred landscape: The buried history of the Holy Land since*
1948 (Berkeley, 2000).

24. This section relies on Emanouel Hareouveni, *The settlements of Israel and*
their archaeological sites (Givatayim-Ramat Gan, 1979) (Hebrew), and Ze'ev Vilnay,
The settlements in Israel (Hebrew) (Tel Aviv, 1951).

25. As an example of how the process worked, see discussion on the Committee for Fixing Names of Settlements under the Auspices of the National Institutions in "Names for new settlements" (Hebrew) *Davar,* Feb. 16, 1952.

26. Benvenisti, *Sacred landscape,* 12–14.

27. Hanna Bitan, ed., *1948–1998, fifty years of settlement: Atlas of names of settle-*
ments and localities in Israel (Hebrew) (Jerusalem, 1999).

28. Eliyahu Ha-Cohen, "General introduction to the songs of the moshavoth
during the first aliyah," in *The first moshavoth: Chapters in the history of the yishuv,*
a teachers' guide (Hebrew) (Tel Aviv, 1978), 81–93.

29. Chaim Nachmun Bialik, *Birkhat Am: Collected writings of Chaim Nachmun*
Bialik (Hebrew) (Tel Aviv, 1959), 6–7. This translation is by Betsy Rosenberg.

30. Typical of this genre is "Song of the Road," written by Natan Alterman with music by Daniel Sambursky during the Third Aliyah for the pioneering work brigades (*gedudei avodah*), who supported themselves by building roads, often through the financing of the Mandate or Jewish national institutions. See Yehuda Erez, "Pathmakers to the Israeli song," in Yehuda Erez, ed., *The book of the third aliyah* (Hebrew) (Tel Aviv, 1964); Yaffa Berlowitz, " 'The scale of our manual work, our star is work': The songs of labor as folk songs (1882–1948)" (Hebrew) *Iton 77*, 63 (April 1985): 24–28.

31. Yoram Bar-Gal, *Moledet and geography in a hundred years of Zionist education* (Hebrew) (Tel Aviv, 1993).

32. Jehoash Hirshberg, *Music in the Jewish community of Palestine 1880–1948* (Oxford, 1995), 78–109, 147–48.

33. Eric Hobsbaum, "Inventing tradition," in Eric Hobsbaum and Terence Ranger, eds., *The invention of tradition* (Cambridge, 1983), 1.

34. Hirschberg, *Music in the Jewish community of Palestine 1880–1948*, 184–203.

35. Gila Dobkin, *Hora songs—Their origins, history and their place in the context of Israeli songs* (Hebrew) (M.A. thesis, Department of Musicology, Faculty of Arts, Tel Aviv University, 1985).

36. Quoted in Dalia Manor, "Biblical Zionism in Bezalel Art," *Israel Studies*, 6: 1 (Spring 2001): 66.

37. Nurit Shilo-Cohen, ed., *Bezalel 1906–1929* (Jerusalem, 1983); *Boris Schatz: His life and work* (Jerusalem, 1925).

38. A brief, accessible discussion of this phenomenon can be found in Dalia Manor, "Framing the native: Esther Raab's visual poetics," *Israel Studies*, 4: 1 (Spring 1999): 234–57.

39. See Tamar Katriel, *Talking straight: Dugri speech in Israeli sabra culture* (New York, 1986), and Oz Almog, *The sabra: The creation of the new Jew* (Berkeley, 2000).

40. S. Ilan Troen, "The construction of a secular Jewish identity: European and American influences in Israeli education," in Deborah Dash Moore and S. Ilan Troen, eds., *Divergent Jewish cultures: Israel & America* (New Haven, 2001), 27–52.

41. The idea of "reconstituting" became a frequent and prominent trope leading up to the decision for partition and creation of a Jewish state. A typical example of the position is found in David Ben-Gurion's Archives before the United Nations Special Committee on Palestine on July 4, 1947: On July the 24th 1925, the Mandate for Palestine was confirmed by the Council of the League of Nations. The Mandate embodied the Balfour Declaration and he added a meaningful amplification. After citing in a preamble the text of the declaration it added, "recognition has thereby been given to the *historical connection* of the Jewish people with Palestine and to the grounds for *reconstituting* (not *constituting*—emphasis by Ben-Gurion) their national home in that country." "Evidence of Mr. David Ben-Gurion before U.N.S.C.O.P., 4th July 1947," Ben-Gurion Archives, Sede Boker.

Chapter 8. The Science and Politics of National Development

Epigraph: Mark Twain, *Innocents abroad or the new pilgrim's progress* (London, 1916), 449; David Ben-Gurion, *Like stars and dust: Essays from Israel's Government Year Book* (Sede Boker, 1997), 68–69.

1. Amir Bar-Or, "The army's role in Israeli strategic planning: A documentary record," *Israel Studies*, 1: 2 (Fall 1996): 98–121.

2. Arieh Sharon, *Physical planning in Israel* (Jerusalem, 1951).

3. Martin Buber, *Paths in utopia* (London, 1949).

4. Moshe Mossek, *Palestine immigration policy under Sir Herbert Samuel: British, Zionist and Arab attitudes* (London, 1978), 7, 157–61.

5. Mossek, *Palestine immigration policy*, 258–60; *British White Paper, Cmd. 1700*, 22–29.

6. *British White Paper, Cmd. 1700*, 17–21; Royal Institute of International Affairs, *Great Britain and Palestine, 1915–1945* (London, 1946), 60–70.

7. Robert A. Macalister, *A century of excavation in Palestine* (London, 1925); David Amiran, "The pattern of settlement in Palestine," *Israel Exploration Journal*, 3: 2 (1953): 68; *Statistical abstract of Palestine, 1944–45*, 273.

8. Claude R. Conder, "The fertility of ancient Palestine," *Palestine Exploration Fund Quarterly Statement* (July 1876): 32.

9. Charles Warren, *The land of promise* (London, 1875), 5–6.

10. Ellsworth Huntington, *Palestine and its transformation* (Boston, 1911), 4–5, 39. The book was also intended to bring a Christian message. Huntington also wished to demonstrate how the natural environment "prepared the way for the teachings of Christ." Because there was much water for supporting life during the time of the Romans, the population present to receive Christ's teachings was large. Among the proofs was that in 30 A.D., at the time of the Baptism of Christ, "the sea [of Galilee] stood high." Later, in 333 A.D., "the Dead Sea stood as low as now. A dry era." The ensuing climatic catastrophe served to disperse the people of Palestine and therefore contributed to the dissemination of Christian teachings. Huntington was also writing in a new scientific tradition that endeavored to study climatic changes and the influence of these changes on history. See also Hubert Lamb, *Climate: Present, past and future* (London, 1972), xxv–xxvi.

11. Huntington, *Palestine and its transformation*, 281–82.

12. David Ben-Gurion and Yitzhak Ben-Zvi, *Eretz Israel in the past and in the present* (Hebrew), trans. from Yiddish by David Niv (Jerusalem, 1979). In three years, 25,000 copies were sold, yielding funds that provided the main support of the American Poalei Zion, who subsidized the writing of the book.

13. Ben-Gurion and Ben-Zvi, *Eretz Israel*, 223. The formula by which they arrived at this number is interesting, if naive. They investigated how many people were living in various parts of the country at the time and compared this with the numbers indicated by archaeological or Biblically based textual evidence. In this way, they demonstrated that in many locations the contemporary population was but one-tenth of the ancient one. The conclusion was simple: because 1 million people were presently living in the area they examined, then 10 million could live there in the future. Ben-Gurion and Ben-Zvi, *Eretz Israel*, 214–22.

14. Ben-Gurion and Ben-Zvi, *Eretz Israel*, 227. For a history of the phrase "a land without a people for a people without a land," see Adam M. Garfinkle, "On the origin, meaning, use and abuse of a phrase," *Middle Eastern Studies*, 27: 4 (October 1991), 540–50.

15. William F. Albright, *The archaeology of Palestine and the Bible* (Cambridge, Mass., 1974).

16. Nelson Glueck, *Rivers in the desert: A history of the Negev* (New York, 1968), xii, 283. See also Michael Evenari, "Twenty-five years of research on runoff desert agriculture in the Middle East," in Louis Berkofsky, David Faiman and Joseph Gil, eds., *Settling the desert* (Sede Boker, 1981), 3–28.

17. Adolf Reifenberg, "The struggle between the 'Desert and the Sown,'" in *Desert research: Proceedings, international symposium held in Jerusalem, May 7–14, 1952,* sponsored by the Research Council of Israel and the United Nations Educational, Scientific, and Cultural Organization (Jerusalem, 1953): 378–91.

18. Magen Broshi, "The population of western Palestine in the Roman-Byzantine period," *Bulletin of the American Schools of Oriental Research* (1980): 1–10.

19. Aryeh Issar, "Climatic changes as the critical factor in the settlement and abandonment of the desert frontier in Israel," Sede Boker, unpublished paper, November 1987; Aryeh Issar and Haim Tsoar, "Who is to blame for the desertification of the Negev, Israel?" S. I. Solomon, M. Beran, and W. Hogg, eds., *Proceedings of a conference on: The influence of climatic change and climatic variability on the hydrologic regime and water resources: International Assocation of Hydrological Sciences, publication no. 168* (Vancouver, 1987): 577–83.

20. Walter C. Lowdermilk, *Palestine: Land of promise* (London, 1944).

21. Jean Gottmann, *Megalopolis: The urbanized northeastern seaboard of the United States* (New York, 1961).

22. Jean Gottmann, *Études sur L'état d'Israël et le Moyen Orient, 1935–1958* (Paris, 1959). His impact on Palestinian geography was such that when the Hebrew University decided to establish a chair in his discipline soon after the creation of the state, he was invited to be its first incumbent. This and other personal information derives from an interview with Jean Gottmann.

23. Robert Nathan, Oscar Gass, and Daniel Creamer, *Palestine: Problem and promise, an economic study* (Washington, D.C., 1946), v–vi.

24. Observations are from a personal interview with Robert Nathan.

25. Arthur Ruppin, *Arthur Ruppin: Memoirs, diaries, letters,* edited by Alex Bein (New York, 1971).

26. Arthur Ruppin, "The selection of the fittest," in *Three decades of Palestine* (Jerusalem, 1936), 66–80.

27. Arthur Ruppin, "Settling German Jews in Palestine," in *Three decades of Palestine,* 278.

28. Ruppin, *Arthur Ruppin,* 307–8.

29. Ibid., 283–316.

30. Alfred Bonné, *Twenty years of economic research in Palestine* (Jerusalem, 1942), 8.

31. See "Planning Committee," Box IV (Ben-Gurion Archives, Sede Boker).

32. David Ben-Gurion, *The reconstruction programme: An address to the Joint Meeting of the Elected Assembly of Palestine and the Zionist General Council, March 24, 1943,* Central Zionist Archives, S25/1943.

33. Chaim Weizmann to Harry S. Truman, Dec. 12, 1945. *Weizmann Papers* (New Brunswick, N.J., 1979), vol. 22, 78.

34. "Planning Committee," Boxes IV, X, XI, XXXIV (Ben-Gurion Archives, Sede Boker).

35. Sharon, *Physical planning in Israel,* and Erika Spiegel, *New towns in Israel* (Stuttgart, 1966). The economic side of the Sharon Plan is examined in a concurrent report: Abraham Gruenbaum, *Four year development plan of Israel 1950–1953* (Hebrew) (Tel Aviv, 1950).

Chapter 9. From New Towns to Development Towns

1. In addition to the materials cited below, there is a very large literature on regional planning in Israel that achieved international interest. Among the

key pieces in this literature are, for the Jezreel Valley, Artur Glikson, *Regional planning and development* (Leiden, 1955); for the Lakhish region, Ra'anan Weitz et al., *The Lakhish region: Background study for research in regional development planning* (Rehovoth, 1970).

2. Arieh Sharon, *Physical planning in Israel* (Jerusalem, 1951), 69.

3. Ra'anan Weitz and Avshalom Rokach, *Agricultural development: Planning and implementation: Israel case study* (Dordrecht, Holland, 1968), xiii.

4. See Elisha Efrat, *The new towns of Israel (1948–1988)* (München, 1989). See also Shlomo Sevirski and Menachem Sushan, *New towns towards a different tomorrow* (Hebrew) (Haifa, 1985); Alexander Berler, *New towns in Israel* (Hebrew) (Jerusalem, 1970); and David Amiram and Arieh Shachar, *Development towns in Israel* (Jerusalem, 1969).

5. Frederic Osborn and Arnold Whittick, *The new towns: The answer to megalopolis* (London, 1969). For background see Stanley Buder, *Visionaries and planners: The garden city movement and the modern community* (New York, 1990).

6. Osborn and Whittick, *The new towns*, 159.

7. Erika Spiegal, *New towns in Israel* (Stuttgart, 1966), 9.

8. Ann Louise Strong, *Planned urban environments: Sweden, Finland, Israel, The Netherlands, France* (Baltimore, Md., 1971), xxix–xxx.

9. Eliezer Brutzkus, "Aims and possibilities of national planning" (Hebrew) *Habinyan*, no. 3 (1938).

10. Eliezer Brutzkus, "The question of urban settlement" (Hebrew) *Handasa Ve'adrichalut*, no. 5 (1945): 13–14.

11. Eliezer Brutzkus, "The new cities in the framework of national and regional planning," *Journal of the Association of Engineers and Architects in Israel* (*JAEAI*), 12: 2 (April–May, 1956): 7–9; and Eliezer Brutzkus, "New towns in the framework of national and regional planning" (Hebrew) *Handasa Ve'adrichalut*, 14: 2 (1956): 7–9.

12. Eliezer Brutzkus, *Physical planning in Israel: Problems and achievements* (Jerusalem, 1964), 17.

13. These issues are considered from different points of view in S. Ilan Troen, "The transformation of Zionist planning policy: From agricultural settlements to an urban network," *Planning Perspectives*, vol. 3 (January 1988): 3–23; S. Ilan Troen "Calculating the 'economic absorptive capacity' of Palestine: A study of the political uses of scientific research," *Contemporary Jewry*, 10: 2 (1989): 19–38.

14. "Symposium on planning and development problems," *Journal of the Association of Engineers and Architects in Palestine* (*JAEAP*), 2: 2 (December 1943). See especially David Horowitz, "The economy of Eretz Yisrael on the conclusion of the war and its opportunities," 5–8; and Ya'acov Shiffman, "Urban development: The size of the city," *JAEAP*, 4: 5 (August–September 1943), 8–13. For a markedly different view of city size see Itzhak Rokach, "Tel-Aviv's struggle for expansion," *JAEAP*, 4: 5 (August–September 1943), 1–2. Rokach, the city's mayor, complains that the city is being artificially constrained by the British. A decade later, as minister of the interior, he effectively employed his powers to rectify this by opposing Israeli planners who operated in the anticentralization tradition expressed here.

15. Reportage on British thinking and practice was constant. See, for example, Thomas Sharp, "The development of the English countryside," *JAEAP*, 3: 3

(October 1942); B. Krougliakoff, "The reconstruction of London," *JAEAP*, 2: 3 (October–November 1941); and C. Wilson Brown, "The housing problem in the United Kingdom: report submitted to the Government of Palestine," *JAEAP*, vol. 8 (September 1945).

16. See files of the *Va'adat Tikun* (Planning Committee) at the Ben-Gurion Archives in Sede Boker for June 10, 1945, for reports and discussions of Richard Kauffmann, Ya'acov Ben-Sira, and Alexander Klein on physical planning. See especially Ya'acov Ben-Sira, "Existing urban centers and their development," and "Theses on town planning legislation," as appendixes to a letter and internal paper for the Planning Committee to architect Richard Kauffmann. Also valuable for the significance of the Barlow Report is a letter by Dr. Kornikov, secretary of the subcommittee for planning, to Richard Kauffmann, Aug. 31, 1945. Kauffmann was a key member of the committee that finalized and signed the national Master Plan in 1950.

17. Ministry of Agriculture, *Project Beit She'an: Agricultural planning* (Hebrew) (Tel Aviv, 1968), and see the file "Beit She'an" in the Kressel Collection. See also "The Gate to the Garden of Eden," *Jerusalem Post*, Sept. 12, 1973.

18. *Davar*, May 2, 1948. Flight began on a large scale in early May 1948 as news of Jewish victories spread panic among the residents of Beit She'an. Women and children were sent to Transjordan.

19. Keren Hayesod—United Jewish Appeal, *Contributions to the history of the settlements in Israel* (Hebrew) (Jerusalem, August 1952). The pamphlet reflects the agricultural bias that characterized Zionist planning in the prewar period. It opens with the following declaration: "Agricultural colonization has always been at the centre of the interest and concerns of the Keren Hayesod. Most of its budget has gone for the establishment and support of hundreds of agricultural settlements. Now, after three years of effort, the Keren Hayesod can examine with satisfaction those hundreds of settlements, moshavim, and kibbutzim, which have been established by it in all the different parts of the country, from Dan to Eilat. These settlements represent most of the agricultural settlements in the state, its backbone and a source for its life." The exclusively agricultural focus continues well after Independence. The regional council of which the city is part acknowledged its neglect of urban concerns. See Ministry of Agriculture, *Project Beit She'an*.

20. "A colony in the making in Beit She'an" (Hebrew) *Davar*, June 30, 1949.

21. "Beit She'an—The forgotten city" (Hebrew) *Dapim*, 1954.

22. Ibid.

23. Ruth Bondi, "Beit She'an: The forgotten among the cities of Israel" (Hebrew) *Davar*, Jan. 6, 1955.

24. Originally, the Hebrew name of the town was *Kiryat Yosef* (the city of Yosef [Trumpeldor]). The families of the seven who died with him in defense of the settlement demanded that all be memorialized. This caused the change of name to Kiryat Shemona (the city of eight). The information presented here on Kiryat Shemona is derived from a composite of newspaper cuttings and pamphlets at the Kressel Collection. In addition, Kiryat Shemona's Department of Culture, Youth and Sport published throughout 1980 a series of 25 pamphlets, entitled *Pirkey Kiryat-Shemona* (in Hebrew) commemorating the origins and early history of the city.

25. "Here a city will rise in the north" (Hebrew) *Davar*, Jan. 16, 1950.

26. Raphael Bashan, *30 Years of Kiryat Malachi 1951–1981* (Hebrew) (Ramat-Gan, 1981).

27. Ibid.

28. Bashan, *30 Years of Kiryat Malachi,* 19–21.

29. See "Kiryat Malachi" in the Kressel Collection.

30. *4,000 and another forty years* (Hebrew) (Ashkelon, 1990). This excellent anniversary volume of the city's founding contains most of the historical information on which this section draws. See also *Ashkelon: A summary of six years of work 1959–1965* (Hebrew) (Ashkelon, 1965), and *Ashkelon: New developments* (World Zionist Organization, Project Planning Department, 1973) (Central Zionist Archives, File 36267 Gimmel). A fascinating contemporary account of the problems Ashkelon encountered was provided by Tel Aviv's Municipal Engineer. See Ya'acov Ben-Sira, "The problem of physical planning" (Hebrew) *Molad,* vol. 10 (1952–53): 130–39. A useful collection of materials is also found in Ze'ev Vilnay, *New and ancient Ashkelon* (Hebrew) (Ashkelon, 1963).

31. World Zionist Organization, *Ashkelon reborn* (Tel Aviv, 1952).

32. There is a good collection of materials in the Beer-Sheva file at the Kressel Collection. Especially useful for detailing the role of the Histadrut is "Beer-Sheva towards its second quarter century" (Hebrew) *Davar,* Sept. 24, 1950, and A.D. Meshulam, "The contribution of the Histadrut to the development of Beer-Sheva" (Hebrew) *Davar,* July 22, 1979; Mordechai Artzieli, "Sapir—Beer-Sheva's patron" (Hebrew) *Ha'aretz,* Dec. 28, 1972. For a particularly valuable account of the role Sapir played in affecting the outcome of settlements, see the biography of the industrialist brought by Sapir to Kiryat Gat, a nearby Negev development town: Israel Pollak, *Stormy times* (Hebrew) (Jerusalem, 1988). The most comprehensive study on the city is Yehuda Gradus and Eli Stern, eds., *Beer-Sheva* (Hebrew) (Jerusalem, 1979).

33. Frederick A. Lazin, *Politics and policy implementation: Project renewal in Israel* (New York, 1994).

34. Benjamin Akzin and Yehezkiel Dror, *Israel: High pressure planning* (Syracuse, N.Y., 1966).

Chapter 10. Israeli Villages

1. The most comprehensive study of population change during the war is Arnon Golan, *Wartime spatial changes within the State of Israel, 1948–1950* (Hebrew) (Sede Boker, 2001).

2. Arnon Golan, "The transfer to Jewish control of abandoned Arab lands during the War of Independence," in S. Ilan Troen and Noah Lucas, eds., *Israel: The first decade of Independence* (Albany, N.Y., 1995), 403–40.

3. The salience of the army in the Israeli planning experience continues through the present. For example, the Minister of Defense provides final approval of all housing in the West Bank communities in Judea and Samaria. That is, the various ministries make plans and allocate resources, including the Ministry of Housing. It does not have, however, authority to carry out decisions without agreement from the Defense Ministry. For a recent example see "Ministry has 30,200 new homes on tap for territories," *Ha'aretz,* Jan. 9, 1998 (English edition).

4. The manner of the departure of Palestinian Arabs from their homes and

lands has become a contested issue in current Israeli historiography. The works by Benny Morris are the most important critical analyses of what occurred. See note 6. A similar view appeared in a 1949 story that has become part of the canon of modern Hebrew literature: Yizhar Smilansky, *Hirbat Hizha* (Hebrew) (Tel Aviv, 1989), 31–78.

5. Golan, *Wartime spatial changes*.

6. Perhaps the best and most controversial source in the story of appropriation of land from Arabs for Jewish settlement is found in the writings of Josef Weitz, who was head of the Land Department of the Jewish National Fund. Among the most important writings are Joseph Weitz, *In the course of settling the country* (Hebrew) (Jerusalem, 1960), *The struggle for the land* (Tel Aviv, 1952), and especially, *My diary and letters to my sons* (Hebrew), vols. 2–4 (Ramat Gan, 1965). In particular, this third work is the subject of intense scrutiny and diverse interpretations. See Benny Morris, *The birth of the Palestinian refugee problem, 1947–1949* (Cambridge, 1987), especially chaps. 4–8, and *1948 and After: Israel and the Palestinians* (Oxford, 1994), chaps. 4–7; Arnon Golan, "Changes in the settlement map in areas abandoned by the Arab population as a consequence of the War of Independence, on the area on which the State of Israel was established" (Hebrew) (unpublished Ph.D. thesis, Hebrew University, 1993).

7. Abraham Gruenbaum, *Four year development plan of Israel 1950–1953* (Hebrew) (Tel Aviv, 1950), 1–15.

8. On the issue of incursions see Benny Morris, *Israel's border wars 1949–1956: Arab infiltration, Israeli retaliation, and the countdown to the Suez war* (Oxford, 1993). A criticism of Morris and an alternative interpretation is found in Mordechai Bar-On, "Small wars, big wars: Security debates during Israel's first decade," *Israel Studies* 5: 2 (Fall 2000), 107–27.

9. David Koren, *Nahal: Military with added values* (Hebrew) (Tel Aviv, 1997).

10. David Ben-Gurion, *Like stars and dust: Essays from Israel's government year book* (Sede Boker, 1997), 46–47.

11. Moshe Mossek, *Palestine immigration policy under Sir Herbert Samuel: British, Zionist and Arab attitudes* (London, 1978).

12. "And [Joshua] said unto the people: Pass on, and compass the city, and let the *halutz* pass on before the ark of the Lord. And it came to pass, when Joshua had spoken unto the people, that the seven priests hearing the seven trumpets of rams' horns passed on before the Lord, and blew with the trumpets; and the ark of the covenant of the Lord followed them. And the *halutz* went before the priests that blew the trumpets" (Joshua, VI: 7–9). For an interesting discussion of the origin and use of the word, see Henry Near, *Frontiersmen and halutzim: The image of the pioneer in North America and pre-state Jewish Palestine* (Haifa, January 1987), 2–8.

13. Eli Tzur, "Mapam and the European and Oriental immigrations," in Troen and Lucas, eds. *Israel: First decade of Independence*, 543–56.

14. Edwin Samuel, *Handbook of the Jewish communal villages in Palestine* (Jerusalem, 1945), 10–11.

15. "Ben-Gurion's remarks in the Knesseth, 16 January 1950" (Hebrew), *Divrei Haknesseth* (Jerusalem, 1950), 536.

16. For an interesting discussion of this episode see Ze'ev Tsahor, "I am 'bosh venichlam'—The kibbutz and the absorption of immigrants" (Hebrew), *Vision and reckoning: Ben-Gurion: Ideology and politics* (Tel Aviv, 1994), 194–210.

17. Yishai Geva, "The settlement tradition after statehood" (Hebrew) *Iyunim bekumat Israel*, 5 (1985): 262–303; and Yossi Ben-Artzi, "Changes in settlement preferences with statehood: A historical perspective" (Hebrew), in V. Pilavski, ed., *The transition from Yishuv to state, 1947–1949: Continuity and change* (Haifa: 1990), 173–85.

18. Livia Appelbaum and H. Margolis, *The moshav—Patterns of organizational change* (Hebrew) (Rehovoth, 1979); and Ovadia Shapiro, *Rural settlements of new immigrants in Israel: Development problems of new rural communities* (Rehovoth, 1971).

19. Alex Weingrod, *Reluctant pioneers: Village development in Israel* (Ithaca, N.Y., 1966).

20. Moshe Schwarz, Raphael Bar-El, Rachel Finkel, and Ariela Nesher, *Moshav-based industry in Israel* (Rehovoth, 1986).

21. Dorothy Willner, *Nation building and community in Israel* (Princeton, N.J., 1969); Ann Louise Strong, *Planned urban environments*, 127–201; Erika Spiegel, *New towns in Israel;* and Arie Schahar, "Israel's development towns: Valuation of national urbanization policy," *Journal of the American Institute of Planners,* 37 (1971): 362–72.

22. Schwarz et al., *Moshav-based industry in Israel,* 8 ff.

23. Alfred Bonné, "Town and city in the Hebrew Land of Israel," in Martin Buber, ed., *Towards the character of the Hebrew village in Eretz Israel* (Hebrew) (Jerusalem, 1946), 27.

24. Ibid., 33–35.

25. Ya'acov Vardi, "The water resources of Judea and Samaria," *Elazar papers: Symposium on Judea and Samaria* (Hebrew) 5 (1982), 33–38; and David Kahan, *Agriculture and water resources in the West Bank and Gaza* (Jerusalem, 1987). The crisis in water management has reached catastrophic proportions and is under intense, public review. The dangers and problems for Israeli agriculture posed by inadequate water supply have been analyzed in a very critical report by the state comptroller. It notes that Israel has been exporting its water to largely European markets in the form of fruits, vegetables, cotton, and flowers. Also, water allocation historically reflects a settlement policy that has favored the development of agricultural settlements. The problem has become so serious that waters from the Mediterranean might infiltrate into the aquifers, thereby compromising their use for agricultural as well as domestic and industrial consumption. See State Comptroller, *Report on the administration of water in Israel* (Hebrew) (Jerusalem, 1990).

26. Haim Barkai, *Growth patterns of the kibbutz economy* (Amsterdam, 1977); N. Gutberg, *Issues in the problems of industry in settlement* (Jerusalem, 1982), in Central Zionist Archives (hereafter, CZA), File 55.906/G.

27. Barkai, *Growth patterns,* 126–27; and Raphael Bar-El, ed., *Rural industrialization in Israel* (Boulder, Colo., 1987).

28. David Newman and Livia Appelbaum, *Between village and suburb: New settlement forms in Israel* (Hebrew) (Rehovoth, 1989), 46–47. Important analyses as well as statistics are found in Meron Benvenisti, *The shepherds war: Collected essays (1981–1989)* (Jerusalem, 1989); and Meron Benvenisti and Shlomo Khayat, *The West Bank and Gaza atlas* (Jerusalem, 1988).

29. *The industrial village: An opportunity for aliyah* (Jerusalem, 1974), in CZA, File 37303. See also *Community villages* (Jerusalem, 1989); *Zionism and industry*

(Hebrew) (Tel Aviv, 1989); and *Industrialization of rural settlements,* Jerusalem, May 1973, in *Ra'anan Weitz Papers,* CZA, File 36077/73. The best overview of settlement policy and history after 1967 is Elisha Efrat, *Geography and politics in Israel since 1967* (London, 1988)

30. Rehavam Zeevi, "Introduction" (Hebrew), *Elazar papers on settlement and security* (Tel Aviv, 1980), vol. 3 (1980), 16.

31. David Newman, *The impact of Gush Emunim: Politics and settlement in the West Bank* (London, 1985).

32. There is a large literature critical of Jewish settlement on the West Bank. Within Israel, the most systematic and scientifically rooted are the materials produced by the West Bank Data Project, headed by Meron Benvenisti. Several key works are listed above. See also Geoffrey Aronson, *Creating facts: Israel, Palestinians and the West Bank* (Washington, D.C., 1987).

33. *Master plan for settlement of Samaria and Judea: Plan for regional development for the years 1983–86* (Hebrew) (Jerusalem, 1983). See also *Rural settlement for the years 1978–1982* (Jerusalem, 1978). On the possible impact of Soviet Jewish immigration see Nadav Shragai, "Building hidden from the Eye" (Hebrew) *Ha'aretz,* Jan. 28, 1991.

34. S. Ilan Troen, "The diffusion of an urban social science: France, England and the United States in the nineteenth century," *Comparative Social Research,* 9 (Spring 1986): 247–66.

Chapter 11. Establishing a Capital

Epigraph: Psalms 137:6; "From the summit of Mount Scopus," popular folk song by Avigdor Ha'meiri.

1. There is a voluminous literature on the city and its history. A good place to begin for readers of Hebrew is Hagit Lavsky, ed., *Jerusalem in Zionist vision and realization: Collected essays* (Hebrew) (Jerusalem, 1989). The following, often based on Hebrew originals, are available in English: Yehoshua Ben-Arieh, *A city reflected in its times: New Jerusalem—The beginnings* (Jerusalem, 1979); Yehoshua Ben-Arieh, *Jerusalem in the 19th century: Emergence of the New City* (Jerusalem, 1986); Meron Benvenisti, *City of stone: The hidden history of Jerusalem* (Berkeley, 1996); Martin Gilbert, *Jerusalem in the twentieth century* (New York, 1996); Amos Elon, *Jerusalem: City of mirrors* (London, 1990); Dov Joseph, *The faithful city: The siege of Jerusalem, 1948* (New York, 1960); Arieh Sharon, *Planning Jerusalem: The Old City and its environs* (London, 1973). The premier scholar of Jerusalem's modern architectural and planning history is David Kroyanker, whose works are cited below.

2. David Kroyanker, *Architecture in Jerusalem: Building during the period of the British Mandate* (Hebrew) (Jerusalem, 1989). See also David Kroyanker, *Jerusalem: Neighborhoods and houses: Periods and styles* (Hebrew) (Jerusalem, 1966).

3. For demographic data on the evolution of the city see Usiel Schmelz, *Modern Jerusalem's demographic evolution* (Jerusalem, 1987).

4. A particularly colorful description of Allenby's entry as opposed to the Kaiser's is found in Bertha Spafford Vester, *Our Jerusalem: An American family in the Holy City 1881–1949* (Beirut, 1950), 278–80.

5. Henry Kendall, ed., *Jerusalem, the city plan: Preservation and development during the British Mandate 1918–1948* (London, 1948).

6. Alan Gordon Cunningham, "Foreword," in Kendall, ed., *Jerusalem, the city plan*, v.

7. The extent to which the division compromised and diminished the Arab share of the city is a subject of passionate debate and polemics. For example, see Sami Tamari, ed., *Jerusalem 1948: The Arab neighbourhoods and their fate in the war* (Jerusalem, 1999).

8. An early and very useful presentation of the challenge of transforming Jerusalem is Government of Israel, *Jerusalem 1948–1951: Three years of reconstruction* (Jerusalem, 1952).

9. Documentation of the chronic lack of employment and the calls for assistance from the government is found in the Jerusalem Municipal Archives (JMA). Early problems are detailed in the *Monthly survey of the work situation* (Hebrew), found in boxes in section JMA/4/1/U. The *Half-year survey for the period January–June 1950* (Hebrew) (Document #78) noted that "the first part of 1950 was a turning point for the development of Jerusalem. . . . The turnabout was especially striking in the civil service sector. More than 600 clerks found work in this short period." No such surge in employment was the result of industry. City officials consciously relied on government and Jewish Agency budgets rather than private capital and industry for development and for support of the city's inhabitants.

10. *Memorandum on the location of the Hebrew University*, Jan. 8, 1953, Central Zionist Archives, File 3654/5544/Gimmel.

11. Saul B. Cohen and Nurit Kliot, "Israel's place-names as reflection of continuity and change in nation-building," *Names*, 29: 3 (1991), 227–46; and Saul B. Cohen and Nurit Kliot, "Place-names in Israel's ideological struggle over the administered territories," *Annals of the Association of American Geographers*, 82: 4 (December 1992), 653–80.

12. For a re-creation of the ceremony see Maoz Azaryahu, "Mount Herzl: The creation of Israel's national cemetery," *Israel Studies*, 1: 2 (Fall 1996), 46–74. See also his *State cults: Celebrating independence and commemorating the fallen in Israel 1948–1956* (Hebrew) (Sede Boker, 1995).

13. Omer Bartov, "Chambers of horror: Holocaust museums in Israel and the United States," *Israel Studies* 2: 2 (Fall 1997), 66–87.

14. Abraham Rabinovich, "On building a fortress," *Jerusalem Post*, Nov. 8, 1994.

15. "If I do not remember . . ." (Hebrew) *Davar*, Sept. 23, 1949.

16. The settlement of the corridor leading to Jerusalem became a central concern of settlement authorities and, particularly, the army. An account of the significance of this project among the planners within the general staff and relations with the Jewish Agency experts has been recorded in an interview with the officer in charge of planning settlements in border regions. See the interview with Col. Aharon Harsina, Aug. 3, 1976, Oral History Section, IDF Archives. For a detailed analysis of what went wrong in the battle for Jerusalem and how its defenses need to be strengthened, including through the building of settlements in the corridor up to the city, see "If I do not remember . . ." (Hebrew) *Davar*, Sept. 23, 1949.

17. Abraham Rabinovich quoted by Christopher Walker, "100,000 Jews to live on seized Jerusalem land," *Times* (London), March 19, 1980.

18. "Jerusalem is ours and shall remain ours declares President Chaim Weizmann during his visit to the city" (Hebrew) *Yedioth Aharonoth,* Dec. 2, 1948.

Chapter 12. Contested Metropolis

1. For a concise survey see Chaim Herzog, *The Arab–Israeli wars: War and peace in the Middle East from the War of Independence through Lebanon* (New York, 1984), 143–92.

2. A variety of sources provide essential demographic, statistical information together with maps. See, for example, Shlomo Karniel and Hava Gordon, *Jerusalem: A metropolitan atlas and guide* (Hebrew) (Tel Aviv, 1993). Essential sources for research are the publications of the Institute for Jerusalem Studies. For example, see *Jerusalem's business center and the outer suburbs: Discussion paper no. 2* (Hebrew) (Jerusalem, 1980).

3. On the battle for Jerusalem see Uzi Narkiss, *The liberation of Jerusalem: The battle of 1967* (London, 1983); and Herzog, *The Arab-Israeli wars,* 167–84.

4. "Ancient Jerusalem is captured by the forces of the IDF. The Temple Mount is in our hands. The Israeli Flag flies over the Western Wall," in *Composite from Davar, 5 June 1967 to 10 June 1967, supplement for Jerusalem Day* (Hebrew), *Davar.*

5. Leora Eren Frucht, "A mount too far?" *Jerusalem Post,* Jan. 5, 2001. The article quotes Professor Shlomo Avineri, a well-known secular, leftist intellectual: "The Temple Mount is a national symbol for the Zionist movement. While as a secular person I have no religious connection to the place, it does symbolize historical continuity of unparalleled duration in world history. . . . I find it very difficult to imagine a nation giving up a core symbol of its identity voluntarily. . . . Nations have lost places which symbolized historical identity and continuity when they lost wars or were defeated. I know of no case in which a modern nation has been ready to give up something as central as the Temple Mount is to the Jewish people."

6. S. Ilan Troen and Zaki Shalom, "Ben-Gurion's diary for the 1967 war: Introduction and diary excerpts," *Israel Studies,* 4: 2 (Fall 1999), 195–220.

7. A compilation of plans for 1967 with an exposition of its assumptions is found in Avihai Hashimshoni, Joseph Schweid, and Zion Hashimshoni, *Jerusalem master plan,* 2 vols. (Jerusalem, 1972). The same study contains considerable historical information about the pre-1967 period.

8. Teddy Kollek, longtime mayor of Jerusalem, used the occasion to begin clearing land around the city's walls to create, where possible, a greenbelt. He related that the idea came from reading Kendall's *The Jerusalem plan* and observed that the British "never had the courage or the money to implement it." Teddy Kollek, *For Jerusalem: A life by Teddy Kollek* (London, 1978), 201.

9. Ministry of the Interior, *Report of the Investigating Committee on Jerusalem's Borders, headed by Chaim Kaberski, Ministry of the Interior, August 1991* (Hebrew) (Jerusalem, 1991).

10. Daniel Elazar, "Minority opinion," in *Report of the Committee for Investigating Jerusalem's Borders,* 41–46.

11. Dani Rubinstein, "A wall that fell and dividers that remained," *Supplement for Jerusalem day, 1967–1977* (Hebrew) *Davar,* May 13, 1977.

12. The Ministry of the Interior argued: "Strengthening the position of the

capital city is seen by the [Kaberski] Committee as a paramount national value, of greater importance than any other consideration." It went on to explain that this required building sufficient housing to absorb new immigrants that were coming from the former Soviet Union and elsewhere. This was to ensure a proper balance between Jews and Arabs. *Report of the Investigating Committee on Jerusalem's Borders*, 14–21.

13. "Deri signed on administrative orders to expand Jerusalem by 15,000 dunams" (Hebrew) *Ha'aretz*, May 12, 1993. Minister of the Interior Arieh Deri signed administrative orders to expand Jerusalem by 15,000 dunams on May 11, 1993. In effect, this was a compromise of the original plan of Kaberski, who argued for an expansion of 30,000 dunams that would include the large, wealthy, and influential suburb of Mevassereth Zion. This suburb successfully lobbied to be excluded. Nevertheless, the rationale behind expansion was upheld, albeit in more modest proportions.

14. Yossi Naim, *Metropolitan Jerusalem—Program of concepts* (Hebrew) (Jerusalem, 1984), 1, 5.

15. Uzi Benzimon, "Returning to the mount" (Hebrew) *Ha'aretz*, Dec. 5, 1969.

16. Yossi Feintuch, *U.S. policy on Jerusalem* (New York, 1987), 123 ff.

17. The planting of trees, a highly political act understood by both Jews and Arabs, resulted in intense competition. See Shaul E. Cohen, *The politics of planting: Israeli–Palestinian competition for control of land in the Jerusalem periphery* (Chicago, 1993). The Kaberski Committee, for example, contains a report by the JNF arguing for their involvement in planting in the valleys and maintaining the hilltops for Jewish settlement. See *Report of the Investigating Committee on Jerusalem's Borders*, 34–35.

18. A detailed analysis of the social and economic problems of the city after the first decade of unification is found in Yuval Elitzur, "Employment in Jerusalem: Growth without roots" (Hebrew) in a "Special Supplement: 10 years to the reunification of Jerusalem" (Hebrew) *Davar*, May 13, 1977.

19. In Chapter 11, we saw how the same problem appeared in the post-Independence period. This remained a constant problem. See, for example, Tuvia Mendelssohn, "Not enough is being done to fix Jerusalem's status as capitol of Israel" (Hebrew), and Aharon Geva, "Increase of children and old people deepens the city's social problems" (Hebrew) *Davar*, May 20, 1974.

20. Although the original article was published in *Foreign Affairs* in 1976 when he was Foreign Minister, Yigal Allon reanalyzed his proposals in "The West Bank and Gaza within the framework of a Middle East peace settlement," *Middle East Review*, 12: 2 (Winter 1979–80): 15–18.

21. "Exiting Minister approves plan for Jerusalem line to settlement," *Middle East Newsline* (*menl@actcom.co.il*), May 28, 1999.

22. Christopher Walker, "100,000 Jews to live on seized Jerusalem land," *Times* (London), March 19, 1980.

23. For a critical review of Israeli expropriation policy see B'Tselem, "Building a Jewish neighborhood on 'Har Homah'—The background and the danger," Feb. 25, 1997 (*www.btselem.org*).

24. Nadav Shragai records the competition between Jews and Arabs for land in "New Jewish zone bought in Jerusalem" (Hebrew) *Ha'aretz*, March 23, 2000. The establishment of fictitious companies to represent Arab interests is revealed

in internal documents of the Palestinian National Authority. See Aaron Lerner, "Text of PLO letters on Jerusalem and support for Israeli Parties," Oct. 23, 1995 (*www.israelinsider.com/views/authors/lerner*).

25. Kollek, *For Jerusalem,* 217–19.

26. According to the census report made public on the thirty-third anniversary of the city's reunification, out of a total population of 650,000 there were 450,000 Jews and 200,000 Arabs. "Jerusalem population reaches 650,000" (Hebrew) *Ma'ariv,* June 2, 2000.

27. Lily Galili and Ori Nir, "City of strangers" (Hebrew) *Ha'aretz,* Nov. 27, 2000. For other examples of the same observations see "Jews and Arabs live separately; in Jerusalem the majority are indifferent to creating personal contact between the two peoples" (Hebrew) *Ha'aretz,* July 18, 1969; Eliyahu Amikam, "Jerusalem is divided again" (Hebrew) *Yedioth Aharonot,* Aug. 6, 1976; Yehuda Litani, "Jerusalem 1980: Between declarations and reality—The capital of the West Bank" (Hebrew) *Ha'aretz,* July 9, 1980.

28. Izhak Galnoor, *The partition of Palestine: Decision crossroads in the Zionist movement* (Albany, N.Y., 1995); and Yosef Katz, *Partner to partition: The Jewish Agency's partition plan in the mandate era* (London, 1998).

29. Ian Lustick, "The borders of the eruv in Jerusalem" (Hebrew) *Ha'aretz,* Dec. 28, 1999.

30. Gideon Weigert, *Israel's presence in East Jerusalem* (Jerusalem, 1973).

31. Michael Romann and Alex Weingrod, *Living together separately: Arabs and Jews in contemporary Israel* (Princeton, N.J., 1991). For a further graphic analysis of the segregation patterns see Usiel Oskar Schmelz, *Modern Jerusalem's demographic evolution* (Jerusalem, 1987), 114–15.

32. There is a large literature on the actual social, political, and economic divisions of the city. Key readings are Meron Benvenisti, *Jerusalem, the torn city* (Minneapolis, 1976); Joel Kraemer, ed., *Jerusalem problems and prospects* (New York, 1980); Saul B. Cohen, *Bridging the four walls* (New York, 1977); A. Chesin, B. Hutman, and A. Melamed, *Separate and unequal: The inside story of Israeli rule in East Jerusalem* (Cambridge, Mass., 1999).

33. Romann and Weingrod, *Living together separately.*

34. Itamar Marcus, *The new Palestinian Authority school textbooks for grades one and six* (Jerusalem, 2000).

35. Romann and Weingrod, *Living together separately,* 195. For a concise discussion of the borough plan and its rationale see Kollek, *For Jerusalem,* 248–51. The idea survives in one form or another on the Israeli side because it attempts to square the circle of maintaining Israeli sovereignty and permitting Palestinian autonomy. See, for example, Nadav Shragai, "Return of the quarters plan" (Hebrew) *Ha'aretz,* June 18, 2000.

36. See Menachem Klein, *Jerusalem: The contested city* (London, 2001); Ruth Lapidoth and Moshe Hirsch, eds., *The Jerusalem question and its resolution: Selected documents* (Dordrecht, The Netherlands, 1994); Moshe Hirsch, Deborah Couriel, and Ruth Lapidoth, *Whither Jerusalem? Proposals and positions concerning the future of Jerusalem* (The Hague, 1995); Ghada Karmi, ed., *Jerusalem today: What future for the peace process?* (Ithaca, N.Y., 1996).

37. Bernard Lewis, *The political language of Islam* (Chicago, Ill., 1991), 73–80.

38. David Clayman, "Update on what Israelis are thinking, reading, doing and saying," *American Jewish Congress: Report #224, 14 January, 2001* (ajcongis@act-

com.co.il). Many Israelis are ready to compromise over the Temple Mount. For example, just after Foreign Minister Shlomo Ben-Ami returned from talks in Washington with the American government and the Palestinian Authority, *Ma'ariv* editorialized that "The Temple Mount is not the people's raison d'être in the country." The editors observed that "For dozens of years, the Temple Mount has—in practice—belonged to the Palestinians," and added that "if the American proposal is accepted, the *de facto* situation will become *de jure*, that's all." *Ma'ariv* went on to editorialize that "Our true *raison d'être* is peace." Similarly, *Ha'aretz* admitted that "The effort to enlarge the Israeli claim on the eastern part of Jerusalem, and focus it on the celebrated sites of the Old City and the Temple Mount, has succeeded only partially: reality is now forcing Israel to share its control over the 'Holy Basin' with the Palestinian people." The calculation was of "peace for territory" even when heavily laden with the deepest religious and historical sentiments. *Ha'aretz* concluded: "At the end of the day, the Arab-Israeli dispute over Jerusalem revolves around a hub of symbols, not around elements fundamental to existence; this is an area worthy of making the necessary compromise." *Editorials from the Hebrew Press–Dec. 26, 2000, Israel-Mideast (divinfo@mfa.gov.il).*

39. *Arutz-7 News Brief: Friday, January 12, 2001 (neteditor@israelnationalnews. com).*

40. Romann and Weingrod, *Living together separately*, 99–124.

Epilogue

1. Curiously, there are no English translations of the massive work done through the "Israel 2020" project. A convenient Hebrew summary is Adam Mazor et al., *"Israel 2020": Master Plan for Israel in the 21st century; summary report* (Hebrew) (Haifa, 1997).

2. Gideon Biger, "Zionist considerations for determining the borders of Eretz-Israel at the beginning of the British Mandate, *Iyunim Betkumat Israel: Studies in Zionism, the Yishuv and the State of Israel*, vol. 10 (2000), 89–102.

3. Shlomo Gazit and Ariel Levit, "Security perspectives and geopolitical scenarios for Israel after 2000" (Hebrew), in Mazor et al., *Israel 2020*, vol. 2 (Haifa, 1993), sec. 3.

4. An important barometer of the change in Israel's national temperament and ideology is Yaron Ezrahi, *Rubber bullets: Power and conscience in modern Israel* (New York, 1997).

5. S. Ilan Troen, "Frontier myths and their applications in America and Israel: a transnational perspective," *Journal of American History*, 86: 3 (December 1999): 1209–30.

6. "Prejudice by nationality," *Ha'aretz*, March 29, 1998.

7. For extended analysis of changes in the Israeli legal system, particularly during the Barak incumbency as chief justice, see the special section on "Law and the transformation of Israeli society," *Israel Studies*, 3 (Fall 1998): 1–192. See also *Judgement in Jerusalem: Chief Justice Simon Agranat and the Zionist century* (Berkeley, 1997).

8. Bagatz 6698/95, *Quaadan vs. Israel Lands Authority, et al.* For a review of comments on this case see Gerald M. Steinberg, "'The poor in your own city shall have precedence': A new-Zionist critique of the Katzir-Qaadan decision,"

Jerusalem Viewpoints (Jerusalem Center for Public Affairs), no. 445, Jan. 1, 2001. For a critical perspective on how Israel employs its powers to the disadvantage of Arabs see Oren Yiftachel, "The internal frontier: Territorial control and ethnic relations in Israel," *Regional Studies,* 30: 5 (1996), 493–508. Both critics and supporters of Israel's policy on the control of land for political purposes can readily document their case. The former generally argue the rights of citizens as opposed to the latter who point to security requirements.

9. Yoram Bar-Gal, *Moledet and geography in a century of Zionist education* (Hebrew) (Tel Aviv, 1993); Ruth Firer, *The agents of Zionist education* (Hebrew) (Tel Aviv, 1985).

10. Philip Warburg, *Investing in Israel's environmental future* (Washington, D.C., 1996), 7–9.

11. The problems of open land versus security, whether located in strings of settlements or concentrated in cities, is common to proposals for settling Jews in the Galilee or the Negev. See Zafrir Rinat, "The incredible shrinking land," *Ha'aretz,* April 9, 2001.

12. Tomas L. Friedman, "It's time for Palestinians to get priorities right," *International Herald Tribune,* March 7, 2001.

Index

Aaronsohn, Aaron, 297*n*34
Aaronsohn, Ran, 300*n*33
Abercrombie, Patrick, 125–26, 146–47, 175, 193, 238–39
Achdut Ha'avodah (Unity of Labor) political party, 109
Acre: Haifa compared with, 119, 238; Zionist urban planning and, 113–14, 125–26
Adams, Frank, 297*n*26
Afridar development company, 201
Afula settlement, 113–14, 136–40, 307*n*27
agricultural policy: American influence on Zionist models, 31–34, 297*n*34; Arab farmers in Palestine, 44–50, 53–59; archaeology and politics concerning, 171–74; defense strategy incorporated with, 62–69; economic pressures on, 219–24; European Jewish settlers inexperience and, 16–22; foreign experts' influence in, 20–22, 175–78; Kiryat Malachi settlement and, 199–200; mixed farming concept and, 21–22; mythology of rural life and, 112; post-Independence pioneer settlements and, 213–19; priority of, in settlement planning, 16–22, 102–11; religious law in governing regulations for, 10; Sharon Master Plan and, 185–87; size of settlements and, 38–41; training institutions for (*hachsharoth*), 19; urban settlements as alternative to, 94–*n*25

Ahad Ha-Am, 54, 295*n*1
'Al-'Aksa intifada, 283–84
'Al-'Azaryah settlement, 267
Albright, William F., 173–74
Allenby, Edmund (General), 119–20, 238, 240
Alliance Israélite Universelle, 5
Allon, Yigal, 272, 321*n*20
Alon Shevut settlement, 272
Alterman, Natan, 153–54, 310*n*30
Altneuland (Old-New Land) (Herzl), 20, 22–23, 37, 53, 58–59; Haifa described in, 116; industrial development inspired by, 129–30; utopian vision in, 85–89, 94–95, 113–14, 303*n*16
"American Palestine Institute," 177
American pioneer settlements, Zionist settlement models based on, 29–34
American Poalei Zion, 311*n*12
Americans: The Colonial Experience, The (Boorstin), 294*n*4
American Schools of Oriental Research, 172–73
American Zionism, 29–34, 122–23, 297*n*34
Anderson, Benedict, 141
Arab architecture, "imagined communities" paradigm and, 147–48
Arab-Jewish tensions: economic conditions and, 42–61; economic policy and, 59–61; future issues in, 283–84; Jewish takeover of Arab lands and, 212–13; partition as solution

Arab-Jewish tensions (*continued*)
to, 60–61; segregation of Jerusalem
and, 275–80; socioeconomic inequalities and, 47–53; strategic
planning of kibbutzim and, 69–78;
"transfer" of Arabs from Palestine
and, 47–48, 299n6; Zionist settlement models and impact of, 32
Arab League, 283–84
Arabs in Palestine. *See* Palestinian
Arabs
Arab villages and buildings, 149–51,
196–98, 201, 210–13, 315n4, 316n6.
See also specific village names
Arad settlement, 136
Arafat, Yasser, 278–79, 284
Aranne, Zalman, 158
Arcadian mythology, colonization in-
fluenced by, 17–22, 295n5
architectural style: development
towns (*ayarot pituach*) and Zionist in-
fluence in, 190–95; "imagined com-
munities" paradigm and, 147–48;
Zionist ideology and, 156
Ariel settlement, 229
Arlosoroff, Haim, 151
Ashdod settlement, 206
Ashkelon settlement, 200–201, 205,
315n30
Ashkenazi Jews: in Haifa, 116; settle-
ment ideology among, 6
Association of Engineers and Archi-
tects in Palestine (AEAP), 192
Australian settlements, development
towns (*ayarot pituach*) modeled on,
190–95
Avineri, Shlomo, 320n5
Axis Powers, Zionist economic plan-
ning and, 180–81

Baerwald, Alexander, 148
Balfour Declaration, 29; foreign experts in Palestine following, 174–
75; immigration policy under,
168–70; Jerusalem's evolution and,
236–43; Jewish National Home and,
55; Jewish National Homeland
promised by, 95–96; land grants ex-

cluded from, 48; legitimacy of Zion-
ism with, 42–45; "reconstitution"
ideology and, 310n41; Zionist "imag-
ined communities" and, 144–48
Balfouria moshav, 138
Bank Hapoalim, 205
Barak, Aharon, 289, 323n7
Barak, Ehud (Prime Minister), 232,
278–79, 284
Bar-Giora settlement, 79
Barlow Report of 1940, 193, 309n17,
314n16
Bauhaus movement, Zionist urban
planning and, 104–11, 133, 142–48,
239, 305n34
Bayside Land Corporation, 124–25
Be'eri settlement, 151
Beer-Sheva settlement, 136, 202–5,
286, 315n32
Beer Tuvia moshav, 199
Begin, Menachem, 243, 273–74
Beit Alpha kibbutz, 69
Beitar Illit settlement, 273
Beit Eshel kibbutz, 74
Beit Ha'aravah kibbutz, 128, 134, 139
Beit HaChinuch (House of Education),
108–11
Beit Hakarem, 144
Beit She'an settlement, 70–78, 195–
97, 246, 314n18
Beit Yosef, 196
Bellamy, Edward, 23, 296n18
Ben-Ami, Shlomo, 323n38
Ben-Gurion, David, 46, 76, 128, 135,
310n41; Declaration of Indepen-
dence read by, 210; on history of
Palestine, 172–73, 311nn12–13; on
Israeli army, 214, 216; kibbutz
movement and, 217–19; Planning
Committee of, 181–82, 191–93,
205–7; Ruppin's correspondence
with, 179–81; Six Day War dis-
cussed by, 261–62; expansion of Je-
rusalem's borders and, 265–68
Ben Menachem (Kugel), Tzadok, 154
Ben-Shemen, 23
Ben-Sira, Ya'acov, 146–47, 192, 201,
314n16

Benvenisti, Meron, 318n32
Ben-Zvi, Yad, 307n22
Ben-Zvi, Yitzhak, 172–73, 221, 311nn12–13
Bergmann, Hugo, 221–22
Bezalel School of Arts and Crafts, 156–57
Bialik, Chaim Nachman, 95, 153
biblical imagery: architecture of Zionism and, 156–57; in covenantal takanoth, 8–9; in Jerusalem street names, 248; post-Independence invocation of, 149–50
biblical topography, 170
Bilu'im settlement, mythology concerning, 10–11
Birkhat Am (Bialik), 153
Blanckenhorn, Max, 130–31
"blue boxes," for funding colonization, 18, 76
Bonfils, Adrien, 115–16, 234–36
Bonné, Alfred, 180–82, 192, 222–24
Book of Joshua, 216, 316n12
Book of the Covenant of Menucha ve-Nachalah, The, 8
Boorstin, Daniel J., 294n4, 302n7
"boosters," evolution of Tel Aviv and, 89, 91–93, 302n7
Borochov, Ber, 54
Bourdillon, B. H., 120–21
Bourneville, England, 129
Brandeis, Louis, 30, 122, 297n34
Brenner, Yosef Haim, 151
"brith" (covenant), colonies' use of, 8
B'rith Shalom (Covenant of Peace), 59
British Mandate: Arab-Jewish tensions concerning, 47–50, 53–56; "economic absorptive capacity" concept, 168–70; economic policy and, 51–53, 299n14; foreign experts' influence during, 175–78; Haganah and, 79; Haifa under, 119–23; immigration policies under, 216–17; industrial development under, 50, 123–28, 133; planning of Jerusalem during, 235–43; Jewish National Home concept and, 55; naming

rules for settlements under, 150–52; partition plan and, 49–50, 299n9; "reconstitution" ideology and, 310n41; settlement planning under, 29–31, 142–48, 309n17; urban development during, 90–111, 238–39; Zionists' relations with, 43–47, 178–82
Broshi, Magen, 174
Brutzkus, Eliezer, 190–92
Buber, Martin, 59, 220–24
Buildings of the People (*binyanei ha-ooma*), 252–53

Cabet, Etienne, 23
"Canaanite" movement, 157
capital sources for settlements, 96–97, 100–102
Census of Industry, 178
Census of Palestine, 295n18
Chermayeff, Serge, 143
Churchill, Winston, 128
citriculture, Zionist agricultural policy and, 21, 53–56, 122
"City of Strangers," Jerusalem as, 275–77, 322n27
class tensions: agricultural policies influenced by, 37; Arab-Jewish tensions and, 51–53; blurring of, in covenantal communities, 7–12; Dead Sea industrial development and, 133–36; Herzl's utopian theory and, 86–89; in Tel Aviv, 94–111
Clinton, Bill (president), 278–79, 284
Cohen, Waley, 122
collective imperative: in covenantal communities, 9–12; in early Jewish settlements, 6–7; medieval Europe as model for, 34–37
colonization: impact on Arabs of, 44–45; kibbutz as military outpost and, 64–69; post-Independence evolution of, 208–9, 216–19; "rurban" settlement policy, 230–32; strategic imperatives guiding, 73–78; urban settlement patterns, 94–111; utopian theory and, 85–89; Zionist ideology and, xiv–xv, 57–59, 300n33

colonization societies, funding of Zionist settlements by, 18–22
commonwealths: Herzl's conception of, 22–28; moshavoth settlements as, 13–14
communitarianism, in early *moshavoth*, 5–7
Conder, Claude R., 170–72
"Confidential Memorandum" for developing Haifa, 120
Contributions to the History of the Settlements in Israel (Hayesod), 314n19
cooperative socialism: Herzl's model for, 23–28, 87, 296n18; medieval Europe as model for, 34–37; for moshavoth settlements, 13–14, 25–28
Cory, H. T., 30, 175
covenantal communities: biblical imagery in, 8; historical evolution of, 3–14; self-government in, 12–14; social ideals and, 7–12; Tel Aviv as, 91; traditions of, 5–7
Creamer, Daniel, 177, 182
cultural policy: Jerusalem as cultural symbol, 234, 261–64; Mount Herzl National Cemetery as reflection of, 248–53; Tel Aviv as center of, 94–95; Zionist ideology reinforced with, 152–59
Cunningham, Alan Gordon (Sir), 241–42

Dahr-el-'Amar (Sheikh), 114–15
dairy farming, Zionist settlements' embrace of, 38, 49
dancing, in Zionist settlements, 156
Davar (Hebrew newspaper), 256, 305n35
"Davidka," 134
Dead Sea, industrial development around, 128–36
Dead Sea Works, 307n22
Defense Ministry: headquarters in Tel Aviv, 239; settlement planning and, 206–7, 211–13, 315n3
defense strategies: corridor settlements to Jerusalem, 256–58, 274–75, 319n16; "Israel 2020" develop-

ment plan and, 282–84; Jerusalem security and defense policies, 268–75; role of Jerusalem in, 234, 253–58; "rurban" settlements and, 230–32; settlement planning and, 69–78; settlement planning influenced by, 206–7, 210–13; urban planning in Haifa and, 120–22; village as military outpost and, 65–69
Degania settlement, 24–25, 41; evolution of, 231; as kibbutz prototype, 101
Deri, Arieh, 321n13
Der Neuer Mensch (New Man) philosophy, 108–11
development towns (*ayarot pituach*): Afula settlement, 139–40; Ashkelon settlement, 200–201; Beer-Sheva, 202–4; Beit She'an as model of, 195–97; comparisons of success and failure, 204–7; economic pressures on, 220; international context of, 187–89; Jerusalem as example of, 246; Kiryat Malachi settlement, 199–200; Kiryat Shemona settlement, 198, 314n24; Sharon Master Plan and development of, 185–87; Zionist ideology and, 190–95
Dimona settlement, 136
din ha'tenu'ah (decree of the movement), 74
diversification: *meshek me'ourav* initiative, 25; Zionist reluctance concerning, 21–22
Dizengoff, Meir, 89–90, 95–97, 100–102, 302n8, 304n22; national policy and influence of, 164, 167
Druze, Zionist agricultural policy and, 114–16, 133–34

Eastern Talpioth, 270
East Jerusalem, Israeli expansion into, 269–70, 272–73, 276
ecological issues, vs. security concerns, 290–92
"economic absorptive capacity" concept: archaeology and politics in assessment of, 169–74; foreign experts' assessment of, 174–78;

immigration policies and, 168–69; Law of Return and, 182–83

economic policy: absorptive capacity of Palestine, calculations of, 168–69; Arab/Jewish relations and, 42–61; archeology and politics concerning, 169–74; British Mandate and, 51–53, 299n14; competing models for settlements and, 29–31; development towns (ayarot pituach) following, 189; foreign experts' influence on, 174–78; industrial development in Haifa and, 122–28; institutionalization of research concerning, 178–82; "Israel 2020" development plan and primacy of, 284–92; Jerusalem's development and unification and, 243–46, 271, 319nn8–9; law of return and, 182–83; settlement patterns and, 16–22, 38–41, 219–24; size of Zionist settlements and, 38–41; Tel Aviv's development and, 89–111

educational system: Arab-Jewish disparities in, 52–53; Beit HaChinuch (House of Education) concept and, 108–11; in Tel Aviv, 94

Egypt, Israeli attack on air bases in, 260

Eilat settlement, 206, 269

Ein Gev settlement, 64–69

Einstein, Albert, 145

Elazar settlement, 272

Elazari-Volcani, Yitzhak (Yitzhak Wilkansky): British agricultural reports dismissed by, 49–50; Jewish Agency for Palestine and, 46; medieval Europe colonial model and, 35–37; settlement models and, 22–26, 29, 31, 40–41, 58, 298n51; size of settlements discussed by, 37–39, 56–57

Electric Cable and Wire Works, 123

Epstein, Yitzhak, 54

Eretz Israel in the Past and in the Present (Ben-Gurion and Ben-Zvi), 172, 311nn12–13

Errand into the Wilderness (Miller), 294n4

Eshkol, Levi (Shkolnik), 38–39, 199

Etudes sur L'état d'Isräel et le Moyen Orient (1935–1958) (Gottmann), 176, 312n22

European culture: denial of, after Independence, 149–50, 156–59; development towns (ayarot pituach) and, 207; settlement patterns influenced by, 16–17; Tel Aviv as model of, 91–111; urban settlements modeled on, 140; Zionist "imagined communities" and, 141–42, 146–48, 151–52

Ezrahi, Yaron, 323n4

fedayeen, kibbutz as military outpost and infiltration by, 63–64

"Fertility of Ancient Palestine," 171

Fifth Aliyah, industrial development during, 123

First Aliyah: religious law in covenants of, 9–12; settlement planning during, 90; songs composed for, 153

First Census of Industries: Taken in 1928 by the Trade Section of the Department of Customs, Excise and Trade, 123–24

folk music and culture, Zionist development of, 155–59

Foreign Affairs, 272

Founding Myths of Israel, The (Sternhell), 294n5

Fourier, Charles, 23, 108

Fox movie studios, 154

French Hill settlement, 269, 274

Frutarom Essences, 123

Gaon of Vilna, migrations to Palestine from Eastern Europe, 4

garden city design: Afula settlement and, 138–40; development towns (ayarot pituach), 188–89; evolution of Tel Aviv and, 90–94; working-class housing projects and, 104–11; Zionist "imagined communities" and, 144–48

Garnier, Louis, 143

Gass, Oscar, 177, 182

Geddes, Patrick, 100, 144–46, 175, 238–39, 241–42, 309n13

Gedera, 5

General Assembly, moshavoth settlements and, 13–14

George, Henry, 104

German Templer colonies: in Haifa, 117–20; Zionist settlements based on, 29–31, 33

Gesamtkultur ideology, Zionist urban planning and, 109

Gilo, 270

Givat Brenner kibbutz, 151

Givat Haim kibbutz, 151

Giv'at Ha-mivtar, 269

Giv'at Ram (Jerusalem), 255

Giv'at Shapira, 269

Giv'at Ze'ev, 273

Glueck, Nelson, 173

Goren, Shlomo (Rabbi), 262–64

Gottmann, Jean, 176, 312*n*22

Government Year Book, 214

Granovsky, Abraham (Granot), 54, 56–58, 135

Great Britain, new town developments in, 204–5

Greater London Plan (Abercrombie), 193

Greenbackers, 32

Gropius, Walter, 143

group worship, covenantal communities as source for, 9

Gruber, Mordecai, 199–200

Gush Emunim movement, "rurban" settlements and, 230–32

Gush Etzion settlement, 271–73

Gutman, Nahum, 156–57

Guttmacher, Eliahu (Rabbi), 150

Gvulot kibbutz, 74

Ha'aretz (newspaper), 289, 323*n*38

Hadassah Medical Center, 237, 245, 259, 269

Hadera moshav: Afula and, 137–40; social ideology of, 11–12; working-class suburbs in, 110

Hadley, Arthur T., 171

Haganah (Defense) organization *See also* Defense Ministry: formation of, 79–81; kibbutz as military outpost and, 63; Plan D of, 164; secret weapons testing at Dead Sea by, 134–36;

settlement planning and, 206, 210–11

Haifa: Afula and, 137–40; capitalism and development of, 114–19, 282–84; ecological issues in, 291–92; European influence in planning of, 142–48; industrial development in, 122–28, 244; Jewish settlements in, 73; working-class suburbs in, 110; Zionist planning in, 113–14, 238–39, 269

Halakha: sanitation regulations governed by, 10; settlement organization and, 294*n*7

haluka (charitable dole), funding of Zionist settlements as, 19–20

halutzim (pioneers): biblical inspiration for, 216, 316*n*12; as Dead Sea industrial workers, 133–36; "rurban" settlements and, 230–32

Handasa ve'adrichalut, 190

Ha'Ogen kibbutz, 151

Har Adar, 273

harosheth (industrial pioneering), 133–36

Harsina, Aharon (Colonel), 319*n*16

Hasidim, Hadera community and, 11

ha-Shomer: cooperative self-defense in, 13–14, 79; size of settlements determined by, 39

"Hatikvah," 257–58

health services, Arab-Jewish disparities in, 52–53

Hebrew University, 131, 145, 178, 182, 220–24, 312*n*22; agriculture faculty of, 24; Mt. Scopus campus of, 245, 254, 259, 269

Hechalutz youth organization, 216

Hedjaz railway, development of, 116

Henriques, Cyril, 297*n*26

Hershey, Pennsylvania, 129

Herzl, Theodore, 296*n*14; 296*n*17; agricultural policy influenced by, 37; burial in National Cemetery, 249; Haifa's development and, 116, 122, 127, 240; industrial development inspired by, 129–30; *Judenstaat* vision of, 51; national policy and influence of, 164, 167; New Society concept of, 22–28, 40, 296n14; 296n17; utopian vision of, 85–89, 94–95, 113, 135; World Zionist Organization founded by, 7, 20, 45, 58–59

Herzlia settlement, 117–18

"hierarchical" population model, development towns (ayarot pituach) policy and, 191

Hilfsverein der deutschen Juden, 116–17, 121

Hillel Pharmaceutical Works, 123

Hirbat Hizha, 316n4

Histadrut (Jewish Federation of Labor). See also Labor party politics: Afula settlement and, 136–37, 139–40; Ashkelon settlement and, 201; Beer-Sheva development and, 315n32; cultural policies of, 108–9, 155–56; development towns (ayarot pituach) investment by, 204–7; headquarters in Jerusalem of, 239; industrial development and, 123, 133–34; Kiryat Shemona settlement and, 198; Zionist labor ideology and housing policies of, 102–11

historiography: archaeology and politics in Palestine and, 169–74; concerning Jerusalem, 234, 246–47; takeover of Arab lands and, 211–12, 316n4; Zionist ideology and, 113–14, 154–59

Hobshawn, Eric, 156

Holliday, Clifford, 90–91, 238–39, 307n20

Holocaust survivors, settlements for, 216

Holon housing development, 105–6

Holzhausen, Rudolf, 236–37

homesteading, Zionist settlement policies and concept of, 16–17, 33–34

Hoofien, Eliezer, 182, 192

Hope Simpson Report, 49, 56–57, 169

hora, creation of, 156

Horowitz, David, 182, 192, 313n14

housing policies: in Haifa, 125–26; Jerusalem expansion and, 269–71; in Tel Aviv, 103–11, 304n31, 305n33

Hovevei Zion (Lovers of Zion), 7; biblical imagery in founding document of, 8–9; funding of Zionist settlements by, 18, 45; lack of profitability in, 295n1

Howard, Ebenezer, 23, 90, 125, 145, 188

Hoy Artzi, Moladati, 153

Hulda settlement, 23

Huleh swamp, Jewish settlements in, 73

Human Development Index (HDI), 299n14

Hungarian Jews, settlements in Palestine by, 5

Huntington, Ellsworth, 171–73, 311n10

Hurva synagogue, 4

Hussein, King of Jordan, 259–60

"imagined communities," Zionist variation of, 141–59

immigration policy: absorptive capacity of Palestine and, 168–69; development towns (ayarot pituach) planning and, 196–97, 207; Herzl's vision of, 86–89; during interwar period, 143–48; in Jerusalem, 236–43, 245–46; Jewish majority in Palestine achieved with, 47–50; Law of Return and, 182–83; post-Independence changes in, 164, 167–68, 216–19; post World War II patterns of, 51–53; Sharon Master Plan and, 184–87; size of settlements impacted by, 40–41; unification of Jerusalem and, 267–68, 320n12

Imperial Chemical Industries, 122

imperial interests: "imagined communities" paradigm and, 146–48; Haifa in Zionist planning, 119–22

income distribution, Arab-Jewish disparities in, 52–53

individualism: Herzl's utopian theory and, 87–88; Homestead Act of 1862 as codification of, 16–17; Zionist settlement policies and ideology of, 16–22, 295n1 industrial development. *See also* science and technology: in Dead Sea region, 128–36; Kiryat Shemona settlement and, 198; in villages, 224–25; Zionist urban planning and, 50, 112–14, 122–28, 178–82, 307*n*16

intifada: Palestinian Arab nationalism and, 56; at Temple Mount, 254

Iraqi oil fields, British development of, 120

irrigation systems, Zionist settlements and development of, 30–31

Israel, independent state of. *See also* War of Independence: Afula's failure linked to, 136–40; Dead Sea development and, 135–36; demographics and boundaries following, 164–67; development towns (*ayarot pituach*) following, 188–89, 193–96; impact on Haifa of, 127–28; Jerusalem in, 243; Jewish Agency for Palestine as forerunner of, 46–47; potential contributions to Arabs from, 54–55; razing of Arab villages after, 149; settlement planning following, 167–68, 208–32; Zionist cultural campaign for, 154–59

Israel Bonds, creation of, 307*n*16

"Israel 2020" development plan, 281–92

Israel Defense Forces (IDF), 63, 79, 211

Israel Land Authority, 291–92

Israel Museum, 253

Jabotinsky, Vladimir, 96, 176

Jaffa: Arab-Jewish tensions concerning, 48; comparisons with Tel Aviv, 89–90; garden city planning in, 105–6; as immigration port, 88–89; suburban development around, 101

Jaffa orange, development of, 21

Jerusalem. *See also* East Jerusalem; West Jerusalem: architectural styles in, 148; under British Mandate, 235–43; corridor settlement strategy for, 256–58, 319*n*16; economic challenges in, 243–46, 256–58, 319*nn*8–9; establishment as capital, 233–58; future planning for, 286;

Jewish control of Holy Sites in, 261–64; Jordanian attack on, 260; naming protocols in, 247–48; National Cemetery in, 248–53; Old City expansion, 259, 273–75, 320*n*2; partition of, 243, 259–60, 275–77; population statistics concerning, 267–68, 275, 322*n*26; post-1967 expansion and development, 257–58; Six-Day War and security challenges in, 268–75; strategic imperatives in, 253–58, 283–84; symbolic significance of, 246–47; unification as Jewish city, 264–68; working-class suburbs of, 110, 144; Yom Kippur war and expansion of, 271–74

Jerusalem Municipal Archives (JMA), 319*n*9

"Jerusalem of Gold," 261

Jewish Agency for Palestine, 46–47, 135; Absorption Department, 196–97; Beit She'an settlement planning and, 196–97; corridor settlements around Jerusalem, strategy for, 256–58, 319*n*16; development towns (*ayarot pituach*) policy and, 193–95, 205–7; Economic Research Institute, 180–82; immigration policies in, 216; Kiryat Malachi settlement and, 199; partition plan accepted by, 163–64, 275–77; Settlement Department, 206, 211, 226

"Jewish bubble": Arab-Jewish tensions and, 50, 59, 60–61, 299*n*9; cultural characteristics of, 158–59

"Jewish Consciousness," 157–58

Jewish National Fund (Keren Kayemeth), 18, 74, 76; cultural efforts of, 155–56; financing of Tel Aviv with, 92; housing projects funded by, 101–2, 104, 109–10; industrial development in Haifa and, 124–25; settlement planning and, 211–12

Jewish National Homeland, 55; British Mandate and establishment of, 175–78; immigration policy for creation of, 168–69

"Jewish presence" concept, rural settlement planning and, 209

Jordan (Hashemite Kingdom): Dead Sea development and, 135–36; evolution of Jerusalem and, 242–43; Six-Day War and, 259–61
Jordanian Arab Legion, 134
Jordan Valley Authority (JVA), 31, 176–78
jubilee year (yovel), covenantal laws and observance of, 10
Judea, settlement expansion in, 226–28, 231–32
Judenstaat, Herzl's vision of, 51
judicial authority, in moshavoth settlements, 13–14

Kaberski, Haim, 266–68, 271, 320n12, 321nn13–14; 321n17
Kaiser Wilhelm, 296n14
Kalandia settlement, 267
Kalia settlement, 128–36, 139, 150–51
Kaplan, Eliezer, 182, 192
Katamon Quarter (Jerusalem), 254–55
Kauffmann, Richard, 64, 67, 125–27, 131–33, 301n6, 307n20; Afula settlement and, 136–37, 139–40; Planning Committee and, 182; Sharon Master Plan and, 314n16; Zionist "imagined communities" and, 143–48
Kaznelson, Berl (Dov Beer), 151
kehillah kedoshah (holy community), 9
Kendall, Henry, 146, 241–42, 320n8
"Key for the Settlement of Various Zones in Palestine," 39
Kfar Daniel settlement, 272
Kfar Darom settlement, 76
Kfar Etzion settlement, 271–72
Kfar Ruppin settlement, 196
Kfar Saba settlement, 146
Kfar Tabor settlement, 79
Kfar Warburg settlement, 74
Khalsa settlement, 198
kibbutzim: American influence in, 31–34; Arab labor on, 58–59; Ben-Gurion's dispute with, 217–19; communal characteristics of, 25–28; cultural development in, 155–56; defense strategy and role of, 62–81, 282–84; "development towns" and, 139–40; economic pressures on, 15–22, 220–24; historical back-

ground concerning, 4–5, 113–14; industrialization of, 224–25; limits of, 59–61; as preferred model, xiv–xv, 37–41, 65–69, 213–19; ring pattern established for, 65–69; Sharon Master Plan and, 185–87; urban settlements compared with, 111
Kimshonim (Thistles) (Raab), 157
Kiryat Anavim settlement, 273
Kiryat Avoda (City of Work), 105
Kiryat Gat settlement, 213, 315n32
Kiryat Malachi settlement, 199–200
Kiryat Shemona settlement, 198, 246, 314n24
Kisch, Frederick (Colonel), 79–80
Kishon River, Haifa industrial development and, 125–28
Kitchener, Horatio, 170
Klausner, Yosef, 91
Klein, A., 125–26, 131–32
Knesseth: "Basic Law-Jerusalem" of, 275; location in Jerusalem, 245, 255; of Mapam, 76, 78; unification of Jerusalem and, 266
Kollek, Teddy, 277, 320n8, 322n35
kollelim, settlement patterns influenced by, 6–7
Kovetz Shchunat Ha-Ovdim (Hebrew newspaper), 305n35
Kroyanker, David, 318n1
Krupp, Germany, 129
Kupat Holim (workers' Sick Fund), 137–38
Kuznets, Simon, 177
kvutza (settlement): historical evolution of, 4, 16–22; model of, xiv–xv

"labor brigades," Dead Sea industrial workers as, 133–36
Labor party politics. See also Histadrut (Jewish Federation of Labor): Ben-Gurion and, 218–19; Dead Sea industrial development and, 128–36; development towns (ayarot pituach) and, 204–7; expansion of Jerusalem and, 273–75; Haifa's development and, 114; settlement patterns and, 34–37, 230–32; Zionist ideology and, 102–11, 310n30

Lakhish region, evolution of, 213, 272
Land of Promise, The (Warren), 171
Law of Return, settlement policies and, 182–83
Lawrence, T. E., 53
League of Nations, legitimacy of Zionism under Covenant of, 42–46
legal system: evolution of, post-Independence, 289–92, 323n7; moshavoth court system, 13–14
Lehman, Herbert, 122
Likud Party, 243, 257, 272, 283
Lipman, Jacob, 297n26
literacy rates, Arab-Jewish disparities in, 52–53
living standards: potential improvements for Arab population, 53–56; Zionist policies concerning, 56–59
Loan Fund, support for Jerusalem from, 245–45
Lockridge, Kenneth A., 294n4
Looking Backward, 2000–1887 (Bellamy), 296n18
Lowdermilk, Walter Clay, 31, 175–76
Lévy, Lazar, 21

Ma'aleh Adumim, 272–73
Ma'aloth Dafna, 269
Ma'ariv, 323n38
MacLean, William (Sir), 240–43
Magnes, Judah, 297n34
Mahler, Gustav, 86
Majdal (Arab village), 201
mamlachtiyut (statism), 218
Maoz Haim, 196
Mar Elias (Jerusalem), 255
Marshall, Louis, 122
Mead, Elwood, 30–33, 39–40, 175, 297nn26–27
Mear, Frank, 145
Me'a She'arim, takanoth of, 8
mechanization: agricultural expansion and, 223–24; Zionist opposition to, 35–37
medieval Europe, Zionist settlements modeled on, 29–31, 34–37
Megalopolis (Gottmann), 176
Meir, Golda, 273

Meltzer, Shimshon, 154
Mendelson, Eric, 143
Merchavia kibbutz, 138
meshek ezer, introduction of, 38
Metzer, Jacob, 299n14
Mevassereth Zion suburb, 321n13
middle class, Tel Aviv as center for, 94–111, 304n25
Middle East, nationalism and primacy of religion in, 60–61, 300n38
Migdal Adar, 272
Migdal Oz, 272
Mikve Israel: agricultural training farm, 19, 24, 37, 296n14; establishment of, 5
military outposts, Zionist settlements as, 62–81
Miller, Perry, 294n4
millet system, development of, 301n38
mitzpim settlements, 74–78, 226
mitzvoth, agricultural regulations and fulfillment of, 10
mixed Arab-Jewish settlements, absence of, in Palestine, 51–53
Mi Yivneh Bayit be-Tel Aviv?, 153
Mi yivneh hagalil?, 153
Mond, Alfred (Lord Melchett), 122
Montefiore, Moses, 5
Morris, Benny, 299n6, 316n4
Mosaica factory, 123
moshavoth settlements: agricultural training for, 19–22; Arab labor on, 36–37, 58–59; Ben-Gurion's support of, 218–19; biblical imagery as inspiration for, 8–9; communal characteristics of, 25–28; covenantal traditions of, 5–7; defense strategies and role of, 65–69; "development towns" and, 139–40; economic pressures in, 15–41, 219–20, 295n1; funding of, 18–22, 296n8; historical evolution of, 4–14, 294n3; industrial development and, 226–32; limits of, 59–61; model of, xiv–xv; naming rules for, 150–52; new models sought for, 22–28; post-Independence evolution of, 218–19; self-governance in, 12–14; Sharon

Master Plan and, 185–87; WZO preference for, 40–41
moshav shitufi (smallholder's settlement), kibbutz/moshav evolution
into, 15–16
Mosul oil pipeline, 120–23, 239
motion pictures, reaffirmation of Zionism in, 154–59
Motzkin, Leo, 54
Mount Carmel, housing development
involving, 126, 269
"Mount Herzl," designation and consecration of, 249–52
Mount of Olives cemetery, 259
Mount Scopus: expansion of Jerusalem and, 237, 245, 254; Jordan's
control of, 259; during Six-Day
War, 260; West Jerusalem linked
to, 269
music: in post-Independence Israel,
257–58, 261; reaffirmation of Zionism in, 152–56, 310n30

Nahalal settlement, 127, 137, 143–44;
defensive design of, 64–69, 301n6
Nahal Oz kibbutz, 214–16
Nahal settlements (No'ar Halutzi Lochem), 214–16
Naharayim settlement, 129
nakba (Arab collective memory), 210–
11
Nakhalat Yehuda housing estate, 39
naming protocols: Jerusalem street
names, 247–48; rules and principles for, in pre- and post-Independence, 149–52
Nasser, Gamal, 260
Nathan, Robert, 177–78, 182
National Cemetery, design and cultural significance of, 248–53
nationalism: agricultural policy impacted by, 35–37; "imagined communities" paradigm and, 147–48;
of Palestinian Arabs, 55–56; settlement ideology and, 6–7, 24, 294n5,
297n21; Zionism and, 60–61
Nazareth, Afula and, 138
Negba settlement, 73–74, 76

Negev, Jewish settlements in, 73, 75–
76
neighborhood design, covenantal
laws and, 10
Nesher Cement Factory, 123
Ness Ziona settlement, 5; Kaiser Wil-
helm's visit to, 296n14; social ideals
in, 8
Netanyahu, Binyamin, 272–73
Neudorf (new village) model, Herzl's
conception of, 22–23
Neveh Ya'acov settlement, 270, 274
*New England Town: The First Hundred
Years; Dedham Massachusetts, 1636–
1736, The* (Lockridge), 294n4
New England towns, *moshavoth* settle-
ment model and, 6–7, 294n4
New Lanark, Scotland, 108, 129
New Middle East, The (Peres), 54
New Society, Herzl's vision of, 22–28,
40
new towns. *See* development towns
(*ayarot pituach*)
New Towns Act (Great Britain), 204
Nineteenth Zionist Congress, 196
1967 War. *See* Six-Day War (1967)
Nir David kibbutz, 196
nonagricultural settlements. *See also*
"rurban" settlements: evolution of,
xiv–xv; Zionists' prejudice against,
20–22
Nordau, Max, 54
Novomeysky, Moshe, 128–36
Nusseibah, Anwar, 267

Ofakim settlement, 246
Oriental Jews, settlement planning
and, 216–17, 219
Osborn, Frederic, 188
Oslo Accords, 54–55, 284, 292
Ottoman Empire: archaeology and
politics concerning, 171–74; impact
on Arabs of dissolution of, 44–47;
Jerusalem during, 235–36; Jewish
communities during, 12; nationalism and religious primacy in, 60,
300n38
Owen, Robert, 21, 108, 129

Palestine: British census statistics concerning, 12, 295n18; legitimation of Zionism and expansion of, 43–61; partition of, 47–50, 60–61, 69, 159, 240–43, 295n18, 299n9; transfer of Arabs from, allegations concerning, 47–48, 299n6

Palestine: Problems and Promise, An Economic Study (Nathan, Gass, and Creamer), 177–78, 182

Palestine and Its Transformation (Huntington), 171–72, 311n10

Palestine Blue Book, 178

Palestine Economic Corporation, 122, 124–25, 307n16

Palestine Electric Corporation, 50, 123, 129, 135

Palestine Exploration Fund, 170–71

Palestine Foundation Fund (Keren Hayesod), 18, 102–11, 154, 314n19

Palestine Jewish Colonization Association, 18; settlement models of, 33–34

Palestine Liberation Organization (PLO), 54–56, 284

Palestine Potash Company, 50, 128–36, 307n22

Palestine State, proposals for, 285–92

Palestine Zionist Executive, 123

Palestinian Arabs: accommodation of, 232; agricultural policy and, 56–59; archaeology and politics concerning, 170–74; attacks on kibbutzim by, 63–81; as Dead Sea industrial workers, 133–36; dispossession by force of, 58–59, 300n34; distribution of, in Jerusalem, 265–67; dominance in rural areas of, 51–53; economic relations with Israelis, future plans for, 286–92; impact of Zionism on, 42–61; Jerusalem's Jewish expansion and, 242–43, 257–58, 265–68, 270–71, 319n7, 321n17; labor on moshavoth settlements by, 36–37; land purchases by Jews from, 274–75, 321n24; Law of Return opposed by, 183; Mount of Olives cemetery desecration, 259–60;

nationalist identity sought by, 55–56; opposition to Jewish settlements from, 70–78; Palestinian State proposals and, 285–92; partition plan and, 163–64; segregation in Jerusalem of, 275–77, 322n35; socioeconomic inequalities of, 51–53, 58–59; takeover of land from, 211–13, 315n4, 316n6; Temple Mount dispute and, 277–80; urban settlements and, 90–111; War of Independence and, 164–67, 209–10

Palestinian Authority, 139, 292, 321n24; Dead Sea development and, 135–36; Israeli compromises with, 273; Temple Mount negotiations, 262–64, 278–79, 323n38

Palmach troops, 81, 213–14, 218

Palmyra Glass, 123

paternalism, funding of Zionist settlements as, 20–22

Pathways in Utopia (Buber), 221

Peel Commission, 47, 52, 60, 69–70, 73, 275

Pen, Alexander, 153

Peres, Shimon, 54–55, 288

Petach Tikva, 5, 110

Petrie, Flinders (Sir), 170

petrochemical industry, Zionist development of, 122–28

Pirkey Kiryat-Shemona, 314n24

Pisgat Ze'ev, 274

Planning Committee (Va'adat Tikon), 180–83, 191–92

polar population policy, 191–95

politics: archaeological research in Palestine and, 169–74; debate over rurban settlements and, 230–32; development town planning and, 205–7; expansion of Jerusalem boundaries and, 265–68, 321n13; kibbutz settlements and, 217–19; lack of middle class presence in, 100, 304nn25–26; Zionist institutionalization of research and, 178–82

population distribution: development towns (*ayarot pituach*) and, 190–95,

313n14; "Israel 2020" plan and, 285-92; in Jerusalem, 266-67; polar population policy, 191-95
Populist movement, American agriculture and, 32
Progress and Poverty (George), 104
proletarian architecture, Zionists' embrace of, 108-11
public convocations, of early settlements, 11-12
Pullman, Illinois, 129
Puritans, Zionist settlers compared with, 6-12

Quakers, colonization efforts of, 22, 296n11

Raab, Esther, 157-58
rabbis, authority of, in moshavoth settlements, 13-14
Rabin, Yitzhak, 250-52, 255, 272-74
railway development in Haifa, 116-19, 122
Ramat Eshkol settlement, 269-70
Ramat Rachel kibbutz, 151, 255, 266
Ramot settlement, 270
Ratner, Yochanan (Eugen), 79-80, 147-48, 159
"Red Vienna" concept, urban planning in Tel Aviv and, 104-11, 305n34
Rehovoth settlement: agricultural research station at, 23-24; biblical imagery in founding document of, 8; communal characteristics of, 25; Kaiser Wilhelm's visit to, 296n14; origin of name, 150; social ideology of, 11; suburbs near, 39
Reifenberg, Adolf, 173-74
religion: Jerusalem's significance in, 234-35; nationalism and primacy of, in Arab world, 60-61, 300n38
Report of the Experts, The, 31, 39-40, 175
Research Council of Israel, 173
research initiatives, Zionist institutionalization of, 178-82
Revisionist Party, 273

Revivim kibbutz, 74
"Right of Return" principle, Arab-Jewish tensions concerning, 60-61
right-wing groups: expansion of Jerusalem and, 273; rurban settlements and, 230-32, 318n32
Rishon le-Zion settlement, 5; experts' misperceptions concerning, 20; Kaiser Wilhelm's visit to, 296n14; origin of name, 150; takanoth of, 11
Robinson, Edward, 170
Rochdale cooperative movement, 22, 40, 296n18; Herzl's utopian theory and, 87; urban housing design and, 109-11
Rogers, William, 269
Rokach, Itzhak, 313n14
"rootedness" metaphor, in Zionist architecture, 156-57
Rosh Pina settlement, 5; origin of name, 150; public convocations in, 295n16; silk-growing experiment and, 21
Rosh Tsurim settlement, 272
Rothschild, Edmund de (Baron), 7; funding of Zionist settlements by, 18-20, 25, 29, 33, 45, 88, 151; offerings to Tel Aviv by, 92; silk-growing experiment and, 21-22
Royal Geographical Society, 130, 152
Royal Institute of British Architects, 146
Ruhama settlement, 74
Ruppin, Arthur, 23-24, 29, 31, 41, 69, 178-80, 182, 297n27
rural communities in Palestine, Arab-Jewish segregation in, 51-53
"rurban" settlements: economic pressures and evolution of, 220; post-1967 expansion of, 226-32; post-Independence evolution of, 208-9; strategic purpose of, 66-69, 283-84; urban communities and, 256-57
Ruttenberg, Pinchas, 70, 123, 129-30, 135
Ryerson, Knowles, 297n26

sabbatical year (*sh'mitah*), covenantal laws and observance of, 10
sabra, Zionist creation of, 157–58
Sacher, Harry, 121
Sadat, Anwar, 273–74
Samaria, settlement expansion in, 226–28, 231–32
Sambursky, Daniel, 154–55, 310n30
Schatz, Boris, 156–57
Schiff, Jacob, 297n34
Schmitt, Peter J., 295n5
Schocken department stores, 143
Schwartz, Mark, 31
science and technology. *See also* industrial development: Haifa's Technion and, 116; Herzl's vision of, 87–89; in State of Israel, 167–68
Sde Eliahu kibbutz, 150
Second Aliyah: agricultural policies during, 36; hora created during, 156; moshav/kibbutz experiments during, 23; secular settlements during, 9–12; songs composed for, 153
Second Temple site, 262–64
secular socialist ideologies, in covenantal communities, 9–12
security concerns. *See* defense strategies
"Security Principles in the Planning of Agricultural Settlements and Workers' Villages," 66
Sede Boker kibbutz, 217
Seetzen, Ulrich, 130
"Selection of the Fittest, The," 179
self-defense: as cooperative ideal, 13–14; kibbutzim as instruments of, 65–78
self-determination principle, Zionist ideology and, 19–22, 43
self-government, covenantal communities' ideal of, 12–14
Sephardim: in Haifa, 116; roots of settlement ideology among, 6
settlement patterns, covenantal communities, 3–14
settlement planning. *See also* specific settlements: agricultural bias in, 102–11; American influence on, 31–34; Arab-Jewish tensions con-

cerning, 47–61; competing models for, 29–31; covenantal communities, development of, 3–14, 293n1; defense strategies and, 63–81; economic pressures on, 16–22, 219–24; foreign experts' influence in, 16–22, 176–78; historical evolution of, xiv–xv; ideological imperatives in, 6–7, 294n5; international culture of, 29–31, 297n24; "Israel 2020" proposals for, 288–92, 323–24n8; Jewish Agency for Palestine's influence on, 46–47; Law of Return and, 182–83; medieval Europe as model for, 34–37; naming trends in, 149–50; political strategies as factor in, 268–75; post-Independence paradigms, 167–68, 208, 213–32; "rurban" settlements evolution, 226–32; size considerations in, 37–41; War of Independence and, 209–13
Sha'ar Ha-Negev kibbutz, 73
Shabbath Nachamu, significance of, 12, 294n15
Sharon, Arieh, 108, 143–48, 167
Sharon Master Plan for settlements, 167–68, 183–87, 193–96, 222, 231; Jerusalem ignored in, 246
Shchunat Borochov satellite city, 109–11, 198–99
Shell Oil, 122
Shemen manufacturing plant, 123
Shemer, Naomi, 261
Shertok, Moshe (Sharett), 69, 301n10
Shlonsky, Avraham, 153–54
Shulkan Aruch (code of Jewish law), 10
"siege mentality," Israeli development of Jerusalem and, 257–58
silk-growing, settlement, experiments with, 21–22
Sinai: Israeli invasion of, 260; kibbutzim as military outposts in, 63–64
Six-Day War (1967): impact on Arabs of, 275–77; Jerusalem's development after, 259–80; kibbutz as military outpost and, 64–65
small business enterprises: emergence of, 50; importance of, in Yishuv,

95–111; lack of Arab participation in, 52

Smilanski, Moshe, 298n51

"Social Character of the Hebrew Village in Eretz Israel, The," 221

socialism: agricultural policies influenced by, 36–37; American experts' opposition to, 33–34; in covenantal communities, 7–12; settlement ideology and, 6–7, 9–12, 294n5; urban settlement planning and, 101–11

social services, Arab-Jewish disparities in, 52–53

Society for Jewish Folk Music, 155

Sokolow, Nachum, 113

Sollel Boneh building company, 205

Song of Songs, 155

Song of the Hammer, 155

Song of the Morning, 155

"Song of the Road," 310n30

Song of the Valley, 155

South African Zionist Federation, 201

spatially controlled society concept, 105

Spiegel, Erika, 188

Statistical Abstract of Palestine, 1944–45, 170

Stern, Albert, 122

Stern, Frederick, 122

Sternhell, Zeev, 294n5

stockade and tower settlements, 69, 74, 80, 196, 301n10; 301n13; defense strategy and, 282–84; ideological motives for, 231

Strahorn, Arthur, 297n26

Straits of Tiran blockade, 260

Strong, Ann Louise, 188–89

Suez Canal, Haifa as alternative to, 120–21

Syria, Six-Day War and, 260

Szold, Robert, 122

Ta'anakh region, settlements as military outposts in, 68–69

Taggar, Tsiona, 157–58

takanoth (bylaws): in covenantal communities, 7–12; urban housing regulations, 110–11

Talmon, Jacob, 221

Talmud, post-Independence celebration of, 149–50

Talpioth settlement, 144, 146–47, 266

Technion school (Haifa), 116–17, 176, 239

Tekoah settlement, 272

Tel Amal kibbutz, 69, 196

Tel Aviv: Bauhaus influence on, 142–48; development of, 89–100, 238–40, 244, 282–84; funding sources for, 101–2; future planning for, 286; garden city design in, 105–11; Haifa compared with, 127; as industrial-technical center, 95–111, 113–14; inner-city housing estates in, 108–11; Jordanian attack on, 260; music in commemoration of, 154; pluralism in politics of, 101–11; population and size of, 101–11, 192; Sharon Master Plan and, 184–85

"Tel Aviv Shore," 154–55

Tel Hai settlement, 198

Tel Or settlement, 129

Templer societies, 33

Temple Mount: cultural symbolism of, 252; military activities at, 254; negotiations over, 262–64, 278–79, 320n5, 323n38

Tennessee Valley Authority (TVA), 31

"thickening" ('ibuiy) concept for defensive settlements, 256

Third Aliyah: pioneering work brigades in, 310n30; secular settlements during, 9–12

Tiberias, suburbs of, 110

Tirat Zvi kibbutz, 196

Tnuvah, Zionist farms' production of, 49

To a New Life (Le-chaim chadashim), 154

Tomorrow: A Peaceful Path to Reform (Howard), 90, 188

"Town and Country Planning in Palestine," 90

Town Planning Institute (London), 146

Toynbee, Arnold, 121

transit camps (*ma'abarot*), at Beit She'an, 196–97

tree planting competition, Arab-Jewish tensions in Jerusalem over, 270, 321*n*17
Trumpeldor, Josef, 198, 314*n*24
Tschernichowsky, Shaul, 95, 153
Turkish occupation of Palestine: development of Tel Aviv and, 90–91, 93; Haifa during, 116–19, 122; Jerusalem during, 237–38
Tuviyahu, David, 205
tzrif (hut), 217

ultra-Orthodox Jews, settlements for, 273–74
United Jewish Appeal. *See* Palestine Foundation Fund (Keren Hayesod)
United Nations: Resolution 194, 212; Special Committee on Palestine (UNSCOP), 55; vote for partition in, 159, 163–64, 310*n*41
United States, Zionist settlement planning and influence of, 29–34, 297*n*34
urban settlements: Afula settlement, 136–40; Arab-Jewish segregation in, 51–53; comparison of alternative plans, 112–40; development towns (*ayarot pituach*), 187–89, 191–95; evolution of Tel Aviv, 89–111; expansion of Jerusalem and, 265–68; Haifa as, 113–28; historical evolution of, 6–7; impact of war on, 254–58; industrial development and, 128–36; population growth in, 21, 101–11; post-Independence planning of, 167–68; potential Arab employment opportunities in, 53–56; "rurban" settlements and, 228–32; Sharon Master Plan and, 185–87; Zionist ideology and, 16–22, 85–89, 112–14
Ussishkin, Menachem, 54
Uthwatt report of 1942, 309*n*17
utopian theory: Israeli national programming and, 167–68; potential improvements for Arab population linked to, 53–56; Zionist settlement models and, 22–28, 296*n*18

Van der Rohe, Mies, 143
Vienna, Tel Aviv as model for, 91, 303*n*11
Vilna, colonization society in, 11–12
Volkswohnungspaläste workers' housing, 108–11
von Hofmannsthal, Hugo, 86
Vulcan Foundries, 123

Warburg, Felix, 122
Warburg, Otto, 29, 131
War of Independence. *See also* Israel, independent state of; Six-Day War (1967); Yom Kippur War: impact on Jerusalem, 242–43; settlement planning and, 209–13; Sharon Master Plan and, 184–85; strategic function of kibbutz during, 64–69; takeover of Arab villages during, 211–13; UN partition plan and, 164–67
Warren, Charles, 170–71
water management policies, 224, 317*n*25
wealth distribution, Arab-Jewish disparities in, 52–53
Weill, Shraga, 76, 78
Weitz, Josef, 74–76, 211–13, 316*n*6
Weitz, Raanan, 226
Weizmann, Chaim, 30–31, 122, 181
West Bank: Israeli annexation of, 256–58, 260–64; rurban settlements on, 229–32, 318*n*32; Yom Kippur War and Jewish expansion in, 271–74
West Bank Data Project, 318*n*32
Western cultural bias, influence on Zionism of, 46–47
Western (Wailing) Wall, Israeli possession of, 261–64, 278–79
West Jerusalem: cultural significance of, 246–47; evolution of, 243; expansion and development of, 256–58; Mt. Scopus linked to, 269; post-Independence success of, 259–60
Whittick, Arnold, 188
wine production, Zionist settlements' experiments with, 22

Wohnhöfe urban workers' housing, 106–11

Wohnkultur concept, Zionist urban planning and, 109

World Zionist Organization (WZO), 7; agricultural research station of, 23–24; American influence in, 31–34, 297n34; Beit She'an settlement planning and, 196–97; collective land ownership concept and, 104–11; Degania developed by, 101–11; Department for Urban and Commercial Development, 97; foreign experts recruited by, 175; funding sources for, 18–19, 101–2; institutionalization of research and, 178–82; international support for, 44–47, 58–59; medieval Europe colonial model and, 35–37; settlement policies of, 15–22, 24–31, 211, 295n2; size of settlements determined by, 38–41, 298n51; urban development and, 238; Zionist "imagined communities" and, 144–48

Wright, Frank Lloyd, 143

Yad Mordechai kibbutz, 76

Yad Vashem (Israeli Holocaust Memorial), 252–53

Yavneh, 24

Yishuv (Jewish community in Palestine): agricultural training institutions in (hachsharoth), 19; Balfour Declaration and legitimation of, 42; British Mandate and development of, 49–50, 299n9; cultural development during, 154–59; Dead Sea industrial development and ideology of, 134–36; development towns (*ayarot pituach*) policy and, 191–95; dominance of Tel Aviv in, 93; economic development under British Mandate, 51–53, 299n14; historical statistics concerning, xiii–xv; impact on Arabs of, 42–47, 55–56; naming rules under, 150–52; strate-

gic imperatives of, 70–78; urban-industrial development under, 95–111, 192–95

Yom Kippur War, Jewish territorial expansion following, 271–75

Y'sod Hama'ala moshava, 5, 21

Zichron Ya'acov settlement, 5, 151, 297n34; agricultural experiments in, 22; experts' misperceptions concerning, 20

Zionist Congress, 7

Zionist ideology: anti-urban bias in, 100, 304n26; Arab homeland ignored by, 55–56; Arab-Jewish tensions and, 42–61; archaeological research and politics of, 169–74; biblical imagery in covenants of, 8–12; British Mandate and, 193–95; centrality of village concept to, 220–24; covenantal communities and, 3–14, 293n1; cultural reaffirmation of, 152–59; defense strategy and, 69–81; design concepts and, 149–59; development towns (*ayarot pituach*) and ideology of, 190–95; economic policy and, 59–61; European roots of, 142–48; Haifa development and, 122–28, 307n16; "imagined communities" concept and, 141–59; imperial context of, 119–22; institutionalization of research and, 178–82; Jerusalem's economic development and, 244–46; misperceptions concerning agriculture and, 20–22; naming rules and principles of, 149–51; national identity and, 60–61; post-Independence planning and, 167–68, 208–32; "reconstitution" concept and, 159, 310n41; strategic imperatives of, 69–78; Tel Aviv's development and, 89–111; utopian theory and, 85–89, 135–36; War of Independence and, 164–67

Zionist Organization of America, 31

CPSIA information can be obtained at www.ICGtesting.com
Printed in the USA
241996LV00002B/24/P

9 780300 178531